POLES APART

To Bill TRAU —
34th Troop Carrier Squadron, 315th Group
With appreciation for what you
have done!

George F. Cholewczyński

POLES APART

The Polish Airborne
at the
Battle of Arnhem

by

George F. Cholewczynski

Sarpedon, New York
Greenhill Books, London

Published by
Sarpedon Publishers, Inc.
166 Fifth Avenue, New York, NY 10010
and
Greenhill Books, Lionel Leventhal Limited
Park House, 1 Russell Gardens, London NW11 9NN

Copyright © 1993 by George F. Cholewczynski

A version of this work was published in Dutch as *De Polen
van Driel* in 1990 by Uitgeverij Lunet, Naarden, The Netherlands.
Edited by Jan Bouman.

Library of Congress Cataloging-in-Publication Data available.

ISBN: 0-9627613-5-4

British Library Cataloguing in Publication Data available.

ISBN 1-85367-165-7

10 9 8 7 6 5 4 3 2 1

Book and cover design by Libby Braden

MANUFACTURED IN THE UNITED STATES OF AMERICA

This book is dedicated to
those who fought for freedom,
and did not live to see the fruits
of their efforts.

Contents

MAPS

PHOTO CREDITS

Photographs in this book are reproduced courtesy of the following individuals and institutions.

Photo page 1: Dr. S. Sosabowski via J.Z. Raschke (top left); Sikorski Institute, London (top right); Polish Airborne Forces Association (bottom). Photo page 2: Pilsudski Institute, New York (top); Pilsudski Institute, New York (bottom). Photo page 3: Kazimierz Janiga (top); Marek Gramski (bottom). Photo page 4: Sikorski Institute, London (top); Sikorski Institute, London (bottom). Photo page 5: Sikorski Institute, London (top, center and bottom). Photo page 6: Sikorski Institute, London (top left, top right); Dave Mondt (bottom). Photo page 7: Sikorski Institute, London (top left, top right and bottom). Photo page 8: Airborne Museum, Oosterbeek (top); Cora Baltussen (bottom left); Benjamin Jansen (bottom right). Photo page 9: Michal Iwaskow (top); Jerzy Dyrda (center); Sikorski Institute, London (bottom). Photo page 10: Sikorski Institute, London (top left); Boleslaw Kuzniar (top center); Stanislaw Nosecki (top right); Michal Lasek (middle row, left and center); Piotr Wawiorko (middle row, right); Sikorski Institute, London (bottom left); Zbigniew Hrehorow (bottom center); Stefan Kaczmarek (bottom right); Photo page 11: Sikorski Institute, London (top); Michal Iwaskow (center); Photo page 12: Sikorski Institute, London (top); Pilsudski Institute, New York (bottom). Photo page 13: Berry de Reuss (top); Bundesarchiv, Koblenz (bottom). Photo page 14: U.S. Air Force (top); Sikorski Institute, London (bottom). Photo page 15: A.L.A. Kremer-Kingma (top); J. Leuseden via Geert Maassen (center); Sikorski Institute, London (bottom). Photo page 16: Sikorski Institute, London (top and bottom).

Acknowledgments

The author would like to extend special thanks to Jan Szygenda (Past President, Polish Airborne Forces Association/USA) and Jan J. Lorys (Past Chairman, Polish Airborne Forces Association), both former Brigade officers, who have read my work since I began this project, and have offered countless suggestions. Also deserving of special mention are Teddy Roy (Tadeusz Rojewski) and Wojciech Drzewienkiewicz, who cheerfully helped me retrace the paths in Fife, Scotland, and the English Midlands where Polish paratroopers' boots had tread.

Concerning preparation of the manuscript, I must pay homage to the people who helped by ruthlessly inflicting on me the rules of English grammar: James McGovern and Michael W. Leonard. Mr. Leonard, a reserve naval officer and noted military artist, also provided great assistance in matters of military protocol and tactics. At Sarpedon Publishers, Donn Teal, for his editing expertise, and Libby Braden, for her aesthetic creativity, are owed a special thanks, as is Dr. Jan Koniarek in New Jersey for his valuable help with the photographs. A special salute, too, is accorded Ms. Marie K. Erickson, who, despite being a merciless taskmaster and former junior-high-school English teacher, always made me look forward to our meetings.

The countless hours and efforts on the long and lonely road of writing this book were lightened by my friend Gerard M. Devlin. I am in awe of Jerry's performance in his three careers, those of soldier, author and family man. All three of these came to bear over the years as he constantly encouraged me when my strength flagged or tasks seemed impossible. I am proud to call myself a friend of this wonerul human being.

Poles Apart is based on years of diligent research, both from official sources and from interviews with the participants themselves, beginning in 1982. It is natural that in the decades since the 1940s events can have become altered in the minds of witnesses. By virtue of the fact that the soldiers who fought at Arnhem–Oosterbeek–Driel were under terrific stress, many accounts, even those written very shortly after the events, show discrepancies, especially concerning what time, or even on what day, certain incidents took place. As far as possible, recent interviews have been confirmed by official records and other contemporary accounts, or by other interviews. Events that could not be independently confirmed have been evaluated by the author, and his judgment has been based on their probability and the reliability of *other* information provided by the particular veteran. The author believes all of the events in this narrative to be accurately presented, and responsibility for all statements and opinions in this book are his alone.

The archives of the Polish Institute and Sikorski Museum, in London, were important to this work. The shelves containing the Brigade's reports and records formed the backbone of my research, along with the Institute's Photo Archive. I would like to thank the entire staff of the Institute, and in particular Captain Waclaw Milewski, Captain Ryszard Dembinski, Captain Stanislaw Zurakowski, Andrzej Suchcitz and Krzysztof Barbarski for their help and kindness. The staff of the Polish Institute, which is one of the focal points of Polish life in London, is always very busy, but the way they responded to my requests and needs gave this author the feeling that when he passed through the Institute's door, it was as if he were entering a second home across the ocean.

The Pilsudski Institute in New York, while not having the massive documentation on the Parachute Brigade that is available in London, has also been very helpful, and its photo collection provided a needed backup for that in the Sikorski archives.

I am also grateful to Post 36, Polish Army Veterans in America (SWAP), Passaic, NJ, for their interest and support.

I would like to express my thanks to the various chapters of the Polish Airborne Forces Association for the way they have welcomed me to their reunions, and for their quarterly official publication, *Spadochron*. In its pages the lives of the Polish paratroopers, both now and in the past, are featured. (I've learned much, unfortunately even from the obituaries.) J. Zbigniew Raschke deserves special mention for his memoir, *"Pieklo"* (Hell), which appeared in No. 63, December 1974, and No. 65, June 1975, and I owe him thanks for permission to quote from his work.

I would also like to thank the late Mrs. Kathryn Morgan Ryan for her conversation and correspondence, in addition to her permission to examine her late husband's research materials for *A Bridge Too Far*, contained in the Cornelius Ryan Collection, Ohio University Libraries, Athens, Ohio. Special thanks are also extended to Sheppard Black, Archival and Special Collections Librarian, who dealt with my requests for the Polish, and some of the British and Dutch, files with speed and accuracy. These were not only invaluable for their content—which opened new avenues of thought and information—but also for their confirmation of many interviews that were undertaken by this author.

This book could not have been written without the help of the sons and daughters of the Netherlanders who lived through the events. Geert Maassen, Jr., municipal archivist; Robert Voskuil, noted expert on the battle; and Berry de Reus, custodian of the Airborne Museum, all grew up in Oosterbeek as the devastated town was being rebuilt. They, like many of their contemporaries, have devoted much energy in gathering and preserving the events of 1944 for future generations. I came first as a researcher, but returned again and again as a friend to these people, who provided me with documents, translated Dutch (a language that is almost as "impossible" as Polish), arranged interviews, accompanied me to the touching memorial services, and walked with me through the woods and fields so that I could better understand the terrain and situations of 1944. I am greatly in debt to them for their many hours of selfless labor spent at desks and in darkrooms assisting the preparation of this book.

Among the people of The Netherlands who lived through those dark days of occupation and the battles of September 1944, I must give special mention, with affection, to Cora and her late brother, Albert J. Baltussen. Events of war have carved a unique place in the hearts of the Polish paratroopers for the Baltussen family. I thank them for overcoming their natural modesty to answer my constant questions. I must indeed make mention of Cora's insight and humanity, which not only caused me to reevaluate some of the material I had written, but made me realize I had met a very special person.

A word of special thanks goes to Gerard and Jo Maassen for the warmth and generosity they have shown to the Polish-American author whom their son once dragged home. Their hospitality and cheerfulness have made my visits to Oosterbeek something to look forward to.

Last but far from least, my deep gratitude to my mother, Jadwiga Cholewczynski, and my brother Henry and his wife Beverly, for their patience and assistance over the long years I spent working on this project.

Should the reader care to learn more about the history of Poland, of which her parachute Brigade is only a microscopic part, I recommend two authors who write in English. Neil Acherson's book *The Struggles for Poland* was written to accompany a television documentary series; it offers a crisp and highly readable look at Poland during this century. Norman Davies' gigantic and well-written work *God's Playground*, as well as his shorter books, stand as comprehensive histories in English of a nation that has been misunderstood, when not ignored, in the pages of history.

The author strongly recommends that if the reader visits either Oosterbeek or London he or she should visit the Airborne Museum housed in the historic Hotel Hartenstein or the Sikorski Museum at 20 Princes Gate. The exhibits in both are all-embracing and fantastic, and the love of the museum staffs for their subjects is readily apparent and will be long remembered.

Foreword

The legitimate Polish government in London during World War II had at its disposal an army composed of two parts: Polish armed forces based in Britain and the Polish armed forces in Poland, the latter known as the *Armija Krajowa,* or "Home Army." My father and I were "Poles apart" – separated by distance. He was in Britain and I was in Poland, but we were united by a common respect for each other, perhaps more than the normal affection between father and son, and, of course, by our mutual wish to fight for the common cause.

In September 1941 the 1st Polish Independent Parachute Brigade Group was formed by my father, in spite of extreme difficulties from several quarters. Specially selected men from the Brigade were vigorously trained to be dropped into occupied Poland, to instruct and to help the Polish Home Army. In Poland they were to be known as the *Cichociemni,* or the "Silent and Unseen," and the total number exceeded three hundred men. Many were killed in battle, some were murdered by the occupying enemy, some were sent to Siberia by the second occupying enemy, and some were even executed soon after the war by the Warsaw regime.

The aim of the Home Army was: (a) to train and organize the military force that would face the enemy in future uprisings, and (b) to form active commando units involved in fighting and continuous harassment of the occupiers.

I myself commanded such a unit in the area of Warsaw and, through this fact, came in direct contact with members of the "Silent and Unseen" and indirect contact with my father. They were, of course, his soldiers. In Warsaw the names of the Brigade and its commander were very popular right from the beginning. The Brigade was not supposed to be used on the Western Front, but was to be sent by air—the shortest way—to liberate Poland.

News about the Brigade was often broadcast by the BBC, and later by the Voice of America, printed by the underground press, and repeated by practically everybody in Warsaw. One of our crack commando units adopted the sign of the parachute as its emblem and wore it on their tunics.

I met one of the "Silent and Unseen" for the first time at a special course for officers involved in diversion and sabotage. One of the instructors, Dr. Alfred Paszkowski, a colonel in the Medical Corps, gave a lecture in my house on medical service in the guerrilla war. He noticed, to his great astonishment, a photograph of my father. He exclaimed: "This is my commanding officer!" I replied, "He happens to be my father." A long conversation followed, and he brought me so much welcome news of my father and his work.

This particular course of instruction, and other similar ones, lasted approximately four months and covered the subjects of modern weapons, use of high explosives (including plastic), unarmed combat, and the tactics of underground warfare. Each course ended with a theoretical and practical examination.

When visitors arrived from Britain, I received not only welcome news, but also some photographs of my father and his paratroopers during their training. I treasured one photo in particular. It was taken on June 15, 1944, at Cupar, Scotland. It showed my father being presented with the Brigade's colors by the President of the Polish Republic.

A short time later, on August 1, the general uprising, OPERATION TEMPEST, erupted in Warsaw. This was a supreme act of heroism and sacrifice by the people of Warsaw and the Home Army—the political wisdom of which will have to be judged, in my opinion, by future generations and by history. From the first day, we waited and hoped for the arrival of our Brigade to help us in our unequal struggle. Our hopes were encouraged by the arrival of weapons and supplies dropped from airplanes flying from England and Italy.

On September 18, in the early afternoon of a sunny autumn day, we heard the sound of heavy bombers from a distance. They were coming in wave after wave above the burning city. The whole sky blossomed with countless parachutes. In spite of enemy action, people ran into the streets shouting with joy, "They are coming—our paratroopers are coming!"

Then came the great disappointment of realizing that this was only a supply of weapons and equipment on a grand scale. And most of this, unfortunately, was dropped on the part of the city that was occupied by the Germans! At that time 90 percent of the city was in the hands of the enemy. We learned the next day that a flotilla of 110 American Flying Fortresses had flown from Britain with the much-needed equipment. It was only during this late stage of the uprising that Stalin permitted them to land and refuel in Soviet-occupied territory.

Our hopes of ever seeing the Brigade coming to liberate the city were crushed when we heard the news of Operation MARKET GARDEN. In spite of the promises of the Supreme Allied Commander, the Polish Parachute Brigade did not go to Poland, but was dropped instead with their British and American comrades in Holland.

On the 8th of May, 1945, the war in Europe ended and the second, Communist, occupation of Poland followed, for a much longer time. The people of Warsaw had to wait forty-seven more years for the arrival of the Brigade in their city. On September 26, 1992, the Brigade assembled on Marshal Pilsudski Square in the center of the capital and laid a wreath on the Tomb of the Unknown Warrior. They followed with a march-past in front of an enthusiastic public.

Two days later, the Brigade arrived in the ancient capital of Krakow, to attend the unveiling of a monument to General Sosabowski—three months after what would have been his 100th birthday—on the 48th anniversary of the Arnhem battle.

Dr. Stanislaw Sosabowski
Dorset, England
1993

1

A Huge Wall of Fire and Steel

1645 to 1730 Hours,
September 21, 1944

Flying over the GARDEN corridor, those soldiers who could see out the doors and windows of their twin-engined aircraft witnessed signs of the fierce fighting below. Burning buildings, debris and shell craters became more numerous as the formation flew farther north. In places there were jams of motionless vehicles, hopelessly tangled in traffic far heavier than the few roads north could possibly bear. American crew chiefs indicated with their fingers that they would be over the drop zone in fifteen minutes. Throughout the formation, paratroopers strapped on their rimless steel helmets covered with netting and strips of burlap, the Polish eagle stenciled in yellow paint on the front now barely visible.

In the Dakota with the number "100" chalked on its nose, the stickmaster, Lieutenant Jerzy Dyrda, observed the Brigade's commander. The lieutenant had been General Sosabowski's adjutant and interpreter long before the Brigade's inception in Scotland on September 23, 1941. At Sosabowski's side during many conferences and meetings, Dyrda was more than a staff officer: of all of the men in the Brigade he probably knew best the intelligent, talented, headstrong and frequently abrasive fifty-two-year-old general. Throughout the flight from England, Sosabowski had smiled often and displayed an air of confidence, showing no hint of fear. Usually a man of great emotion, Sosabowski could not afford to reveal his true feelings now.

As the 71-plane formation flew over Holland, the other end of Europe blazed as the population of Warsaw desperately fought a battle of annihilation against the Germans. Seven weeks before, the city had risen after five years of occupation. The 1st Polish Independent Parachute Brigade had been raised specifically to participate in this bid for freedom.

Instead, attached to the British 1st Airborne Division, it was jumping into Operation MARKET GARDEN, one of the most daring operations ever attempted and the largest airborne battle in history.

Five days before, the British had landed in Holland with the mission of capturing the bridge over the Neder Rijn (Lower Rhine) at Arnhem. The American 82nd and 101st Airborne Divisions had been assigned to seize the bridges near Nijmegen and Eindhoven, respectively. Scheduled to jump on the third day of the operation, the Poles had been delayed by bad weather. From the beginning, General Sosabowski objected to operations that seemed to be "pulled like rabbits from hats." He felt that the plans created by the British I Airborne Corps throughout the months of August and September 1944 were overly ambitious and flawed. Unfortunately, as he looked down from his plane at the scarred Dutch countryside rolling past, he found his melancholy predictions confirmed. He had received little information about the battle from his British superiors but had heard reports that the Polish glider lift, which had taken off two days before with the Brigade's heavy weapons, transport and supplies, had been decimated while landing on the north side of the river. Even if these reports were untrue, the Polish paratroopers now en route would be landing unsupported in the open fields around Driel. Sosabowski hoped he would not find Germans on the drop zone; he did not relish his men, armed only with rifles and grenades, having to fight Panzers as they had in Poland five Septembers before.

The anxious troopers heard the stickmaster's shouts of "Action stations!" over the roar of the engines, as red lights beside the open doors of the Dakotas lit. Men rose into the aisles dragging their kit bags in front of them as snap-hooks clicked, attaching static lines to the cable that ran along the starboard side of the cabin. In all of the aircraft the reactions were the same: legs felt like rubber while the soldiers, dry-mouthed, either muttered prayers, bit their lips or did both while waiting for the green light to flash.

After passing Nijmegen, some of the aircraft began to buck. The thumps the men felt were accompanied by puffs of smoke and steel fragments that rattled on the aluminum skins of the Dakotas. Nevertheless, troop-carrier pilots maintained their formations magnificently as they throttled back their engines and tightened their "V's" for the approaching jump.

The German anti-aircraft fire rapidly increased in strength and intensity as the Allied planes neared their destination, the drop zone outside the village of Driel on the southern bank of the Neder Rijn. The heavy German guns across the river joined the light flak from Elst and the railroad bridge. From all around the drop zone, machine guns and even rifles opened fire on the unarmored, unarmed Dakotas. The tight "V"s of the twin-engined American transports were surrounded by smoke and intersected by flashing tracer bullets.

To the men in the bucking aircraft the wait for the green light seemed an eternity. In Plane 111, Private J. Zbigniew Raschke muttered a "Hail Mary" as he heard a whispered farewell come from among the men standing in front of him. The plane jolted. "We got it in the wing. . .!" the corporal standing near Raschke shouted at the top of his lungs. "The wing is on fire!" Raschke indeed saw smoke pouring from a hole in the left wing. With eyes riveted on the bulkhead, he waited for the light to change to green. The light finally flashed, and the column of impatient men pushed their way out the door.

At the door of plane 100, Lieutenant Dyrda was almost paralyzed by the fear of burning to death in a transport aircraft that did not have self-sealing fuel tanks. The lieutenant was certain that his last hour of life was passing: "Before us was a huge wall of fire and steel." Looking out the door, Dyrda recognized the drop zone from the briefing. The soldiers ringing it were obviously not British; they were shooting at the slow-moving aircraft. At 1715 the green light flashed, and the lieutenant went out the door. Without a word, General Sosabowski followed. Hanging under his parachute, Dyrda saw two aircraft losing altitude across the formation. Both trailed smoke and fire as paratroopers continued to tumble from them.

Following the General, Captain Jan Lorys, the Brigade's operations officer, jumped out into a sky flashing with zigzagging bullets and bursting shells. Despite the explosions on the field below, and bullets buzzing around him "like many busy bees," the captain was "strangely happy." Lorys saw that "this was a real battle and, after so many years of waiting and the frustration of so many previously canceled operations," he was glad to be in it.

When the energetic Sosabowski landed, he lost no time getting to his feet, and ran to the Brigade headquarters' assembly point while shouting instructions and encouragement to his men. Captain Lorys landed softly and, as he was removing his harness and oversmock, noticed parachutes drifting east toward the railroad embankment, which bristled with machine-gun fire.

Lance Sergeant Cadet Tadeusz Herman, at the end of the stick on plane 54, carrying part of the 2nd Battalion's headquarters, jumped late. Half of the 18-man stick was out of the aircraft when it was hit. The remaining men lost valuable seconds trying to remain standing as the stricken aircraft twisted and bucked in the barrage. Jumping last, Herman came down on the east side of the embankment.

Herman did not realize that he was alone and surrounded by Germans. "Everybody was shooting at me. I figured that they were making some kind of mistake." The cadet jumped into a water-filled ditch, bullets whizzing all around him. Herman watched a grenade sail toward him "as if in slow motion." He ducked under the water and, coming up for air, found Germans standing along the edge of the ditch. An officer with a pistol in his hand smiled, "Hello, English, for you the war is over." The officer then politely asked Herman for a "souvenir," pointing to the cadet's pistol and commando knife. The amazed Herman finally realized that he had not landed on the drop zone.

In Plane 113, 2nd Lieutenant Szczesny Relidzinski, stickmaster of the headquarters signal center, stood near the open door next to the plane's flight engineer. Both clutched folding bicycles, which would be thrown out before the stick jumped. The red light flashed to green and there was a jolt as the motorcycle slung below the aircraft was released. The bicycles flew out the door, followed by the signal officer. A blast of wind hit Relidzinski full in the face. Eyes squeezed shut and shoulders hunched, he waited for his parachute to open. The harness jerked, and the officer looked up between his hands and noticed that the chute had inflated beautifully, all of its panels intact. Above his canopy, Relidzinski saw the rest of his stick leaving the plane. Glancing below, he saw yellow parachutes with the signal company's equipment containers drifting downwards. Adjusting his lines, the signal officer became aware of gunfire coming from several directions. Distracted by the shooting, the lieutenant did not check his descent and slammed into the ground. His parachute folded lightly around him on this breezeless day as the gunfire increased in intensity. Relidzinski hugged the ground and released his parachute harness.

The crew chief of plane 65 stood on an armored flak vest watching as Lieutenant Albert Smaczny, commander of the 3rd Battalion's 8th Company, went past him and out the door. In the air, Smaczny could hear the sounds of individual rifles among the bursts of machine-gun fire. The rising arcs of yellow tracer bullets "seemed unreal" and looking up, the lieutenant saw two bullet holes in his parachute canopy. Smaczny whispered a prayer of thanks as his feet touched the soft farmland of the Betuwe. Getting out of his harness, the officer heard the familiar shouts of General Sosabowski through the noise of battle.

Jumping fifth behind Lieutenant Smaczny was his radioman, Lance Corporal Boleslaw Kuzniar. As Kuzniar pulled at his lift web to steer his parachute, he felt a blast of air so strong that "I thought my helmet would be torn off." Pulling on his web, the lance corporal avoided landing in a ditch, coming to earth 35 meters from it. Still shaken by his trouble in the air, Kuzniar twisted the quick-release buckle on his chest and hit it smartly. As the parachute harness fell away, odd little fountains of dirt rose a meter ahead of him, and then to his left. The radioman realized that somebody was actually trying to kill him. Overcoming his shock, Kuzniar somersaulted backwards like a circus acrobat until he found himself in the ditch.

Preoccupied with trying to assemble his company, Lieutenant Smaczny was unable to enjoy the sight of his general in action. Four 8th Company men had been wounded while still in the air; one was shot three times in the abdomen. As Smaczny looked him over, he saw signs of other bullets: three dents in a row in the soldier's armored vest. The lieutenant had previously doubted the value of the vest, but this battlefield testimony made him a believer. Gathering his company, the commander forbade the men to abandon their vests, which had earlier been second in popularity to gas masks as items discarded on the drop zone. When a head count was taken, the 8th Company was missing over 40 men, including two officers.

Standing twelfth in his stick, Private Piotr Wawiorko paid no attention to the thumping around plane 110. Sliding his snap-hook with his left hand, the signaler put his leg and kit bag out the door, and "I was gone." Swaying under his inflated parachute, Wawiorko carefully lowered his kit bag, which was connected to his parachute harness by a 20-foot suspension line. "Somehow my mind was working as if this was a training exercise," and Wawiorko wondered, "Why the hell are they wasting all that blank ammunition and petards." The arcing tracers snapped him back to reality, however, as the private saw himself surrounded by brightly colored supply parachutes and paratroopers descending to earth. His kit bag hit the ground softly, followed by the man.

Wawiorko landed standing on his feet, his parachute delicately draped around him. Quickly discarding his jump gear, he joined another soldier from his stick. The pair saw Captain/Father Franciszek Mientki, the

Brigade's chief chaplain, pacing in a circle around his kit bag, praying from his missal. The soldiers approached the chaplain, who had jumped with their stick, to see if he needed any help. The priest ignored the men and continued to pray from his book. With shrugs of their shoulders, the two soldiers started for their assembly area.

Captain/Father Alfred Bednorz, 2nd Battalion chaplain, pushed his way past the toothless American crew chief and out the door of the Dakota. Ignoring the shooting all around him, the chaplain remembered his jump drill and calmly lowered his kit bag. Hanging in the air, the priest saw the Driel church tower and smiled to himself, thinking of the soldier in his stick on plane 38 who said during the flight, "During the jump, the chaplain before anything else should look for a church tower, so we can follow him to the safety of the rectory cellar." Bednorz's musing ended when his kit bag broke loose with a jerk and hurtled to earth, leaving its tattered line flopping below the chaplain. After landing in a ditch full of water, the Father went to look for the missing bag, which contained his field chapel. Spotted by three Germans, who began shooting at him, the priest ran back to the safety of the ditch, pursued by machine-gun bullets, which whizzed around his head. Giving up his kit bag for lost, Bednorz found two bags of medical supplies and hoisted them on his back, starting toward his assembly point.

As the 5th Company, 2nd Battalion jumped, Private Michal Jakutczyk glanced at plane 34's crew chief, standing petrified in a flak vest with eyes glazed over. Ignoring the shooting around him, Jakutczyk checked his canopy and lowered his kit bag. The rifleman came to earth 50 meters from a chattering Spandau. Seconds later, a member of his platoon landed in the open a mere 20 meters from the machine gun, and hugging the earth, frantically called for help. In a moment, a cadet from the same "V" of aircraft landed beside the exposed man. Preoccupied with firing at the pair, the Germans were startled as a bicycle dropped on them from the sky. Its parachute covered the machine gun nest completely, and Jakutczyk and the two other Polish soldiers got to their feet and took prisoner the Germans, who were swimming in the parachute silk. The prisoners and the captured Spandau were turned over to an officer.

The 2nd Battalion quickly assembled by the Baarskamp and took a head count. The medical section and some of the headquarters personnel were missing. Two men had been killed. One, a soldier who had his helmet shot away with the top of his head while still in the air, lay where he landed. His face was pale from blood loss, but otherwise bore a peaceful expression. This shocking sight of their comrade demoralized the many soldiers who passed him on their way to the assembly areas. To Private Jakutczyk's relief, his own platoon had gathered intact.

The anti-tank squadron's supply officer, 2nd Lieutenant Zbigniew Bossowski, jumped from plane 99. Some of the men in the squadron were Poles forcibly conscripted earlier by the Germans and were veterans of Rommel's Afrika Korps. Now serving their motherland under assumed names, their odd "veteran's status" was to prove of great value. Bossowski landed in a water-filled ditch, and the area was immediately raked by a Spandau. Unable to move, the lieutenant heard one of his troopers shout, in perfect colloquial Wehrmacht German, "Stop shooting at us, you horse's ass!" To the officer's surprise, the machine gun stopped!

When the flak began, Sergeant Wojciech Juhas of the engineer company pushed his way to the door of plane 43. Despite the warnings from the American aircrew, Juhas wanted to watch the spectacle. The plane bucked and rolled "like a ship in a storm." The crew chief told Juhas not to worry about the folding bicycles, that he would throw them out. The green light flashed, and Juhas was out the door. Suspended under his parachute, Juhas watched his Dakota drone on, but no bicycles followed. The sergeant muttered a curse, and then put them out of his mind. On the ground, Juhas began unpacking his supply containers, constantly looking up to make sure that those men and bikes still coming down would not land on him. The stick grouped around their bear-like sergeant and reported their radio operator had been wounded. The sappers loaded their equipment onto trolleys and started walking towards the Baarskamp farm.

Plane 62 bucked so much from the anti-aircraft fire that only a few men managed to stay on their feet. One trooper fell, and became so tangled that the flight engineer unhooked him, fating him to return to England. The green light flashed, and the overburdened troopers prodded their kit bags toward the open door. Under his parachute canopy Private Mieczyslaw Chwastek struggled with the release pin for his kit bag. He finally pulled it only two meters above the ground, and the bag slammed into the field, breaking the stock of Chwastek's rifle. Under heavy fire, the rifleman looked through his equipment for anything with which he might lash his rifle back together.

Behind Chwastek, the parachute of his friend and squaddy Private Michal Lasek drifted over a ditch from which General Sosabowski shouted through his cupped hands, "Boys, this is not a farce." On hitting the ground, Lasek tried to make sense of the situation, with "Germans hitting us from all directions. We were crawling, confused and dazed, because if you stood up, for sure the German tommy gunners would get you, and just as surely you would be left on the drop zone." Without having unpacked his weapons, the private crawled over to a young trooper from his platoon who was sprawled in shock amidst the shooting on the drop zone. He lay still in his parachute harness, the sleeve of his Denison smock and the arm in it hanging by thread of fabric and flesh. Lasek put a tourniquet on the man and eased him out of his equipment. Across the drop zone, Lasek saw troopers gradually organizing by section, starting to move in combat formation across the drop zone.

Private Raschke exited his burning Dakota and felt himself falling "like a toy doll." A tug on his harness told him that his parachute had opened. Gray ribbons of smoke threaded their way upwards between the descending parachutes. Raschke drifted towards the railroad embankment, from which tracers were reaching out to touch the suspended paratroopers. Releasing his kit bag and pulling on his parachute straps, Raschke prayed aloud for deliverance. Hitting the ground, the cryptographer lay still "like a corpse" as bullets flew around him. Armed with a short-ranged Sten gun and unable to return fire, he began dragging himself and his kit bag filled with cypher sheets to cover. When a lull came in the firing, the cryptographer gained his feet and sprinted towards a ditch as the Germans opened a fusillade at his running form. Out of breath but in one piece, Raschke reached cover and worked his way through the ditches and canals toward the headquarters assembly point at the Baarskamp farm.

Major Malaszkiewicz's parachute opened above him. The Brigade's chief-of-staff glanced at his watch and noticed it was exactly 1723. Looking off in the distance, the major spotted the blue water of the Neder Rijn less than 3 kilometers away. Smoke was pouring from Arnhem and Oosterbeek, but the river itself was "quiet and devoid of life." A series of shell bursts snapped the officer into realizing that this was not a training exercise. Hitting the ground in a somersault, Malaszkiewicz collapsed his parachute. After loading a magazine into his Sten gun, he slung his map case over his shoulder and started walking in the direction of the river. Quickly the major met other soldiers from his stick. Their "peaceful stroll" was shattered when gunfire erupted from a building across one of the broad fields. The marching column wordlessly rearranged itself into a skirmish line and surged forward. There was no need to press an attack;

the shooting stopped and the headquarters troops saw paratroopers push six Germans with their hands on their heads out of the building.

The 2nd Engineer platoon began to gather around its commander, 2nd Lieutenant Mieczyslaw Grunbaum. The orderly assembly was interrupted when a machine gun cut loose from behind a hedge. For years Grunbaum had thought about his martyred country and his Jewish relatives who remained there. He could not wait to come to grips with the enemy, and now, covered by a shower of grenades, the engineer officer led a charge that flanked the hedge. The embroiled paratroopers pumped round after round into their tormentors. With the bodies of the *Ubermenschen* underfoot, the lieutenant reloaded his Sten gun, "knees trembling and feeling weak like a tiny kitten, rather than seven feet tall."

As the sounds of gunfire petered out across the drop zone, they were replaced by loud Polish voices: "8th Company over here . . ." "I saw them going . . ." "4th Company, pick it up . . ." "Anti-tank Squadron . . ." "Where is Sergeant . . ." "Get that man to . . ." The Brigade began to sort itself out. Supply containers were recovered and opened, and their contents divided among the troops. An occasional odd shot or machine-gun burst echoed across the fields as more and more troops appeared from odd corners of the drop zone. The soldiers tried to orient themselves. Four hours earlier, they had been in peaceful England; then, in the span of minutes, they had been thrown into heavy combat. The General divided his attention between Lieutenant Dyrda's interrogation of the prisoners and watching his signalers trying to contact the Brigade's different units. Seemingly calm and at ease, Sosabowski munched on the fruit that grew in the orchards. But the commander's demeanor was just a mask. The Poles had orders to get across the river by ferry and reinforce the hard-pressed British 1st Airborne Division as quickly as possible.

On September 21, 1944, the 1st Polish Independent Parachute Brigade landed in Driel, Holland as part of Operation MARKET GARDEN, the largest airborne operation in history. These men had traveled from all over Europe to join the Polish Army in Exile in Britain. Defeat, hunger and captivity were among the obstacles overcome by the men whom Nazi propaganda cynically referred to as "General Sikorski's Tourists." Those men who reached the coast of Fife in Scotland were given a gray beret and earned the privilege to wear the silver diving eagle insignia of the Polish paratroopers on their breasts. Becoming a paratrooper was the promise of a way to get home.

Most of these men were never to see Poland again. In common with their countrymen fighting on other fronts, they impressed their allies—soldiers and civilian alike—with a pathos and love of country unsurpassed among fighting troops in the Second World War. They joined their commander, Major General Stanislaw Sosabowski, in writing a story of blind courage, endless frustration and twisted fate. This is that story.

2

Education of the Soldier and Citizen
1892 to Summer 1939

Occupying the heartland of Europe, Poland had been a constitutional monarchy beginning in 1791. Once a commonwealth that stretched from the Baltic to the Black Sea, the nation suffered gradual dismemberment by its powerful neighbors, Russia, Prussia and Austria, and in 1795 actually disappeared from the map of Europe.

The culture of Poland and its people had been vital, modern and forward-looking. The nation was fervently Catholic, but had always practiced religious tolerance, and was one of the few nations of the then-Western world that did not have a religious war in its history. Following its dissolution, the country abruptly fell into a morass of foreign tyranny that sought to eradicate the nation's spiritual and cultural values. Many of the "best and brightest" people left Poland, unable to live under the conquering powers. An opportunity to regain their country's freedom came with the rise of Napoleon in France, the nation where most of the emigrés had gone. The young conqueror raised several Polish legions, whose members proved to be superb soldiers. With Napoleon's assurances that Poland would be reborn, the legions' ranks constantly increased, and the reward for this service was the creation of the Grand Duchy of Warsaw. In 1812, however, the hope for Poland's resurrection died in the snows of Russia, where the Poles formed a large segment of the French leader's Grand Armée.

After the defeat of Napoleon, Russia, Prussia and Austria reoccupied the parts of Poland they had previously partitioned, but in a compromise permitted a small "Kingdom of Poland," centered on Warsaw, to exist. This situation lasted for fifteen years, until the officers of the Kingdom's army revolted in 1830 and won a victory at Grochow, outside of

Warsaw. The rebellion was crushed by the Czar the following spring, and the Kingdom of Poland was annexed by Russia. Again came a new wave of emigration and, as in the past, many went to France.

The remnants of the Polish gentry again revolted against the Russians in 1863, and this insurrection too was crushed. The Czar instituted a rigid policy of "Russification": all universities were closed, spies flooded the country and the Polish language was forbidden in schools, the courts and local government.

In Prussia, Bismarck was busy uniting the German states, and saw the German-ruled Poles' patriotism and high birth rate as threats. While the Polish population under Germany was not inclined to insurrection, an increasing non-Germanic element within Prussia was by itself intolerable to the Teutonic "Iron Chancellor." A "Kulturkampf" was instituted that was aimed directly at the Poles and their religion. From then on all schooling would be in the hands of the civil authorities. German schoolmasters were brought in en masse, and German was adopted as the official language. Even a sign on the street could no longer be in Polish. But the Slavs had little interest in the German "civilizing" mission and even resisted Prussian attempts to buy their farmlands.

The circumstances in the Austrian-ruled parts of Poland were different. The Polish language was widely used in all sectors of life, and the population was allowed considerable latitude, even in local governmental administration. But Austria was a Ruritanian empire, and those who had power and influence seemed to prefer waltzing in Vienna to developing the provinces. Poland, fortunately, lay in the furthest backwater of the empire and received little attention. Nevertheless, in economic terms, the wretched state of the peasants under Austrian rule began to equal that of the long-suffering population in those parts of Poland under the rule of Russia.

It was in Austrian Poland that Stanislaw Franciszek Sosabowski was born on May 8, 1892. Stanislawow, his place of birth, was a city where the steppes in the fertile bend of the Dniester River met the Carpathian Mountains. Stanislaw was the second oldest of two boys and two girls fathered by Franciszek Sosabowski, a clerical worker for the Austrian national railroad. Young Stanislaw had the privilege of attending school, and at the age of eleven, while attending gymnasium, he became the head of the family when his father died. A meager widow's pension was not enough to keep the family from sinking into poverty. Still, the bright boy did not abandon his education, but helped support his family by tutoring his classmates.

The school was almost totally Polish, and both the teacher and the students were highly patriotic. It was there that Sosabowski joined "The Falcons," a Polish gymnastic society that was also a semi-underground independence organization. Besides discussing Polish history and politics, the members also trained with rifles that were provided by the government, ostensibly for national defense. These units became part of a clandestine "Sharpshooters" organization, and were to provide a cadre for a Polish Army when the opportunity would present itself. In 1912, Sosabowski was selected for secret training as a Polish officer, and commanded the Sharpshooters in Stanislawow. He was also involved in the secret raising of a Polish Boy Scout troop in the area.

In 1914, the world shuddered when Austrian Archduke Ferdinand was assassinated and Europe plunged into total war. While many Poles flocked to the Polish Legion of the Austrian Army under Jozef Pilsudski, the Poles of Lwow and Stanislawow waited for the call of their own nationalist leaders. Unknown to the Sharpshooters, there were political differences between Pilsudski and the Polish patriots in the region. These units never joined the Legion and as a result were forcibly mobilized into the Austrian Imperial Army. Sosabowski found himself a corporal cadet wearing the pike-gray uniform of the 58th Infantry Regiment.

The opening moves of World War I found a Russian offensive attempting to take the Austrian fortress city of Przemsyl. Through the long winter, Corporal Cadet Sosabowski saw his regiment fritter away. Those men not disabled by Russian shells and bullets were laid low by the soldier's traditional companions: lice and dysentery. The corruption of the Imperial supply system provided little except an extra income for corrupt quartermasters. Men froze for lack of overcoats; the delivery of rations was uncertain, and soldiers actually died of starvation. By the end of the first year of the war, Sergeant Cadet Sosabowski was one of three surviving members of his original company of 250 men.

The following summer, Sergeant Major Cadet Sosabowski taught survival to replacement officers of the Austrian Army. During June 1915, Sosabowski was wounded in the right leg by a shrapnel ball, leaving damaged nerves and a pronounced limp. Sent to recuperate in what was to become Czechoslovakia, Sosabowski was accompanied by his wife. It was there that she bore him his first child, a boy named Stanislaw. Late in 1917 the cadet was finally commissioned an officer in Franz Jozef's army, and given assignment as a staff officer to the Archduke's headquarters in Bolzano on the Tyrolian front.

During his "busy work" in the Imperial Staff's archives, many secret orders and reports passed through Sosabowski's hands. By early 1918, the conclusion of the war was foreseeable. Sosabowski arranged his transfer to Lublin, Poland, to await coming events. Russia was out of the war and in the depths of revolution. All of Poland was in either German or Austrian hands. Pilsudski was in prison, having refused to fight for the new "Kingdom of Poland," a puppet state created by the Germans. The Central Powers were visibly losing the war, and there was the obvious possibility that Poland would be reborn. Already there were missions to Woodrow Wilson and Georges Clemenceau, who supported, for both political and sentimental reasons, the establishment of a free and independent Poland. In these last months of war, Sosabowski organized officers of Polish background for the inevitable.

By the beginning of November, the soldiers in Lublin were removing the Austrian cockades from their caps and replacing them with the Polish White Eagle. Their primary purpose was not to fight the remains of the demoralized polyglot Austrian Army, but to disarm them, send them home, and insure that none of the large military warehouses were removed or destroyed. There were five railroad battalions stationed in Lublin. Fortunately, they consisted mainly of Hungarians, who were sympathetic to the Poles. The work was long and arduous, but accomplished without incident, and, with the German evacuation of Warsaw, de facto Polish independence was achieved. Sosabowski remained in Lublin, working on the quartermaster staff in the headquarters of the Lublin Military District.

Since his wounded leg precluded front-line service during the battles against the Bolsheviks, the Ukrainians and the German Freikorps during 1919–20, Major Sosabowski found himself in Spa, Belgium, with the Polish mission to the Interallied Council,* as a specialist in supply and materiel matters. This was of extreme importance, as it was Sosabowski's bureau that decided what needs (of the many) had priority, and how they would be transported to the reborn nation.

---

*An international body was created by the victorious Allies to administer the terms of the Armistice with Germany. Military commissions, headquartered in Spa, were composed to deal with hostile border disputes between the newly created nations of Central and Eastern Europe.

Finally and truly independent after over 120 years of foreign occupation, there was still little cause for celebration in Poland. Border fighting continued until 1921, and even the eventual peace provided little respite. The country was devastated. Armies had passed back and forth, leaving destruction and death in their wake. All industry was destroyed, and 85 percent of the nation's population was unemployed. Half of the farms remained uncultivated, either ruined by war or with their owners dead or crippled in battle. Civilians who had fled the fighting only slowly drifted back to what remained of their homes. Transportation was in shambles and practically every bridge and railroad line had been destroyed.

As if the destruction of war had not been enough, trying to create a nation from three separate administrations proved a nightmare. The railroads—even if they had been undamaged—were built to the standards of three different nations, and ran on two different gauges. There was no experienced civil administration in the formerly German areas, and differing versions existed in the former Austrian and Russian provinces. There were three codes of laws from the previous administrations and, in Warsaw, a separate Codex that was a carryover from the old Kingdom of Poland. A Herculean task faced the Poles in creating a nation out of the shambles that remained. This they attacked with verve and energy.

Sosabowski returned to Poland to carry on normal staff duties. It was not only the civil and legal administrations that suffered from divided backgrounds; a similar situation existed in the military. The soldiers had been trained by three completely different armies. Using their religious background as an excuse, the Prussians did not commission Poles, but in the trenches they did form a large part of the German non-commissioned officer corps. The Russian and Austrian armies did commission Poles as officers, and many of them succumbed to the status and privilege of this class within those societies. With this type of officer, the energetic Sosabowski was always at loggerheads, and he rapidly acquired an army-wide reputation as a troublesome "kicking stallion."

Major Sosabowski began taking courses at the young (but already highly respected) Polish Army General Staff College in 1922. Polish soldiers had proven themselves many times throughout the centuries, but, unlike the other powers of Europe, the nation had passed more than a hundred years without any academy of higher military education. A sense of identity for the Polish Army was not the problem—it was in establishing a sound, long-term military policy, and providing the physical and intellectual means to field an army in the swiftly changing atmosphere of the twentieth century. The staff needed to study and propagate the tactical innovations executed on the battlefields during the years 1914–21. It needed a plan for integrating the nation's population, territory and resources in a framework of defense for a nation surrounded by large and hostile neighbors.

Sosabowski was posted to the General Staff after completing staff college. He again concerned himself with supply matters and in planning for strategic reserves of materiel in case of war. Doubtless this was important work, but the driven officer longed for a line command. As the years passed, the limp resulting from his shrapnel wound gradually disappeared and he had come to regain his former athleticism.

In 1927, Sosabowski was promoted to lieutenant colonel and given command of a battalion of the 75th Infantry Regiment, stationed at Rybnik in Silesia. Just seven years earlier, the Poles had been embroiled with the Freikorps in several vicious conflicts in this border region. The units stationed there received first draw of the latest equipment and also the best manpower. The battalion commander demanded that the large German population that remained see only exemplary standards and conduct on the part of the Polish soldiers in the area. Discipline was strict, as was Sosabowski's reputation as a commander.

A year later, Sosabowski was assigned deputy command of the 3rd Highland Rifle Regiment. This was a Silesian regiment, and an elite mountain infantry unit at that. Besides wearing a distinctive uniform, the regiment had the pleasure of being garrisoned in the lovely mountain city of Bielsko. Sosabowski was at home in this positive atmosphere, and spent much of his time on skis. However, garrison life with a divisional headquarters nearby did not appeal to this independent man, and he frequently found himself crossing swords with superiors who did not always agree with the "Sosabowski way" of doing things. This did not, however, prevent excellent fitness reports, which stated that he was always considered to be an asset to the unit.

Late in 1929, Lieutenant Colonel Stanislaw Sosabowski was invited to join the faculty of Warsaw's General Staff College. Soon, specializing in supply matters, he acquired the nickname of "The Shopkeeper" within the army. He was, of course, electrified by the responsibility of educating staff officers, and emphasized the necessity of personal leadership and solid logistical support in military operations. His book *Education of the Soldier and Citizen* was published in 1932 and became a standard text in military education. It was an unusual book on the private soldier as a member of a free society, and about the need for military leadership to be mindful of a soldier's dignity in order to lead troops with respect and responsibility.

Students at the school remembered the excessively robust and bombastic lieutenant colonel as an aggressive and ambitious climber. However, he also left a stronger impression as an energetic and precise organizer not given to theatrics. Aside from normal academic work, Sosabowski edited scholarly military journals, for which he also wrote dozens of articles. In 1935 a second book, *Quartermastership in the Field*, was published.

These were happy days for Sosabowski. Income from the publications allowed his family to live in a small villa in the Warsaw suburb of Zoliborz. A second son, Jacek, was born in 1922. The staff college professor spent as much time with his children as possible, often vacationing in the Tatra Mountains. Though strict, he never struck his children or even raised his voice. A disapproving look was usually sufficient to accomplish discipline: his brow would curl down, and his normally warm, blue-gray eyes would turn icy. The intense glare would take on the uncompromising effect of gun barrels. If a child misbehaved, the look was unavoidable, and unmistakable, and there was no further need for words.

Lieutenant Colonel Sosabowski was promoted to full professorship at the staff college, but his heart was set on commanding an infantry regiment. In 1937, this wish was granted. Leaving the bustling capital for rural Zamosc, Sosabowski took command of the 9th Infantry Regiment. He inherited a unit poor in morale and lacking in cohesiveness. Distractions were few in the small town, provided only by alcohol and a single movie theater. The new commander saw to it that there was more time off for the young officers from the hard daily work at their units, and arranged for passes for them to visit Warsaw or Lublin on weekends. The municipality itself had previously been a Russian garrison town and the local citizens were still not well disposed to soldiers, no matter what their uniform. A point had to be made to create more interplay with the townspeople, including invitations to regimental dances and functions.

For the conscripted common soldier, Sosabowski put into deed the writings of his first book. He saw the soldier's time away from a wretched village or a depression-wracked city as an opportunity for his education as a citizen. This was extended to the soldier's family, and the Colonel made arrangements with the railroad authorities for a certain number of free or discounted tickets so family members could see their sons and brothers march in ceremonies. Afterwards, the families were invited to soldiers' dinners under the open sky. The success of the Colonel's approach became apparent when the regiment won the Divisional Shooting Award and that winter went on to win another award for skiing.

While Sosabowski's eldest son, Stanislaw, was studying at the Army Medical College, the younger, Jacek, was killed in a tragic firearms accident. Sosabowski was shattered, and felt that commanding a regiment at this time was beyond him. In January 1939, he reported personally to the Ministry of Defense in Warsaw and asked to be relieved of his command of the 9th Infantry Regiment.

Shortly afterwards, in March 1939, Sosabowski was promoted to full colonel. With promotion came an offer of command of the 21st Infantry Regiment. Sosabowski, while still deeply emotional over the loss of his son, accepted the offer, which did much to bring him out of his grief. The unit was the famous "Children of Warsaw" Infantry Regiment, and it had long, traditional ties to the city.

The unit had seen its first action in the streets of Warsaw in 1794 against the Russians. It was later resurrected by the Kingdom of Poland in 1815, and received the title "Children of Warsaw" when it fought (again against the Russians) at the battle in the Warsaw suburb of Grochow in 1830. The regiment was reborn on November 11, 1918, from the cadre of an underground independence organization. From that day on, it had been quartered in the city's citadel, and in military protocol was the capital's premier garrison unit. Many of the unit's soldiers were recruited from the city's rougher neighborhoods, but even hardcore "jailbirds" had respect for their strict but fair commander. The regiment was not only a crack combat unit trained to a high military standard, the 21st was also acknowledged for its "spit and polish" parade appearance.

On Constitution Day (May 3) 1939, the soldiers of the "Children of Warsaw" Infantry Regiment led the capital's parade. Colonel Sosabowski, mounted on a white horse, rode at their head, listening to the cheers of men, women and children. The huge ceremonial march proceeded down Warsaw's broad boulevards, which were decked in red-and-white flags. None of the thousands of spectators that beautiful spring day could visualize the parade that would take place a mere six months later. Then, only soldiers in coal-scuttle helmets would line the avenues. The fluttering flags would be red-and-white, but with the addition of a black, twisted cross. A man with a small black mustache would take the salute, and, for millions of people around the globe, a familiar world would have ended and a dangerous new one begun.

3

The Soldiers Known as the "Children of Warsaw"

August to September 1939

With the rise of Adolf Hitler, Germany attempted to redeem the blows its collective psyche had suffered as a result of defeat during the First World War and its "punishment" afterwards. The Nazi philosophy was based on a premise of German superiority over other races, particularly Jews and Slavs, who were viewed as subhumans. Under Hitler, Germany embarked on a massive program of rearmament and the expansion of its armed forces, subsequently adopting a policy of intimidation towards its neighbors. After the Germans seized Czechoslovakia in 1938, in defiance of the spirit of the agreements made at Munich, France and Britain began to re-evaluate their politics of appeasement. When the Nazis increased their anti-Polish propaganda throughout the summer of 1939, it also became apparent that Hitler had designs on his eastern neighbor.

In 1939, the young Polish state comprised parts of what had formerly been East Prussia, along with other formerly German-ruled territories east of the Oder River. The Germanic city of Danzig had been stripped from Germany and a "corridor" of Polish territory now bordered on the Baltic Sea, separating East Prussia from the rest of Germany. Hitler's propaganda viewed the Poles as unworthy usurpers of German lands and sought to magnify any injustices committed by Poles against German citizens along the border areas.

The Polish situation was unenviable. With the German occupation of Czechoslovakia, Poland now had to face its racial and political enemy not only on its western frontier and on its narrow corridor to the sea, but also along its southern border. The twenty-year-old Polish Republic had struggled desperately throughout the Depression years of the 1930s to rebuild from the ravages of war and create from a polyglot bureaucracy a modern state. Despite the pressing needs of education, industry and infrastructure, the bulk of spending had to fall to defense. However, although by 1939 Poland was spending over 50 percent of its gross national product on defense, the struggling nation was hard-pressed to keep pace with its enemy. Poland's total defense expenditure between 1936 and 1939 was less than 10 percent of what Germany had spent on its air force in 1939 alone.

When Germany demanded the return of the Free City of Danzig* to the Reich, France and Britain worried about Hitler's increasing power. Despite—perhaps because of—the Polish rejection of French and British advice to seek an alliance with the Soviet Union, the Allies entered into common defense treaties with Poland. The Poles obviously would not bow to Hitler's demands, and their new Allies sought to advise them on defense. The foreign "experts," looking at maps, suggested that the Poles, with no natural defense lines in their flat country, abandon much of their territory and fall back behind their rivers to defend only the central part of the nation. This strategy was impossible for the Poles. Not only was there great emotional attachment to the Corridor, Polish Silesia, and other areas outside of central Poland, much of the nation's population and industrial resources were there. Leaving the periphery of the nation undefended would only allow Hitler to cut pieces off Poland like a sausage. Britain and France promised that in the event Hitler attacked his neighbor, they would declare war against Germany. Noting their Allies' assurances, the Poles girded themselves for whatever lay ahead.

In 1939, the Polish Army's annual summer maneuvers were canceled as a result of the worsening political situation. Colonel Sosabowski was ordered to return with his regiment to Warsaw on August 22. Arriving at the Citadel the following evening, the Colonel saw feverish preparations taking place. That very night the capital was rocked by news of a "Non-Aggression Pact," signed in Moscow, that forged an alliance between Hitler and Stalin. Sosabowski was issued mobilization orders that were to take effect on August 24, the following day. General mobilization was still not taking place; the British and French had requested a postponement so as not to provoke the Germans. The 8th Infantry Division, however, which counted the "Children of Warsaw" Regiment in its ranks, received orders to move north to the border with East Prussia.

---

*The port of Danzig (now Gdansk) was made a Free City under the supervision of the League of Nations following WWI. The German population of the ancient Polish city resented the Polish regulation of the port, the postal system and a small military base.

During the late afternoon of August 26, Sosabowski reviewed his troops, battalion by battalion. After over twenty-five years of military experience, encompassing training, combat and higher education, the Colonel was confident of himself and his men. They began a night march to Opinogora, sensing the strong possibility of war.

As the "Children of Warsaw" slogged towards the border, most of the ships of the Polish Navy slipped out of indefensible Gdynia and sailed for Britain. The planes of the Polish Air Force moved to primitive combat airfields away from their main bases. The French and British were still opposed to the Poles' carrying out a general mobilization, for this might serve to provoke Hitler. Despite the wishes of their allies, the Poles discretely carried out their mobilization by mail.

On August 31, the German battleship *Schleswig-Holstein*, on a "goodwill" visit to Danzig, weighed anchor and moved across the harbor. In the German border city of Gleiwitz, not far from the barracks of the Poles' 75th Infantry Regiment in Rybnik, the radio show being broadcast was suddenly interrupted. Shots rang out as "Polish" soldiers grabbed the microphone and babbled a political diatribe in Polish. Then the transmitter went dead. Journalists visiting the site the next morning saw a corpse in Polish uniform. The "attackers" were actually SS men, and the corpse was that of a concentration camp inmate, poisoned and left at the radio station as "proof" of Polish provocation.

At 4:45 on the morning of September 1, 1939, the *Schleswig-Holstein* opened fire point-blank against the Polish ammunition dump at Westerplatte in Danzig harbor. In the pre-dawn twilight, heavily laden German aircraft crossed the Polish border and ruthlessly began bombing both military and civilian targets. All along the border, the roar of diesel engines and the screeching of metal rent the dawn as German tanks swept across the border. On the frontier with East Prussia, the German Third Army, consisting of three infantry divisions, the "Kempf" Panzer Division and a cavalry brigade, crossed into northern Mazowsze and attacked units of the Polish Army Modlin. Under an umbrella of screeching Stuka dive bombers, the Third Army attacked the Polish 20th Infantry occupying the border fortifications at Mlawa. After heavy fighting the Germans managed to achieve only a minor breakthrough, but the Polish positions at Mlawa were under extreme pressure.

The dawn of that historic first day of September found the 21st Infantry Regiment in a stand-down. In the eight days since its "secret" mobilization, the regiment's soldiers had covered 150 kilometers in five days of marching. The following days were spent in intensive labor constructing field fortifications, and the exhausted soldiers were finally having a much-needed day of rest. Colonel Sosabowski made his last command preparations as the regiment received fresh horses.

The next day, the "Children of Warsaw" remained in their positions. All was quiet except for enemy bombers flying at high altitude in "V" formations in the direction of Warsaw. The division commander called his regimental commanders to his headquarters for final orders. The Poles' 20th Division was fighting for its life on the border, both taking and inflicting heavy casualties. German Panzer and motorized infantry units had broken through the Polish line and were moving on Warsaw. That night, the 8th Division was to march to the 20th's aid, and a few hours before dusk, with the 21st Infantry on the 8th Division's left flank, the march to battle began.

By dawn the soldiers known as the "Children of Warsaw" had moved beyond the village of Radomko. Colonel Sosabowski was troubled by the division's deployment. He had protested the large gaps between his battalions and, even more, the gaps between the division's regiments and the lack of contact with neighboring units. For his bother, Sosabowski was bluntly told to follow orders. The chatter of machine-gun fire announced that patrols sent ahead of the march column had run into the enemy. The Colonel spurred his horse forward, and saw soldiers clad in field gray moving among the trees. In short order the enemy machine guns were joined by mortars and artillery. Coming straight from a march, and without any artillery support, the 21st launched a bravura assault that stopped the German advance.

Colonel Sosabowski was justifiably proud of his men. Fighting went on throughout the day, the experienced commander watching his command closely through binoculars. The Colonel was impressed with the conduct of his officers and NCOs. They were calm under fire, and the troops responded well to their leadership and inspiration. Unknown to the Polish soldiers, their division had run into the German 12th Pommern Infantry Division, and had brought its advance on Warsaw to a halt. But the "Children of Warsaw" were at the end of their tether. The Polish regiment had taken a fair number of casualties itself, and was in urgent need of reinforcement. At sunset Sosabowski telephoned divisional headquarters and was assured the arrival of a fresh battalion at 2200 hours. This was the last he ever heard from headquarters or of the promised reinforcements.

As night fell, the 21st's positions were flown over by aircraft and surrounded by the sounds of skirmishers and tank engines. Obviously cut off, Sosabowski ordered a two kilometer withdrawal to better defensive terrain, which began at 0330. By dawn the troops were digging in. The "Children of Warsaw" found themselves in the open, the nearest cover being the Opinogora forest. To the south, smoke rose from the town of Ciechanow, which, unknown to Sosabowski, was now occupied by a German motorized column.

On September 3, France and Britain finally declared war on Hitler, and gave him three days to withdraw his army from Poland. The Luftwaffe had caused great havoc, bombing and strafing soldiers and civilians alike. Apart from the indiscriminate raiding of cities, the initial specific targets were, however, the railroads: the late mobilization and the bombing of the transportation system would leave many reservists stranded and unable to join their units. The revolutionary German "Blitzkrieg" had cut through the Polish Corridor and left many breaks in the Polish defensive lines. The invader was rapidly approaching Warsaw.

Colonel Sosabowski's problem was serious; his regiment was cut off in the open, exhausted from combat and days of marching, and had not eaten in twenty-four hours. The risk of moving 11 kilometers through open country to the cover of a forest was preferable to waiting for help that would not come, or eventual discovery by the Germans. In broad daylight the troops moved out.

The route to the forest gave silent testimony to the fate of the remainder of the 8th Division. Sosabowski knew nothing of what had happened to the rest of his division. The German 1st Cavalry Brigade and the "Kempf" Panzer Division overwhelmed the Polish Mazowiecka Cavalry Brigade, which was protecting the 8th Division's left flank. As the German drive continued, the enemy rolled over all of the units of the 8th Division except the 21st Infantry Regiment.

The "Children of Warsaw" passed all manner of abandoned materiel: rifles, artillery and munitions, most of it in usable condition. Colonel Sosabowski was horrified. It was reminiscent of scenes he had witnessed over twenty years before, when the two former empires, the Czar's and the Kaiser's, had bumbled into battle. But now there was a difference: this was a Polish defeat. Sosabowski stomached his disappointment and moved through the ranks, talking to and encouraging his troops. Fearful of air attack, the exhausted soldiers shuffled on. Upon reaching the village of Lekowa, the last village before the beginnings of the forest, Sosabowski was approached by a captain from the divisional staff. The officer saluted and announced to Sosabowski that he was now in command of the remains of the 8th Division.

Gathered around the village were the survivors from units of both the 8th and 20th Divisions. Together they totaled four battalions of infantry, two batteries of artillery and two companies of tankettes. Sosabowski now had almost 5,000 exhausted and defeated men under his command. There was no food and, more important, no information, other than that from peasants, that there were many German tanks in the area.

The forest would obviously be a refuge for only a few hours. So, after calling for a short rest, Sosabowski briefed the unit commanders on his plans. The group's objective was to get to Modlin, divided into two columns, each 5 kilometers long and including guns, tankettes and wagons. In this dangerous situation the normal Polish tactical doctrine of carrying out movement at night was even more critical. Contact with the enemy was to be avoided under any circumstance.

To prevent panic, Sosabowski issued very strict orders against any shooting. For emphasis, the soldiers were to remove their rifle bolts and carry them in their pockets. Any excess equipment was to be systematically destroyed, and two motorcycle couriers were sent to make contact with the headquarters of Army Modlin. Lightly screened by cavalry, the column moved off. In a report written in 1945, Major Stefan Obrebowski, commander of the 21st Infantry's 3rd Battalion, paid tribute to his men:

> The soldiers' conduct, despite the forced march and the lack of food and sleep, could only be described as magnificent, morale-exemplary: no indiscipline, no discarding of equipment. The soldiers were driven as if by their own free will. Moving silently, they regarded the situation as temporary, and that their hour would come. Orders were carried out willingly and without delay. The company commanders moved the entire time on foot, their horses given to the exhausted riflemen. They helped carry equipment, were last to be fed, and slept only when their men were taken care of.

The columns reached the village of Zalesie as the sun rose on September 5. What provisions the village could spare were requisitioned, giving many men the first food that they had in forty-eight hours. As many soldiers as possible were packed into barns and houses to sleep and make preparations for the coming evening.

That night, Sosabowski's group crossed the River Wrke and burned the bridges behind them. The tankers were about to destroy their vehicles for lack of fuel, when by a stroke of luck they found some drums of gasoline at an abandoned airfield. In the distance, rifle shots were heard as the screening soldiers ran into a German patrol, but the skirmish was quickly broken off, as movement had priority. At dawn, the Sosabowski group was met by two trucks carrying provisions sent from the Modlin fortress. The lieutenant in command swore that the road to Modlin was open. As these trucks had obviously gotten through, Sosabowski decided not to stop, but to push on.

Colonel Sosabowski and his group reached the Modlin fortress on September 7, after four days behind enemy lines. While Modlin prepared to meet the German advance — at that time about to be renewed — Sosabowski went on to Jablonna to give his report. He then traveled to Warsaw to check on his regiment's supply column, and to see how his family was faring. The journey proved depressing. The towns and villages along the way were shattered by bombs and abandoned by panicked civilians. The bodies of men, women, children and farm animals lay bloated and rotting in the sun. The edges of the road were strewn with personal belongings as groups of homeless people shouted requests for news when they saw the officer drive by. Plumes of black smoke on the horizon showed the way to Warsaw.

Upon entering the city the repulsive sight of the war raining down on the heads and homes of innocent civilians increased in horror and intensity. Putrid odors came from the once beautiful buildings that lined the capital's streets and avenues, now burned out or reduced to heaps of rubble. The civilians in the streets were filthy, and met Sosabowski's looks with hollow stares. Warsaw had been under constant aerial bombardment since the first day of the war.

Arriving at the Citadel, Sosabowski discovered his supply train there. It had returned when the 8th Division was shattered. It was immediately ordered to join the rest of the regiment at Modlin. Then, racing to his house in Zoliborz, the Colonel discovered that his wife and sister had already left the city, and that there was no word of his son, Stanislaw, who was deputy commander of a hospital train.

Poland's situation on that eighth day of September was critical. Communications between the General Staff and field commands over the country's overworked telephone and telegraph systems had been marginal at best, and broke down completely when the General Staff evacuated Warsaw. Krakow had fallen and the Polish Army was in almost total disarray. The mechanized German divisions rapidly outpaced the Polish soldiers, who could depend only on the legs of men or horses for maneuver. Herculean efforts on the part of field commanders frequently rewelded the shattered remains of combat units into organized groups, and in vicious fighting, the Polish rear guards shielded their retreating comrades. The remains of Army Modlin would hold the giant Napoleonic fortress of the same name as a roadblock to the Germans advancing southward on Warsaw from East Prussia. The "Children of Warsaw" were ordered to fall back to their mother city and aid in her defense.

The tanks of the 4th Panzer Division had already probed the streets of the Warsaw neighborhood of Ochota on September 8. Two days later, German tanks ran down its broad avenues in an attempt to push into the center of the capital. The Germans were building up their strength on the outskirts of the city, but their ring was not complete.

On September 10, the Poles' 21st Infantry Regiment, strengthened by the 8th Division's machine-gun company and other divisional units, left Modlin for Warsaw. Over Colonel Sosabowski's protests, the march took place in daylight. The commander drove his column hard, and even when attacked by Stukas, seeing over twenty men killed and scores wounded, he managed to get the column moving within an hour. The regiment reached Struga-Zielonka in the late afternoon, and there dug into defensive positions. Three days later, on September 13, the regiment was ordered to move to the Praga district of Warsaw on the east bank of the Vistula River.

During the early hours of September 14, the "Children of Warsaw" started occupying the streets and avenues of Warsaw's eastern suburb of Grochow. They passed a monument to the men of their regiment who had stood in the January frosts 108 years before and kept the Czar's army from the city. Colonel Sosabowski received reinforcements in the form of two battalions of the 336th (Reserve) Infantry Regiment, and an artillery battalion. His orders were to keep the Germans away from the Poniatowski and Kierbedzia bridges, which crossed the wide Vistula into the city's center. The fields of 1831 were now built over with gas works, large factories and the city's slaughterhouse. The areas between were crowded with apartment buildings, houses and shops that made up the working-class community. The soldiers immediately began building barricades of earth and rubble across the avenues. At the intersection of Grochow Street and Washington Avenue, an earthen redoubt was constructed that would be the center of the sector's defense. The main defensive liability was the broad open area to the southeast, and the woods of the Saska Kepa park, which ran along the river. Ammunition for small arms was not a problem; the Pocisk ammunition factory was located in Sosabowski's defensive sector. But artillery munitions were scarce. The Colonel established his headquarters in the Motlot factory, which had previously manufactured aircraft components, and waited.

The bombardment on the morning of September 15 was heavier than usual. Sosabowski was informed that a large German column supported by tanks was moving from the city of Minsk Mazowiecki. The German infantry was still in marching order as it approached the positions of the 21st Regiment's 1st Battalion. The battalion opened up a hurricane of fire that took the Germans by surprise. Polish machine guns and rifles cracked as the enemy tried to deploy into assault formations. Stalled, the Germans brought direct artillery fire and tanks to bear on the Polish positions. Polish 37mm Bofors anti-tank guns positioned down the avenue knocked out two of the tanks, but the attack made progress as the Germans gained a section of a factory worker's colony in the extreme eastern section of Grochow. A platoon of Polish riflemen were wiped out as they covered the withdrawal of the rest of their company, but the German attack was held at the next street. By 1900 hours, all was comparatively quiet. Sosabowski's command tallied a loss of 320 men killed, wounded or missing.

September 16 dawned relatively quiet in Grochow. Behind the soldiers' backs the drone of aircraft engines and the explosion of bombs continued throughout the day as the Luftwaffe persisted in its attempts to punish the city into submission. Early in the afternoon, an automobile flying a white flag and escorted by two tanks drove towards the Polish barricade on Grochow street. Colonel Sosabowski crossed the barricade and, speaking German, asked the enemy officer what he wanted. The German replied that he carried a request for the surrender of the city. Sosabowski passed along the request to the commander of Army Group Warsaw, General Juliusz Rommel.* It came as no surprise to Sosabowski

---

*Lieutenant General Juliusz K. Rommel (1881–1967) was no relation to the German "Desert Fox."

that the request was spurned.

Less than two hours after the German messenger returned to his lines, a furious artillery bombardment began, most of the shells falling on the Polish redoubt. An hour later, at 1700 hours, the Germans began moving against all of the Polish positions in Grochow. The Poles waited until the attackers had approached within 100 meters of their positions before opening a withering fire with rifles, machine guns and mortars. The German artillery responded by pasting the rear of the Polish positions. After three hours of heavy fighting, the enemy gave up its attempts to reach the barricade. By sunset, all was quiet except for the moans of the wounded lying among the dozens of bodies in the street in front of the Polish positions.

During the night, Major Stefan Obrebowski led 300 men of his battalion on a daring raid behind the German lines. Each man carried two grenades, a bottle of gasoline, and ten 1-kilogram demolition charges. Civilians coming into Grochow had told Colonel Sosabowski that the Germans had a large number of tanks parked behind the Wawer Woods. Sosabowski ordered the raid to destroy the steel monsters before they came rolling into the suburb. The expedition destroyed two staff cars, along with their passengers, as well as an armored car, before a prisoner confirmed that there had indeed been tanks there, but they had withdrawn that night. At dawn the raiders returned to their lines, but before noon were out again, this time part of a general advance to reclaim lost streets.

The Polish advance went slowly but well. Fighting was often bitter in the narrow alleys and between the houses of the Grochow industrial neighborhood where some of the Polish soldiers had grown up. The Germans, expertly skilled with their machines, were less inclined towards combat that was face-to-face. A dozen machine guns were captured, along with 130 prisoners. The machine guns were put to good use, but the prisoners were a problem: with every man needed for defense, and the food supply critical, the prisoners were sent across the river into the city after only the briefest interrogation. Of greater interest was a German lieutenant colonel, the deputy commander of the 11th East Prussian Infantry Division's 23rd Infantry Regiment. The officer's crestfallen demeanor showed that his division had failed in its assignment to take the Vistula bridges.

After midnight, Captain Stanislaw Jachnik rode a motorcycle out to the Polish units and recalled them behind the barricades. The captain, who had been one of Colonel Sosabowski's students at the General Staff College, had been unable to join his unit earlier, at the front, and was in Grochow when the 21st Infantry marched in. Sosabowski had little difficulty convincing his bright former pupil to stay. As the Poles regained their old positions, the enemy displayed a change in tactics. No longer would the Germans go parading down the streets expecting everyone to be humbled by the sounds of their jack boots and tank treads. Instead, they decided to lay back, and then to dump all the explosives and incendiaries possible on Grochow from their numerous guns and aircraft.

The morning brought shocking news. That day, September 17, Russia had invaded Poland. Stalin had held up his end of the secret bargain with Hitler and was now moving into the eastern region. There was as yet no activity on the part of Poland's allies, despite the fact that they had declared war on Germany on September 3. The twenty-one-year-old republic was being smothered by its larger, eastern and western neighbors. The defenders of Warsaw could look only to God, or to the weapons still clenched in their hands.

The days in Grochow settled into endless harrowing hours of artillery bombardment. The shelling was punctuated only when German aircraft leisurely circled the area before picking their targets. Movement during daylight was impossible. At night the Polish soldiers sallied from their defenses to sweep the areas in front of their positions. Saska Kepa Park was kept clear, but the fighting was bloody. The threat of night combat in the streets and inside houses forced the Germans to "occupy" the area only lightly. They held only odd houses, and had pulled their main line farther back. But the constant patrols were demanding and took a physical and mental toll on the hard-pressed Polish defenders. When they discovered a Nazi-occupied building, it was either set ablaze or blown up. The price the Poles paid was high, with daily losses in killed and wounded in the labyrinth of streets and alleys. The soldiers would return before dawn exhausted, and sleep as if they were dead men, despite the hurricane of explosions around them.

The young Dr. Sosabowski, the Colonel's son, was discovered to be working in a hospital set up in railroad cars in a tunnel under Warsaw Central Station. His father had heard rumors that he had been killed, along with the entire hospital train when it had been bombed. Though casualties had been heavy, he had survived and attached himself to a railroad sapper's train, and had gotten back to Warsaw. The Colonel visited his son every chance he had, after reporting to the nearby bank building where the headquarters for the defense of Warsaw was located.

There was plenty of work for the doctor at Warsaw Central Station, but little for the sappers in the skills in which they had been trained. Colonel Sosabowski remembered some abandoned and untended railroad freight wagons, loaded with artillery ammunition, behind the German lines. At nightfall, a battalion-sized force swept the area, and behind them came the railroad sappers in a donkey locomotive found undamaged at Grochow Station. Amazingly, the raid did not attract undue enemy reaction, and the ammunition was pulled behind the Polish lines.

Colonel Sosabowski's command problems multiplied, however. Food was scarce, and ammunition even scarcer. The Germans, in a move to apply pressure on the already overburdened defenders, refused to allow any civilians to cross their lines and leave the besieged, burning city. The Colonel organized policemen who had been evacuated from western Poland to keep order and help provide provisions and shelter for the many civilians in Grochow. Then, Sosabowski's office in the Motlot factory received a direct hit while the colonel slept. He was unscratched, but his car and the regiment's radio equipment were destroyed. He moved his headquarters to the city's slaughterhouse, which had not received a hit during the entire siege. The pens and stalls where swine and cattle had waited for their inevitable meeting with the knife were now crowded with the regiment's horses. The gentle animals remained composed despite the madness all around them, and the sight of them had a calming effect on the soldiers who moved through the new headquarters.

Days went by and casualties mounted. Replacements came in, either soldiers of the 21st Infantry who had only now reached their unit because of the haphazard mobilization, or volunteers from other units. There were incidents of wounded men refusing to leave their posts, and some who had been evacuated for medical attention, "escaping" from hospitals and returning to the front lines at Grochow.

At the "Children of Warsaw's" backs, the city that was their mother starved and burned. On the days and nights of September 25 and 26, the German bombardment reached a crescendo. The Luftwaffe put up a maximum effort, flying hundreds of sorties. The Polish Air Force had long been swept from the skies, but not before they had taken a heavy toll of the enemy with them in aerial combat. Polish anti-aircraft guns pointed to the sky, impotent, their ammunition long expended. In a particularly vicious move, the Germans targeted the ruins of Warsaw's Jewish quarter for massive incendiary bombing on the Day of Atonement, Yom Kippur.

The next day, the bombardment ceased. It was the first time in almost a month that an hour had passed in Warsaw with no explosion heard. The city had suffered over 40,000 of its citizens killed, and more than 10 percent of its buildings destroyed. The population had been starved and shaken by the bombardment. The soldiers in Grochow sat in the sun for the first time in twelve days, trying to make sense out of the many rumors. Colonel Sosabowski went to General Rommel's headquarters for information, but was told verbally that an armistice was being arranged. The next morning, Sosabowski was called to headquarters, informed that the city had capitulated, and was given the terms of surrender.

4

Poland Is Not Lost...
As Long as We Are Alive
October 1939 to June 1940

The five infantry battalions that defended Grochow were each visited by their commander, Colonel Sosabowski. In one of its last acts before capitulation, the headquarters of Army Warsaw approved decorations for the men of the 21st Infantry Regiment. Two hundred soldiers were cited for decoration with the Cross of Valor, and ten, including the regiment's commander, were decorated with Poland's highest military award, the *Virtuti Militari*. In addition, the regimental standard of the "Children of Warsaw" was decorated with the *Virtuti Militari*, in recognition of the unit's outstanding conduct in the twenty-seven-day campaign. The Colonel told his men that he was proud of them, and that the defeat was not final. They knew, as did Polish soldiers in years gone by, in the words of the national anthem, that "Poland is not lost.... As long as we are alive."

The defenders of Grochow were marched into captivity with the rest of the Warsaw garrison. Colonel Sosabowski found his son, and the pair went as prisoners together. In a matter of days both had escaped. On October 5, 1939, Adolf Hitler took the salute of the massed German forces that paraded past the tribune set up on the Ale Ujazdowska boulevard. But during the days before the conquering army had its triumphal celebration, fugitive Polish army officers had met; people of different backgrounds and from different political parties were drawn together to form an underground Polish state. Its military arm would eventually be known as the *Armija Krajowa* (the Home Army), or the AK. The Sosabowskis, both father and son, naturally were part of it.

Poland was divided once again, and this time not between archaic monarchies but between ruthless totalitarian dictatorships. The eastern provinces of Poland were annexed by the Soviet Union and the rest of the country by Hitler's Germany. The parts of Poland taken by Hitler were the heartland of the nation. The western territories (consisting of the corridor to the sea, Poznan, Polish Silesia, and the industrial center of Lodz) were annexed directly into the German Reich. The rest of German-occupied Poland was left a self-standing entity named the "General Gouvernement." During the brutal winter of 1939–40, tens of thousands of Poles were expelled from the western territories to occupied Poland, where the occupier immediately began putting into effect the racial theories that were a pillar of the Nazi philosophy. In many parts of the nation the leaders of Polish society—politicians, professors, business leaders, priests, and even Boy Scouts—were arrested or executed.

The German planners foresaw that Poland would provide natural resources, and an expendable labor pool that would be deprived of all human rights and education, and on whose backs the "Thousand Year Reich" could be built. The only group of humanity other than the Slavs that the Nazis judged to be greater *Untermenschen* were the Jews. The world's largest community of Jews lived in Poland, and they were soon isolated in ghettos. The Germans would eventually open large death camps capable of killing thousands of people daily as a means of ridding the world of so-called "inferior people." As if the depression of defeat and the terror of occupation were not enough for the Poles to bear, their occupiers would eventually bring Jews from all corners of Europe to be killed in their country, in installations whose only purpose was genocide.

In the parts of Poland seized by Stalin, the Soviets in twenty-one months of occupation managed to far outdistance in brutality and cold-bloodedness the attempts of the Czars to obliterate Poland in 125 years of occupation. The 200,000 Polish soldiers who had been taken prisoner in 1939 were sent east to the Gulags and labor camps. Like the Nazis, the Soviets singled out the elite for extermination, executing thousands of Polish officers and disposing of the bodies in hastily dug mass graves.

By early 1940, the Soviets had begun deportation of the civilian population that was "too Polish" to be assimilated into the Soviet empire. The teenaged son of a veteran of Pilsudski's Legion, Boleslaw Kuzniar, lived near Zabaraz, a place made famous by the historical novels of Henryk Sienkiewicz (author of *Quo Vadis?*, *With Fire and Sword*, etc.). On the night of February 10, when the temperature was 40 degrees below zero, entire Polish families were told that they were an "undesirable element," and were taken to the town's railroad yard and loaded onto railroad wagons. Kuzniar remembers:

> We traveled to our destination for twenty days, a place called
> Stepkova in the Urals, in freight wagons, forty persons to a car,
> guarded by Russian soldiers.
>
> We were not to go out, except for a few people who fetched
> buckets of millet gruel or coal. There was a hole in the floor of
> the freight wagon that was used as a toilet, and in the middle
> stood a stove to keep us warm. Because of the lack of proper
> food and milk, babies and small children became ill, or even died.
> We heard of cases where the dead bodies of babies were thrown
> out of the wagon into the snow. The guards would not let us
> bury them.
>
> Until 1942 we worked in the forests, cutting trees under
> very poor conditions: bad food and no proper clothes. In
> wintertime we still had to go to work, even when the temper-
> ature was 45 degrees below zero. The people who were not used
> to hard work as laborers (teachers, clerks, etc.) could not adapt
> themselves to the conditions and quite often died of overwork
> or starvation.

The experiences of Boleslaw Kuzniar were not so terrible in some
circumstances, and worse in others, for the almost two million Poles who
survived deportation into the hinterlands of the Soviet Union. The worst
may have been the fate of the Poles who were sent to mine lead and gold
north of the Arctic Circle. The best lot may have fallen to those who were
dumped in Russia or Soviet Central Asia, where they were left to shift
for themselves and find work wherever they might—for this was a society
where "He who does not work, does not eat." Needless to say, for Poles
everywhere it seemed that their nation had entered a nightmare that might
never end.

Colonel Sosabowski had spent the early days of occupation traveling
to different parts of Poland trying to organize the military underground.
Sosabowski's new orders were to go to Lublin, and then to Russian-
occupied Lwow on a liaison mission, and then on to Rumania and
Hungary to report to his clandestine superiors on the activities of the
Polish underground. On November 21, 1939, Colonel Sosabowski went
to Warsaw Central Railroad Station. After hugging his son, the Colonel
got on the train for Lublin. He did not know that later, after crossing

the border into Hungary on December 15, he would never see his homeland again.

After the defeat of Poland, many soldiers and officers had fled to Hungary or Rumania. Interned there, the Poles thought instinctively that the Germans would be defeated by the French and the British, and sought to join the reforming Polish Army in France. Though Hungary and Rumania were both under pressure from Germany, they were sympathetic to the Poles; the terms of internment were not strict, and ultimately many thousands of Poles made it to France.

Reporting to the Polish Embassy in Budapest, Colonel Sosabowski gave the military authorities his report on underground activities, and the radio codes, ciphers and wavelengths used by the group in Lwow. The Colonel then told of how the underground in Warsaw was critically short of cash with which to carry on its activities. Sosabowski asked that the money be made ready for his return to Warsaw as quickly as possible. He was told that his report would be communicated to the Polish headquarters in France, and after their reply, further orders would be issued. That same day, Sosabowski was informed that he was to report to Paris in person. On December 20, Sosabowski left Budapest for Milan on a civilian airliner, and from there traveled to Paris by train.

France had declared war on Germany simultaneously with Great Britain on September 3, 1939. Six days later, the Polish ambassador in Paris signed an agreement permitting the raising of a Polish Division in France. That nation already had a Polish population of almost a half-million. France had been a traditional haven for Polish exiles and political refugees since the time of the partitions. Apart from political refuge, many Poles had also emigrated to France for economic reasons. These people were employed primarily in the country's mines and factories. It was a reasonable assumption that the Polish Legions of the time of Napoleon and of World War I would be revived.

While Poland was being overrun, France went through the motions of threat and mobilization. The nation had been demoralized by its massive losses suffered during the First World War and the French Army had been traumatized into a defensive psychology. Much of the French male population had been killed or maimed in the trenches, and the nation's cohesiveness and psyche had similarly suffered. The economic depression made recovery very difficult. Politically, France had flirted with socialism shortly before the outbreak of war, and appeasement had

become an unspoken doctrine of its foreign policy. The new war with
Germany was not popular, and the rank and file of the newly mobilized
army resented their service. The military sat behind the Maginot Line
and, save for a well-publicized "offensive" seizing several hectares of
German territory, did nothing.

Following the surrender of Warsaw, a Polish government-in-exile was
formed in Paris. The choice of the leader of both civil and military sectors
was most fortunate: General Wladyslaw Sikorski. This very talented and
respected hero of the 1920 Russo–Polish War, and one-time Chief of the
Polish General Staff, had had serious differences with the Pilsudski regime.
Sikorski had spent many of the inter-war years living in France. There
he wrote his theories of modern warfare, which predicted the Blitzkrieg.
He had many friends among the French officer corps and was considered
an unofficial Polish military ambassador to France.

Though some French officers were sympathetic to the Poles, the
general picture in France was bleak. The French populace resented the
Poles for dragging them into an unpopular war, and the opinion of them
in French military circles was also poor. The French military thought the
Polish armed forces were incompetent to have lost their country so
swiftly. This was complicated by widespread belief in enemy propaganda
that falsely portrayed the Polish Air Force as having been destroyed on
the ground and told falsely of an army on horseback that charged tanks
with lances. The French refused to listen to the first victims of the
Blitzkrieg, and failed to acknowledge the advent of this new form of
modern war. Relying on the lessons learned in the trenches two decades
before, France insisted on a defensive posture. Against this background,
Colonel Sosabowski arrived in Paris on December 21. Personally
debriefed by General Sikorski, Sosabowski was posted to General
Kazimierz Sosnkowski's staff to organize communications, supply and
liaison with the underground army and government in Poland.

The contrast between Paris and occupied Poland was great. The "City
of Light" still glowed in the evenings as in peacetime. The cafés were
crowded and a "business as usual" atmosphere prevailed through the
Christmas season. Many of the Polish officers bickered among themselves,
trying to fix blame for the defeat. Colonel Sosabowski immediately began
working on his reports about the underground, trying to establish a
network to get couriers and supplies to it.

During the middle of January, Sosabowski was appointed Deputy

Commander of the Polish 1st Infantry Division. Thoroughly disgusted with Paris, the Colonel was glad to return to a combat unit. His joy was short-lived. Arriving at the Division's headquarters at Coëtquidan, a training camp southwest of Rennes, in Brittany. Sosabowski was shocked at what he saw. The sloppiness and poor discipline of the French Army was beginning to spread to the Poles. Granted, many were French natives and were unused to military discipline, but the state of affairs appalled the strict Colonel. Rather than training, the soldiers sat in cafés, and drunkenness was common. The stone barracks had broken windows and the stoves were useless. Only one thin blanket was issued per man, and this did not keep out Brittany's bitter cold in January. The soldiers were clad in old horizon-blue uniforms and had been issued a handful of rifles dating back to the Franco–Prussian War.

Trying to get the division combat-ready, Sosabowski was continually frustrated by the French military's attitudes, both towards the Poles and on how to defeat the Germans. All the same, General Sikorski was under pressure to get the Polish divisions combat-ready, notwithstanding the fact that the French withheld both recruits and equipment. The Polish 1st Division went to the Maginot Line (ironically posted on the few hectares seized from Germany in September 1939), in mid-April 1940. Sosabowski was attending an artillery course for divisional staff officers and did not go with them. By this time, three further infantry divisions and a mechanized cavalry and mountain brigade had been established. Sosabowski was appointed Deputy Commander of the 4th Infantry, forming in the port city of Sables d'Olonne. Arriving on April 15, Sosabowski faced another repetition of his experience in Coëtquidan.

However, by now the "Phony War" atmosphere was broken by the German invasions of Denmark and Norway. The Polish "Podhale" Mountain Brigade, along with French Foreign Legion units and the Chasseurs Alpins, were sent to the frozen fjords of Norway. Crack German mountain troops were temporarily defeated, and the port of Narvik was seized. The elite French troops held their Polish comrades in very high esteem during the bloody mountain fighting.

With dawn of May 10, 1940, the skies above Rotterdam, Dordrecht and Moerdijk echoed the drone of tri-motored aircraft. Suddenly, hundreds of parachutes blossomed in the sky. German paratroopers quickly seized the strategic bridges over the rivers on roads leading to the heart of Holland. In Belgium, gliders and paratroopers took forts and bridges. Tanks rolled over the borders of both countries, sweeping away the defenders before them. The French armies were mauled as they moved into Belgium to try to stem the advance. In two days, the main armored forces of the invaders had moved through the "impassable" Ardennes Forest, crossing the French border to reach the Meuse River at Sedan. On May 13, waves of Stuka dive bombers screeched down on the defenders while German infantry and engineers crossed the river barrier in rubber boats. The Maginot Line was outflanked, and a wedge driven between the British Expeditionary Force now in Flanders and the main body of the French Army.

At this point, the Poles' 4th Infantry Division was only a cadre formation of 3,000 soldiers. The only weapons on hand were some ancient Gras rifles. The quartering situation became worse as refugees started flooding the area, and civilian authorities started evicting the Poles from their billets. On May 24, the unit received orders to move to Partenay, south of the Loire River. They were also informed that the 4th Division would find reinforcements waiting for it there. Arriving in Partenay, the division staff could find no sign of the promised reinforcements.

Colonel Sosabowski hurried to Sikorski's headquarters in Paris for any further orders and information, especially about the reinforcements. Polish Army Headquarters was preparing to leave the city as the Germans advanced. Although the roads were clogged with refugees, the Parisians still behaved as if there was no war. Sosabowski returned from Paris on June 15, the same day reinforcements finally arrived. Unfortunately they were raw recruits from the Calais and Lille districts, and had absolutely no military experience. The next day, the 4th Infantry Division was ordered to move to Saintes, some 100 kilomters to the south. This was impossible, as the unit had no transport. Polish Headquarters had supposedly moved there, but due to a total lack of communications, the 4th Division simply sat and waited.

The situation was coming apart. The British had been evacuated from Flanders through Dunkirk. Paris had been declared an open city on June 14, and subsequently was entered by the Germans. Three days later, France asked for an armistice from Hitler. The Polish 4th Division's staff began drawing up plans for an evacuation through the nearby port of La Rochelle.

General Dreszer, the divisional commander, sent Deputy Commander Colonel Sosabowski to Saintes to receive instructions as to the division's fate. En route, Sosabowski's car was stolen, and an ancient, struggling

Citroën was found. After forty-eight hours of searching, Sosabowski finally located Polish Army Headquarters and received orders for evacuation. The journey back to his division was a nightmare. In their panic, refugees packed the roads with carts, autos and baby carriages. Drunken French soldiers who had thrown away their weapons, shouted, "La guerre est finie!" Worse, French military police refused to let the Colonel pass through some villages, suspecting anyone unfamiliar of being a German paratrooper. The panic in France was even worse than in Poland nine months before. The old Citroën eventually broke down, and Sosabowski had a motorcycle courier take the evacuation order to the division while he remained in Saintes for still another night.

General Sikorski issued orders that all Polish units were to try to escape to Britain. In the disastrous French campaign, the Polish units had acquitted themselves well: the 2nd Infantry Division covered the retreat of the French XLVth Corps, and then marched across the Swiss border into internment; the 3rd Division was marginally better manned and equipped than the 4th, but was still only partially trained (it was destroyed in combat in Brittany). General Stanislaw Maczek's 10th Mechanized Cavalry Brigade suffered 75 percent losses in Champagne before it destroyed its remaining tanks and struck out for the coast. The 1st Grenadier Division (formerly the 1st Infantry Division) provided the rearguard for the French XX Corps as it retreated behind the armistice line. Its commander, General Boleslaw Duch, made the difficult decision to ignore General Sikorski's orders. He felt that there should be no chance for recrimination against the Polish Army in this debacle. The unit fought until it was down to half its strength, and was almost totally surrounded when Duch finally gave the order to escape to Britain. Few of the men made it.

In Saintes, a sympathetic French officer showed Colonel Sosabowski a secret order that forbade the evacuation of Polish units from France as part of the armistice agreement with the Germans.

Leaving Saintes by automobile, Colonel Sosabowski hoped to catch up with his division at La Rochelle, and then get to England. Just a few kilometers outside of Saintes, Sosabowski found his former student—and the man who was his chief of staff at the end of the siege of Warsaw—standing on the side of the road. Captain Stanislaw Jachnik was squeezed into the overloaded car, and off they went. Driving through the night, Sosabowski's car ran through a French military police roadblock on the way to La Rochelle, scattering the gendarmes. Another car filled with

Polish soldiers fell in behind Sosabowski's, and all went well until, in an otherwise deserted village just outside of La Rochelle, Sosabowski's car was disabled after a head-on collision with another vehicle. Captain Jachnik took an injured member of the party in the other Polish car, with orders to return for the rest of the group. After two hours of waiting, Sosabowski and his men felt abandoned as the sky to the east began to glow with the ominous first signs of dawn.

The personnel of the 4th Division were having their own adventures in La Rochelle. A stricken Greek freighter was belching oily smoke in the harbor, fortunately with no one aboard. During the evening, as troops were embarking, an orange rocket went up into the sky from behind the dockside buildings. The embarkation was stopped, and those already on board got off the ship. As the troops moved off the concrete mole in the bright moonlight, they heard a sound that had burned into their consciousness since September 1939: the unsynchronized groans of Heinkel engines—which grew louder. Soon the whistle of falling bombs was heard and, in their terror, every soldier thought that each was aimed at him. When the bombers left, the ship on which the soldiers had planned to escape to England was burning, and a British collier, the SS *Abderpool*, was entering the harbor. Her master was going to leave at first light. Embarkation began again immediately.

As he walked towards the port city, Colonel Sosabowski flagged down a French Army truck full of civilians going in that direction. Sosabowski sat with the driver in case Captain Jachnik was met on his way back. The captain and the injured officer were found at the entrance to La Rochelle. As the sun was beginning to break over the horizon, the group had a wild drive trying to find the quay at which the evacuation ship had docked. When the *Abderpool* was found, the gangway had already been removed. Cheers rose from the crowded decks as the Colonel followed Jachnik and the injured officer up a rope ladder as the ship cast off its mooring lines.

General Dreszer told Colonel Sosabowski to assume command of all troops on board. There were over 3,000 on the vessel. A number of officers' wives and their children, and a handful of French, British, Belgian and Dutch personnel were also embarked. People crowded every part of the collier: the decks, the corridors, the coal bunkers and even the masts. There were a few cabins for the ship's officers, and humble berthing spaces for the ship's crew in the forecastle. Only two toilets were on the entire vessel. Everyone was dirty, hungry, frightened and exhausted.

Still within sight of land, terror gripped the ship when the sound of twin unsynchronized aircraft engines was heard in the distance. Wide-open, bloodshot eyes strained at the skies to spot the source of the familiar, terrorizing noise. The soldiers did not have the chance to run anywhere on the crowded iron vessel. The ship was so full that many could not even duck down. Each man dealt with his terror in his own way: some prayed, some whistled, some lost control of their bowels. From the ship's stern, Oerlikon cannons barked, and the offending aircraft kept its distance, and then turned away.

Colonel Sosabowski spoke to the ship's captain through an interpreter. The captain was awaiting Admiralty orders concerning when, and at which British port, the ship might dock. In the meantime, the ship was trying to put as much distance between it and France as possible. Sosabowski spoke to the crowded ship through a megaphone, explaining the situation, and calling for strict obedience. Food was collected and then divided. Any machine guns brought aboard were positioned, should there be any more visitors with black crosses on their wings. The ship plodded westward.

The weather was hot. The men waited on line for hours to reach the few containers for drinking water, and even longer to use one of the two toilets. This continued for three days. The men's beards grew as they numbly tried to comprehend the disaster that had befallen them. The Poles on board had been beaten brutally and chased out of two countries in less than a year. Looking out to sea as the sun set again, they pondered their fate. They had no country and, seemingly, no future.

5

Good Scotch Whisky

July 1940 to September 1941

Late in the evening of June 21, 1940, Colonel Sosabowski was informed that the *Abderpool* would be entering Plymouth harbor the next morning. As the sun rose, the Colonel gave orders that everybody should shave and the last of the rationed water was used to this end. Sosabowski wanted his troops to be presentable for their new hosts. For the officers and men aboard the ship, this gesture toward hygiene was the beginning of a return to normalcy. Though they were hungry, their uniforms were dirty and their tired eyes were bloodshot, at least they would be freshly shaven.

Sosabowski ordered that the dead and wounded were to be brought ashore first. There were not many of these, and after the ambulances moved off, the troops started down the gangways. 2nd Lieutenant Kazimierz Janiga remembers the figure of the Colonel strutting back and forth along the pier like a bantam rooster (and making just as much noise), supervising the unloading. Sosabowski wanted a proper unloading because the dock was lined with people watching, and he also wanted to underline that *he* was in charge.

British NCOs broke the assemblage into manageable groups and escorted them to separate railroad platforms. The green-uniformed girls of the WVS (Women's Voluntary Service) greeted them with carts, smiles and the words, "Cigarette, biscuit, cup of tea?" The question of what the British were to do with these new arrivals in their now chaotic nation, as they simultaneously received their own evacuated army and prepared for an invasion by the enemy, was quickly answered. Within hours, trains were taking the Polish soldiers to Scotland.

The exhausted men gradually became cognizant of their new surroundings. What a contrast this was to France: no fires, no drunken

42

soldiers tossing away their weapons, everything calm...a smile, a cigarette, cup of tea? The trains moved north. There were many hours to catch up on lost sleep, and many new things to learn. The toilets on the train were most welcome after the interminable waiting on the *Abderpool*. Unfortunately, the red chain on the lavatory ceiling was mistaken for a means of flushing the convenience, and all too often the trains came to screeching halts while still another soldier learned from an angry conductor that the pedal on the floor was there for such a purpose. And in the stations where the trains came to a halt there always appeared the smiling women in green hats: "Cup of tea, cigarette, sandwich?" France was in ashes, but in Britain pretty women were smiling.

The next morning, the trains entered Glasgow and billets for the Poles were arranged in schools. As the soldiers marched through the streets, the citizens of the grimy industrial metropolis applauded the new arrivals—a startling contrast to France. Sosabowski was given command of all Polish troops in Glasgow, and his first act was to confine everybody to their billets. It wasn't until the third day that he allowed his people permission to see something of the city. Glasgow granted free public transportation to all those wearing Polish uniform, and the men welcomed the opportunity to take a look at this strange new land, have a bite to eat, and wash the shame and depression of their days in France from themselves.

There were new customs to learn. In the words of Lieutenant Janiga: "Where is the first place a Polish patriot and Catholic would go? To a tavern naturally, so we might find the real 'atmosphere' of the country." Unable to find one where French was spoken, and armed with an English vocabulary that consisted of two words ("whisky" and "beer"), six officers in Janiga's party decided on a local, where wartime austerity had yet to make its impact on the quality and variety of available libation. The officers asked for and received a round and, as on the Continent, did not pay, but they returned to their table to acclimatize themselves to their "Glaswegian atmosphere," leaving the publican with his hand out. The six decided to sample another beverage (several times), leaving both Scottish customers and owner disturbed and amazed. Who were these men in strange uniforms speaking a strange language? An army of occupation that expected to drink for free? A bus ride was one thing; good Scotch whisky was another. This went on for much of the afternoon, with the publican showing a restraint uncharacteristic for Glasgow. Finally, having sampled enough "atmosphere," the officers rose and, pulling pound notes from their pockets, asked for their check in French. The Scots gave a sigh of relief.

It was from these kind of beginnings that a Polish-Scottish love affair formed. The Poles had finally found their foils in honesty and stubbornness. They admired the toughness of the Scottish soldiers and workers, whose levels of hospitality and friendliness were comparable to their own. Very often, the exiles would finish a meal in a restaurant and, upon asking the waiter for the check, were told that the meal had already been paid for.

The Poles were shortly moved from Glasgow to a tent city at Biggar. The camp held over 2,000 officers and only a handful of NCOs and soldiers. The British were perplexed that so many officers of the Polish forces had made it out of France, and so few of the troops. Much of the Polish Army in France was led by regular and reserve officers who had come out of Poland, while most of the ranks consisted of members of the Polish community in France, who were discharged so that they might return home and care for their families after the armistice. This was most obvious in the 4th Division, which had just begun to fill its ranks, yet had almost a full officer contingent. Colonel Sosabowski began as early as June 27 to organize a brigade structure for the tent camp at Biggar.

Major General Burhardt-Bukacki, Polish commander in Scotland, appointed Sosabowski to command a new formation, the Canadian Officers Cadre Brigade. This was to be sent to Canada to recruit members of the large North American Polish community, as had been done during the last war. Officers were again in a majority, and were so organized that each rifle company would eventually provide the staff for an infantry regiment, and the NCOs would comprise a training company. Though the British provided some weapons, many of these were requisitioned from other Polish units. Only 30 percent of the Brigade was armed with rifles brought from France. On July 20, the Brigade relocated to Eliock near Kilmarnock.

Immediately after Dunkirk and the general evacuation from France, German air attacks on Britain began in earnest. Coastal shipping was being bombed in the Channel and the entire island kingdom treated the threat of invasion very seriously. After the shocking German airborne assault on Holland, extensive anti-parachutist exercises were held. The Scottish Home Guard dragged out sporting guns, claymores and pikes, and were joined by the Polish soldiers of the equally ill-equipped Canadian Cadre

Brigade. 2nd Lieutenant Janiga remembers Home Guardsmen proudly showing off an anti-tank barricade they had built. Two concrete block walls were built halfway across the pavement from opposite sides of a road leading into a village. The beaming Scots had slowed a sedan representing a tank to a crawl, and crept through the obstacle in an "S" maneuver. Remembering how the Panzers had left the roads and moved cross-country, smashing through Polish and French villages, Janiga did not know whether to laugh or cry. He forced a smile and nodded his approval.

On August 15, Sosabowski was informed that the Brigade would not be going to Canada. In its stead, a general was sent on this mission, and the unit was renamed the 4th Cadre Rifle Brigade (the number "4" was retained to continue the tradition of the 4th Division formed in France). The Polish units in Scotland were reorganized as the Polish I Corps, and General Sikorski went on an inspection tour to survey his army. On September 5, Sikorski visited the Brigade. The unit turned out smartly, Sosabowski at its head, and Commander-in-Chief Burhardt-Bukacki was impressed with what he saw. Many of the other Polish formations remained idle, blaming their lack of weapons or lack of a mission, while Sosabowski, working with what little he had, managed to create a viable military formation.

By the end of summer 1940, the German attempt to achieve air superiority in what came to be known as the "Battle of Britain" had failed. Had it succeeded, an invasion certainly would have followed, and Britain might well have shared the fate of France and Poland. RAF Fighter Command was all that stood between Hitler and the British shores, and by the end of the battle, one out of every eight pilots in Fighter Command was a veteran from the Polish Air Force. Despite becoming operational well into the affair, 303 Polish Squadron ended the battle as the squadron with the single-highest toll taken of German aircraft, and the experienced Polish pilots had the highest "kill-to-loss" ratio in Fighter Command. The fighter pilots managed to place the perception of the Polish armed forces in a new light, and this paid much of the new arrivals' "room rent" in Britain.

On October 8, Sosabowski was confirmed as Brigade commander and was given new orders. Though the Germans had been frustrated in the air, fear of invasion still loomed large and the majority of Polish army units in Scotland were given the mission of coastal defense. The 4th Rifle Brigade, assigned a 24-kilometer sector of the Kingdom of Fife's coastline, moved its headquarters to Leven on October 20, 1940. As is typical in this part of Scotland, the Poles were welcomed with open arms. The mines and the factories of this Lowland Scottish area were separated by farms and rolling hills. The North Sea lapped at the shores and subjected eastern Scotland to its brooding weather. The villages held many curiosities for the Poles, not the least of which was the statue of sailor Alexander Selkirk in Lower Largo. Almost three centuries before, Selkirk left his home in Fife to become a stranger in a strange land. The Poles felt a kinship with this man who was known to literature as Daniel Defoe's Robinson Crusoe.

Through the fall and winter the Brigade set to its assignment of coastal defense. Sosabowski would not tolerate idleness, and even the officers were put to digging trenches and stringing wire. While the Brigade gradually acquired modern arms from available stocks, another avenue of endeavor also became apparent: during General Sikorski's inspection in September, he mentioned that he was looking for candidates to be parachuted into Poland to support the underground army.

A group of 20 officers was sent to the British Commando School at Inverlochy Castle near Fort William, the first of thirteen groups that would be sent there from September 1940 until May 1942. Sent ostensibly to participate in a "Rifleman Course," their actual purpose was to learn various commando methods of sabotage, unarmed combat, disguise and other tactics of covert warfare. As an adjunct to their training, in February 1941 the first Polish students were sent to the British Parachute Training School at Ringway Airport near Manchester.

The men returning from Ringway regaled their comrades with animated tales of their parachute training, and their enthusiasm spread to the colonel of the Brigade. While the rest of the Brigade undertook ski training during the unusually snowy Scottish winter, Sosabowski thought about Poland. As the Ringway graduates boasted about their training, Sosabowski pondered the reality that the "shortest way" back to Poland would be by air. In his office on the second floor of the Leven YMCA, Sosabowski made up his mind to form a Polish Parachute Brigade.

Poland had been one of the first countries to develop a military parachuting program. The first jumps from aircraft took place in 1922 to test methods for emergency situations, and by 1929, Irvin parachutes were being domestically manufactured. In Poland, the love of all aspects of aviation during the inter-war period was almost as intense as in

Germany. The LOPP (*Liga Obrony Powietrznej Panstwa*, or "League for National Air Defense") sponsored enthusiastically attended courses in both powered flight and gliding. The LOPP erected its first parachute tower near Warsaw in 1936, and by 1939 there were seventeen parachuting towers throughout the country. Polish Boy Scouts also undertook parachute training, and gave a demonstration jump at the 5th International Scouting Jamboree near The Hague in August 1937.

The army began examining military applications of parachuting after massive Soviet demonstrations in 1936. At first, officer cadets did tower jumps as a character-building experience. In September 1937, the first military parachuting course was initiated, with the objective of creating parachute sabotage and diversion units. In September 1938, a 24-man unit armed with pistols, grenades, light machine guns and demolition materials parachuted as a sabotage/diversion team during the annual maneuvers; their success prompted the Ministry of Defense to open the Military Parachuting Center at Bydgoszcz in May 1939.

The Bydgoszcz Center graduated the first class of eighty officers and NCOs in June 1939. Besides training jumpers, the center kept busy developing special communications equipment and weapons, and the containers to drop them with the parachutists. In August 1939, a second class commenced, but the outbreak of war prevented its graduation. The Center was ordered to evacuate, but its aircraft were destroyed in an air raid on September 1 and all structure was lost when the Center's trucks were bombed near Lowicz several days later. The Military Parachuting Center was dispersed and its personnel tried to make their way to safety individually.

Unfortunately, the majority of the paratroopers and instructors from the Bydgoszcz Center ended up behind barbed wire or in graves in Poland, France or Norway. However, two of the best instructors did manage to reach England: Air Force pilots Lieutenant Jerzy Gorecki and Lieutenant Julian Gebolys. As the British were just beginning their military parachuting program, these veteran instructors were gladly welcomed at Ringway.

It is difficult to look at parachuting in 1940 from a contemporary perspective. In 1938, man had only experienced his first thirty-five years of powered flight and parachuting had only in the past decade been removed from the province of stuntmen and daredevils. Notwithstanding the developmental state of parachuting, the Polish advances were noteworthy: Lieutenant Gebolys discovered that by changing the shape of the parachute's canopy by manipulating the lines, the parachutist was able to alter direction, minimize oscillation and have some control over the speed of his descent. Prior to this innovation, parachutists just hung under their parachute and landed as fate and the winds blew them. The British doctrine stated that the parachutist was to land facing the direction of his drift and take the shock of landing in a forward roll. Using the British method, if a backwards landing was imminent, the riser straps were pulled by opposite hands (left hand pulling the right riser, and vice versa), reversing the position under the canopy. This was considerably better than the German technique, where a single riser was attached out of reach halfway down the parachutist's back (the Luftwaffe's paratroopers jumped from a low altitude, with a small parachute for a speedy descent, and attempted to land on their hands and knees—not a method to guarantee a maximum number of combat-ready troops during an assault). Gebolys introduced the British to pulling on the risers, individually, or in concert, to alter the shape of the canopy. These methods were adopted by the British, and later by the Americans, and became known as the "Polish Method" of parachuting.

Lieutenants Gorecki and Gebolys were already on the staff of the Parachute Training School at Ringway when the first Polish students arrived from Scotland. Their relations with the school's head, Wing Commander Maurice Newnham, were first-rate. Gorecki and Gebolys were the natural choices for training the Polish students and, as more and more Poles arrived for training at Ringway, an autonomous Polish section was created at the school. The Polish instruction staff gradually became fleshed out with the more promising graduates from Sosabowski's Brigade.

As trucks rolled down the winding road from Leven to Largo, the cattle in the fields peered over stone walls as the air reverberated with melodic voices recalling earlier days as Boy Scouts or soldiers in Poland. Interspersed were thickly accented versions of "My Bonnie Lies Over the Ocean" and the "Beer Barrel Polka," along with more recent compositions with lyrics in both languages about the red-haired local girls. Taking a sharp left turn down a side road, the trucks downshifted as they went up a hill for 50 meters. They drove past a lovely stone church and turned left down a country lane, passing a sign that read, "War Department Property/Entrance Strictly Forbidden." The singing stopped as the trucks passed another sign, this time in both Polish and English: "THE MONKEY GROVE. If You Are Looking for Death, Come in for a While." The soldiers had arrived at what was known officially as Unit 140, Polish Forces, but better known and feared by the name painted on the sign.

Monkey Grove was established on the grounds of Largo House, a stone mansion built in 1750 that, by 1940, was providing offices and storage for military supplies. In the stable, the loft had holes put in the floor and barrels inserted, matching the size and shape of the floor exit of the Whitley bomber, the paratroop transport of the time. But it was the grounds of the manor house that were the real reason for Monkey Grove's existence. In a thickly wooded corner of the estate, the Brigade's sappers, under the direction of Lieutenant Ludomir Mazurek, built an obstacle course of devilish contraptions that stretched every muscle and honed mind and body for the rigors of parachute training. Men, scantily clad in athletic shorts, were swinging on trapezes, walking balance beams, climbing, jumping, tumbling, all at double time with instructors constantly shouting, "Legs together...go...get down...go...get up...go...legs together...go...faster...go...this time do it right...go...go... go..." The candidates went through the two-week course in groups of forty to fifty. The students finished bruised and battered, but also alert and strong. Every member of the Brigade, regardless of assignment, even administrative personnel, surgeons and chaplains, had to pass through Monkey Grove. The price of failure was to repeat the two-week course. The mark of Monkey Grove's usefulness was that the Polish section at Ringway had proportionately half the injuries of the British parachute school.

Much of what was accomplished was subsidized with the Brigade's own resources. The officers and men even used their own money to purchase needed items. The Brigade sought to build a parachuting tower similar to those that existed in Poland before the war. Polish Army Headquarters arranged a grant of £500, and with the help of Lieutenant Gebolys, the Polish Army Corps of Engineers Research Department produced the drawings. A Scottish construction firm erected the steel tower near an ancient stone ruin, the sole remains of a castle where Mary, Queen of Scots, entertained guests; the tower was opened on July 20, 1941. A trooper was suspended from a parachute held by a cable from the 100-foot-high tower. The cable could stop the soldier at any point during his descent, so the instructor, using a loudspeaker, could chastise him for any error while he was suspended in the air. British visitors from Ringway were so impressed with the structure that they built their own, and the design was adopted throughout the Commonwealth.

With the foundations for Polish parachuting laid, the search for a suitable insignia commenced. The only indication that a man was a qualified paratrooper was a small badge that was presented by either of the parachute manufacturers (the firms "GQ" or "Irvin") and worn above the breast pocket. Among the Poles in Scotland was architect Marian Walentinowicz, who was also the talented illustrator of a very popular series of children's comic books. In Scotland, he prepared the cover illustration for a new edition of a novel about Polish-German relations during the partitions: *Ziemia Gromadzi Prochy* (The Earth Creates Ashes). This showed a white eagle, diving into combat through a stormy sky with talons extended. The illustration so caught the eye of the newly qualified Polish paratroopers that the design was reproduced in metal, submitted and officially accepted by Polish headquarters in London on June 21, 1941. The reverse had the motto, *"Tobie Ojczyzno"* (For You, Motherland) and a serial number. The first 500 were designated for the Commander-in-Chief's disposition, and the remainder given to the Brigade. The insignia was awarded along with a similarly numbered document, and only on completion of training. Provisions were made to have the eagle's beak and talons plated in gold, denoting completion of a combat jump.

The first 500 badges set aside for disposition by General Sikorski were to be given to a special Polish parachute unit: the *Cichociemni* (the Silent and Unseen). These men and women were chosen and trained for clandestine warfare and courier service with the underground army in Poland. Many had originally been with the 4th Cadre Rifle Brigade, where they had received their parachute training. Volunteers came from throughout the Polish forces, and all received their preliminary training at Monkey Grove.

The Brigade had opened a survival school for both itself and the *Cichociemni*. Lieutenant Jan Pic, a former Scoutmaster and expert in survival, headed the school. It was located in the forests of Dunkeld, on the Duke of Atholl's estate, 25 kilometers north of Perth. There the soldiers were taught shelter building, concealment, escape and evasion, and food gathering. Aside from the traditional building of traps and snares for small game familiar to any Boy Scout, Pic added mushroom gathering, long a staple of Polish diet, but virtually unknown in Britain and Western Europe. Commandos from many of the Allied nations were also participants in this course.

By September 23, 1941, almost 400 Polish soldiers had qualified as paratroopers and the 4th Brigade was ordered to give a demonstration of what it had learned. The objective was a British coastal battery atop a hill at Kincraig Point. General Sikorski was there to distribute the first parachute badges to the 4th Cadre Rifle Brigade after the exercise. Wing Commander Newnham and other British military and civil dignitaries were invited, but as word spread, the fields were crowded with many additional spectators. Lysander aircraft piloted by Poles overflew the battery, dropping phosphorus smoke bottles. The Lysanders were followed by Whitley bombers borrowed from Ringway. The Whitleys flew in single-line formation and, just over the objective, tiny black dots appeared below their bellies. In seconds, parachutes bloomed over the dots, and the crowd loudly cheered its enthusiasm. The paratroopers handily took the battery and demonstrated other maneuvers. After a short ceremony during which the badges were distributed, Sikorski gave a speech. He ended with the words: ". . . There will come a time when like victorious eagles you will dive on the enemy, and with this you will be the first to free our country. . . . From this day, you will be the 1st Polish Parachute Brigade!" And so, September 23 was established as the Polish Parachute Brigade's Holy Day.

By September 1941, the German Army had enmeshed itself in a titanic struggle with the Soviet Union, Hitler having turned on his former ally the previous June. Though German aircraft still dropped bombs on Britain, the bulk of their war effort had necessarily become devoted to the conquest of Russia. At sea, Britain was in the midst of a desperate struggle against the U-Boats, but the only place where her army saw combat was in the North African desert. There, the Polish Carpathian Brigade moved into Tobruk to relieve the besieged Australian garrison.

With the forced entrance of the Soviets into the Allied camp, General Sikorski had signed a pact with Stalin for the organization of a Polish Army in Russia from the almost two million Poles deported there. In Moscow, the very day after the ceremonies at Kincraig, Stalin endorsed the Atlantic Charter, which contained a provision concerning the self-determination of nations.

Also by September 1941, Poland had endured two years of occupation, the most brutal of any nation under the Nazi heel. The country's Jewish population had been isolated in ghettos and was being systematically exterminated in death camps set up on Polish soil. In addition to the Jews, the Nazis had systematically earmarked the Poles for slave labor, and eventual murder. Large parts of Poland had been annexed directly to the German Reich, and those citizens not imprisoned or expelled were forced to serve in the German Wehrmacht. The underground AK (*Armija Krajowa,* or Home Army) had not only earlier reported the massive German preparations for the invasion of Russia, but as Poland became an active military rear area, underground intelligence, sabotage and diversionary activities had increased. In Warsaw, a student of the Academy of Military Medicine continued his studies underground while serving as a full-time soldier in the AK. He was 2nd Lieutenant Stanislaw Sosabowski, who had last seen his father almost two years before.

6

The Shortest Way

September 1941 to December 1943

The plan for the establishment of a Polish Parachute Brigade by General Sikorski at Kincraig was confirmed by written orders eleven days later, October 4, 1941. The Brigade was to be used especially for operations in Poland, a policy endorsed by previous British-Polish military discussions that permitted 5 percent of the Polish forces in Britain to be at the sole disposal of the Polish Commander-in-Chief. The *Cichociemni* were included in this 5 percent.

The fact that the Parachute Brigade was listed in the Polish order of battle did not necessarily mean that an effective military unit existed. In autumn 1941 there were less than 400 qualified paratroopers between the *Cichociemni* and the Parachute Brigade, and all of the Polish armed forces had critical recruiting problems. New volunteers who had escaped from Poland were becoming fewer and farther between, and practically every available Pole in the West was already in uniform. As in the past, Colonel Sosabowski ignored all difficulties, and tried with all means available to prepare the Brigade for its mission of being the first unit to participate in the liberation of Poland. Despite the recruiting competition between services, a slow but steady stream of volunteers continued to drift towards Fife, and thence through the gates at Monkey Grove.

The British high command was beginning to look at the developments in Scotland with increasing interest. Their airborne forces had already been established under the command of Major General F.A.M. ("Boy") Browning. As a young subaltern with the Grenadier Guards, Browning had survived a brave and distinguished career in the front-line trenches during World War I. In manners and appearance, he was a person who seemed almost a creation of Hollywood. Educated at Eton and Sandhurst, he married author Daphne du Maurier, and was a paragon of the affectations associated with the British Brigade of Guards. Dressed in the best-tailored uniforms, Browning's turnout was immaculate. His charm and manners were beyond reproach, and in impressiveness were second only to his organizational abilities and energy.

The first meeting between Colonel Sosabowski and General Browning was in November 1941, when the Pole visited the British airborne commander at his headquarters in England. There could not have been a greater contrast between the cool Browning and the temperamental Sosabowski in background, but the two were soon exchanging varied tactical and organizational views based on their long, but different, experiences. The meeting was extremely cordial, except when Browning intimated that he would like to see the Polish Parachute Brigade take part in operations in the West. Sosabowski replied that he was under Polish Government, rather than British War Office, orders and that the decision was not Browning's to make. A positive result of the visit for Sosabowski came after Browning persuaded the War Office to allow the Airborne Command to deal with the Polish Brigade directly, rather than through normal channels. This arrangement eased the difficulties the Poles were experiencing in receiving the special uniforms and equipment required for airborne training and eventual operations.

Another problem facing the Poles was the fact that the British naturally still had priority for the use of the facilities at Ringway, while Sosabowski's men waited for parachute training. The Poles were totally dependent on the RAF for aircraft, as they did not have any transports of their own. The infamous British weather also played havoc with training schedules. The frequent rainy days grounded aircraft time and again, sometimes obliterating the Polish portion of the schedule. In fact, all parachutists training in Britain had to depend on balloon jumps for much of their training.

When possible, the aircraft that the paratroopers jumped from was the Whitley bomber, which was already obsolete at the beginning of the war. It was too slow to survive bombing missions, but this turned out to be an advantage for parachute jumping. The ventral turret was removed, and this proved to be a ready-made exit for paratroopers. The Whitley was very far from being loved, but it was the only aircraft available. The paratroopers sat opposite each other, legs herring-boned, on the aluminum deck. The plane's interior reeked of petrol, exhaust fumes, and the nervous perspiration of the men, past and present, who had anticipated jumping out of the hole in the floor, and into space. Smoking was prohibited because of the fumes, and the poorly lit interior was so noisy that instructions had to be shouted. When the green light flashed, the paratroopers jumped in succession from opposite sides of the hole. A perfect jump from the Whitley was difficult, and it was the lucky paratrooper who managed to complete training without having smashed his face on the sides of the exit hole. This was known as "ringing the bell." The Polish Paratroopers sang the song:

> "The Whitley soars through the clouds like a tomb . . .
> Inside are ten paratroopers as if they were dead . . .
> All faces having expressions like Scotland's gloom . . .
> As the sweat runs in streams from off of their heads!"

On April 27, 1942, Colonel Sosabowski attended an important conference in London along with the commanders of all of the major Polish Army formations in Britain. With the critical manpower crisis, General Sikorski had to evaluate the future of the Polish forces in Britain. The British were interested in staffing the Polish Air Force, Navy, and General Maczek's armored division forming in Scotland. Beyond this, General Sikorski wanted to see the Parachute Brigade in an operational state. The 1st "Scotland" Rifle Brigade was in the highest state of operational readiness of all the Polish units in Britain, but after heated discussions, Sikorski ruled that the Brigade would be broken up and its personnel distributed as needed. Sosabowski was promised 300 enlisted men from this formation. This decision had two points of significance for Sosabowski and his own brigade: (1) at this point the parachute Brigade was still top-heavy with officers, and the ranks were severely undermanned, and (2) the decision underlined the fact that the Parachute Brigade was an important, integral part of the Polish forces. In addition to the men who would be provided by disbanding the Scotland Rifle Brigade, Sikorski also promised Sosabowski that he would make available reinforcements from the Middle East in the near future.

The Polish Parachute Brigade was to have a structure different from conventional infantry or airborne forces. A brigade normally consisted of three rifle battalions, while a division was composed of three brigades, which had to depend on divisional units for service and support (engineers, artillery, signals, medical, supply, etc.). The Polish Parachute Brigade's mission required that all service and support units be organic to the

Brigade. These units would have to be raised and trained. As the Brigade was to provide its own service and support units, and would not have to look to any higher formations, Sosabowski's Brigade was in short course renamed the 1st Independent Parachute Brigade.

The armies of the other nations in exile in Britain also had a need for parachute troops. To ease the strain at Ringway, which was busy turning out Britain's airborne forces, the Poles were asked to help in training. A total of 238 Frenchmen, 172 Norwegians, 2 Czechs, 4 Belgians and 4 Dutchmen qualified, and were awarded the Polish paratroopers' badge. The French personnel were primarily from the air force, and hated the Nazis with a rabidity that almost equaled that of the Poles; they appreciated the fact that the Poles instructed them in French, and had Continental manners. The Norwegian paratroopers were formed into a parachute commando company, and immediately became involved in special operations, including the famous raid on the Vemork heavy water plant. Following a mission in their homeland, the Norwegian paratroopers presented Colonel Sosabowski with a silver cigarette box. It was suitably inscribed, and inlaid with pieces of colored Norwegian flint that they had carried back from the raid.

The appeal of the Norwegians' being the first to return to their homeland by "The Shortest Way" was met by the enthusiasm and longing of the Polish soldiers to be fighting on their own native soil. Some, meanwhile, made the tortuous journey across many borders from Poland to England so they might return – armed – to free their suffering country. Others, who had avoided capture, continued to come from France in small numbers, many having seen service in the growing French Résistance. More men came after Spain released the Polish soldiers interned after the fall of France in the Miranda del Erbo concentration camp, where they had rotted among the Republicans and Communists captured by Franco's forces during that country's civil war. After the Allied invasion of North Africa, more Poles came from the Vichy French forced-labor camps in the "Hot Siberia" of the deserts of Morocco and Algeria. But it was from the frozen, real Siberia that the Brigade was to receive its largest contingent of soldiers.

After the Nazis had turned on the Soviet Union, Great Britain no longer saw itself standing alone against Hitler, and offered Stalin its support. The Poles were in the curious position of becoming de facto allies of the power that had invaded, and then deported, almost two million of its citizens. Through the efforts of the Polish Commander-in-Chief, General Wladyslaw Sikorski, an agreement was reached with Stalin. The Poles in Soviet captivity were given amnesty (though their "crime" was never explained to them) and provisions were made for a Polish Army to be formed in the Soviet Union. The gates of the labor camps were swung open, and hundreds of thousands of starved, sick and exhausted Polish men, women and children began to make their way to Buzhaluk, where the Polish Army was being formed.

The Soviets clamored for the Poles to take part in the bloody fighting against the Germans, who were now at the gates of Moscow, but only slowly provided weapons, and were even slower to provide food to the rapidly increasing numbers of Poles who flocked to their colors. Many thousands had died in captivity, and continued to die as disease swept the camps and people succumbed to starvation. The Polish government continued to inquire about 16,000 officers, who were known to have fallen into Soviet hands, and had yet to appear. Stalin did not have a concrete answer to General Sikorski's queries about the missing men, and implied that they had escaped to Manchuria. The Soviets cut the rations further, and soon began encouraging the gathered Poles to leave. In August 1942, the first of 115,000 Poles who would leave Russia crossed the Caspian Sea and arrived in Iran.

After all of their possessions were burned, and all of the hair was shaved from their bodies, the soldiers were deloused and given new uniforms. The Poles who had left the "Godless land" were slowly fed until they could eat normal meals, and their training as soldiers began again in earnest under the warm sun. The Polish soldiers began a trek that was Biblical in more ways than one as they crossed Iraq to Syria and then to Palestine. Though the majority of them would eventually end up fighting in Italy, some of the men who had come out of Russia would be sent to Britain to replace losses suffered by the Polish Air Force and Navy, and to fill out the ranks of the under-strength army units in Scotland.

The British had been victorious at El Alamein, and had taken thousands of Germans and Italians prisoner. Rather than divert manpower to guard them, and ship food through the U-Boat blockade to feed them, the captured enemies were loaded on empty ships returning to the United States to be interned in prisoner-of-war camps there. Polish soldiers were delivered to Scotland. There, representatives from the different branches of the Polish armed forces greeted the new arrivals, and gave "sales pitches" describing the advantages of their particular service. Of course, the Parachute Brigade had its recruiters there too.

At Kirkcaldy, Scotland, Private Michal Lasek and his friend, Private Mieczyslaw Chwastek, listened to the representatives of the other services. The pair had been together since leaving Russia, where Chwastek's mother, sister and two younger brothers had died. After listening to the boring speeches, a junior officer from the Parachute Brigade gave a rousing talk about the special nature of his unit, and about how it would be the first to return to Poland. He then spread open a parachute in a demonstration of how to collapse it. A strong gust of wind filled the chute, and dragged the officer face first across a cow pasture. Lasek was convinced, thinking, "If this is what happens to officers in this unit, I want to be part of it." He and Chwastek both volunteered to become paratroopers.

The Germans' final defeat in Africa had an unusual benefit for the Brigade in that it brought more men into its ranks. Among the thousands of prisoners were Poles whose homes were in the territories annexed to the Reich. The men had been forcibly conscripted into the Wehrmacht, and then by the Allies in North Africa. After segregation, interviews, and verification in the prisoner of war camps, many joined the Polish armed forces to fight for their motherland. Many of these unusual "veterans" brought their skills and knowledge of the enemy to the Brigade.

The Parachute Brigade also attracted volunteers from the Polish communities of America. After the United States entered the war in December 1941, however, the majority returned to the U.S. armed forces. Nevertheless, there was one "Polish" American volunteer in whose veins did not flow one drop of Polish blood, and despite the fact that there was no comparison between the Polish and the American armed forces in pay, equipment and privileges, Richard K. Tice decided to remain with these men, with whom he had become so close. Tice joined the Polish Army in Canada in September 1941, unable to speak a single word of Polish. The towering Yank immediately became one of the most popular persons there. Fair-haired and with a smile always on his face, Tice possessed a warm and sincere personality, and won the immediate affection of Poles and Scots alike when the Canadian Poles had crossed the Atlantic. He was a crack shot with any infantry weapon, but most loved firing a revolver from the hip. Because of his unusual and accurate marksmanship, his Polish comrades soon called him "The Cowboy" behind his back.

During 1943 the Brigade opened an Officer Cadet School in Falkland.

The Polish system of educating and commissioning officers followed a Central European pattern that was unusual in the West. The officer candidate did not automatically receive his commission upon graduation. Rather, the candidate was usually graduated with an NCO rank commensurate with his standing in the class, and the notation that he was a cadet. Thus, a graduate would hold the rank of Lance Sergeant Cadet (which would place him in the top 20 percent of his class). The cadet could later be commissioned in annual promotions, or by his deeds on the field of battle.

One of the cadets who was graduated as a *commissioned* officer was Richard Tice. Colonel Sosabowski recognized the great propaganda potential of the American volunteer, and chose him to attend the school, despite his struggles to learn the difficult Polish language. It is an indication of how well-liked Tice was by the men of the Brigade that this author has not heard a single word of resentment towards him, despite the fact that his attendance took a place that could have been filled by a Polish candidate who was possibly more worthy.

The Brigade naturally owed much to the man who founded and shaped it, Stanislaw Sosabowski. In matters military, Sosabowski was a martinet, but not without a sense of humor. He favored young officers who could think quickly and come back with a smart answer or excuse, and saw these people as the future of his nation. He despised selfishness, incompetence and poor soldierly bearing. He looked out for the welfare of his men, and did his best to continue their outside education in the hope that they might be better citizens after the end of hostilities.

A measure of the Colonel's concern for the welfare of his men, and for the people of Poland, came when the Polish paratroopers received their back pay in February 1943. The pay was made retroactive to the time the man had qualified, and some men were due to receive quite a bit of money. Sosabowski stipulated that it was not to be paid directly to the soldiers, but bank accounts would be established for them. It did not matter if it was withdrawn a week later to be squandered on cards, wine or women, but it did give many men pause to think about the future. A voluntary collection was held (and God help the soldier who did not "volunteer"!), at which the soldiers were asked to donate 20 percent of their windfall to aid the widows and orphans of Home Army soldiers in Poland. A total of £7,500 was collected, and in fact was carried to Poland by the *Cichociemni*, where it was distributed to those in desperate need.

The Colonel was very active, and set a standard that was difficult to match for many younger men. Sosabowski was fifty years old when he went to Ringway and qualified as a parachutist. He neither drank nor smoked, but was enough of a realist to accept vices in others, provided that they did not hinder performance either as soldiers or as people. Sosabowski was a person not easily forgotten by those who had met him. Of medium height, the Colonel weighed 82 kilograms and was lean and athletic. His most striking feature was his blue eyes, set deep, and topped by heavy brows that seemed to be hanging in a perpetual frown. They seemed to constantly scrutinize everyone and everything, and gave the impression that they could penetrate anything on which they focused. Sosabowski's eyes spoke before his mouth, but as emphatic as they were in anger or displeasure, they likewise would sparkle with felicity before a wide smile came to his lips and then spread across the rest of his face.

On November 21, 1942, General Browning presented a standard to the Brigade as a New Year's gift from the 1st Airborne Division. The same wine color as the British Airborne beret, the banner had a light blue Pegasus insignia in its center, and both Polish and British paratroopers insignia embroidered in the corners of the fly end. It was inscribed: "TO 1 POLISH PARACHUTE BRIGADE FROM AIRBORNE DIVISION NEW YEAR 1943." Browning presented the standard to the Brigade with the words: "This is a symbol of our brotherhood of arms, which will be sealed on the battlefield with our mutual enemy."

Colonel Sosabowski was pleased with the gift, but had set his heart on a special standard for a special unit. Sosabowski had requested of some of the officers who had left the Brigade to join the *Cichociemni* that when they returned to Poland they ask the people of occupied Warsaw to present a proper Polish military standard to the Brigade. It was Sosabowski's dream to return to the city with it. The *Cichociemni* men had jumped into Poland a long time before, and there had been no word of their fate; therefore, any thoughts about a standard for the Parachute Brigade were trivial in comparison.

During the dark early hours of December 28, 1941, six men suspended from parachutes had drifted to earth far away from Scotland. Unfortunately, they landed not in occupied Poland, but in the territory that had been annexed to the German Reich. In the ensuing fight, two of the *Cichociemni* were killed by the alerted Germans while they covered the escape of their comrades. The survivors lost all of their equipment, but managed to reach Warsaw with the military orders and currency they had carried from England intact.

The leader of the group, Captain Maciej Kalenkiewicz, had been wounded and was left in the care of an underground medical unit. While recuperating, Kalenkiewicz met with Maria Kann and author Zofia Kossak. The captain told them of the Parachute Brigade and of its desire to have a standard from the city they sought to liberate. The women of Warsaw gathered the scarce materials and worked on the flag under the noses of the Gestapo, who were everywhere in the city. The standard was given a deeper historical significance when the ruby-red silk robe of Cardinal Dunajewski, a nineteenth-century Polish patriot, was donated to form the body of the banner.

After nearly a year of work, the flag was finished. The standard was designed in the traditional pattern of Polish military colors: a red Maltese cross on a white field. One side bore the Polish eagle and the arms of Warsaw. The reverse had St. Michael the Archangel (the patron saint of paratroopers) embroidered in the center. Above the image was the inscription, "WARSZAWA 1942," and below, "SURGE POLONIA" (Arise, Poland). Both sides of the flag had the diving-eagle Polish paratroopers badge embroidered in silver thread in the four corners.

In a secret ceremony on November 3, 1942, the color was consecrated in Warsaw's Canon church. In attendance were Zofia Kossak and Maria Kann, who were to be known as the Brigade's godmothers. The Polish Army was represented by three *Cichociemni*: Captain Kalenkiewicz, Lieutenant Mieczyslaw Eckhardt (pseudonym: "Stork") and 2nd Lieutenant Jan Marek. All three had been in the Parachute Brigade before joining the *Cichociemni*, and none would survive the war. After the solemn ceremony, the flag was hidden away; there was no way to get the flag to the men so far away, to whom it was dedicated.

The warm relations between General Browning and Colonel Sosabowski allowed the Brigade to receive needed equipment. In March 1943, the Brigade was to take part in field exercises that were to be observed by Polish Premier and General Sikorski and exiled Polish President Raczkiewicz. Browning was invited, and had arrived a day early. He sat down to have a drink with Colonel Sosabowski and his adjutant and interpreter, Lieutenant Jerzy Dyrda. Dyrda, who was an industrialist in Poland before the war, was immensely talented, both in languages and as a negotiator. The three sat alone in the Brigade's officer's club in Leven, when Browning told the Polish colonel that he understood the problems that he had with recruitment, and proposed the formation of a British-

Polish Airborne Division under Sosabowski's command; the troops that were lacking would be made up by the British. Dyrda was stunned both by the proposal, and by Sosabowski's immediate response: "That is impossible. This Brigade has to go to Poland! That is the order of General Sikorski!"

A look of disappointment came over Browning's face, and he replied, "Please don't worry. When the proper time comes, the entire division will jump into Poland. I myself will go with you." Sosabowski repeated himself, and stated that he would be seeing General Sikorski the next day, and would take the matter up with him. After Browning left, Lieutenant Dyrda told his chief that he should have been more tactful with the British general, who did not stay to see the Polish exercises the following day. In the months that followed, there were requests from the British War Office to move the Polish Parachute Brigade south to England, on the pretext that the training facilities would be better there.

While the Allies prosecuted the war militarily, the Polish government in England also had to fight on the political front. The Poles had the unusual balancing act of trying to work in harmony with the Anglo-Americans, and at the same time trying to maintain some sort of relationship with the Soviet Union. This difficult task was becoming harder and harder as time passed. The British working class had been left-leaning in previous decades, and was a fertile ground for the anti-Polish propaganda soon spread by the Soviets. While Roosevelt and Churchill courted Stalin for their own reasons, an increasing amount of Soviet propaganda was directed against the London Poles. In January 1943, the Soviets declared that all non-ethnic Poles who had lived in the territory seized in 1939 were citizens of the USSR. Four months later came shocking news – and, from all places, German radio.

In a broadcast on April 13, 1943, German radio announced the discovery of mass graves near the village of Katyn, Russia. The Germans claimed that they had found the corpses of 10,000 Polish officers. All had their hands tied behind their backs, and had been executed by a single bullet to the back of the head. The Polish government was in a difficult position. Preliminary indentification (from documents found on the bodies) by the Germans pointed to the fact that these men were part of the group of 16,000 officers in Soviet captivity who had not reported to the Polish Army in Russia. Radio Moscow announced two days later that the Nazis had committed the atrocity. The Polish government knew that both dictatorships were capable of the crime, but the overwhelming evidence pointed to the murders having been committed by the Soviets. When the Polish government requested an investigation by the International Red Cross, the Soviet Union broke off all diplomatic relations with the Polish government in London.

The Western Allies could not understand that the Poles were fighting for their very existence, and urged them to come to an understanding with the Soviets. Roosevelt and Churchill were committed to winning the war, and they needed Stalin and his vast armies to defeat Hitler in the quickest possible manner. Amid Stalin's demands that the Anglo-Americans open a second front in Europe, the Polish efforts to save their country were viewed more and more as petty and self-centered, and destructive to the alliance against Hitler.

On July 3, 1943, the Poles were struck by yet another disaster in a seemingly unending stream of tragedy when General Sikorski was killed in a plane crash at Gibraltar. The death of the man who was both the Polish Premier and Commander-in-Chief of the armed forces deeply shook the Polish community. It was especially hard on the Parachute Brigade, which realized that he had done everything possible for its development. Colonel Sosabowski, who had always enjoyed close relations with the general, took a parachute company to London, where they formed part of Sikorski's honor guard as he lay in state in Westminster Abbey. Even Sikorski's political enemies realized that he was one of the few Poles who had both the political skill and the access to the world's leaders that was needed to represent Poland's national interests.

Life, however, was not just pain, homesickness, hard work and strict discipline for the men who wore the gray berets. The years the Polish soldiers had been in Scotland had in many ways been idyllic compared to the horrible events happening in the world around them. This land of mountains and clouds, and air that smelled both of clover-filled cow pastures and the sea, became a second home to many of the Slavs, who found themselves staying there. The people of Fife, who had worked small farms, dug coal, made linoleum or caught fish, had led in many ways an isolated existence. The arrival of the Poles, especially in the beginning, when the majority were officers, gave the Scots a view of people that they "had only seen in the cinema." The Poles put great stock in gracious manners, and showed a pronounced deference to women. Many a teen-aged girl's heart took flight when she had her hand kissed, and would feel as if she were "the only person in the world" when she had a Pole as an escort. The pretty red-haired girls never had to spend a night at home with all of the charming and eager men around. Many of these relationships led to the altar.

The most holy and sentimental time for the Poles is the Christmas Eve "Vigil" supper, and in 1940 the soldiers so far away from their homes and families shared this time with their Scottish hosts. Though language was a barrier, the ritual and warmth of the occasion cemented a lasting bond with the Scots. The Polish soldiers never overlooked an opportunity to sing, and Fife was now filled with beautiful and melodious song, the words of which were incomprehensible to the Scots. The soldiers never neglected an opportunity to stage a review either, and the audiences were always full of Scots. After a review of Polish cabaret jokes, paratroopers would take the stage in kilts and would perform music-hall songs in thickly accented approximations of a Scottish brogue. The performances were frequently finished with a few simple (and dreadful) jokes that would leave the audience roaring simply from the absurd but pleasant presentation by their friends onstage.

On September 23, 1943, the Parachute Brigade celebrated its second anniversary. The occasion was highlighted by the presentation of a standard by the County of Fife. The banner had been beautifully embroidered by the women of Fife, and was presented to the Brigade at a ceremony that was attended by two of the Poles' longtime Scottish friends: Lady Victoria Weymss, Lady-in-Waiting to the Queen, and Lord Eglin, Lord-Lieutenant of Fife. When the Brigade marched, the flag that was presented by General Browning of the 1st Airborne Division was joined by the lovely banner that displayed both the white eagle and Scottish thistle, and proved to be a tangible reminder of the happy relations the Poles had enjoyed with their hosts.

The fall and winter passed with the Brigade taking part in exercises with the troops of the British 52nd Lowland Division. Colonel Sosabowski enjoyed a warm, professional relationship with his new Commander-in-Chief, General Kazimierz Sosnkowski. Sosnkowski was an old-line soldier who had coordinated efforts between the Poles in London and the AK in Poland. He was relentlessly suspicious of the intentions of both the Soviets and the Anglo-American Allies for Poland. At the end of November, Churchill, Roosevelt and Stalin met in Teheran, where the latter two rejected the British Prime Minister's plan to invade the Balkans. Unknown at the time, the three powerful men, without consulting the Poles, had moved the Polish border westward, and had ceded to Stalin the parts of Poland he had seized in 1939.

On December 16, 1943, Colonel Sosabowski was decorated with "The Most Excellent Order of the British Empire," with the rank of Commander. He then left with Lieutenant Dyrda for the United States and Canada to observe airborne methods and training, and also to investigate the possibilities of obtaining transport aircraft.

During his visit to the United States, Sosabowski visited the U.S. Airborne Command Center at Fort Benning, Georgia, where under almost constantly sunny skies hundreds of paratroopers were turned out. He later saw division-sized exercises at Fort Bragg, North Carolina, and was impressed by the sight of a drop by over a thousand paratroopers.

Colonel Sosabowski then visited the General Staff College at Fort Leavenworth, Kansas. During the visit Sosabowski and Lieutenant Dyrda were escorted by a Colonel Schallenberg. Touring the operations room, the American Colonel took the Poles into a small adjoining chamber and pulled back a curtain, exposing a wall-sized map of Europe. Over the map was a label, "Spheres of Influence." A thick black line followed the Elbe River and divided Europe between the Anglo-Americans and the Soviets. Lieutenant Dyrda was shocked, both by the map, and by the violent curses that came from Sosabowski. In all the years he had known him, the lieutenant had never heard his chief curse. Dyrda then looked at the American officer. His name was that of a typical Junker. He wondered if the man, with an obvious German background, was mocking them. Dyrda only saw pity in his face.

After Fort Leavenworth, the Polish officers moved on to Indianapolis, Indiana, to visit the headquarters of Air Transport Command and hold discussions with its commander, General Bruce Evans. Colonel Sosabowski and Lieutenant Dyrda had flown throughout their time in the United States on the excellent C-47 (known to the British as the Dakota) transport plane. To his dismay, Sosabowski learned that, due to Lend-Lease agreements, the Polish armed forces could receive American equipment only through British channels. After six weeks in North America, the Polish airborne officers returned to Britain. It was now 1944, and a new chapter of history was unfolding.

7

Poles Apart

January to September 1944

Upon his return to Britain from the United States, Colonel Sosabowski enthusiastically stated the case for the C-47 transport. Fitted with extra fuel tanks, the Dakotas would be able to transport the Parachute Brigade to Poland and then land at Russian-held airfields. Sosabowski's desire to get the Brigade to Poland overrode his normal sense of reason. The perceived range of the Dakota that was engraved in the Colonel's mind was a result of an encounter with a group of American pilots in Indiana who, joyously warmed by whiskey, sang the praises of the aircraft with the eloquence of Texans. While the Dakota might reach Poland with extra fuel tanks, this represented the extreme fringe of the aircraft's range, and did not take into account that such a trip would require a straight flight between two points. German air defenses would make this highly improbable, and a northern route across Sweden was out of the question. Furthermore, the Brigade's mission, in light of the general situation in early 1944, was strategically impossible. Sosabowski's lack of sound judgment was due in part to his desperation on learning the results of the conference at Teheran while in the United States. Had the Allies pursued a Balkan strategy, it might have been possible to fly to Poland from Yugoslavia or Hungary, but learning that Poland was to be in the Soviet "sphere of influence" made the Colonel's despair acute.

By 1944, the British Isles were host to hundreds of thousands of American soldiers, sailors and airmen preparing for the invasion of the Continent. Having been at war longer than the United States, and having suffered more casualties, the British, however, were coping with a severe manpower shortage. Out of concern not to be overshadowed by their giant ally, they sought to marshal every resource available, and the sole remaining Allied unit in Britain not committed to Supreme Headquarters Allied Expeditionary Forces (SHAEF) was the 1st Polish Parachute Brigade. The British were also mindful of the resources they had expended on the Polish Brigade and sought to reap some benefit from their investment. Early in March 1944, the British sent to Polish Headquarters a formal inquiry asking under what circumstances might the Parachute Brigade be released for operations on the Continent.

Coincidental with this request, Colonel Peto, Chief of the 4th British Liaison Mission in Scotland, visited Colonel Sosabowski in Leven. When he suggested that General Montgomery was "very keen" on having the Brigade with him for operations in the coming invasion, before it was used for its primary mission in Poland, Sosabowski lost his temper with Peto, telling him sternly that the Polish Commander-in-Chief, General Sosnkowski, alone decided how and where the Brigade was to be used. Despite his reception, Peto reported to Montgomery that the Polish Parachute Brigade was a valuable tactical unit. Two days later, at a meeting at British Airborne Headquarters, General Browning told Sosabowski that he had heard, "through the grapevine," that the Polish Brigade would be joining his command for operations in Europe, and pointed out the advantage of receiving new combat equipment. The pressure on the Poles was becoming more and more overt.

On March 11, General Sosnkowski received from the offices of Field Marshal Sir Alan Brooke, Chief of the Imperial General Staff, a letter offering conditions for the Brigade entering operations under SHAEF. Briefly, these were:

(1) The Brigade would be a reserve for the Allied Airborne Forces, and would not be used in the initial stages of the invasion.

(2) Should the Brigade suffer severe casualties (on the order of 25 percent), it would be withdrawn from operations.

(3) If the opportunity arose for the Brigade's employment in Poland, every effort (with no guarantee) would be made to secure aircraft to transport it there.

The matter was now in the hands of the highest Polish political and military authorities.

In the meantime, Montgomery was inspecting units that were to be under his command during the coming invasion. On March 13, he was scheduled to visit General Maczek's Polish 1st Armored Division in Scotland. Montgomery requested that the Parachute Brigade be represented, and he was impressed with what he saw.

While debating the implications of the British request, General Sosnkowski conferred with Colonel Sosabowski on the matter. The brigade group was organized to have over 4,000 soldiers. It was felt that the Brigade could still take part in operations with 3,000 men, but in March 1944 it could only muster 2,200. Despite the freshly raised 4th Battalion's being broken up to reinforce the other three, they each had less than 450 riflemen each. With the manpower barrel scraped, there was little realistic possibility of filling the ranks.

Sosabowski also put forth the matter of training. The British had priority for the use of Ringway. In the buildup before the invasion, the British were raising two airborne divisions, while the Poles were still waiting patiently for space at Ringway to train parachutists to fill one brigade. Aside from qualifying men as paratroops, the matter of training the soldiers in specialties took even more time. The Polish Parachute Brigade had not yet had the opportunity to conduct parachute exercises at even the company level. Sosabowski also wanted the Brigade to have an organic glider-pilot unit to transport the Brigade's heavy equipment, but this program was not even at an embryonic stage.

The Polish government replied to the British with a counterproposal for the Brigade's use in Western Europe:

(1) The Brigade would be used in one major operation, or some minor actions.

(2) It would be withdrawn if it suffered more than 15 percent casualties.

(3) It would not be used during the early stages of the invasion.

(4) There should be a firmer statement about the use of aircraft to transport the Brigade to Poland.

In addition, Colonel Sosabowski submitted a further request that the Brigade maintain its Polish identity, and not be merged with British units. The decision was a difficult one for all sectors of the Polish government. Even the AK was consulted on the decision. The die was cast for service in the West, and the Brigade accelerated its training program.

Meetings and discussions about the use of the Brigade in operations on the Western front took place all through the spring in Polish governmental and military bureaus. At the end of one such exhausting meeting in London on April 29, General Sosnkowski pulled a package wrapped in paper and string from his desk and handed it to Colonel Sosabowski. Opening the package, Sosabowski discovered the standard that the women of Warsaw had secretly made for the Parachute Brigade.

Hidden since its consecration in November 1942, it was transported to Italy a scant twelve days before on a Dakota bearing underground political and military leaders from occupied Poland as part of Operation MOST (Bridge).

Arriving with the colors were letters to the Brigade from its godmothers. One of them, Zofia Kossak, was now in Auschwitz, arrested for possessing underground newspapers. Of the *Cichociemni* who had dropped into Poland and passed on the request for a standard, Lieutenant Eckhardt ("Stork") was dead. After a successful period in which his detachment of saboteurs had destroyed a number of enemy military trains, he had been captured by German anti-partisan troops. After being brutally tortured, Eckhardt had hanged himself in his cell to avoid compromising his comrades. During the late spring of 1944, Major Kalenkiewicz was recovering near Wilno from the amputation of his hand due to wounds suffered fighting the Germans. He was surrounded by his trained and well-armed partisan regiment.

The standard was unfinished, as the woman of Warsaw were unable to obtain the silver fringe that normally edged Polish colors in their impoverished and brutalized city. While this was being added to the banner in England, a staff and pole top were needed. The eagle that traditionally sat atop the staff of Polish military colors would have as deep a meaning as the flag itself. The colors of the Polish 21st Infantry Regiment had found their way to England. The pole top of the "Children of Warsaw" Regiment commanded so masterfully by Sosabowski in 1939 was used to mold the eagle for the pole top of the Parachute Brigade's colors. Colonel Sosabowski had hoped to wait for the Brigade's Holy Day for the presentation of the colors, but in light of the new situation, there was no time to wait until September.

All of the soul-searching and negotiation about how and when to fight the Germans ended when General Sosnkowski received a letter from the Imperial General Staff requesting use of the Brigade, without any stipulations whatsoever. The Polish government agreed to this request the same day the Allies invaded France, and it was confirmed by SHAEF one week later. On June 15, 1944, the entire Brigade was to be brought together in Cupar, Scotland.

On the morning of June 14, Colonel Sosabowski's battledress jacket and beret were stolen from his quarters. Several hours later, they had been returned with the insignia of a Major General in their place. Daily orders, which included confirmation of Sosabowski's promotion, were seen by some of the headquarters personnel. In celebration of "Pop's" promotion, they took silver shilling coins and fashioned them into general's insignia. Sosabowski was deeply moved by this heartfelt gesture from his men.

The next day, the entire Brigade was brought together for the first time in its existence, on the athletic field of Cupar. In attendance were President Raczkiewicz, and members of the Polish General Staff. After High Mass, General Sosabowski read his order of the day. It concluded with the words: "The time of our labors in battle approaches. The nation...waits for us in confidence....Warsaw believes that this standard will lead victory to her walls."

The letters from the women of Warsaw, written almost two years before, were read before the Brigade. The color was blessed and presented by Vice President Stanislawski, who had brought it from Poland, to the President of the Republic. President Raczkiewicz then passed it to General Sosabowski. After speeches by many of the dignitaries, the color was paraded before each unit in the Brigade. After the many speeches, the soldiers wondered about the future. Following the ceremonies, they returned to their billets and began packing for the move south to England.

On June 20, members of General Browning's staff announced that the Polish Parachute Brigade would have an equipment priority to get the unit ready for action. Two days later, Browning's chief of operations, Lieutenant Colonel Charles Mackenzie, arrived in Leven to inform General Sosabowski that the Polish Brigade was needed for an operation on July 6. The Polish commander was flabbergasted. He had long insisted that it would be at least August before his Brigade would be ready for combat. Called to Browning's headquarters on June 25, Sosabowski argued the case that he was not prepared to lead a half-trained brigade into combat. While the meeting further strained the increasingly stormy relations between the two, it produced a positive result in that Major General Ernest "Eric" Down was appointed to assist the Poles in their preparations.

The Polish Parachute Brigade began moving from Scotland to the English Midlands on June 29. The benediction was provided by the tears of the local girls. After four years, the Scots were sad to see their extraordinary guests leave. The move was completed on July 3. Brigade headquarters was located in Stamford, and units were billeted as far away as Peterborough. The 1st Airborne Division was located nearby at Grantham and provided great support in equipping the Poles. As the 6th

Airborne Division was in Normandy, it was most likely that the Polish Brigade would be involved in operations with the 1st Airborne Division. General Sosabowski met its commander, Major General Robert E. "Roy" Urquhart. The tall Scot was a veteran infantry officer appointed to command the 1st Airborne Division despite being an "outsider," who had had no previous airborne experience.* Urquhart quickly won the respect of his command. General Sosabowski regarded the solid, reliable and pleasant commander with satisfaction. Their relationship was professional, that of soldiers, rather than that of any real friendship, but Urquhart, unlike many other British generals, seemed to have some understanding of the position and the pressures on the frequently abrasive Sosabowski.

The Brigade began operational training on July 8. It must be stressed that all of the Polish paratroop units had led separate existences in Scotland. The rifle platoons and companies had been spread all over Fife, hoping that their presence might provide security against the threat of enemy agents being landed on the isolated coast. Apart from learning to jump from a Dakota, the soldiers had now to learn to function as a cohesive unit. Aside from basic infantry training and parachute instruction, there had been little further coordinated training within the battalions. Due to the Brigade's mission, many men had attended urban warfare courses in the bombed-out ruins of Southampton, and the Polish Armored Division had schooled many men in anti-tank tactics. However, many of the special schools that were in existence during the Brigade's early years had since received other priorities, or had been closed due to their expense.

The Brigade was extremely busy in the Midlands as it underwent its parachute conversion training from Whitleys to the Dakotas. The Dakota was a comfortable aircraft that allowed the paratroopers to leave through the side door like "gentlemen," rather than dropping from a ventral orifice. The lack of coordinated parachute training was rectified with a vengeance and the Brigade was confined to barracks practically all summer as it made both day and night jumps.

The preparations for action pleased Lieutenant Albert Smaczny of the 8th Company. Smaczny had joined the Brigade in 1941 after seeing combat in France. To him, the war was a personal matter. Before

---

*General Urquhart had served on the staff of the 51st Highland Division during the North African campaign and had commanded the 231st Independent Brigade Group in the invasion of Sicily.

hostilities, Smaczny had been an officer of the counterintelligence division of the Polish National Police, investigating subversive activities by the German minority in his native Silesia. Captured in 1939, he escaped, only to have his sixteen-year-old brother murdered by the Gestapo in reprisal. From the time he had learned of his brother's death, Smaczny no longer saw the Germans as a political enemy to be fought, but had been left with a deep, implacable hatred for the Teutonic conquerors. Friends in the Polish Air Force based in Britain had explained the impossibility of air-transporting the Brigade to Poland unless the Soviets permitted refueling on their terrain. General Sosabowski had explained to his officers that the odds of the Brigade's getting to Poland would be better from the Continent after fighting the Germans there. The years of preparation left Smaczny, like many others in the Brigade, anxious to come to grips with the enemy under practically any circumstance.

After training jumps on the platoon level, company-size jumps were scheduled. On the morning of July 8, the 8th Company was to jump as a battle group, yet the night before there was unease in the ranks. Lance Corporal Kuzniar, Lieutenant Smaczny's radio man, would not be taking part in the jump because he was hard at work in the Signal Company preparing for a coming night jump. After supper, Kuzniar's replacement, Private Jozef Podolski, told signaler Lance Corporal Stanislaw Matlak that he felt that he would not return from the maneuver. Matlak replied, "Why not?" and insisted that everything would be alright. To this, Podolski pulled a one-pound note from his wallet and bet Matlak the money against his own return. Podolski asked Kuzniar to witness the bet involving such a large sum of money. Puzzled, Matlak asked Podolski what he should do with the money if he really did win the bet. Podolski glibly replied, "Buy me a wreath."

Private Podolski was not the only man feeling anxious about the coming jump. 2nd Lieutenant Stanislaw Trybus told Lieutenant Smaczny that he had felt sick since the early morning, having had a dark premonition. As the stick commanders gave the containers slung under the aircraft a final check, Trybus gave a weak smile in Smaczny's direction, waved and climbed aboard his airplane. The Dakotas were soon airborne. Sitting by the door, Smaczny watched the other aircraft in the formation. In the "V" of three aircraft behind Smaczny's, the left-hand aircraft sharply banked toward the center one. The Dakota in the middle quickly gained altitude to avoid his neighbor, which then crashed wings with the right-hand plane in the formation. Within seconds, the two smashed airplanes were tumbling towards the ground, followed by a single parachute.

Two days later, twenty-six coffins lay in ranks of four in a large single grave. The grave was near that of General Sikorski in the Polish Air Force cemetery in Newark. The largest wreath lay on Private Podolski's coffin. The single parachute seen floating to earth belonged to an American flight engineer who was sitting near the aircraft's open door. He was wearing a chest-type parachute with a rip cord. There had been absolutely no chance of escape for the Polish paratroopers, whose chutes were on their backs, and were opened by a static line. Seven American aircrew also died in the collision.

Aside from giving the paratroopers' morale a shattering blow, the tragedy left a large gap in the 3rd Battalion. Two officers, two cadets, ten noncommissioned officers and twelve riflemen were missing from the already under-strength ranks. The entire battalion experienced a reshuffling to fill in the stricken 8th Company. This gave 2nd Lieutenant Tice, bored with his work in the Anti-tank Squadron, an opportunity to transfer to a platoon command in the 7th Company. The preparations for action continued with battalion jumps and, finally, after July 30, exercises as an entire brigade group.

To better utilize the available airborne resources, SHAEF formed the First Allied Airborne Army. The Army was composed of two corps, the U.S. XVIII Airborne Corps (82nd, 101st and the arriving 17th Airborne Divisions) and the British I Airborne Corps (1st and 6th Airborne Divisions, the 52nd Lowland [Airlanding] Division, and the Polish 1st Independent Parachute Brigade), as well as British and American Troop Carrier Commands. The British felt very strongly that the Army's commander should be General Browning. This was overruled by Eisenhower, who chose Lieutenant Lewis Brereton, former commander of the U.S. 9th Air Force. Browning was appointed Deputy Army Commander, a position in addition to his command of British I Airborne Corps.

As the Polish Parachute Brigade was winding up its operational training, events in Eastern Europe unfolded with the same lightning speed as had those in France. The Russian summer offensive had barreled through Byelorussia and the Ukraine and across the old border into Poland. As the Soviet armies hit German resistance at Wilno and Wolyn, the Polish Home Army rose in open warfare, attacking German lines of supply and communication. After briefly embracing the AK as "comrades in arms," within hours the Soviets began denouncing the AK as "bandit groups," arresting or executing Polish officers, and forcibly conscripting the soldiers into their commissar-led "Polish Peoples Army." After hearing the news from Wilno, Major Kalenkiewicz withdrew his regiment from in front of the Soviet advance. On July 22, the Red Army took Lublin, and the Soviet-sponsored "Union of Polish Patriots" proclaimed themselves to be the legitimate Polish government. The Red juggernaut smashed the German defenses and was swiftly approaching Warsaw. Nearing the city, the Soviet-sponsored "Radio Kosciuszko" broadcasted appeals to the capital to rise against the Germans, proclaiming, "The hour of liberation is at hand."

In Warsaw itself, scenes reminiscent of 1918 were repeated as withdrawing Wehrmacht units moved through the streets of the city. The Germans began by evacuating their military depots and civilian administration. The AK in Warsaw consisted of over 35,000 armed men and women, restive after nearly five years of brutal occupation. Since October 1943 over 7,000 people had been killed in random street executions alone. With the sighting of Russian tanks in one of Warsaw's eastern suburbs, the AK commander, General Tadeusz Komorowski (pseudonym "Bor"), gave orders to begin the inevitable national uprising.

During the late afternoon of August 1, 1944, soldiers of the Home Army threaded their way among the crowds returning from work. At 1700 hours, gunfire rippled through the city as German strongpoints were attacked. After twenty-four hours, much of the city center was in the hands of the AK. Red-and-white banners flew from the rooftops for the first time in many years. The notes of Chopin's previously forbidden polonaises wafted through the August air as civilians built barricades to consolidate the insurgents' gains. Throughout the liberated districts, joy was unrestrained—except in the headquarters of the AK.

The Germans withstood the AK's attacks on the Vistula bridges, and still held the broad avenues leading to them. The AK held several districts, but unfortunately the only means of communication were through the city's sewer system. The AK had also planned on seizing airfields to permit the Parachute Brigade and supplies to be flown in, but the crucial attack on Okecie airport had failed. Aside from its military importance, Okecie was to be the conduit to bring in the constitutional government-in-exile in London in order to forestall the designs that Stalin had on the Polish Republic.

Five days before the uprising in Warsaw, a radio message from General Bor was received in London: "WE ARE READY AT ANY MOMENT TO FIGHT FOR WARSAW. THE PARACHUTE BRIGADE'S INVOLVEMENT IN THIS BATTLE WILL HAVE TITANIC POLITICAL AND TACTICAL SIGNIFICANCE . . . "

The Brigade had now been under British command for six weeks. The Polish High Command approached the British with a request to divert part of the Brigade, a battalion, or even a company, to Warsaw. This was refused. Amid insinuations that he had been dragging his feet, Sosabowski said he had been told by Brigadier Peto that the Brigade would be considered ready for operations by the beginning of August.

On July 22, Adolf Hitler had just barely survived an assassination plot by elements within the German Army. Just fifteen days after the attempt on his life, Hitler gave orders to ruthlessly crush the rebellion in Warsaw and wipe the city from the map. Aside from available Wehrmacht and Waffen SS troops, a motley collection of Russian and Ukrainian renegades and an SS battalion recruited from German prisons were committed to this end. On August 5, therefore, Warsaw's Wola District was the scene of events rare to Europe since the Dark Ages. In the course of the enemy's taking three streets, the residents were pushed into courtyards. After the buildings had been looted and the women raped, the civilians were shot. On this single day, by conservative estimate, 10,000 people were murdered in Wola.

On the first day of the uprising, "Kolegium A" Company of the elite Kedyw captured a Waffen SS depot. Seized were rations, boots and hundreds of camouflage smocks, which with the addition of a red-and-white armband became the "uniform" of the Warsaw insurgents. The unit was led by Lieutenant Stanislaw Sosabowski. Over the years, the younger Sosabowski had been awarded three Crosses of Valor, and had earned a reputation as one of the bravest and ablest commanders in Kedyw. For the next few days the insurgents consolidated their positions. On August 7, Lieutenant Sosabowski was inspecting his company's positions overlooking the Wola District. During the relatively quiet afternoon, a shot from a German sniper struck the officer in his left cheekbone and blinded him.

Stalin, meanwhile, publicly dismissed the Polish insurgents as "adventurers" and "bandits." He refused the Western Allies permission to refuel aircraft on Soviet-held terrain after supply drops, though such permission was granted for planes landing after bombing raids over

Germany. British, South African and Polish aircrews flying from Italy suffered ghastly losses in attempts to drop a few planeloads of supplies on the tortured city.

On August 13, the Polish 1st Parachute Battalion stationed at Easton-on-the-Hill was lined up outside its mess hall for its evening meal. Some men refused to enter the mess hall as a sign of protest against the Allies' not sending the Brigade to Warsaw. All of the officers and men eventually decided to join the fast. While sympathetic to his men's motivation, General Sosabowski could in no way permit such a breach of military discipline, which amounted to a hunger strike. Given his strained situation with General Browning, and the fact that operational orders would be shortly forthcoming, Sosabowski praised the noble aim of the action but stressed that each soldier must maintain his fitness, as they might be going into battle at any moment. In light of the strict rationing imposed on the civilian population, the uneaten food was given to the village church for distribution to children and needy families. That night the Brigade was confined to barracks as the soldiers cleaned their weapons and packed haversacks with what they would need in the field; orders had been given to expect imminent movement to airfields for a combat operation.

After the American breakout from Normandy, General Omar Bradley planned a wide sweep east around Paris with the U.S. Third Army. This maneuver required units of the 1st Allied Airborne Army to fill a gap that would be created in the line, and to seize roads and bridges ahead of the advancing Americans. Known as Operation TRANSFIGURE, planning commenced on August 6.

Due to a shortage of troop-carrier aircraft, the drops were to be divided over two days. The first day would see the U.S. 101st Airborne Division and the British 52nd Lowland Division committed. The next day would see parachute landings by the British 1st Airborne Division and the 1st Polish Parachute Brigade. The Polish objective was Rambouillette, southeast of Paris. On August 13 all troops were confined to barracks in preparation for the commencement of the operation three days thence.

General Bradley's long-term plans were changed by the speed of General George Patton's race across Brittany. The Germans retreated, and were caught in a pincer at Falaise. Advancing from the north with the First Canadian Army was General Maczek's 1st Polish Armored

Division. Moving at the point of the Canadian advance, the Poles seized Chambois and Hill 262 on August 19. This hill stood astride the only route out of the Falaise pocket. For three days, without resupply of food, water or ammunition, outnumbered even by their prisoners, the Poles were hit with constant assaults by frantic and fanatic German troops from elite divisions trying to escape the encirclement. Bottled up, the enemy troops trapped in the pocket were slaughtered by wave after wave of Allied fighter-bombers. Though many Germans managed to escape, most of their formations were shattered (including a parachute and four SS Panzer divisions). German casualties included 50,000 taken prisoner, 10,000 killed, 500 tanks destroyed and other serious materiel losses. After Falaise, the Germans were being cleared out of France, and due to the rapidity of the Allied advance, Paris was taken and Operation TRANFIGURE canceled.

With the greater availability of transport aircraft after the conclusion of airborne operations in southern France, the staff of 1st Allied Airborne Army formulated Operation LINNET. The U.S. 82nd and 101st Airborne Divisions and the British 1st Airborne Division with the Polish Parachute Brigade were to drop near Tournai, Belgium. Thus, the airborne units were envisioned to move ahead of, and speed the advance of, the British and American armies moving across that country. The troops were again sealed in their barracks and D-Day was set for the afternoon of September 3. American ground forces, however, overran Tournai the night before the operation was to begin, and once again the assault was canceled.

Anxious to maintain the strategic momentum, an alternative plan to LINNET was already in place: LINNET II. As General Hodges' U.S. First Army approached the German border, it was planned that the LINNET forces would drop ahead of Hodges' advance near Aachen. This plan would have vaulted the Allies over the Siegfried Line. When Montgomery (who was promoted to the rank of Field Marshal on September 1) heard of this operation, and that it would favor American, rather than British, ground forces, he flew into such a rage that it threatened to cause a serious rift in SHAEF. Upon hearing of Montgomery's tantrum, General Browning argued for a postponement, stating that the operation was too hastily planned. Told to carry out his orders by General Brereton, Browning refused, saying that his divisional commanders would protest in writing. When Brereton relieved him of his command of the operation, Browning submitted his resignation from the staff of the First Allied

Airborne Army. In the face of a major command breakdown at the highest levels, Eisenhower canceled LINNET II.

With the cancellation of the operation, Browning withdrew his resignation. In a fence-mending move, Brereton offered Browning command of Operation COMET. The 1st Airborne Division and the Polish Parachute Brigade were to seize bridges over the rivers at Arnhem and Nijmegen in The Netherlands, then drive east to outflank the Ruhr. Not only would this operation support Montgomery, but the British I Airborne Corps had already studied the proposed mission. The troops, who by now were in complete readiness for an operation, were scheduled to take off on September 8.

General Browning issued his orders for COMET: the British 1st Airborne Division and the Polish Parachute Brigade were to seize the bridges over the rivers Maas at Grave, Waal at Nijmegen, and Neder Rijn at Arnhem. British ground forces would pass over them to form a bridgehead and allow the airlift of the 52nd Lowland Division into the area. The Polish task was to land near Grave and relieve Brigadier Hackett's 4th Parachute Brigade holding the bridge, or capture it if this had not already transpired.

During the staff and planning sessions for COMET, General Sosabowski was struck, while listening to the plans, by the casual approach of the British commanders and staff officers. The pugnacious Hackett raised his voice several times, but General Urquhart particularly remembers Sosabowski's interruptions: "The Germans . . . what will the Germans be doing while all of this is going on?" The Polish general thought that the fundamental error in this planning was faulty intelligence that gave the impression that the enemy forces in Holland were second- or third-rate. He felt that if the Allies could see the strategic advantages of flanking a "vulnerable" Ruhr, so could the Germans, and they would never allow it.

Aside from the fact that General Sosabowski thought the entire plan was too ambitious, his specific objections to COMET were:

(1) The drop zone was 4 kilometers away from the objective, thereby compromising the element of surprise.

(2) The entire operation would be under enemy observation from the Groesbeek Heights.

(3) If the enemy held the bridges, or if they were destroyed, no other means of crossing the rivers were available.

The weather on September 8 did not permit the execution of

COMET. That day General Sosabowski met with General Urquhart and stated that the bridge at Mook should be taken as insurance. He also urged that the crossings of the Maas and Maas/Waal canal near Heuman and Malden should be seized, and explained his worries about the Germans holding the Groesbeek area.

The next morning a telephone call from the 1st Airborne Division confirmed the change of the Polish objective to Mook and the Maas/Waal crossings. Still bothered, General Sosabowski arranged a meeting with General Urquhart at Cottesmore Airfield. On arrival, Sosabowski found Brigadier Hackett with Urquhart. The fiery Pole immediately came to the point and demanded written orders confirming his Brigade's role in COMET. Urquhart was shocked, and asked for an explanation. Sosabowski stated his lack of confidence in the operation and explained his responsibility to the Polish government for the Brigade, and his anticipation of its demise. Urquhart listened and apparently was so moved by these arguments that he flew with Sosabowski to Browning's headquarters at Rickmansworth.

At 1st Airborne Corps Headquarters, General Urquhart met first with General Browning. Then it was General Sosabowski's turn. Browning told Sosabowski that he could speak freely and in privacy. The Pole frankly explained that he felt the mission had no chance for success, and that it would be suicide to attempt it with the forces available. Browning stated that Sosabowski's points were well taken, and he was in agreement with them, but that he had his orders. Much to the Pole's aggravation, Browning smiled and said, "My dear Sosabowski, the Red Devils and the gallant Poles can do anything."

The written confirmation of General Sosabowski's orders never came. The day after Sosabowski's meeting with General Urquhart a re-evaluation of German strength caused Field Marshal Montgomery to postpone the operation for another twenty-four hours. COMET was canceled on September 10, 1944. That same day, planning commenced on the combined air and ground operation code-named MARKET GARDEN.

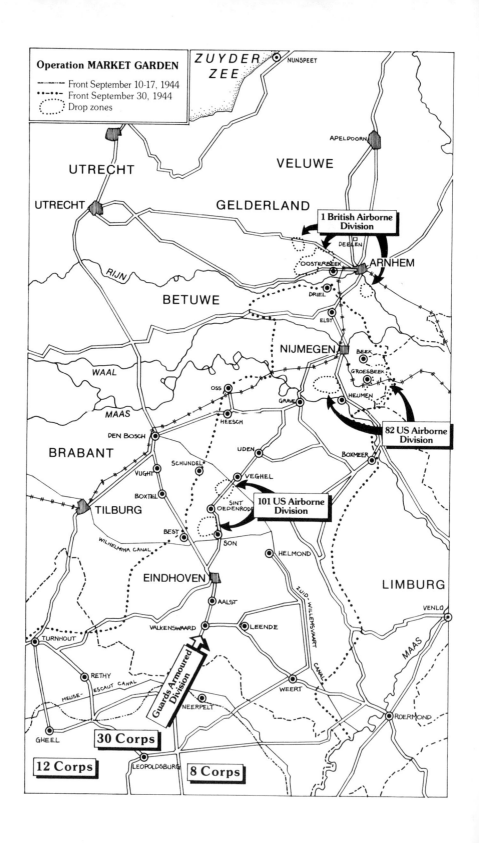

8

An Operation Named
MARKET GARDEN
September 10 to 17, 1944

The Airborne Corps staff, expanding the plans it had already made for COMET, presented its outline for Operation MARKET, the airborne end of the offensive, at General Urquhart's Moor Park headquarters. In addition to the 1st Airborne Division and the Polish Parachute Brigade, the U.S. 82nd and 101st Airborne Divisions were to participate under General Browning's overall command. Rather than taking the river crossings in both the Arnhem and Nijmegen region, the British and Polish airborne units were now to concentrate only on the Neder Rijn crossings by Arnhem. The crossings in the Nijmegen/Grave* area would be the sole mission of the 82nd Airborne Division.

Farther south, the 101st Airborne Division's task was to take the city of Eindhoven and the canal and river crossings north of the town. Overall, in MARKET, as the largest airborne operation in history, the paratroopers were to lay an "airborne carpet" in preparation for the second part of the offensive, which was code-named GARDEN.

In GARDEN, General Horrocks' XXX Corps of the Second British Army was to break across the Dutch frontier, roll through a 127-kilometer corridor across airborne-held bridges, cross the Neder Rijn, outflank the Ruhr and, possibly, bring the war to an end sometime in 1944.

As missions were laid out, General Sosabowski became "very upset" because the British seemingly assumed that the Germans would allow their sacred Rhine to be flanked. Disconcerted by their sanguine attitude as

---

*Studying the maps, the 82nd's commander, Brigadier General James Gavin, immediately realized the importance of the Groesbeek Heights and the Grave crossings. These same opinions had led General Sosabowski to confront General Browning during the planning stages of Operation COMET.

the briefing continued, he felt that the British estimate of German forces in the area was grossly understated. The biggest shock came when General Urquhart revealed that the dropping and landing zones for the 1st Airborne Division would be over 10 kilometers from the most critical objective, the Arnhem bridge. In Sosabowski's words, "We had lost the one indispensable element an airborne operation needs: surprise! Any fool of a German would immediately know our plans."

While Sosabowski digested the fact that it would be at least five hours after the drop before his objective could be reached, the operation's lift schedule was announced. Due to a shortage of aircraft, the assault would take place in three lifts in as many days. Sosabowski was dismayed that the troop carriers would fly only one lift a day. If two were flown, it would have been possible to have all the forces in place within 36 hours.

Given his orders, General Sosabowski was again astonished at the casualness with which his British counterparts received the briefing. They sat about, cross-legged, looking bored. When General Urquhart asked if there were any questions, nobody spoke. Sosabowski felt very alone. In an interview shortly before his death, he stated that he had already said too much during the briefings for earlier operations: "I wanted to say something, but I couldn't. I was unpopular enough, already, and who would have listened?" Sosabowski returned to his headquarters in Stamford. The next morning, the Polish general presented his staff with the orders for the new operation and his decisions on how the Polish Brigade would fulfill its assigned tasks.

The plan for the taking of the bridges at Arnhem stipulated that on D-Day, Sunday, September 17, 1st Airborne Division's Headquarters, Brigadier Gerald Lathbury's 1st Parachute Brigade, and Brigadier Philip Hicks's 1st Airlanding Brigade would land in Holland. The 1st Parachute Brigade would immediately proceed east to the city of Arnhem and seize the road and rail bridges. The 1st Airlanding Brigade would accompany the division's artillery and heavy equipment by glider. The three airlanding infantry battalions would stay behind to protect the LZs and DZs for the arrival of Brigadier Hackett's 4th Parachute Brigade and additional gliders the following day. The Airlanding Brigade would then organize supply-dropping zones on the western outskirts of the city while the 4th Parachute Brigade was taking the high ground in northern Arnhem. On D + 2, Tuesday, September 19, the Polish Brigade would jump into a drop zone immediately south of the bridges (a location that was deemed "unsuitable" for landing on D-Day), cross over or capture them, and then take up defensive positions in eastern Arnhem.

On September 14, General Sosabowski went with his Chief-of-Staff, Major Ryszard Malaszkiewicz, for a second MARKET GARDEN conference with General Urquhart. Sosabowski again stated his worries about how his brigade was to cross the river and hook up with the 1st Airborne Division. Urquhart assured the Polish general that it was essential that the British Division would hold the bridges for the Poles to cross. He further assured Sosabowski that the drop zone would be held, and that the Polish jeeps would be there to gather the supply containers. The next question from Sosabowski concerned the defense of Arnhem. The British Division and the Polish Brigade were to defend an 18-kilometer front. He feared that the 1st Division would not be able to complete its allotted missions, leaving the Poles jumping into enemy hands and fighting for their drop zone. Urquhart agreed that such a situation was possible, though not probable, as no serious enemy resistance was expected in the area.

During all of this planning, Polish paratroopers were already on the Continent. A seaborne lift, consisting of 200 men, 113 vehicles and three 6-pounder anti-tank guns, had departed for France on August 16 in conjunction with Operation TRANSFIGURE. This was to transport the Brigade's vehicles, supplies and spare guns to provide replacements for the artillery units that were yet to cross the channel. The men of the sea-lift had seen the Brigade's first, albeit minor, action when they took prisoner some German stragglers near their camp in Belgium. The sea-lift paratroopers were frequently visited by the recently Belgian Polish community, who begged to be allowed to join the Polish Army.

After the Brigade's glider allotment was cut further, it became apparent that the Polish light artillery battery would not be able to go into action with the Brigade by air. A second sealift was organized to bring the eight 75mm howitzers and their ammunition to the Continent. The Poles were finally allotted two glider lifts: ten gliders on D + 1, and the main lift of thirty-five gliders, landing at Johannahoeve on D + 2, coinciding with the Brigade's parachute drop south of the river. All of the sub-units were to pack a minimum of their heavy equipment on their gliders. The Airborne Anti-tank Artillery Squadron's fifteen all-important 6-pounder guns and jeeps would be carried with only a driver and a skeleton crew of two men per gun. The rest of the anti-tank crews would arrive with the parachute lift.

The Brigade staff went about repeating the grueling work that had been performed for the abortive previous operation. The orders received by General Sosabowski at conferences were in turn passed on to the Brigade staff late in the afternoon. Working completely isolated, for security reasons, the staff planned the mission of each sub-unit down to the last detail. Here the units were divided into individual planeloads. Then the Brigade staff officers would have to decide upon assembly areas on the ground; what signals were to be used for assembly; the lines of march for each rifle company; where the Brigade's heavy weapons would be sighted, and what support fire they would provide; the locations of first-aid stations; what routes and means would be used to evacuate the wounded; and hundreds of other items to hone the plan down to the most meticulous detail.

Excellent aerial photos were provided. From these, sand tables were constructed, detailed to the last tree for briefings down to the platoon level. Working through the night, the staff would have the operations orders ready as the sun was rising. They were then given to the units, who studied them through the day. As a result of the questions and comments from the units after they had studied their instructions, another night was spent making any necessary revisions.

The operational plans caused much concern among the staff officers working on the planning. Some of the Polish staff officers discovered the same casual atmosphere among their British counterparts that had so annoyed General Sosabowski. When Captain Jan Lorys, the Brigade's Tactical Operations Officer, questioned some of his British opposites about contingencies if the bridge were not captured, he was told not to worry. "We will be waiting for you with buses, you will be our guests for a cup of tea."

The 3rd Battalion was briefed by its commander, Captain Waclaw Sobocinski. Receiving the 8th Company's orders, Lieutenant Smaczny, despite assurances that there were few German troops in the area, was disturbed by the instructions. The lieutenant was confident of the Brigade's street-fighting abilities, and thought that the 8th Company would have no problem taking its objective, a factory warehouse several hundred meters from the bridge. Smaczny had studied the maps and photographs for so many hours that he felt, "I could find it blindfolded." While the operational instructions were precise, the lieutenant wondered how he would get his men across the river if the bridge was fortified or had been blown. There was mention that the Dutch underground would round up boats or that the RAF would drop dinghies if needed.

In their barracks and billets the Brigade's soldiers reflected on the events of the past months. The Polish Air Force and Navy had been in action since the beginning of the war. In Italy, General Anders' Polish II Corps had taken the monastery on the crest of Monte Cassino after a week of vicious frontal assaults. For five months, this fortified mountain had defeated the troops of six of the Allied nations until finally, on May 18, 1944, it was the Polish flag that was raised on its ruins, opening the road to Rome. During August, General Maczek's 1st Polish Armored Division wrote a bright chapter in the annals of Polish military history during the bloody fighting in Normandy, and was now pushing its way across Belgium. Many in the Polish Parachute Brigade felt left out of these ranks of military glory, having so far only had a long, frustrating wait. They chafed at some of the less sensitive jeers from men of other Polish services and units that the Polish Parachute Brigade was merely a propaganda formation.

Now it appeared that this might all change, and that they would be leading a spearhead through Germany's "back window." Besides, some rationalized, the Continent was a step closer to fulfilling the Brigade's promise to be the first soldiers to return to Poland. Through all of the frustrations and delays, this thought was never absent from the paratroopers' minds; and, like all Poles around the world, they thought of Warsaw and her agony. Bombardier Nosecki wondered about the fate of Holy Cross Church on the beautiful Nowy Swiat boulevard, where he had been an altar boy. Nosecki had no way of knowing that the church was now a gutted ruin, and had been in German hands for several weeks.

In Warsaw, the soldiers of the AK now held only a few scattered and separated districts, and those were under constant bombardment by artillery and Stukas. When the bombardment would stop, German sappers and SS men assaulted the insurgent positions, while paramilitary formations and German-allied Ukrainians continued their burning, raping, looting and butchery. The aged, the women and the children huddled in cellars in fear of the bombs and shells that had been falling on the city, under siege by the Soviets for six weeks. They were desperately short of food, and the insurgents lacked weapons and ammunition. All the same, the AK continued to fight from their bunkers in the ruins and the barricades on the shattered streets to provide Poland with a Polish future. The now-sporadic radio broadcasts coming from the stricken city spurned the Allies' sympathy, and demanded weapons instead.

While Warsaw went through her agony, the Red Army sat idle across the Vistula River. Churchill and Roosevelt tried to convince Stalin to aid the beleaguered insurgents and, after the costly and limited supply drops from Italy, the Americans pressed for landing areas in Soviet-held territory to be used for large formations of heavy bombers that were available to make mass supply drops over the city. Stalin refused, it suiting him better to have the AK destroyed fighting the Germans and not interfering with his designs for Poland. On August 21, pursuing Red Army units caught up with Major Kalenkiewicz, the remaining courier who had parachuted into Poland with the request for the Parachute Brigade's colors. In a bitter battle with Soviet soldiers, the Major was cornered and killed along with thirty-one soldiers of his regiment.

Meanwhile, the troops of the Polish Parachute Brigade repeated their preparations for all the previous abortive operations. The men pasted maps and aerial photos, cleaned their weapons, and waited for the RAF trucks that would deliver their parachutes. Currency exchange again took place, and again the portrait of Queen Wilhelmina on the crisp bills told the paratroopers that they would be landing somewhere in Holland. Each platoon packed its supply containers with medical supplies, radios, mortars and pioneer tools. An unknown sapper "appropriated" two four-man rescue dinghies from an American airfield and packed them away in one of his company's containers. Trollies and bicycles were rigged with parachutes, to be dropped from below the aircraft or from the door just after the men jumped.

Amid the bustle, the troopers also found time to make their individual preparations. Smokers swamped the NAAFI and crammed their smocks with as many packages of cigarettes as they could carry or afford. Nobody had any idea how long they would be in action. A non-smoker, Private Michal Lasek, made a different sort of purchase for the future. The twenty-year-old bachelor spent four pounds for a gold wedding ring. Not knowing what fate awaited him, the rifleman thought, "It would be worth at least a loaf of bread."

Parachutes were delivered, and the Brigade was confined to barracks to await their drop on the third day of the operation. The waiting began again. Many of the cigarettes gathered for the future were smoked as the men nervously wondered whether this operation would also be canceled. Those who would be lifted into action by glider departed for the airfields.

At Keevil airfield, the gliders for the second lift were being loaded. During the preparations for COMET, the American-made Waco gliders had been exchanged for British Horsas. The Horsa was certainly roomier, but not nearly as easy to load as the Waco. Loading a jeep into a Horsa often meant over an hour of intensive wrestling to get it through the side hatch, and then lashing it down. Upon landing, the glider's tails would be unbolted, and the vehicles driven down metal ramps. The commander of the six men bringing the four jeeps and one trailer of the Brigade's headquarters was Sergeant Cadet Edward Holub. Remembering the many hours of loading and unloading due to the previous delays and cancellations, Holub hoped that this operation would take off. The plywood aircraft could be left loaded for only 48 hours in the humid English climate.

Lieutenant Mleczko's Airborne Anti-tank Squadron's 3rd battery was ready. His seven gliders would be leaving for Arnhem on the second day of the operation. Late in the afternoon on September 15, he was called to Saltby airfield for a briefing by General Sosabowski. After a summary of the general plans and landing zone, Mleczko waited for specific instructions about what to do after landing. The lieutenant kept looking at the General, who was becoming a little embarrassed.

Mleczko was puzzled: "General Sosabowski had always been very sure of himself, and his orders were always very precise and without nonsense." To break the uncomfortable silence, Mleczko asked, "What after landing?" Sosabowski impatiently retorted, "You will join the Brigade." Mleczko reminded the general that the rest of the Brigade would not be landed until the next day, and would take positions miles way from where his battery would be landed. "What in the meantime? What are my exact orders after landing?" Sosabowski barked, "I have none!" The lieutenant stated mildly that he understood. Sosabowski then reminded Mleczko that his men would be the first Polish troops to have a combat role in the operation.

The General and the lieutenant then wished each other luck, and the battery commander returned to Manston airfield. It was late when he arrived, but the station was bustling with activity. Stopping at the canteen, he wondered what briefing he would give to his men. After one brandy, Mleczko's "always positive" attitude towards the operation returned.

In the English Midlands, the morning of Sunday, September 17, glowed in the autumn sun. The lawns and gardens were a gorgeous emerald green under the cloudless skies, a last hurrah before the coming frosts would strip the green from the land. The Brigade's busy preparations were put aside for an hour while the paratroopers attended Mass, a last chance to make peace with God before going into action. Lance Sergeant Cadet Hrehorow attended an open-air Mass in which Father Bednorz gave the 2nd Battalion general absolution, and announced that he would be jumping into action with them.

In Stamford, General Sosabowski leisurely strolled back to his quarters from Mass. The morning was so beautiful that the General had almost completely put the approaching operation out of his mind. But the peaceful scene was interrupted by the approaching roar of many aircraft engines. General Sosabowski looked up as the giant air armada thundered overhead, and hoped that luck would be on General Urquhart's side.

Unable to attend Mass that morning, Lieutenant Kaczmarek from the Brigade's Supply Company was on the road delivering winter underwear to the units. He brought his jeep and trailer to a screeching halt as the hundreds of planes passed overhead. Elated and certain that the war would soon be over, Kaczmarek felt "a joy that almost hurt." But any savoring of the pleasure would have to wait till later; the lieutenant had work to do. After his assignment was completed, Kaczmarek returned to his unit. Just as the first paratroopers were jumping over Holland, the speeding Kaczmarek was stopped by a local constable and given an angry lecture: "Just because there is a war on, soldiers should not think that they can disobey local traffic laws." In a hurry to rejoin the Brigade, Kaczmarek impatiently told the constable, "Write whatever you want."

South of Arnhem, lying between the Neder Rijn and Waal Rivers, was the region known as the Betuwe. A meter below the surface lay a dense clay which accounted for the numerous brickworks along the riverbank. The resulting brick was so hard that most of the streets of Holland were paved with them. But clay was not the real treasure of the Betuwe. From their camp in Nijmegen, Roman soldiers had taught the primitive natives how to steady the course of the river with dikes and drainage ditches. The result, some fifteen centuries later, was one of the most fertile areas in the entire Netherlands.

The Betuwe was bisected by countless drainage ditches and crossed by narrow brick or dirt roads that connectd the area's villages with the farms. As opposed to the primarily Protestant merchants and professionals living north of the river, the residents of the Betuwe were mainly Catholic farmers. Hardworking and frugal, the prosperous farmers tended their cattle in the lush meadows. In the fall they picked the fruit from the apple, cherry, pear and plum orchards that checker-boarded the region. During the spring, throngs of tourists from all over Holland, crossing on the cable ferry from Oosterbeek to Driel, came to view the hectares of fruit trees in bloom.

The center of the village of Driel was dominated by the steeple of its Catholic church. The pastor, W.A.M. Poelman, had long been a pillar of the community. In the years before the war Father Poelman had organized a choir specializing in Gregorian chant. This local choir had became so renowned that people came from all over Holland to hear it. Few came now because of the war, but the sound of the ancient liturgy still flowed from the church windows on Saturday evenings. The priest now had the village organized in sending packages to locals who had been deported for forced labor in the Reich. The women of Driel knitted socks and sweaters, and the pastor made sure that any clothes donated were new, not used. He wanted to be sure that his countrymen in their sad foreign circumstances would know that their friends and relatives at home still cared deeply.

Just south of Driel, on the Honingveldsestraat, lay the 20-hectare Baltussen orchard and jam factory. The tightly knit Baltussen family had run the factory since 1868, and September 1944 promised to be the biggest harvest in many years. What should have been a happy time was marred by years of occupation. Head of one of the most respected families in the Betuwe, the elder Arnold Baltussen was the acting mayor of Driel. He was constantly harassed by two German officers who gathered food in the region for the Wehrmacht. The Germans not only sought to take the factory's production, but also local people for forced labor in Germany. Baltussen had stood up to the occupiers, and told them, "You can take the products of my factory, but you shall never take my people." His efforts saved many of his neighbors, but had hastened his death the year before. With the Germans regrouping after their retreat from France, the Baltussen family bided its time, and hoped that it would all come to an end soon.

Modest and committed Catholics, on September 17 the family was making preparations to celebrate their mother's birthday. At 1140 came the roar of many aircraft engines, followed by the dull thud of exploding bombs. Daughter Cora, a Red Cross nurse, watched as smoke rose from the north bank of the river.

From his family's home behind the Driel dike, Benjamin Jansen also watched the bombardment. The twenty-four-year-old Dutchman, who worked for a neighbor growing flowers and vegetables, went back to his chores. At 1300 hours, the roar of aircraft was again heard. Peering curiously, he watched as gliders detached from their tow planes. Shortly afterwards, more planes came, and in their wake the sky filled with hundreds of parachutes. This spectacle would continue for almost an hour. As the planes made their turns to head back to England, some of them passed directly over the Jansen house.

From the rooftop of her family home, Cora Baltussen watched as the skies over the Veluwe were filled with hundreds of multi-colored parachutes. Happy and singing the "Eindeboven," the Baltussens turned up their illegal radio louder than it had been in many years.

Throughout eastern Holland, from Eindhoven north to Arnhem, British and American paratroopers were jumping from airplanes with the objective of bringing the war to a speedy end. All through the corridor, Dutch civilians and German soldiers alike were taken by surprise as thousands of strong and skilled paratroopers floated to earth in The Netherlands.

Over the heaths near Wolfheze, British paratroops and gliders drifted down silently. It was a textbook jump. The weather was perfect, and there was almost no enemy interference with the landings. The paratroopers finished their assembly and unloading within an hour and a half, and started their long walk to the Arnhem bridges.

The Germans felt the stirrings of panic, but only momentarily. Ignored by Allied intelligence, two SS Panzer Divisions were regrouping and refitting after the bloody beating they had taken in France. Commanded by Obergruppenführer Wilhelm Bittrich, II SS Panzer Corps consisted of the 9th (Hohenstaufen) SS Panzer and 10th (Frundsberg) SS Panzer Divisions. Withdrawn from Poland, where they had helped to stem the Red Army's advance in the spring, they had transferred to Normandy, where they had been mangled during the Allied breakout. Both formations were short of tanks, but could still muster many armored vehicles, and had full compliments of mortars, anti-aircraft weapons and artillery. Their ranks contained young, dedicated Hitlerites who were spoiling to extract vengeance for the mauling they had received in France.

Moving towards Arnhem, parts of the British 1st Airborne Division passed through the village of Wolfheze, which had been heavily bombed that morning, suffering a number of civilian casualties. Despite their losses, the jubilant Dutch citizens thronged around the liberators, and pressed flowers, food and drink on them.

Beyond Wolfheze on the road to Arnhem lay the town of Oosterbeek. This affluent suburb was home to many well-to-do professional people. Vacationers had in the past flocked to the shady town to stay in its comfortable hotels and boarding houses and relax amid the attractive scenery on the bluffs overlooking the Neder Rijn. The hotels, until that morning, were occupied by the headquarters of Field Marshal Walter Model's Army Group B, which hastily evacuated as the first waves of paratroopers were landing.

The three battalions of the 1st Parachute Brigade moved off the drop zones towards the Arnhem Bridge. 2nd Para Battalion, commanded by Lieutenant Colonel Frost, went along the river and made good progress, but the other units soon ran into trouble. Between 3rd Para Battalion, moving down the Utrechtseweg, and the 1st Para Battalion, following the Arnhem–Ede highway, the enemy lay in wait. A Waffen SS training battalion, commanded by Sturmbannführer Sepp Krafft, occupied the woods between the two routes, and quickly established defenses facing Wolfhezeweg. The heavily armed unit immediately began attacking the flanks of the advancing British battalions.

The 2nd Battalion reached the railroad bridge linking Arnhem and Nijmegen, at its crossing of the Neder Rijn between Oosterbeek and Driel, but the bridge was blown in the faces of the paratroopers dispatched to seize it. Undeterred by this event, Lieutenant Colonel Frost pushed his battalion on to Arnhem. At the same time, German armored cars and half-tracks moving from the city reinforced Krafft's mortars and machine guns, and brought the other parachute battalions' advances to a halt. The Division headquarters was still located on the landing zone and, through all of this, no communications could be established with any of the advancing British units. General Urquhart went forward to coordinate movement from Brigadier Gerald Lathbury's headquarters.

The 2nd Battalion moved into the narrow streets of Arnhem and probed towards the bridge. After several minor skirmishes, Frost's paratroopers secured the north end of the bridge. After an assault on the bridge's south end was repulsed, the British quickly consolidated positions in the buildings surrounding the north end. They felt confident that the rest of the division would soon reach them, and began making plans to assault the bridge's south end after dark.

As the sun set, smoked poured from Arnhem. Throughout the afternoon, Benjamin Jansen had heard the sound of gunfire become more and more intense as it traveled from Wolfheze to Oosterbeek. Despite the fall of night, he heard the sounds of singing in the streets of Oosterbeek drift across the river. At the Baltussen house, nobody slept that night. Even when Cora saw the railroad bridge being blown, the euphoria of coming liberation overrode any sense of danger. Throughout Driel, people watched the glowing sky over Arnhem. After over four years under the Nazi heel, they were convinced that liberation by the British was close at hand.

In the billets and barracks of the Polish Parachute Brigade in the English Midlands, the considerable relief that an operation was finally under way was mixed with a fatalism that "the sacrificial goat dies only once," as the men readied themselves for their jump a day and a half thence. The men of the Brigade's advanced party, leaving by glider in the morning, tried to sleep. The rest of the soldiers busied themselves as best they could. In all of the companies, commanders reviewed their missions with their platoon leaders, and grilled them over and over again. In the morning the supply containers would be taken to the airfields.

The barracks were quiet, and no longer filled with either soldiers' griping or good-natured banter, as the Polish paratroopers were lost in thought. Practically every member of the Brigade had had an odyssey worthy of Greek legend before reaching this particular place and time. Images of golden fields ripe with harvest, thatch barns with stork sentinels on their peaks, gas-lit streets echoing the melodies of violins and the soft clumping of horse hooves, spruce-covered mountainsides, mothers, brothers, sisters, wives, lovers—all unseen for many years, appeared before these diverse men. They came from many different backgrounds. They were peasants and nobles, barely literate laborers and professors, but above all they were Poles. They were beyond the normal soldier's cynicism. They were beyond the patriotic propaganda that surrounded them. They were untied by a silver-plated diving eagle that they so proudly wore on their breasts. And maybe now, after all these years, they were taking a step towards home. . . or their graves. Now there was little to do but watch the clock until the appointed hour.

In his headquarters in Stamford, General Sosabowski had made his final preparations. Now there was only time to think. The fact that his heavy weapons and ammunition would be landing across a river from the main body of his brigade gnawed at him. Stanislaw Sosabowski had been a soldier for over thirty years, always in service of the country that he so dearly loved. Five Septembers before, he had marched at the head of his troops from Warsaw to fight the German invaders who were now again immolating the city. In a few days, he would be in action once more—leading the Brigade that he had so laboriously raised and nurtured. The disappointment of not being in Warsaw was mitigated by the fact that a soldier does not choose the place or circumstances of his battles, any more than he could choose his own fate. Before he went to sleep, the General dictated an order:

THE 1st INDEPENDENT PARACHUTE BRIGADE
September 17, 1944
SPECIAL ORDER
To be read in front of all units on September 18th

SOLDIERS OF THE BRIGADE!
I do not know under what conditions we will be celebrating the third anniversary of the existence of the Brigade—
So, the celebration today in our ranks will be humble, as the Brigade's locations and preparations will permit.
On this day of celebration we reflect with a special sadness on our blameless fate that we are not taking part in the battle for our capital. Warsaw, which presented us with our standard this year—which called for us and challenged us—waits for us in vain.
The fact that we can do nothing, despite our hearts are torn there, does not decrease, but increases our pain and sadness.
Soldiers of the Brigade! In the fourth year of the existence of our Brigade we are entering combat.
It was not up to us that our first action would not take place on the soil of our Motherland.
We will do everything to fulfill our soldierly obligations. In this way we will contribute to the glory of our Motherland, and indirectly come to her aid.
Long Live THE MAJESTIC POLISH REPUBLIC!
Long Live HER PRESIDENT AND COMMANDER-IN-CHIEF!
Long Live and Be Victorious THE ARMIJA KRAJOWA!
Long Live OUR BRIGADE!

Commander 1st Independent Parachute Brigade
(Sosabowski)
Mjr. Gen.

9

Nothing Concrete About the 1st Airborne's Situation

September 18, 1944

In England, September 18 dawned with the diffused light of an overcast sky as the second parachute and glider lifts made their preparations for a takeoff scheduled at 1000 hours. Under clear skies in Arnhem's western outskirts, the troopers of the 1st Parachute Brigade tried to advance and break through to the 2nd Battalion holding the northern end of the Arnhem bridge. Communication within the Division was practically nonexistent. General Urquhart was still with Brigadier Lathbury, who was trying to push his brigade forward as it became entangled in battle near the St. Elisabeth's Hospital. It was near here that the Utrechtseweg was pinched into a bottleneck between the Neder Rijn and the hills of western Arnhem. The Germans held the high ground, and also had the area under direct fire from across the river. Supported by armor, the SS troops dispersed the British spearhead among the narrow streets, and brought their advance to a halt. During this fighting, both Urquhart and Lathbury disappeared as the fighting degenerated into small unit actions.

At the north end of the Arnhem bridge, the 2nd Battalion's defense was well organized in the surrounding buildings. Several attempts to seize the southern end of the bridge during the night had failed, and vicious skirmishing flared until daybreak. In twos and threes, men from other units managed to slip through the German lines and reach the 2nd Battalion's positions. At 0930, the rumble of armored vehicles came from the southern end of the bridge, which the paratroopers optimistically thought to be the arrival of XXX Corps. The black crosses painted on the sides of the dirty yellow vehicles crossing the bridge snapped the defenders to their senses. A ferocious battle began that would go on for almost two hours, leaving twelve vehicles and some of the buildings around the bridge in flames. Lieutenant Colonel Frost's men gathered their wounded, consolidated their defenses and gave up any further thought of seizing the southern end of the bridge.

The surviving German armored vehicles retreated south to Elst. This unit was AA 9 (Aufklärungsabteilung 9), the reconnaissance battalion of the 9th SS Panzer (Hohenstaufen) Division. In addition to vehicles, the unit lost its commander during the attempt to clear the bridge. Licking its wounds, AA 9 reinforced the defenses on the south side of the river. General Bittrich needed the bridge; the only other way to move his units north of the Neder Rijn to reinforce the 10th SS Panzer (Frundsburg) Division fighting the Americans by Nijmegen was by a pontoon ferry not capable of transporting heavy tanks.

On this day, the 4th Parachute Brigade and the extensive second glider lift were scheduled to arrive at 1200 hours. The soldiers of the 1st Airlanding Brigade had spent a sleepless night defending the drop and landing zones. Small patrols of German skirmishers vigorously probed the area during the hours of darkness. As the advance on Arnhem bogged, Brigadier Hicks relieved the 2nd Battalion, South Stafford Regiment, of its assignment to secure the glider landing zone for the coming lift, and sent them to try and break through to the bridge.

Lieutenant Alfons Pronobis, who had parachuted in on D-Day with the mission of terrain orientation for the Polish Brigade, had spent the night in the woods, shaken from a German air attack. At first light, he shaved and moved west along the railroad to greet the Polish element of the glider lift. At 1100, his group reached a small wood on the south rim of the landing zone south of the railroad. Dug in and waiting, Pronobis kept hearing the sounds of sporadic small-arms fire in the distance.

At Manston Airfield, Marek Swiecicki, correspondent for the Polish Ministry of Information, stood outside his glider with the two British pilots. The pilots admired the names that had been chalked on the nose of the aircraft: Krystyna, Irena and Barbara. Three Polish girls, two in England and one in Rumania. The first pilot, Staff Sergeant John Cotterill, handed out chewing gum and looked at the names wistfully. A YMCA wagon dispensed mugs of tea and left a London newspaper. Its banner headline, "ALLIED AIR ARMY INVADES HOLLAND," caught everybody's attention. However, journalist Swiecicki was disappointed with the content, which consisted of an appeal to the people of The Netherlands from the Dutch Government-in-Exile, and superficial biographies of Generals Browning and Brereton. Orders came to embark, and a tractor pulled the Horsa to the runway. Besides the correspondent, glider 899 carried the Liaison Officer to the 1st Airborne Division, Captain Ludwik Zwolanski; artillery officer Alfons Mackowiak; three soldiers; and a jeep with trailer composing the Polish Parachute Brigade's advanced headquarters.

Of the remaining nine gliders allotted to the Poles in this lift, two carried the Engineer Company's heavy equipment. The other seven were loaded with Lieutenant Mleczko's battery. The five guns, two ammunition trailers, seven jeeps, several motorcycles and seventeen men were to precede the rest of the Anti-tank Squadron, due to take off the next day with the main Polish glider lift.

The cloudy sky became gloomier as the takeoff hour, now delayed until 1145 hours, approached. Moments later, the engines of the tow-plane engines parked near glider 899 burst into life. With a gentle tug, the first Polish glider followed its Albemarle tow plane down the runway like a fledgling gosling behind its parent. Watching the ground disappear in the overcast, journalist Marek Swiecicki was sad that, after four years of exile, he felt that he was leaving a dear second home. As the tow planes and gliders struggled to higher altitudes, sunbeams began to pierce the clouds. With a shudder, the gliders hit less dense air as the armada reached the brilliantly sunlit skies over the North Sea.

Halfway across the continent of Europe, Warsaw was in its forty-seventh day of insurrection. The sections of the city held by the insurgents had become even further compressed. Shortly before noon, the shells falling on the Polish positions petered out. The sounds of shells bursting high in the sky, and not in the streets, drew civilians from their subterranean shelters. The harmonious hum of aircraft that they heard was not the all-too-familiar scream of Stukas which for weeks had been pulverizing the metropolis.

Focusing their eyes, unused to daylight, the citizens in the streets saw neat formations of silver four-engined bombers high in the sky. Over the city center, strings of white dots began trailing the formations. Soldiers and civilians alike started shouting, "PARACHUTES! Its our Parachute Brigade!" The people of Warsaw thought that promises heard for years over the radio waves from London were finally being kept. One man in the street knew better. General Bor-Komorowski was privy to the fact that Stalin had finally relented to Anglo-American pressure, and given permission for B-17 bombers to land in Soviet-held territory after completion of missions dropping arms and ammunition to the beleaguered city. The general watched wordlessly as the majority of the parachutes drifted beyond the barricades and into parts of the city that had been held by the AK only a week before.

Over the North Sea off England, the clear skies exposed the multitude of gliders and tow planes that extended in a line over 150 kilometers long. Marek Swiecicki noticed a contrast between Captain Zwolanski and pilot Cotterill in glider 899. Zwolanski gleefully looked over the massive formation, while Cotterill worried over how he would find a place to land among the 296 gliders reinforcing the 1st Airborne Division this day. Over the Dutch coast, heavy anti-aircraft fire burst ineffectually out of range. Further inland the flak continued sporadically, but gradually became more intense as the armada pushed on to its designated landing zone. Removing their now useless lifebelts, the passengers puffed on a last cigarette as they buckled their seatbelts for the final approach.

From his slit trench by the railroad, Lieutenant Pronobis continued his wait. Skirmishing had gone on all morning because a group of Germans had stubbornly dug themselves onto a wooded hill overlooking the landing zone. Just before 1430 hours, the rumble of approaching aircraft was heard, and as they came into view, anti-aircraft fire broke out from the distance. Momentarily awed by the sight of hundreds of four engined aircraft and gliders, Pronobis then felt sorry for the men in the air as more and more shells began bursting around the formation. A Stirling was hit as the tow planes cast off their gliders and began their banking turns to point themselves back to the direction of England. The gliders swooped downwards at a sharp angle as shells began bursting on the narrow field. A Dakota flew over the Polish officer's head trailing smoke from its port engine.

The picture was one of great confusion. The field was covered with gliders with their tails lying askew beside them, bursting shells, scurrying men and jeeps. More gliders skidded to a halt and their hatches flew open. Over this panorama, a glider overshot the landing zone and crashed into the trees. Firefights broke out among the landed gliders as handfuls of Germans infiltrated the landing zone. Pronobis heard an order to withdraw, and as he moved back along the railroad line, he met more and more of the glidermen.

Glider 899 cast off its tow line and its passengers were numbed by the sudden silence. The quiet was short-lived as the sound of gunfire rose from the landing zone. The Horsa slammed into the crowded field and bounced to a halt. In an instant, the men were out the hatch and lying prone around the plywood bird, their Bren gun trained on the woods. Nearby a glider burst into flames. A gigantic Hamilcar glider hit the green field and ground to a halt. Its massive nose opened and disgorged a pair of carriers, which drove across the field to clear the woods. With no fire coming in their direction, the Polish headquarters detachment quickly unloaded its jeep from its glider, and sped away from the LZ.

As Lieutenant Mleczko climbed out of his glider he heard "a constant chatter of machine-gun fire," but knew instinctively that he was out of range. Mleczko counted his gliders and saw that all had arrived safely. The battery's Bren gunners had their weapons pointed at the woods while the rest of the men wordlessly unloaded their jeeps, guns and trailers from the aircraft. The lieutenant silently took great satisfaction in the fact that the years of training and good discipline were obviously paying off. In five minutes the guns were limbered and the battery cleared from the landing zone, leaving behind the empty plywood birds that had carried them there.

Despite the contested landing, over 90 percent of the gliders had arrived and unloaded successfully. Brigadier Hackett's 4th Parachute Brigade jumped north of the glider landing zone onto the heather-covered Ginkel Heath. His troops immediately joined the men of the Airlanding Brigade in the skirmishing on the drop zone. The Germans broke contact as the newly arrived Brigade formed up for its move towards Arnhem. Hackett was met by the 1st Division's Chief of Staff, Lieutenant Colonel Charles Mackenzie, who then informed him of General Urquhart's disappearance and that, in his absence, Brigadier Hicks would be in command of the Division. In trying to keep to the original operational plan, Hicks detached the 11th Parachute Battalion from Hackett's Brigade, ordering it to push on towards the bridge. After a heated discussion between the two brigadiers, Hackett was given the 7th Battalion of the King's Own Scottish Borders (7th KOSB) to replace the unit that had been taken from him.

Across the river, in Driel, the villagers were again treated to the spectacles of mass parachute and glider landings. However, they had also noticed that the flak was much more intense than it had been the day before.

One of the gliders crashed near Heteren. The troops moved down the dike looking for a way to cross the river. The village's German garrison had fled the day before, and the "Drielenaren" went to the dike to see the liberators. Among them was Antoon Verhoef, a twenty-eight-year old member of the underground, who had emerged from a hiding place at his girlfriend's house to greet the Red Devils. The British soldiers passed out cigarettes and chocolates before taking the ferry to the north bank. Antoon was one of the lucky ones who received a cigarette. A neighbor offered him ten guilders for it, but Verhoef refused the fantastic offer.

The jeep carrying Marek Swiecicki sped on to Wolfheze. Stopping in front of a café with British paratroopers dozing in wicker chairs, the correspondent cheerfully shouted, "Hello, boys!" As the soldiers' bloodshot eyes opened, an angry "Shut up!" rose from the group, followed by a chorus of curses. An apologetic British officer in a torn Denison smock told the sheepish reporter that his men had been fighting for almost twenty-four hours straight. The jeep continued on the tree-canopied road to Oosterbeek.

The British and German dead, spaced like milestones along the road, increased Swiecicki's embarrassment over his greeting at the café. Turning east onto Utrechtseweg, the Poles paused by a bullet-riddled Citroën auto, from which hung the corpse of a German general. A minute later, a British officer directed them to Division Headquarters, which had halted at the Hotel Hartenstein on the Utrechtseweg. The jeep turned off the road and onto a tree-lined drive.

The stately structure stood against a background of calm and cool green trees, and contrasted with all of the activity going on about it. Jeeps were arriving and driving off, as soldiers in wine-colored berets bobbed in and out of the elegant white building. Paratroopers were digging slit trenches on the surrounding, neatly trimmed lawn and the correspondent wondered why they were digging in.

Following not far behind the jeep carrying the Polish advanced headquarters came Lieutenant Mleczko's anti-tank battery. Passing dead soldiers and smashed vehicles left by the fighting on the previous day, Mleczko took some comfort in observing that it appeared that the enemy had suffered more. A British soldier flagged down the battery's column as it raced down the Utrechtseweg toward Arnhem. Lieutenant Mleczko was ushered into the Hartenstein, where he was met by a British colonel who informed him that his battery would be given instructions and orders from him. The Polish officer was relieved that he would have someone to turn to until the rest of his Brigade arrived. The colonel told Mleczko to set up his guns to protect the division's headquarters. When the Pole asked from which direction they were most vulnerable, the British officer replied, "The north and the west," but quickly added that Mleczko should regard "the whole perimeter as an island. The Germans are trying to infiltrate from all directions." It was decided to position the guns around the intersection of Utrechtseweg and Oranjeweg, covering both roads.

In Driel, it had become quiet again. During the late afternoon, Arnold Baltussen discovered that the wayward glider troops were not the only British soldiers passing through Driel. He discovered two British soldiers with a German prisoner in tow, who were trying to make contact with the Allied land forces. Arnoldus took them to the Baltussen house, where the Red Devils promptly fell asleep. Just before the curfew hour, they left with the prisoner and returned to Oosterbeek via the ferry.

Back in England, the Polish Parachute Brigade made its final preparations. During the morning, the aircraft of the second lift had roared overhead, but nothing could be seen through the soupy fog. As the soldiers packed their few personal possessions for storage, the Brigade did likewise with its gear. Kitchens were broken down and packed, along with any administrative or household equipment that would not be carried to Holland. The containers loaded with field equipment were taken to the airfields, where they were to be slung from the aircraft in the morning.

In the Brigade's headquarters, the same bustle of final packing went on, along with confirmations of the logistical planning necessary to move the men from their scattered locations to their airfields. The Polish glider lifts reported from their locations far to the south in Gloustershire and Dorset that they were loaded and ready.

Though all seemed to be on schedule, General Sosabowski was troubled by the fact that the only information available about the situation of the MARKET forces, and the 1st Division in particular, was from the newspapers. General Browning had flown into Nijmegen by glider with his I Airborne Corps Headquarters, and had not been able to establish communications with either his bases or with First Allied Airborne Army Headquarters. Sosabowski's chief British liaison officer, Lieutenant Colonel R. George Stevens, was unable to obtain anything further, and there was nothing concrete about the 1st Airborne's situation in Holland. The Polish general, unable to receive any changes in orders, or information from Browning, could now turn only to the First Allied Airborne Army. By doing this, Sosabowski would be breaking the chain of command and, considering the sensitive situation between Browning and the American Brereton, his "sin" would be compounded by the fact that the Polish General would be going to another "foreigner," to boot. In Holland, the 82nd Airborne Division had managed to seize the Grave bridge by landing on both sides of it on D-Day. Further east, General Gavin was securing the Groesbeek Heights and was able to release troops to probe towards the bridge over the river Waal in the center of Nijmegen. But the situation remained unstable, and the 82nd had spent the day trying to consolidate its positions in Groesbeek, receive reinforcements and, at the same time, repulse persistent German attacks.

Farther south, the 101st Airborne Division had taken Eindhoven and all of its D-Day objectives after bitter fighting, except for a canal bridge in Son, which had been blown up in the faces of the troops assigned to take it. The Guards Armored Division, spearheading the GARDEN forces, was still trying to push through to Eindhoven. On D-Day, they had encountered surprisingly stiff resistance, but once through it, decided to make it an early night. It was only during the night of September 18 that the Guards Armored Division reached the embattled Screaming Eagles.

At the Hartenstein, Marek Swiecicki settled in with the other correspondents attached to the 1st Airborne Division. The ground floor of the building was occupied by the division headquarters, so Swiecicki went upstairs to find a corner for himself. Walking through the rooms, the journalist busied himself by leafing through the personal correspondence that littered the floors. The envelopes and letters that had belonged to the German staff officers who had previously occupied the hotel were addressed to, or postmarked in, German cities. After putting together a meal with Sergeant Cotterill, which included a bottle of wine taken from the hotel's cellar, Swiecicki tried to find out something about the military situation. The optimistic news that the Arnhem bridge was held was offset by reports of heavy British casualties and fanatical German resistance. The correspondent composed a brief news dispatch that was sent out over the BBC radio set. His thoughts turned to the fact that, tomorrow, the rest of the Polish Brigade would be arriving, and there would certainly be more news to report.

At 2230, the Baltussens' five dogs announced the return of the two British soldiers who had been there that afternoon. They were now accompanied by two British officers who had planned a journey that would hopefully lead them to Nijmegen. They left just after midnight, escorted to the edge of the village by Arnold Baltussen. Scurrying into a ditch to avoid a German motorcycle that had roared out of the darkness, one of the soldiers injured his ankle. The three British messengers continued their mission while Arnold took the injured man back to his house. The soldier was a cheerful Irishman named Cooney. He declined the Baltussens' offer to stay in their home, and instead took shelter in a shed in an orchard behind the factory.

At the Polish Brigade's headquarters in Stamford, Lieutenant Colonel Stevens returned after making the rounds trying to secure any further intelligence about the ongoing operation. Some information had been confirmed: Browning had landed safely in Holland, communication had not been established with his headquarters in Britain, or with the 1st Airborne Division. Stevens also relayed casualty reports from the troop carrier units, and odd bits gleaned from the BBC net, but had nothing further about the 1st Airborne Division.

General Sosabowski was disturbed by the fact that his Brigade would be jumping into the unknown on the third day of the operation. The element of surprise, so crucial to airborne operations, was now in the hands of the Germans. They would surely be waiting as his troops jumped. In an attempt to get as much rest as possible, the General went to his quarters at 2000, and turned off his light.

10
It's Bad
September 19, 1944

The rays of bright sunlight streaming into the upper floors of the Hotel Hartenstein woke correspondent Marek Swiecicki. The journalist walked outside and looked around. The jeeps now stood under the trees, unloaded, and the Utrechtseweg was quiet in contrast to the busy activity of the day before. Returning to headquarters in pursuit of news, Swiecicki found little. From what he could gather from the staff officers, the Germans were bringing up reserves and were evidently trying to surround the British in Oosterbeek. General Urquhart had managed to slip away from the Germans who had surrounded him in Arnhem, and was again in command of his division. He was out, inspecting his forward positions. This was the day that the Polish Parachute Brigade was to join the 1st Airborne Division in Holland. The Polish glider lift was scheduled to land at the Johannahoeve farm, to be followed shortly by the parachute drop on Drop Zone "K" just south of the Arnhem bridge.

At the Arnhem bridge, the 2nd Para Battalion had survived its second night of battle. The light of day meant that the troopers moving between buildings did so by risking death from sniper or machine-gun fire.

Rations carried by the paratroopers into action had all but run out. The men rifled through cellars for food, and found mostly jars of preserved fruit. They still had radio contact with the airborne artillery, but the Germans had brought up heavy guns of their own, and took many of the British-held buildings under direct fire. The casualties mounted, but the brave men at the bridge remained combative, and their morale was high.

Lieutenant Colonel Frost was mindful that this day would bring the Polish Parachute Brigade, and Frost remembered the original battle plan.

The Polish drop zone was now invested by SS Panzer troops and their armored vehicles. The highly experienced British officer could well imagine the reception that the men in the gray berets would receive as they landed. The colonel had two jeeps with mounted Vickers guns and a carrier ready to charge across the bridge the moment the Polish drop began. This suicidal maneuver might cause confusion among the Germans, and hopefully give the Polish paratroopers some respite as they descended into the hornets' nest that would certainly be stirred as they dropped on top of the heavily armed defenders.

In England, the Polish paratroopers heard through their barracks windows the rumble of trucks shortly before 0600. The men filed out into the foggy morning air, dressed for combat and lugging their field gear behind them. While the stick commanders verified their rosters, the troopers loaded their equipment and then themselves onto the vehicles. As the trucks moved through the villages, people in nightclothes appeared at their windows and waved. The Poles returned the gesture, feeling that they were waving good-bye to Britain.

After an hour, the trucks arrived at Saltby and Spanhoe airfields, seventeen miles apart. They were the respective homes of the US 314th and 315th Troop Carrier Groups. The Brigade Headquarters, the 2nd Battalion and part of the 3rd Battalion would take off from Saltby, whereas the 1st Battalion and the remainder of the 3rd Battalion would depart from Spanhoe. The scene was the same at both airfields, as the trucks drove down the flight line looking for the assigned aircraft marked by numbers chalked on the noses of the Dakotas. As the Poles and American aircrew eyed each other with equal curiosity, the paratroopers unloaded their vehicles. After slinging the equipment containers onto the racks underneath the twin-engined birds, the paratroopers then sat beside them awaiting the signal to put on their chutes and board.

The Polish Parachute Brigade's staff officers and battalion commanders were otherwise engaged. There were still no reports from either the 1st Airborne Division or from General Browning's headquarters in Holland. Nevertheless, despite the lack of communications, the original orders would be followed. The takeoff had been scheduled for 1000 hours, but the weather was terrible and a misty fog blanketed the airfields. The Polish liaison officers conferred with the air base staff on what the possibilities were of taking off that day. The meteorological reports did not look good: the cloud cover varied between 6,500 and 10,000 feet, and extended well over the North Sea. All they could do now was to sit back and hope that the fickle British weather might improve as the day went on.

Farther to the south, weather conditions were better, but still not satisfactory. The takeoff of the thirty-five Polish gliders from Tarrant Rushton and Keevil airfields was postponed for two hours, until 0945.

Meanwhile, in Driel, charred bits of paper fluttered down onto the village from across the river. Bullets and shell fragments whistled around Benjamin Jansen as he milked his employer's cow. He took the cow from the orchard to the safety of the barn. Some villagers were hit by the stray missiles. Prompted by these events, Cora Baltussen helped the village physician, a woman, Dr. Van den Burg, set up a small aid station in the Catholic parish house in the center of the village.

Across the river in Arnhem, more and more German reinforcements, in the form of troops and combat vehicles, began arriving. In addition, an anti-aircraft brigade, with over a hundred guns of all calibers, had arrived, and was being deployed against both air and ground targets. The one item that the Germans had no shortage of was ammunition. It was a rare event in the preceding years when the German soldier could count on lavish artillery support. Now, due to a massive mobilization of its remaining material resources, and increased transports of slave labor, Germany had managed to reach its absolute peak of war production during the months of July, August and September 1944. Much of this production took place in the Ruhr—the final objective of Operation MARKET GARDEN. In fact, it was the short distance from this point of manufacture to Arnhem that accounted for the Germans' being so well supplied with ammunition. To further augment their ground forces, an entire Luftwaffe Jagddivision, consisting of over 300 fighter aircraft, was relieved from its task of intercepting Allied bombers over the Ruhr and put at the disposal of the Germans in Holland. The enemy was tightening the noose around the British 1st Airborne Division.

North of the railroad line, Brigadier Hackett's 4th Parachute Brigade's drive on the Arnhem hills came to a halt at Dreyenscheweg. The street (which became Stationsweg south of the railroad in Oosterbeek) could not be crossed. The troops and armor of the Hohenstaufen Division formed an impenetrable wall that the Red Devils could not breach. The Germans intensified the pressure from the north as reinforcements continued to arrive. During his inspection, General Urquhart decided that Hackett's mission was now pointless, and ordered the 4th Para Brigade to withdraw south of the railroad line and take positions in Oosterbeek. It was expected that the repositioned brigade would then march eastwards, and break through to the Arnhem bridge. However, it was imperative that Hackett's troops hold the Johannahoeve farm, a mere 750 meters from the Dreyenscheweg, until the Polish glider lift, scheduled to arrive at noon, had landed. Urquhart, realizing the situation that the Polish Parachute Brigade faced in Holland, requested that its drop and landing zones be changed. Included was a request that the drop zone for the supplies scheduled to come in that day also be changed, since it was now deep in enemy-held territory.

At the airfields in England, the appointed hour passed, and the Polish paratroopers continued to lounge around the aircraft. As afternoon approached, the "greaseless breakfast" served before dawn had left the men's stomachs rumbling in belated response. YMCA tea wagons served sandwiches on the flight line in place of the rations that were to be consumed after the soldiers had landed in Holland. The Poles passed the time watching the American airmen. The mannerisms and body language of these boisterous, perpetually youthful men were a source of continuous source of curiosity and amusement through an otherwise gloomy wait.

At Tarrant Rushton airfield, WAAFs smiled sweetly as they handed out sandwiches to the Polish anti-tank men. Bombardier Nosecki did not return the pretty women's smiles: he was concerned that there had been no reports about the landing of the Squadron's 3rd battery the day before. Nobody seemed to know anything concerning the operation, now in its third day.

A klaxon suddenly screeched, and the men went to board their gliders. Nosecki wished his friend, Bombardier Jozef Oprych, good luck as he turned for his glider. Nosecki had known Oprych since they were together at Coëtquidan in the winter of 1939. Together they were caught trying to escape from French North Africa, and had spent over two years in a forced-labor camp there. They had now known each other for almost five years. In January 1943, the two were both happily assigned to the Parachute Brigade's anti-tank squadron, where Oprych had gained a reputation as one of the best soccer players in the Brigade.

Getting into glider 131, Nosecki would ride with the 2nd Battery's commander, Lieutenant Jerzy Halpert. Halpert was to be in temporary command of the ten 6-pounder anti-tank guns landing in the glider lift. The squadron's commander, Captain Jan Kanty Wardzala, would be parachuting into Holland with the rest of the gun crews. Until then, the

British glider pilots would assist the fifty-three Polish anti-tank artillerymen who would be arriving by glider until the gunners from the parachute lift joined them.

Shortly before noon, the engines of the Stirling tow planes coughed into life. The obsolete bombers released their brakes and ran down the runways with the Horsa gliders trailing behind them. Black-bellied and invasion-striped, the tugs and gliders stood out prominently against the overcast sky as they quickly formed up and turned east. The glider lift was airborne.

During the morning in Holland, correspondent Swiecicki had tried to compensate for the lack of information in division headquarters by talking to the prisoners held in a stockade converted from a fenced-in tennis court behind the Hartenstein. Among the captives were former residents of the parts of Poland that had been annexed to the Third Reich. Forcibly impressed into the Wehrmacht, the men had endured the horrors of fighting for an enemy that still considered their families *Untermenschen*, and treated them accordingly. The stories Swiecicki's hapless countrymen told him about life in the German Army during its debacle in France were most enlightening. They spoke of how the soldiers frantically discarded their equipment, and even weapons, during their retreat from Normandy. The German rout had continued until the beaten army reached Holland, where it was swiftly reorganized.

At 1300 hours, the rumble of aircraft distracted the attention of everybody in Oosterbeek away from the shelling that had begun during the morning, and that had intensified with each passing hour. The shelling slackened as both Britons and Germans watched the spectacle of multi-engined aircraft flying in from the west in slow, close formation. The fire shifted from the ground to the air as the Germans reacted to the supply mission. Around the Hartenstein, British paratroopers tried to attract the cargo planes' attention by waving colored identification panels, but Marek Swiecicki saw only two or three aircraft release their loads near the hotel. To the northeast, the sky bloomed with multi-colored parachutes. Shells burst amid the yellow, violet, red, blue, khaki, green and orange parachutes. Planes went down in flames as the supplies descended into German hands. From his vantage point at the Hartenstein, General Urquhart watched the horrible, yet strangely beautiful, spectacle, and knew that his request to change the drop zones had not been received in England.

As the formation of the surviving supply aircraft turned and crossed the Neder Rijn, one of the Stirlings, a port engine afire, staggered and lost altitude as it approached Driel. Cora Baltussen, her sister Reit, brother Albert, and three members of the Driel Red Cross team saw the bomber, which had been converted into a supply plane, crash behind the dike. They ran to the river and saw the crew evacuating the burning aircraft. Despite machine-gun bullets whistling around them, the civilians helped drag the shaken aircrew from the burning bomber before it exploded. Of the eight crewmen, two were very badly injured. The bomb aimer's arms were broken and his foot was mangled. The wireless operator's back was broken, and all other of the aircrew had suffered broken bones.

The flyers who could care for themselves were hidden in the local brickworks and a nearby culvert. The two badly injured airmen were loaded onto a horsecart that Antoon Verhoef borrowed from a nearby farm. Taking them to the small hospital established in the parish house, Verhoef was harassed for information about the airmen by a young German soldier armed with a Panzerfaust. Verhoef, of course, "didn't know anything." Other German soldiers scattered throughout the village did not disturb the civilians with the injured airmen. When they reached the small hospital in the center of the village, the young German soldier with the Panzerfaust demanded that Dr. Van den Burg turn over their papers. When the woman doctor refused to do this, the angry soldier shouldered his Panzerfaust and stomped off in the direction of Elst, shouting that he would return with his commander.

In England, the Polish paratroopers still waited beside the Dakotas that they hoped would carry them to the Continent. The clock passed 1300 hours, and there was still no order for takeoff. Hoping that the weather might clear, the Americans postponed the mission once again, until 1500 hours.

High in the sky over England, Bombardier Nosecki relaxed in the dark cavern that was the fuselage of glider 131. He passed the time in idle conversation with his friend, Bombardier Roman Kabat, who sat in the jeep. Finally airborne, Nosecki thought "the flying was nice and smooth, even better than in the powered aircraft during training." But the conversation among the passengers was interrupted as the pilot announced, "We are over the Channel now," and an hour later he said, "We are over Belgium."

In glider 144, Cadet Sergeant Edward Holub, who disliked being in the air in any manner, tried to relax on the glider's folded rubber rescue dinghy. His companions, General Sosabowski's drivers, Lance Corporal Marian Boba and Sergeant Boleslaw Nachman, were calm and seemingly did not share the cadet's discomfort. The pilot was a pleasant Scot from Kinross, Sergeant Henry Blake. Holub had begun his preparations for landing when he felt the glider jerk twice, as the sounds of the tow plane's engines seemed to lose intensity. Then Sergeant Nachman suddenly shouted that the glider had separated from the tow, and that they were going to crash in the ocean.

While passing through a cloud Sergeant Blake had lost sight of his tow plane. Unable to maintain correct position behind the plane, the tow rope had broken as it was buffeted by the bomber's slip stream. The sound of the tow plane faded until there was only the whisper of the wind outside the Horsa. While Holub fumbled with his seatbelt, Nachman tried to knock open the glider's upper escape hatch with his rifle butt. Nachman paused, looking over the pilot's shoulders, and shouted in Polish: "Good!" That was the last thing Holub remembered before waking up in the back of an ambulance. The glider had just managed to reach the Belgian coast, and had bounced off a rooftop before it smashed into the ground. A total of six gliders from the Polish glider lift had been lost over Belgium due to broken or shot-through tow ropes.

North of Oosterbeek, the 4th Parachute Brigade was being very hard pressed. With German activity increasing to the west of Oosterbeek, Hackett's only way of getting his vehicles and guns across the railroad at the level crossing in Wolfheze was now threatened. Strong enemy forces were now starting to move towards Johannahoeve from the Dreyenscheweg.

General Urquhart now ordered Hackett back to Oosterbeek. As the 10th and the 156th Para Battalions, which had been in close combat all day, began their withdrawal, the 7th KOSB still maintained its positions on the southern edge of the open field of the Johannahoeve farm that had been designated as the landing zone for the Polish gliders. The KOSB had suffered some casualties during German air attacks that morning, which had left the farm buildings burning. They were to be the last to leave. Their mission was to protect the Polish glider landing and to provide a rearguard for the rest of the Brigade. As the withdrawing paratroopers moved past their positions, the men of the KOSB wondered if the Polish gliders, now hours overdue, would in fact ever arrive.

Sitting on the grassy railroad embankment, correspondent Marek

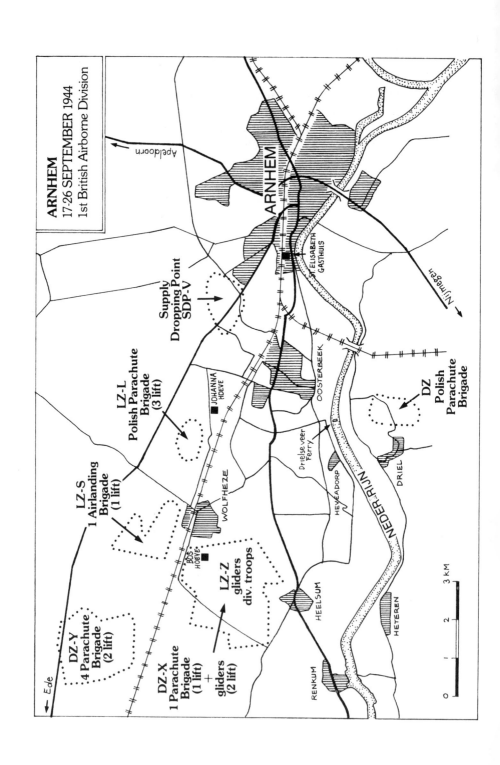

ARNHEM
17-26 SEPTEMBER 1944
1st British Airborne Division

Apeldoorn

ARNHEM

Nijmegen

ST. ELISABETH
GASTHUIS

Supply
Dropping Point
SDP-V

LZ-L
Polish Parachute
Brigade
(3 lift)

OOSTERBEEK

JOHANNA
HOEVE

DZ
Polish
Parachute
Brigade

LZ-S
1 Airlanding
Brigade
(1 lift)

Driel'se veer
Ferry

WOLFHEZE

HEVEADORP

DRIEL

NEDER-RIJN

BOS
HOEVE

LZ-Z
gliders
div. troops

Ede

DZ-Y
4 Parachute
Brigade
(2 lift)

HEELSUM

HETEREN

DZ-X
1 Parachute
Brigade (1 lift)
+
gliders
(2 lift)

RENKUM

0   1   2   3 KM

Swiecicki also awaited the Polish gliders. It was a beautiful September day, and Swiecicki thought with a little envy that he would have rather landed here. The field he had landed on the day before was small, crowded with gliders and surrounded by woods. In the foreground the correspondent watched the Scottish glider infantry in their positions on the edge of the wide and open field. At the other end of the field Swiecicki saw a cool and quiet wood on the horizon. He gazed wistfully at the landscape. If not for the rumble of artillery and the pop-pop of small arms in the distance, he would not have felt that he was in a war zone.

Bombardier Nosecki needed no further announcements from the pilot: "We see it, we hear it, and we understand. We are under fire from German anti-aircraft artillery." The artillerist knew himself how dangerous it was to be a target. His anxiety was increased by the knowledge that the glider was flying slowly, and at low altitude, and could not seek cover in the clouds. One of the shells burst just ahead of the glider, filling the cabin with acrid smoke. Lieutenant Halpert looked out over the pilot's shoulder and shouted, "It's bad!" Another shell burst under glider 131, sending splintered pieces of the floorboards and shrapnel into the ceiling and tearing Nosecki's trousers. Seeing the bombardier's smoking and torn pants, Halpert called to him, asking if he was hurt. Nosecki felt around and, as he replied that he was okay, the glider's pilot let out a groan and grabbed his chest. Putting his bloodied hands back on the control column, the pilot insisted that he would get the glider down safely.

It was getting late on the drop zone; the sun was already far to the west and the trees cast long shadows on discarded containers and parachutes from a supply mission the day before. Marek Swiecicki's ears perked when he heard the hum of aircraft in the distance. The correspondent detected that something was wrong. For many years he had heard many formations of Allied bombers pass overhead on their way to Germany. Swiecicki now heard a strange, inharmonious whining accompanying the low, even cadence of multi-engined aircraft. As the Stirlings cast off their gliders and banked, the journalist realized what was happening. The whine had come from a flight of Messerschmitts, which had overtaken the formation from behind, tearing through it with guns blazing. Staring in disbelief, the correspondent saw a glider, hammered by a Messerschmitt's cannon, "break apart like a matchbox . . . and out fell a jeep, a gun, and people. They looked like toys." The gliders, now in their final approach, dived at the open field while the German fighters chewed at them in the air.

The wounded pilot of glider 131 told his passengers to get ready. Looking out the side window, Bombardier Nosecki saw a glider going down, "lit up like a fireball. In the distance a Stirling was smoking." After some maneuvering, Nosecki's glider hit the ground and skidded to a halt. Then, "greeted by a shower of machine gun fire," the anti-tank men started working on the bolts that held on the aircraft's tail.

Correspondent Swiecicki saw the woods he had so admired "erupt in fire. Everything—mortars, machine guns and even individual rifles." The German fighters made several more firing passes before peeling off. The thin plywood walls of the gliders were pierced by shrapnel and bullets as they landed on the now chaotic field. From the railroad embankment the journalist watched as a Horsa nosed into the ground in a column of dirt that added to those thrown into the air by the bursting shells. He bolted from the railroad embankment towards the field, "to help the medics help the wounded...it was very bad....This beautiful field became a curse to those on it. Insanely, the Grim Reaper was shouting his roll call."

Bombardier Jozef Oprych helped unload the jeep and ammunition trailer, and then his motorcycle from glider 120. 2nd Lieutenant Grabowski ordered Oprych to tell the gun crews to gather the battery's guns by his glider, which had landed at the southern edge of the field. The bombardier had only ridden a few hundred meters when he heard the sound of a Messerschmitt bearing down on him. Suddenly, Oprych was slammed to the dirt. Looking at the wreckage of his motorcycle next to him, he tried to move. Lying on the ground, his leg bleeding profusely, Oprych watched, helpless, as the Messerschmitts flew off and enemy skirmishers came running from the surrounding woods.

Glider 138, carrying a heavy load of jeep and trailer belonging to the 1st Battalion, bumped to a halt. Their weapons ready, 2nd Lieutenant Stefan Sawicki and his driver, Lance Corporal Waclaw Koczan, jumped out of the glider, followed by the two British glider pilots. Sawicki looked around; the field was "a vision of Hell." In the sky above, aircraft were on fire as jeeps pulling anti-tank guns drove west, as specified in their briefing. After his glider's tail was removed, Sawicki was trying to put the unloading ramps in place when he felt a piece of shrapnel burn into his hand. The lieutenant could still flex his fingers, and decided to ignore the wound; he finished putting the ramps in place. As the jeep started its engine, Sawicki looked around for the glider pilots, but they had vanished.

After the jeep was pulled from his glider, Bombardier Nosecki tried unsuccessfully to start his motorcycle. As he hurriedly inspected the engine, Nosecki discovered that the carburetor was shattered, and gasoline had spilled all over the engine. Thankful that the machine had not caught fire during the flight, he abandoned it. Taking shelter behind his glider while German machine-gun bullets stitched it, the bombardier saw Lieutenant Halpert dressing the injured glider pilot's wound. As the group tried to leave, Nosecki spotted some Germans break cover and try to run towards the gliders. Grabbing a Bren gun, the bombardier dropped to the ground and fired a few short bursts. The skirmishers fell to the ground. Nosecki waited, and after a few a moments they sprang to their feet in a run. Touching off another burst, Nosecki heard one of them scream as he pitched backwards.

Nearby, Bombardier Oprych pleaded for help. Nosecki crawled to his friend. Looking at Oprych's shattered leg, he remembered the numerous hours they had played soccer in the many places that fate had sent them. Oprych pointed towards the woods, saying there were two Germans shooting at him. Nosecki had two magazines of ammunition left. Taking aim at the spot two hundred meters away, he fired. Changing magazines, the bombardier gave the trees another burst. The section of woods was quiet, and nothing moved.

Nosecki made his way back to his glider and hailed some British medical orderlies passing in a jeep. He pointed them in the direction of his wounded comrade. A few minutes later, the burly anti-tankman felt great relief when he saw the jeep pass, with a man on a stretcher who, he thought, was his wounded friend.

The overloaded jeep carrying 2nd Lieutenant Sawicki was stuck between the old potato furrows of the farm field. Watching the British retreating down the road as bullets whistled around him and his driver, Sawicki wondered what to do. Alone in the field, he thought about abandoning the jeep and running the 400 meters to cover. However, at this moment he remembered that not only was the jeep carrying crucial ammunition and medical supplies, but also the battalion's best typewriter. He decided to save the vehicle. Some British soldiers were spotted coming across the field in a carrier. The Polish officer hailed them, and together they pushed the jeep free. With bullets buzzing around them, Sawicki and Private Koczan made their way across the field. The lieutenant ran beside the vehicle so he would not weigh it down any more than it was. When he made it to the road, Sawicki was out of breath and, as he climbed into the jeep, it took off after the withdrawing British. The lieutenant then looked at the wound on his hand for the first time. Fortunately, it was slight, so he simply covered it with a field dressing.

At the moment of the Polish glider landings, the Germans, commanded by Sturmbannführer Krafft, began to press their attack against the retreating 4th Para Brigade. At the landing zone's southeast corner, a tragedy within a tragedy occurred. Under attack by Germans, British soldiers, seeing the Poles running for cover, mistook them for the enemy and opened fire. Shot at from everywhere, the embroiled Poles returned a frenzied fire in all directions, even at a platoon of KOSBs who had emerged from their positions to help unload the gliders.* With all of the shooting and confusion on the field, some of the Polish glidermen ran for the nearest cover, and into German hands.

Lieutenant Halpert took stock of his situation. He could account for only two of the jeeps and three of the Anti-tank Squadron's guns. A British officer had commandeered one of the guns to meet a German attack, and that was the last time it was seen. Halpert gathered what was left of his men and followed the retreating British towards the railroad crossing at Wolfheze. Reaching the village, the Dutch came out of their houses and greeted the gunners in English. The civilians were startled when they saw the "POLAND" titles on the newly arrived soldiers' shoulders, and realized that Poles were fighting on their soil. The civilians welcomed the Slavs cordially, and shared with them their dwindling supply of food and drink.

At the airfields in the English Midlands, 1500 hours had arrived and the aircrews still made no movement towards their aircraft. An apologetic American officer informed General Sosabowski that there was no chance for a takeoff that day; it was rescheduled for 1000 hours the next morning. There was nothing further for the Polish Parachute Brigade to do but return to its vacated billets. While transportation from the

---

*A British glider pilot who was at Johannahoeve has described to the author how some British soldiers cupped their hands and, in an attempt to approximate Polish, started shouting, "Come, come" in a deep accent. He explained that the Poles replied to their efforts with gunfire. The author observed to the glider pilot that the way he shouted, the words sounded very much like the German *"Komm, komm,"* and thus might have been the reason for the beleaguered paratroopers' firing in the direction of the sounds.

airfield was available, any further preparations had yet to be made. The General turned to Lieutenant Kaczmarek and barked an order to arrange messing for the Brigade when it had returned to its billets.

Dragging his parachute and field equipment with him, the one-time comedian called the supply depot at Kettering to arrange provisions. In the broken and heavily accented English that had brought such laughter to the Scots, he tried to explain the situation. At first, the supply depot did not want to believe that the Brigade had not taken off. When he finally convinced them that indeed they had not gone, Kaczmarek then had to make arrangements for the rations, and gave the number to be delivered to the various locations scattered between Peterborough and Stamford. Caught between a frustrated General Sosabowski and incredulous British quartermasters, Kaczmarek remembered this as "one of the most difficult moments that I experienced during the war."

When Lieutenant Halpert's guns reached the intersection of the Wolfhezeweg and Utrechtseweg, they were directed to join the rest of the Polish guns near the Hartenstein. The newly arrived guns were sent north on the Oranjeweg, 300 meters north of the intersection with the Utrechtseweg, where the other five Polish anti-tank guns had been positioned. The two 6-pounders were to cover the open area to the west and northwest, should the Germans press their attack from the railroad line. The gunners dug their weapons in quickly while keeping an eye in the direction from which an English officer told them that they could expect an attack.

As the sun went down, the Germans moved cautiously towards Wolfheze. Like the Polish glider arrivals, the British 4th Parachute Brigade had been shattered. Some Poles managed to straggle to the Hartenstein. Others, who had been wounded, were taken to the field hospitals in Wolfheze or Oosterbeek. Still other Poles, not taken prisoner in the woods surrounding Johannahoeve, found refuge with whatever British unit they could attach themselves to. Alone, and not able to speak more than a few words of English, they were forced to endure the battle that raged around them in fear and ignorance. Not far from the darkening field at Johannahoeve farm, Bombardier Oprych had crawled for more than two hours in the direction of Wolfheze. Near the railroad, he found a dug-in anti-tank gun from his squadron. Two men occupied the emplacement, and behind them was a jeep loaded with ammunition. The Polish gunners pulled the wounded bombardier, weak from blood loss, into the their dugout.

In England, Sosabowski's soldiers had arrived at their vacated billets. Lieutenant Kaczmarek was amazed to find that the rations had arrived before the men. The paratroopers were in a poor psychological and physical state. They had been keyed up by years of advanced training and preparation, and then laid helpless by Warsaw's agony. Frustration had only increased with planning and waiting for operations that never took place, and now this: an operation finally under way, and the men kept idle by vacillations of the weather. The hours of waiting beside their aircraft had only increased the soldiers' tension, only to have the crushing crescendo of cancellation again fall upon them. With uniforms wet from rain and drizzle, and the cold sweat of nervous perspiration, the Polish paratroopers tried to choke down the hastily prepared "compo" rations. They took off their boots, smocks and field equipment. Still wearing their damp battledress, they lay down to try to sleep, expecting to return to the airfields at a moment's notice. For most, the tension was so acute that rest was an impossibility.

At twilight, a German self-propelled gun appeared from behind Wolfheze station and approached the Polish anti-tank gun positioned north of the Utrecht-Arnhem railway line. It halted and fired a round that burst near the Polish anti-tank gunners' jeep. The 6-pounder replied with one round, and then another. The self-propelled gun reversed itself on its treads and withdrew. Their jeep wrecked, however, the gunners quickly conferred, and then removed the breechblock from the gun and threw it into the underbrush. The two of them, carrying the wounded Bombardier Oprych under their arms, started for the railway embankment. Crossing over it, they entered a wood. There were the sounds of boots moving in the underbrush and German voices were all around them. Carefully and quietly, the anti-tank men moved through the woods, trying to find a friend.

At the Baltussen factory in Driel, the two British messengers left on their second attempt to reach Nijmegen. In the center of Driel, Dr. Van de Burg checked on the British bomb aimer. Hours before, she had amputated his foot. The bomb aimer was not alone, for several villagers and two wounded German soldiers also lay in the hospital. One of the Germans, a very young soldier, was in critical condition. But every time Cora Baltussen or Father Poelman tried to comfort him, or get his family's address so they might tell them about their son, he replied with a *"Heil Hitler."*

At the Hotel Hartenstein, Marek Swiecicki tried to sort out the day's events. The optimistic mood of the previous day was gone. Blackout rules were strictly enforced around the headquarters, and it was forbidden to smoke cigarettes outside. The correspondent tried to sort out fragments of reality he had seen from the press briefings he was given before the operation. The Germans had obviously proven to be much stronger than expected. The correspondent was especially disturbed by the surprising showing the Luftwaffe had made. Swiecicki, like many people at the time, thought that German airpower had been all but broken. Among the British staff officers, there was consternation that the Polish Parachute Brigade had not arrived to reinforce the beleaguered Red Devils, and a growing apprehension was felt about the fate of 2nd Para Battalion, which was still holding the north end of Arnhem bridge.

In position far up the Oranjeweg from the Hartenstein, Bombardiers Nosecki and Kabat took turns sleeping and standing watch. Told to expect an attack any minute, their gun was ready with a round locked in the breech. Kabat shook Nosecki awake, and the powerfully built man took his turn on watch. Straining his eyes in the darkness, Stanislaw Nosecki could not help but relive the events of that afternoon. He tried to fight off the "awful feeling that the Germans had finished the squadron on the landing zone. So many of the men had lost their lives before they even had a chance to fire." Thinking about the squadron became too painful, and Nosecki nourished the hope that he might still get some rest this night, and that perhaps the events of the day were not real: "Maybe with daylight the rest of us will gather, and things will be better."

At his headquarters in Stamford, General Sosabowski tried to sort out whatever intelligence he could get concerning the battle raging in Holland. Knowing that his glider lift had taken off earlier in the day, Sosabowski finally received the RAF reports, and the news was not good. Twenty-eight gliders were listed as having been successfully released, but there was no confirmation of their fate. Aerial photographs had shown only nine on the landing zone. More disturbing was a sketchy report from Oosterbeek that when the Polish gliders were landing, the landing zone was under heavy fire. Losses were termed as "heavy," and equipment had to be abandoned in burning gliders. Once again Sosabowski dispatched his British liaison officers to gather any further information.

11

Maybe Tomorrow

September 20, 1944

In Oosterbeek, the light of dawn struggled with the low clouds that blanketed the area with a cold drizzle on the morning of Wednesday, September 20. During the night General Urquhart managed, with some success, to contact his units by radio. He called on the heavily engaged Brigadier Hackett to report to Division Headquarters. Urquhart planned to use Hackett's brigade for yet another attempt to break through to Lieutenant Colonel Frost at Arnhem bridge. Just after 0300 hours, a tenuous radio contact with Headquarters, I Airborne Corps in Nijmegen, was obtained. General Browning sought information concerning the Polish drop zone. General Urquhart requested that the Polish drop zone be moved west, to the fields outside Driel, in light of the situation at the bridge. There the Poles could cross the river by ferry and reinforce the Red Devils. The valuable radio contact shortly evaporated when the Germans greeted the sunrise by working over the Oosterbeek pocket with a heavy artillery and mortar bombardment.

With daylight, the anti-tank gunners carrying their wounded comrade, Jozef Oprych, emerged from the woods on the Wolfhezeweg. All night long Germans had been moving through the woods, but the Poles had escaped detection. The road was crowded with jeeps and trailers trying to reach the division. Lying wounded in a roadside garden, Oprych could hear, but not see, the vicious combat that began in the morning and was destined to continue throughout the day.

In England, after an uncomfortable night, the Polish Parachute Brigade again boarded trucks that would take them to the airfields. Arriving at Saltby at 0845 hours, General Sosabowski was given the change in drop zones by Lieutenant Colonel Stevens. Thirty minutes

118

later, the Polish staff officers were verbally informed by the General of the change in the operational plan. The takeoff, scheduled for 1000 hours, was pushed three hours forward. The many days and nights of staff work, the map studies and the briefings were all thrown out the window as new plans had to be formulated in the span of a few short hours. Major Tonn was called from Spanhoe to receive his new instructions as the Brigade's staff officers pored over maps and aerial photographs of the new drop zone, four miles to the west of the old one.

At the side of the taxiway at Saltby airfield, Lieutenant Smaczny found the tension unbearable, and felt his men's faith in the operation eroding bit by bit. To the lieutenant, the sky, though overcast, seemed clear enough for flying. From above, the roar of aircraft engines was heard, and occasionally planes were spotted through breaks in the clouds.

At the Arnhem road bridge, Lieutenant Colonel Frost's 2nd Parachute Battalion still managed to hold ten buildings, the cellars packed with its wounded. The Germans kept throwing attack after attack at the defenders, who fought like lions from their burning buildings. Much of the combat had been hand-to-hand owing to the fact that the Red Devils were running out of ammunition. Starved, and numb from fatigue, the men at the bridge still sent out unanswered radio signals to the Second Army, which they expected to appear any hour. During the morning, the gallant Frost was wounded in both legs, and was carried into one of the crowded cellars.

In Driel, Benjamin Jansen awoke to the sounds of fierce fighting from across the river. From the south, the dull thuds of drum-fire came from the direction of Nijmegen. The excited citizens of Driel gossiped about the Second Army's impending arrival. At the Baltussen farm, five more British soldiers found shelter. They had been taken prisoner in Oosterbeek, but slipped away from their captors and swam across the Neder Rijn during the night. Dutch villagers found them wandering the fields. They took them to the Baltussens, who they knew spoke English and would not turn them away. In addition to the Red Devils, the Baltussens' factory and warehouses sheltered refugees from Oosterbeek, among whom were Jews and members of the underground who were forced to flee their hiding places due to the fighting.

Standing near the Polish anti-tank positions, Marek Swiecicki watched as the exhausted and filthy soldiers of the 4th Parachute Brigade drifted into the Hartenstein area throughout the morning. Suddenly, as Nebelwerfer rockets screeched through the air, the correspondent threw himself to the ground. Tree limbs crashed and clattered on the roadway as explosions and shouts filled the air. When the uproar ceased, Swiecicki turned to his neighbor, Lieutenant Halpert. The lieutenant, who had survived the massacre at Johannahoeve the day before, lay in a pool of blood that was pouring from a savage wound in his leg. He and two other wounded Polish gunners were taken away in an ambulance jeep.

At the two Polish anti-tank guns situated three hundred meters up Oranjeweg, Bombardier Nosecki felt the situation was "a chaotic mess, full of unanswered questions." In his detached position, he felt isolated, yet surrounded: "Not far away we could see German infantry. We have no front cover, the whole situation stinks." Orders eventually came from Lieutenant Mleczko. Men were needed to take the place of those who had become casualties at one of the guns at the crossroads of Utrechtseweg/Oranjeweg. Nosecki was told to grab his gear and get down there.

At Saltby airfield the Brigade Staff hurriedly worked over their new assignment in the wet grass near the dispersal area. The troops prepared to board their aircraft. The meticulously planned operation would now be fought in an improvised manner on new terrain. The rapid re-evaluation of the Brigade's mission from the maps and aerial photographs revealed a drop zone of open fields bordered by orchards that lacked any distinctive landmarks, making assembly and orientation of the units difficult. Furthermore, the fields were bisected by numerous drainage ditches. These obstacles promised to hinder the gathering of equipment and the assembly of the heavily burdened men. General Sosabowski's anger and unease was alleviated by his realization that the change in orders was one of the fortunes of war that a paratrooper, by his very nature, should take in stride. To Sosabowski, his soldiers appeared combative and confident. More distressing to the command group was the fact that the change in orders was not followed with any information about the tactical situation. The total lack of information from the battlefield created a deep apprehension that the 1st Airborne Division might not hold either Arnhem or its bridges.

The Polish liaison officers with the 1st Airborne Division, with a radioman and correspondent Swiecicki in tow, left the Hartenstein to meet their Brigade's parachute lift. Walking through the dark woods in back of the hotel, Swiecicki, having already endured two bombardments that morning, marveled at the peaceful scene yet to be touched by war.

As the group moved towards the river, Dutch faces appeared at the windows of the houses along the tree-lined lanes. From the doorway of one, a plump Dutch woman in a blue dress asked if anything serious was going to happen. The correspondent replied that she should not worry, "We are here."

When the Polish liaison group arrived at the artillery positions in lower Oosterbeek, they rested outside a battery command post while waiting for any further news about the Polish Parachute Brigade's impending landing. The small talk among the Poles came to an abrupt halt when the now-familiar screams of Nebelwerfer rockets again tore the air. Correspondent Swiecicki flew into the house, "whether from instinct, or pushed by explosive concussion," he could not recall. Swiecicki went into the cellar, where the artillerymen stood around a table covered with a map and protractors and quadrants, and ringed with telephones and radios. As the explosions burst outside, and glass shattered on the floor above, the journalist thought: "Bombarded from the west while at the Hartenstein; now here, in another part of the perimeter, bombarded from the east. Surrounded. Were there Germans on the other side of the river? Would the [rest of the] Brigade meet the same fate as the glider lift?"

A field telephone rang. A British officer said that it was headquarters; the Polish drop was postponed for three hours.

The Polish anti-tank squadron suffered further shelling throughout the day. Many of the British glider pilots remained with the Polish guns, filling in for missing gun crew members. As enemy pressure increased on the northern side of the perimeter, skirmish groups of German infantrymen joined the snipers in harassing the gun positions. The 6-pounders replied with high-explosive rounds.

With furious small combats taking place in the woods between the Hartenstein and Wolfheze, tanks and self-propelled guns were reported approaching from the west. Lieutenant Mleczko received a frantic order from Division Headquarters to deal with a self-propelled gun. A jeep and gun with crew limbered up, and zoomed west down Utrechtseweg. Only later was Mleczko informed that a German tank had destroyed the vehicle, the 6-pounder, and killed the crew and a British officer who was guiding them before they could get into position. As more casualties were sent to the field hospital, Mleczko received orders from Division Artillery to prepare to move to new positions near the Oosterbeek church.

Marek Swiecicki and the officers of the Polish liaison group emerged from the cellar of the British battery command post. Down the street, near the church, houses and trees were in flames. The command post building itself tilted crazily, an entire wall blown out. The Polish radio operator, who had taken cover under a jeep, lay badly wounded. He weakly asked forgiveness for the shattered radio that lay beside him. Artillery was still falling, and accompanied the Poles making their way back to the Hartenstein. The neat house where the hefty woman had questioned Swiecicki now had all of its windows blown out. Most of the roof was gone, and a corner of the brick cottage was now a heap of rubble. Near the gate lay a crumpled form in a familiar blue dress. The Poles took shelter in trenches occupied by a group of glider pilots. High-pitched screaming rose over the explosions of artillery and mortar shells. As the correspondent looked, he saw a group of school children, led by a pretty teenage girl, thrashing in panic through the underbrush.

In England, the United States Air Force decided to postpone the takeoff for one more hour in the hope that the fog would disperse. The decision to drop or not to drop would be made over the drop zone. Once again donning their cumbersome equipment and taking a last gulp of tea, the paratroopers boarded the aircraft.

At 1340 hours, Pratt and Whitney engines burst into life with a roar amid clouds of blue exhaust. Throughout the passenger compartments of the Dakotas, smiles of relief flashed across the paratroopers' faces. The ground crew removed the wheel chocks from the leading Dakotas. The pilots released their brakes and the lead aircraft started down the taxiways. The aircraft at the end of the runway gunned their engines, while those in the last serials shut theirs down. The Dakotas then spun around and lumbered back to their dispersal points—the drop had again been called off. The fog and drizzle that covered England were heavier yet over the Channel, with cloud to 9,000 feet.

Cursing, the Polish paratroopers left the Dakotas. Their state of anger was such that some of the American aircrews made sure that they maintained their distance from the livid Poles. At Spanhoe airfield, a Polish sapper could not stand the tension and frustration anymore. He chambered a round in his Sten gun, and before anyone could stop him, put the muzzle under his chin and pulled the trigger.

At sunrise, most of what remained of the 4th Parachute Brigade had withdrawn south of the railroad line. As they pushed towards the Hartenstein, they were constantly harassed by mortars, artillery, machine guns, self-propelled guns and tanks. Casualties mounted, and many officers and NCOs were lost as they continuously led their men in desperate attacks. The attacks allowed the withdrawal to continue, though only to bump up against still more Germans who had to be fought. The last men of the 4th Para Brigade to get into the perimeter did so behind a bayonet charge. Hackett's command now numbered barely 300 men. Crushed by the demise of the 4th Brigade, General Urquhart could no longer think of making another effort to break through to Lieutenant Colonel Frost at the bridge.

The whine of fighter planes distracted Benjamin Jansen from his work on the farm behind the Driel dike. From the haze, over twenty aircraft appeared, and dived on Oosterbeek. Grabbing a pair of field glasses, Jansen focused on the planes and saw swastikas on their tails. The aircraft pulled out of their dives and made a wide circle around Driel. The fighters reformed, and again dived on the town. Several hours later, the deep hum of multi-engined aircraft took the farm hand from his work. Another supply mission was approaching the Oosterbeek perimeter. As the formation passed by Elst, it was greeted by light anti-aircraft fire. Then, as the supply planes crossed the Betuwe, they attracted the attention of heavy anti-aircraft guns near the railroad bridge and from across the river. The sky began to fill with puffs of smoke. Shards of roof tiles clattered to the streets as the shrapnel from the bursting shells fell on Driel. Jansen ran into the barn and curled himself up against a wall.

Driel became quiet again. At the Baltussen house, Cora looked out the window, and saw between sixty and eighty German soldiers beginning to deploy in a ring around the home and factory. The British messengers were still asleep on the floor. Cora tried to wake them, but no matter how hard she shook them, they did not respond. They were "sleeping like stones." She continued to frantically shake them "as if they were door-mats." When she finally roused them, they instinctively drew their pistols. Cora's mother trembled while her daughter bundled the paratroopers into an outbuilding. "We were all praying to our guardian angels, and I looked at my young sister Eef, and said to go and sit on the bench outside." The two women sat down, and calmly began knitting.

As some German soldiers came into the yard, their eyes were riveted on Eef, a stunning eighteen-year-old. Cora rose and greeted the two officers with a *"Guten tag."* They replied that they wanted to search the house; they had heard that there were British soldiers hidden there. Eef looked at the German soldiers. They seemed to be between sixteen and eighteen years old. Eef told them, "You look tired, would you want some water?" Cora calmly told the German officers that the factory, a mere 15 meters away, was "quarters for two German officers and their men, and that they had left an hour ago, and would probably be back soon." As the attractive Eef poured water for the young troops, Cora calmly told them that "it would be impossible, stupid, to hide people where Germans were quartered." Taking notice of how relaxed and correct the women seemed, the German officers called their troops together and left, saying that they still had to continue searching for the British.

Cora and her sister quietly waited in the yard until the field-grays were out of sight. Entering the house, they found the evacuees whom Cora had saved from POW or concentration camps quivering in fear. Cora muttered a prayer to the "brigade of guardian angels who were helping us," and herself began to shake.

Delayed, awaiting orders at the Hartenstein, it was only at 1730 hours when Lieutenant Mleczko joined the remaining six guns of the Anti-tank Squadron in their new positions. During the move Corporal Stanislaw Gorzko had been killed by shellfire while the column drove through the woods south of the Hartenstein. After consulting a British officer, Mleczko positioned his guns to protect the rear of the nearby Royal Artillery positions. Two of the 6-pounders were pointed north, with the rest aimed down the Benedendorpsweg from positions west of the Oosterbeek church. By this time, the Polish gunners had abandoned the heavy camouflage nets that they had previously used to help mask their guns. In their place, chicken-wire fencing had been taken from the gardens of Oosterbeek, attached to the gun shields and woven with natural foliage. In this way the guns could quickly become mobile without sacrificing concealment while in position.

The tons of supplies that had been dropped that afternoon had fallen mostly into German hands. There was still the hope among the British staff that the Polish Parachute Brigade would arrive and help reverse the situation. Again the Polish liaison team left the Hartenstein to meet their Brigade. This time they had a jeep, and their destination was the ferry landing at Heveadorp. The jeep pulled up at the headquarters of the 1st Airlanding Brigade, and the Poles were given a haversack full of apples and a guide. When they reached the Border Regiment's positions on the lower slopes of the Westerbouwing, the Poles settled into slit trenches, and again began their vigil, awaiting the expected parachute drop.

Marek Swiecicki was amazed at the view of the river and the broad polder from his high ground. Eagerly accepting a proffered mess tin full of water, now so rare at the Hartenstein, Swiecicki drank while a British officer briefed him on the situation. The Germans positions were a few dozen meters away. Pointing to the ferry landing, the officer noted that the ferry had been there only a short time ago. The Germans were regularly sweeping the landing and the river with fire.

This was confirmed by the ferry dock, which was now a mass of splintered timbers. The enemy's presence was underlined when a British soldier ran into the open to recover a supply pannier, its parachute still attached. A terrible fusillade of machine-gun fire burst forth as the soldier crawled, dragging the heavy pannier behind him, back to his foxhole. As the Poles watched him make his way to cover, a British soldier came running from the battalion headquarters towards them with a message: The Brigade would not be arriving this day since the weather in England did not permit a takeoff. As the Poles prepared to return to the Hartenstein, they talked among themselves about the situation. Marek volunteered, "Maybe tomorrow. . ." but he did not believe it himself. He was thinking that "tomorrow" the Germans would be there instead.

As the afternoon wore on, more Germans arrived in Driel in trucks and buses from Elst. Ferry operator Peter Hensen had gathered his family and found shelter for them in a culvert under the road to the ferry. At 1800 hours, British fighter planes circled Driel. Benjamin Jansen felt uneasy about the situation, and had his family take shelter in the concrete drain of the cattle barn. As he was going to warn some neighbors, Jansen heard machine guns, explosions and the sounds of fighter planes zooming off. Down Dorpstraat, two German trucks were burning. Hopping on their bicycles, Benjamin and his brother went to take a look. Behind the fiercely burning trucks, five houses were also on fire. Villagers tried to put out the flames with buckets of water, but in vain. Only some livestock were saved.

The British paratroopers cut off on the Wolfhezeweg had repulsed German attacks all day. As the sun was going down, a heavy artillery bombardment fell on the stranded group. The two Polish anti-tank gunners took their wounded comrade, Bombardier Oprych, and put him under a wrecked jeep. They then slipped back into the woods. At twilight the Germans rounded up the last of the paratroopers left west of the Oosterbeek perimeter. They found the wounded bombardier and put him on a truck that delivered him to a captured British field dressing station set up at the Wolfheze psychiatric hospital, and an unknown future as a prisoner of war.

In the English Midlands, the men of the parachute lift again returned to their billets. This time Lieutenant Kaczmarek did not have the difficulty arranging the men's rations that he had had the day before. As vexing as the aborted takeoff was, it did allow time for the Poles to better develop an operation plan for the landing on the new drop zone. The Brigade staff and unit commanders would not get much sleep that night.

The anger and frustration of the Polish paratroopers were minor compared to that felt by their commander. General Sosabowski was almost at the point of rebellion. He was torn between his military orders for an operation now in progress and his obligations to the Polish government and his soldiers who had worked so hard to make the Brigade an actuality. Sosabowski sent Lieutenant Colonel Stevens to gather *any* information about the 1st Airborne Division's situation.

During the afternoon of this day, the troops of the 82nd Airborne Division forced the Waal river in flimsy canvas and plywood boats. This crossing, accomplished in broad daylight, stands among the most gallant small-unit actions of the entire war. Seizing the northern end of the Nijmegen bridge, the Americans were met by Sherman tanks of the 2nd Battalion, Grenadier guards. Despite Lieutenant Colonel Frost's hanging on at Arnhem only 19 kilometers away, the tanks did not move beyond the bridge. The surviving troopers of the 504th Parachute Infantry Regiment's 3rd Battalion, which had bled heavily during the crossing, were livid as the tankers explained that they could not proceed without infantry support. As the sun went down, the tankers brewed tea and waited for their infantry to catch up with them.

The Brigade staff labored through the night to devise a battle plan for the assault on the new drop zone, while the troopers again lay down in their damp uniforms to try and get some sleep. Lieutenant Colonel Stevens was running himself ragged trying to obtain any solid information to give to the agitated General Sosabowski. The British liaison officer returned with rumors, and was again sent on his way. Not having heard from either Generals Urquhart or Browning for two days, Sosabowski was contemplating taking the drastic step of breaking the chain of command and going directly to General Brereton. Totally in the dark, the Polish general was contemplating a refusal to let the Brigade take off unless written orders were issued confirming the Brigade's mission and the enemy situation in Holland. With only a hope that it would get through to Browning, a radiogram was sent requesting such a clarification. At any rate, Brereton could not be reached as he was on the Continent, inspecting his command in the field. Sosabowski then prepared a request for written orders to be sent to First Allied Airborne Army Headquarters in the morning.

The General then lay down to try to sleep. The old soldier slept in fits and spurts, remembering his bloody battles of the past. But his thoughts for the future disquieted him even more. Sosabowski was tormented by the nightmare of possible court martials: by the British for refusing to take off, or by the Poles if his Brigade were to be needlessly sacrificed.

The night skies around Driel glowed orange over Arnhem, Oosterbeek and Nijmegen. Standing outside his home watching the fires, Benjamin Jansen saw people who lived near the railroad bridge fleeing through the village. They told him that many Germans were digging in by the railroad embankment. Among the refugees, a handful of drunken Waffen SS men strode through the town. Whether they were deserters, or were in Driel for a purpose, they put a cold fear into the villagers. The sounds of heavy gunfire continued to drift into Driel from the south, but did not seem to be coming any closer. Until this day, the village had seen little of the actual battle. Benjamin Jansen, farm hand and flower grower, wondered what tomorrow might have in store for little Driel.

In Oosterbeek, Marek Swiecicki was trying to find a place to go to sleep. Not wanting to spend the night in a damp trench, he returned to the Hartenstein. On the ground floor, the Division Headquarters staff labored on by the light of paraffin lamps. Climbing up the stairs, the correspondent found the second floor a contrast. The rooms were dark, the floor deserted. Outside, tracers and shells lit the night with flashes of red. All of the mattresses and blankets had been taken from the well-appointed hotel rooms for the dressing station in the cellar.

Lying down on the wooden slats of an empty bed, the correspondent closed his eyes and immediately was out. A nearby explosion awoke him, and was followed by two more, which shook the entire room. Pulling himself from the bed, Swiecicki went to a room on the other side of the hotel and stretched out on another mattress-less bed. Before he could close his eyes, yet another explosion lit up the room and peppered his blanket with broken glass and plaster. Moving into the corridor, Swiecicki found a bookcase built into the wall. Feeling like a "barbarian," the correspondent pulled the beautifully bound books from the shelf and curled up on it. Thinking that he was, "a man in his rightful place," the writer immediately fell asleep.

12

Third Time Lucky

0430 to 1730 Hours, September 21, 1944

As the sun rose over the Arnhem bridge, the Germans rounded up the last of the British defenders. It had been planned that a brigade of paratroopers was to take and hold this objective until relieved by XXX Corps forty-eight hours later. Lieutenant Colonel Frost's battalion had held it for almost ninety hours, while the ground forces were only now beginning to cross the Waal in any appreciable strength. The Germans had little time to waste; they could not allow the Allies to exploit their positions on the Waal, and the tangle of wrecked vehicles on the Rijn bridge had to be cleared to allow passage of reinforcements south. The German AA 9 was finally able to cross the bridge into Arnhem, where part of it was sent straight into action. The rest of the unit was held in reserve as a mobile "Jagdkommando" in the event of further airborne landings.

The commander of II SS Panzer Corps, General Bittrich, sought this day to eliminate the 1st Airborne Division in Oosterbeek by a coordinated attack on all sides of the perimeter. There had been some early success. Shortly after daybreak, the single platoon of the Border Regiment holding Westerbouwing was pushed off the hill on the western flank of the Oosterbeek perimeter. German paratroopers, all of them NCO school candidates, took the objective in a fanatic and bloody assault, and then repulsed a British counterattack. The heights remained in German hands, and from this dominating terrain the Germans now overlooked the entire southern part of the British perimeter, plus the Heveadorp ferry landing at the foot of the hill.

When the surviving Fallschirmjägers moved down its slopes to the landing, the ferry was nowhere to be seen. Late during the previous night, after seeing to his family's safety, Peter Hensen had cut the ferry adrift. With so many Germans in Driel, the brave ferryman did not want to allow its use by the hated occupiers. The vessel later washed up on the north bank of the river between Heveadorp and Castle Doorwerth, where it lay ignored for the rest of the battle.

Marek Swiecicki walked down the stairs of the Hartenstein. The beautiful hotel was showing the effects of five days of battle. The walls were cracked and scarred, and the floors were covered with plaster and shards of glass. Division Headquarters had already been moved from the ground floor into the hotel's cellar. There, General Urquhart was holding a conference with his commanders concerning the Division's defense. Dividing his forces in two, he charged Brigadier Hicks with command of the western and Brigadier Hackett the eastern sides of the thumb-shaped perimeter that the British airborne forces had been squeezed into.

The Germans had avoided direct assaults against the majority of the British defenses, and instead relied on mortar and artillery fire to kill the defenders in their positions. Snipers had infiltrated the gaps in the lines caused by the shelling, and raised havoc among all echelons. While Urquhart was in conference, the division's artillery had managed to make radio contact with the fire control center of the Second Army's 64th Medium Regiment (Royal Artillery). Aside from having finally established a tenuous radio contact with the ground forces, this contact meant that the 1st Airborne Division would have some support of heavy guns for the remainder of the battle.

The Polish Parachute Brigade once more boarded trucks at their English billets and again made their way to the airfield. Lance Sergeant Hrehorow was filled with a variety of troubled thoughts, but tried to appear "confident and carefree." Looking at the faces of the other men from the 4th company of the 2nd Battalion in his truck, "there seemed to be a point of honor that we were not revealing, even to closest friends, any anxieties or forebodings, and by now, there were plenty of these." Hrehorow's eyes fell on the face of Private Lipman Jakubowicz, who responded with a broad and invulnerable smile. Jakubowicz was a proud Jewish Pole, scrawny and bow-legged, and not at all reflecting the recruiting-poster image of a paratrooper. The man, however, possessed incredible spunk and spirit, and an energy that was infectious. Hrehorow returned the smile, and somehow felt a little less doubtful about the future. It was 0700 when the trucks arrived at the airfields, and in weather that did not seem any better than it had been on the previous two days.

Despite the heavy mist, Lieutenant Smaczny could see quite clearly the Dakotas on the edges of the runways 400 meters away. A report of clear skies over the Channel was relayed by Captain Sobocinski. With the delays, poor food, and seemingly endless waiting, Smaczny was worried about the mood and condition of his men. The lieutenant was also distressed by the lack of any definite information from Holland. He had listened nightly to the BBC, but all he had heard was "the same reassuring pap." The troopers shouldered their equipment, and went to the aircraft with the number "65" chalked on its nose to begin yet another wait.

Walking to plane 111 with the other members of the headquarters company, Private J. Zbigniew Raschke noticed yellow streaks in the gray sky. The sun was trying to break through. "A good omen," thought Raschke. The age-old English expression "Third time lucky. . ." came to the cryptographer's mind. A canteen truck was passing out mugs of tea and mutton sandwiches. Raschke, thinking of the future, grabbed some of the sandwiches and stowed them in his pockets and kit bag, in which he carried some of the Brigade's code charts, and then followed the rest of his stick to the parked Dakota.

General Sosabowski answered a knock at his door to find Lieutenant Colonel Stevens. He had with him a copy of General Urquhart's radiogram from the day before. Given to Stevens as current information, the message gladdened Sosabowski with the news that his drop zone had not been changed again and that the ferry was still in British hands. Stevens also related that the Guards Armored Division had crossed the Waal, and was giving the 1st Airborne Division artillery support. A few minutes later, the phone rang. General Brereton's Chief of Staff replied to General Sosabowski's messages of the night before by confirming the information given by Stevens. Though the General feared that his Brigade might run into German units being pushed north by the Allied ground forces, by following the hasty plans that had been worked out through the night the Poles should be able to link up with the 1st Airborne Division by nightfall, using the ferry. Despite the overcast skies, takeoff was scheduled for 1200 hours.

In Driel, Benjamin Jansen awoke. The sounds of fierce fighting continued to drift across the river from Oosterbeek, but now there was only silence from the direction of Arnhem. Looking across the fields, Jansen saw groups of German soldiers, some with machine guns balanced on their shoulders, trudging east towards the railroad embankment.

Villagers who lived in the area were moving in the opposite direction, carrying their possessions. Already machine guns were trading bursts between the Germans in the "Lange Pas" (a grove of poplar trees near the railroad) and the British in Oosterbeek. As more German soldiers continued to pass through the village, Jansen kept urging his employer to leave.

After meeting with his officers, General Urquhart spoke to the correspondents in the hotel's former reception area. The General began with a review of the operation. Though he tried to put a best face on the situation, Urquhart told the reporters that the division was surrounded, and that the Germans were bringing up reinforcements. Returning to the upper floors of the Hotel Hartenstein, Marek Swiecicki wrote up a radio dispatch. As explosions outside chased them from room to room, Staff Sergeant Cotterill corrected the journalist's written English. The short report was then sent to London over the BBC transmitter.

With the Arnhem bridge now clear, and the units that had invested Frost now uncommitted, Lieutenant Colonel Harzer gave orders for an all-out attack on all sides of the Oosterbeek perimeter as more and more reinforcements arrived in Arnhem. Under an umbrella of heavy mortar and artillery fire, supported by tanks and self-propelled guns, the Germans started nibbling at the British positions. Though they managed to take some, the German assaults suffered from poor coordination. Their attacks were further blunted by the excellent shooting of the British heavy artillery, firing at maximum range from Nijmegen. General Bittrich was more concerned about the threat from Nijmegen, pushing back the British who had crossed the Waal River. Supplies and reinforcements for the hard-pressed Frundsberg Division were now moving south across the Arnhem bridge.

At airfields in England, the Polish troopers apprehensively choked down mugs of tea, wondering whether they would finally take off this day. During the delays, the Poles began hoarding as much extra ammunition as they could find, and packed it away in their pockets and kit bags. In addition to the burdens that the other Allied paratroopers carried, the majority of the Poles wore bullet-proof vests under their Denison and sleeveless jump smocks. Consisting of steel plates covered with webbing, they were of British design and manufacture, and covered the chest, spine and kidneys. Heavy and uncomfortable, the armored vest was very rarely worn by British airborne troops other than glider pilots.

The American aircrews arrived at 1100. It was an hour until the scheduled takeoff, and the heavy mist still hung over the English Midlands. As 1200 approached, there was no improvement in the meteorological situation. The takeoff was postponed, and General Sosabowski sat down for a cup of coffee with the American airfield commander. The recess was disturbed by a message that the weather was breaking up. After a hurried handshake and an exchange of good wishes, the General returned to his waiting troops and spread the word. The soldiers began strapping on their parachutes and equipment and awaited orders to finally board.

At 1245, the hum of aircraft was again heard over the Betuwe as a supply mission made its way to Oosterbeek. Benjamin Jansen saw anti-aircraft fire coming from Arnhem, Oosterbeek and the Doorwerth woods. It was even heavier than it had been on the two previous days. One Dakota crashed in flames on the polder on the north shore of the river. Minutes later, German fighters appeared, and strafed the British positions in Oosterbeek. Finally convincing his employer that they should leave, Jansen borrowed a miller's horse and cart. Loading the cart with pro-visions, and neighbors of all ages, Jansen drove to the center of the village as stray shells landed in the fields. The streets were crowded with other villagers preparing to leave. A farmer told Jansen that he might be able to stay at his son-in-law's farm west of the village, and then asked Jansen if he might return to collect him and his wife afterwards.

At Saltby and Spanhoe airfields, the Polish stickmasters gave the equipment containers slung under their aircraft a final check. They then turned to their men and made sure all were present. Lined up in order of their jump number, the paratroopers gave one another's straps and equipment a last check. Bent under their parachutes, wearing two smocks with pockets crammed with equipment and struggling with their heavy kit bags, the men looked like "two-legged camels" to Lance Sergeant Cadet Hrehorow.

The American ground crews helped the ungainly men up the aluminum steps into the Dakotas. The aircrews received final briefings in small groups on the grass along the taxi strip. They then dispersed and walked to their aircraft, where some of the pilots had a quick word with their stickmasters and then disappeared into their cockpits. The Poles crowded as far forward as they could on the bench seats that ran along both sides of the cabin. Jammed together in a jumble of parachutes, wea-pons and kit bags to keep the aircraft's center of gravity as far forward as possible during the takeoff and the climb, the paratroopers apprehensively hoped that this was finally the real thing.

With puffs of blue smoke the airplanes burst into life. At 1358, the first Dakota released its brakes and lumbered down the taxi strips. Like a procession of dinosaurs, the other Dakotas followed. In threes, the aircraft lined up at the ends of the runways as the hum of Pratt & Whitney engines rose in pitch and intensity before the pilots released their brakes and the planes shot forward.

Their tails rose in the air as they raced down the runway, ever gaining speed. When lift overcame gravity, their wheels left the tarmac, and the Dakotas were airborne. Through the open doors the paratroopers watched the ground slip away as the planes climbed into the fog. In "V" formations of three, the Dakotas struggled through the clouds. The soldiers, taunt as guitar strings, mutely waited for the planes to gain altitude in the gray clouds. Through the windows, the wings were barely visible in the clouds that boiled past. The silence was grim and unnerving: the memories of the collision in July had everybody on edge. Not many meters away, hidden in the murk, was the wingtip of another aircraft.

At 10,000 feet, the Dakotas broke through the cloud ceiling and into bright sunlight, as beautiful blue skies greeted the armada. The fear of collision waned, and stomachs knotted by fear began to relax. The soldiers began to spread out along the bench seats. Flying above the cloud ceiling, it became very cold. The spectacle touched every man who saw it, as above a milky-white carpet of clouds drab-painted Dakotas flew in purposeful formation. In the distance, the sun twinkled off of the canopies and propellors of escorting Spitfires and Mustangs. Soon the steam coming out of the soldiers' mouths was replaced by cigarette smoke. In plane 34, Sergeant Michal Iwaskow's men forgot their tension and exhaustion and began to joke and sing.

Lieutenant Kaczmarek, so impressed by the sight of the massed aircraft warming up on the ground, missed the spectacle in the sky. The plane carrying his supply platoon climbed with the formation into the clouds. But when plane 98 broke through into the sunlit blue sky it was alone. Kaczmarek was flabbergasted; it was as if all the other aircraft had disappeared. After circling some minutes, the Dakota turned east and set off by itself.

Lieutenant Jerzy Lesniak looked out of plane 21. Having climbed through the "pea soup," the Lieutenant shivered as he gazed at the beautiful layer of clouds below. There were no other aircraft to be seen.

One of the pilots came back to tell him, "Well, we're lost." Lesniak thought this an example of the American "strange sense of humor." The plane descended through the clouds again, and soon was flying over water. Going into the cockpit, Lesniak saw that they were approaching land. The pilot told the Polish officer to go back and look out the open cabin door to see if they were over England or the Continent. Watching through the mists, Lesniak saw automobiles being driven on the left side of the road. When the Polish officer reported that they were over England, the pilot replied, "That's all right, I just received a message that we are to turn back. The mission has been canceled." Lesniak went back to his seat, so angry at this point that he "did not care whether we went or not."

While the aircraft from the 314th Troop Carrier Group were trying to break through the clouds, the lead ship of one of the squadrons received an "F" type message over the IX Troop Carrier Command flight control frequency. These messages consisted of a four-letter Morse cypher that was normally repeated four times. The radioman checked his code book, valid until 1800 hours of that day. He could not find the combination that was broadcast in either his code book or on the squadron's briefing sheet. As this frequency was used for recalls (and strict security regulations prohibited replying to such messages), it was assumed that the mission was aborted due to the weather. The lead aircraft transmitted the recall to the other ten planes in its element. These planes were carrying rifle platoons and the headquarters of the 3rd Battalion.

The heavy cloud cover proved disastrous to the mission. Of 114 aircraft involved in the Polish lift, a total of 41 aborted due to weather, or because they had interpreted the radio signal as a recall. The 314th Troop Carrier Group had fourteen aborts, the rest being from the 315th. Besides the eleven planes of the 3rd Battalion, twenty-five of the 1st Battalion, two from the 2nd Battalion and three aircraft of the Brigade headquarters group returned to England.

Lieutenant Smaczny asked all the men in plane 65 if anybody felt sick. The paratroopers all shook their heads and the aircraft remained silent. Lance Corporal Boleslaw Kuzniar watched the faces in the plane. A feeling of foreboding about what they would find on the ground left all the men on the bench seats isolated within themselves. Some soldiers made the sign of the cross. Kuzniar felt a strange feeling come over him: "I felt as if someone else had taken my hand and made the same sign. At that time

I felt something over my head . . . something very powerful, difficult to describe, which literally, slowly, physically flowed over me, from my head to my feet, and I found a strange peace which from that moment never left me during the whole battle."

Private Michal Lasek in plane 62 had withdrawn into himself. He did not feel good about the coming operation but he was not alone in his feelings; *nobody* was talking. Near the door sat Lieutenant Tice, the American volunteer. Besides thinking about leading a platoon in combat, Tice had other things on his mind: his Scottish wife was pregnant. Private Mieczyslaw Chwastek was unnerved by the fact that he was jumping number thirteen in his stick, but took comfort from a picture of the Madonna of Ostra Brama that he had carried in his army paybook. It was a photograph of a copy of the painting that the men of the 3rd Battalion had made, and then presented to the chapel of Mary Stuart's castle in Falkland, where the 3rd Battalion's headquarters had been located. Chwastek sat across the aisle from his friend Lasek. Together the two men had come out of Russia, wound through the middle east to Scotland, trained as paratroopers and then were assigned to the same platoon. They exchanged no words. Lasek was so distracted by the thoughts of what might lay ahead of him that he did not realize, or even care, that this day was his 21st birthday.

Captain Lorys calmly enjoyed the view and watched General Sosabowski. The Brigade commander seemed to be in good humor and moved about the cabin of plane 100. Several times he went forward to talk to the pilot.

The stickmaster, Lieutenant Dyrda, forgot his usual fears about whether his parachute would open or not. He was worried about the Dakotas. They would have to reduce their airspeed to 110 miles per hour for the jump, and did not have self-sealing fuel tanks. Dyrda was terrified by the thought of death by fire. Dyrda tried to put his fears aside, for he knew that he would have to be the first out of the airplane.

After reaching the English Channel, General Sosabowski reached under his seat and pulled out a crate of oranges. With a smile he gave one to each man. Captain Lorys was astonished. "Where did he get them? Oranges were so scarce in England that it was some time since I had even seen one."

The Brigade's Chief of Staff, Major Ryszard Malaszkiewicz, drilled the headquarters personnel in plane 111 over and over again on the Brigade's orders and mission. The Brigade's command group had been divided into three, and was flying in as many aircraft. If for any reason General Sosabowski did not arrive at the battlefield, the deputy commander, Lieutenant Colonel Jachnik, would take command. If both Sosabowski and Jachnik were missing, Major Malaszkiewicz would take command. All of their staffs had full knowledge of the orders and operational plans. After the drill some men feel asleep, drained by stress and tension. Near the front of the cabin a soldier was writing something on a piece of paper. Malaszkiewicz gave him a sharp look and he hid the paper. Writing anything was strictly forbidden.

Over the Channel some aircraft lost their supply containers. Watching the brightly colored parachutes descend into the sea, the paratroopers wondered what unit would be missing needed equipment once it was on the ground. Reaching the coastline, the formation flowed over Belgium. The men's interest increased as they flew over the colored checkerboard fields divided by streams and roads. This was the first time in years that the men had seen the Continent. The nearer they flew towards the enemy, the more the landscape became littered with smoking ruins, smashed aircraft and vehicles.

While the men were watching this violent world go by, below their planes an unusual incident happened. As plane 77 tried to climb over a patch of turbulent air, it stalled. With the aircraft flying nose down, the pilot went into a slow roll to recover. One of the Polish paratroopers, thinking that the plane was in imminent danger of crashing, hooked his static line and pushed past 2nd Lieutenant Leon Prochowski and out the open door.

The stickmaster of plane 43 was Sergeant Wojciech Juhas, a bull-necked, barrel-chested native of Zakopane. Instructor at a ski school before the war, Juhas had guided escaping Polish soldiers across the border until the Gestapo put a reward of 2,000 Reichsmarks on his head. A man of incredible strength and energy, the sergeant was intimidating, but his physical strength was matched by that of his character. He was respected and well liked by his motivated sappers. A combat veteran of the Polish and French campaigns, Juhas lived for the day when he could return to his beloved mountains.

In the same "V" of aircraft as Juhas', 2nd Lieutenant Mieczyslaw Grunbaum wondered how his men were bearing up in plane 42. The tough engineer officer was reassured when he saw one of his men on his knees shortening the fuses for his bangalore torpedos.

At the Hartenstein Hotel, the Polish liaison team again picked up their radios and went off to meet the Brigade's parachute lift. This time a British colonel told them that the Brigade was definitely on the way; he had received a message that it had taken off from England.

As they moved south from the hotel, a passing patrol of Red Devils cautioned the Poles to "keep a lookout for snipers." After they had moved a few meters farther, bullets whistled past them, and the Poles wondered whether these were aimed shots or strays. Correspondent Swiecicki angrily reflected that there was no safety, not even near Division Headquarters.

Another British patrol emerged from the woods and began to argue among themselves about the exact hideaway of a sniper they were hunting, and then gave a warning to the Poles about his possible location in a clearing up ahead. Reaching the area in question, the mortars and artillery stopped "as if in spite." Captain Zwolanski sprinted across the road, and was pursued by bullets from a machine pistol. In an instant, Lieutenant Pronobis, Swiecicki and the three radio men followed at a run. The Schmiesser continued to chatter as the men disappeared over a rise. Stopping to catch their breath, they thought they were safe until they saw fountains of earth erupt all around the slit trenches they had tumbled into. From a nearby dugout, curses in Polish were hurled at the sniper. Marek Swiecicki recognized the voice as that of Captain Mackowiak, who had stayed in the British artillery positions. The captain swore that he would eliminate the "louse," and, refusing any help, disappeared into the brush. From time to time, Mackowiak's progress was measured by the bushes swaying along his path. An hour later the artillery officer appeared. Mackowiak told his comrades that he had found the "bastard" in a corner house, and that the road was now safe.

Benjamin Jansen returned to Driel with his horse and cart to pick up the farmer. Looking down Molenstraat, Jansen saw German troops the entire length of the road. Leaning his bicycle against a fence, he saw his benefactor's cow, badly in need of milking. As he walked to the animal, his feet kicked shell casings from fighter planes in the shaggy grass. As the pail began to fill with milk, he again heard the sound of a formation of approaching aircraft. Once again, German anti-aircraft fire began hammering at yet another supply drop. A few meters away, a bundle of blankets that dropped from the sky without a parachute tumbled across the meadow.

Still flying solo, plane 98 was approaching the Betuwe. The American crew chief was calmly chewing a wad of gum. He looked over at Kaczmarek and said, "All in a days work." The casual American had a calming effect on Kaczmarek, who wondered what had happened to all of the other airplanes. Had they received a recall signal? The Polish officer decided that the pilot "knew what he was doing," and did not give the matter any further thought.

13

Polish Soldiers To Liberate Us?

1710 Hours, September 21, to
0100 Hours, September 22, 1944

At Holland's border with Belgium, a group of 113 vehicles caught in the massive traffic jam were distinguished from the many others only by the black formation sign with the stylized white diving eagle painted on their fenders. Standing around them were 14 officers and 186 men wearing gray berets with Polish eagles on them. The soldiers were impatient because for days they had been tangled in traffic and shunted off to side roads while XXX Corps and the 101st Airborne struggled to keep the corridor open. At 1615 hours, they received the first news about their Brigade since the operation began, through one of Marek Swiecicki's dispatches on the BBC. A half hour later, a formation of Dakotas passed over the convoy. The traffic-bound paratroopers hardly took notice, since in the previous few days they had seen other, larger formations pass overhead. The men certainly would have shown more interest had they known that it was their Brigade passing above.

Inside the planes in the formation, apprehension grew as the Dakotas began to slowly descend to jump altitude. What little conversation there was ceased as the men blew their noses to relieve the pain in their ears caused by the changing air pressure. In the distance, ineffectual flak rose from pockets of Germans who had not yet been rolled over by the "airborne carpet." Those paratroopers who looked out of the windows saw the landscape becoming more and more sinister-looking as the planes flew north.

Marek Swiecicki and the Polish liaison team reached the last artillery positions near the Oosterbeek church. The situation was quiet, and the correspondent looked out over the polder that ran flat and unbelievably open to the edge of the Neder Rijn river 400 meters away. The Poles settled into a 75mm howitzer pit to wait for a promised jeep. Two of the gunners concentrated their attention on the playing cards held tightly in their hands while the rest of the crew tried to wash themselves in a small ditch filled with dirty water. Swiecicki kept his eyes focused on the southern bank of the river, where the Brigade was supposed to land.

Lieutenant Kaczmarek stood at the open door of his solitary Dakota. The red light was on, and the paratroopers were ready to go. The plane had been dogged by light flak since passing Nijmegen, and now the heavy anti-aircraft guns across the river in Oosterbeek were finding the range. The green light flashed, and Kaczmarek pushed himself out the door. Surrounded by puffs of smoke, he waited for his parachute to open. A sudden jerk, and he was drifting to the ground. Surrounded by "so much noise and tracer," the lieutenant thought that "every gun was aimed directly at me." The "feeling of peace and contentment" that had always followed the opening of his parachute during training jumps was replaced by a prayer that he might get down as fast as possible. Kaczmarek's heels dug into the ground, plopping him on his rear end and driving the rim of his helmet into the bridge of his nose. The firing stopped "as if cut by a scissor," as he picked himself up with stars in his eyes and tears rolling down his cheeks.

Releasing his harness and getting out of his jump smock, Kaczmarek saw other members of his platoon approaching. They had already recovered one of the supply containers. A billowing colored parachute betrayed the location of another, half out of the water and embedded in the mud of a drainage ditch. While some of the men began to wrestle with the long white cylinder, others spread out to investigate the now quiet, seemingly peaceful orchards and pastures.

"In Driel it was a beautiful day," Cora Baltussen has recalled. "The last unharvested orchards were laden with fruit. The sun was shining." Cora was on the dike with other members of the Dutch Red Cross, looking for survivors from yet another plane that was shot down. It was one of those September days that reinforced the people of the Betuwe's belief that theirs was one of the richest areas of The Netherlands. She was torn by the extremes: "Beautiful sunshine, beautiful nature, horrible fighting."

Back at his family's house near the Driel dike, Benjamin Jansen was discussing the supply drop with his brother when they again heard the drone of airplanes and bark of anti-aircraft guns. Going to the large dike, the brothers watched still another formation of Dakotas flying over the Betuwe. The heavy German anti-aircraft guns from across the river joined the flak from Elst and the railroad bridge. From the fields surrounding the village, machine guns and even rifles joined the din. The tight formation was surrounded by puffs of smoke and intersected by necklaces of twinkling tracers. Then, as the brothers watched, "in the wink of an eye" the sky filled with parachutes.

Across the river, Marek Swiecicki heard the first approach of the Allied fighter planes providing support, and the furious staccato of anti-aircraft guns accompanying the even rumble of engines of the approaching formation of Dakotas. The crackle of machine guns from across the river joined the "concert," followed by the boom of the German heavy guns in Oosterbeek. Parachutes appeared behind the Dakotas. The memory of the glider lift sent hot flashes through the correspondent's body, and he hoped that the Brigade would not share the same fate. The large dike that protected the Betuwe from the river also hid the events in Driel. Cadet Pajak set up his radio and started repeating the call, "Hallo Cuba, Hallo Cuba, This is Roman, Can you hear me?" The radio replied with static, and the signaler repeated his call.

A frightened young German prisoner flushed from a house, clad in long underwear and a Sten gun in his back, was brought to Lieutenant Kaczmarek. "I was asleep, and they managed to escape" was the reply to Kaczmarek's question about the whereabouts of the rest of his unit. Renewed fire and the sound of approaching aircraft distracted the lieutenant from his interrogation. A formation of Dakotas was over the fields a kilometer to the east, on the other side of the village. Then the sky suddenly blossomed with parachutes. Kaczmarek leveled his Sten gun and told the prisoner, "We are going through the village to see if you are telling the truth. If you run or betray us, you'll get a bullet in the back." Walking through the village, the Poles met only enthusiastic civilians waving orange ribbons and pressing fruit and flowers on them from their neat houses.

From her vantage point on the dike, Cora saw the sky over the Betuwe "filled with hundreds of green parachutes in the wake of the Dakotas. Men were running among bursting shells and tracer bullets trying to get organized." Cora hopped on her "poor old bike" with wooden tires, and rode in the direction of the parachutists 3 kilometers away.

The Poles jumped through a whirlwind of anti-aircraft fire into soft farm fields divided by ditches and wire cattle fences. Some parts of the drop zone were covered by a crossfire from the railroad embankment and pockets of German infantry that had not been withdrawn to Elst to block the Allies advancing from Nijmegen. The Poles had to fight for their drop zone. Shucking their parachutes, the soldiers tried to carry out their tasks however the situation permitted. Some units gathered their containers and moved to their assembly areas, while others were immediately locked into combat with the Germans, who were raising such havoc on the open fields. By 1725 hours, the last paratrooper had touched down on the soil of Holland.

The section of drop zone where the 3rd Battalion landed had the most trouble. Most of its sticks were so hard-pressed that they could only with difficulty gather a few of their containers. Lieutenant Smaczny and his 8th Company was the first unit to reach 3rd Battalion's assembly area at the crossroads one kilometer south of De Nevel. The 8th had taken two prisoners, frightened boys of seventeen or eighteen years of age. After Smaczny gave them cigarettes, and assured them in his flawless German that they wouldn't be killed, they began talking freely. The young prisoners said that they had been billeted on a farm and for two days had been waiting for more paratroopers to be dropped.

A few minutes later, the 9th Company, commanded by Captain Ignacy Gazurek, arrived. Smaczny asked him if he had seen Captain Sobocinski, or anybody else from the Battalion's command group. Gazurek replied in the negative, and added that he was missing between thirty and forty of his own men. The 7th Company trailed in, led by Lieutenant Wieslaw Szczygiel of the Engineer Company. The company commander and over forty men from the 7th Company were missing. It was decided that Captain Gazurek would take over command of the Battalion until Captain Sobocinski showed up. A few minutes later, Lieutenant Slesicki and twenty soldiers from the Battalion Headquarters appeared, but they had no information, only questions about the missing men. The Battalion could muster less than 200 men. They started towards the ferry down the road that they had been briefed on, hoping that the missing sticks would be found.

General Sosabowski had gathered his headquarters, and discovered that his entire staff had landed safely. The signalers had managed to contact all sub-units except for the 1st Battalion and the Anti-tank Squadron. When the corporal working the radio set reported this, Sosabowski replied, "Well done, well done. Keep calling." In a matter of ten minutes, the Anti-tank Squadron reported, leaving everybody wondering what had happened to the 1st Battalion, which had yet to respond. Though nobody spoke, everybody had the same fears: Had they dropped in another location? Had they been attacked in flight? Were they prisoners of the Germans, or dead? Captain Lorys remembered seeing the parachutes drifting beyond the railroad embankment, and hoped that that was not the fate of the missing sticks.

As Cora Baltussen rode her bicycle south, she heard much shouting in a strange language above the din of battle. At Honingveld she saw Allied soldiers 200 meters away. Since she was one of the few English speakers in Driel, Cora went to greet them.

Smiling, she said, "Welcome, Tommies. I am from the Red Cross, what can we do?" The soldiers looked at the Dutch woman seriously and spoke among themselves in an odd language that perplexed her. A red-haired officer then replied in accented English, "We are Polish." The perplexed Cora asked, "Polish soldiers to liberate us? Is that possible?" Lieutenant Tadeusz Lang firmly responded, "Yes, that is possible."

Lieutenants Dyrda and Lang stared at the woman wearing an apron and a Red Cross armband. The Poles had been briefed not to trust anybody. In the background Cora noticed an older soldier with a mustache, leaning against a tree and munching an apple, curiously watching the scene. Asked about the location of the Baarskamp farm, Cora became frantic and tried to dissuade the paratroopers from going there, fearing danger. The day before, a platoon of Germans with machine guns had occupied the farm.

The older man walked over to the group and carefully looked the woman over. Lieutenant Dyrda turned to him and said in Polish, "I think she's all right." Cora then told them of the British paratroopers hidden at the family house, and sent her brother to go and get the Irishman Cooney.

More reports came in to the command group. No one had any idea, or dared to verbalize their horrible thoughts, about what had happened to the missing troops. But on the drop zone, casualties turned out to be surprisingly light. Only four bodies of those killed during the jump had been found. One corpse caused great revulsion and anger in the many men who saw it. A signaler from the 2nd Battalion landed with his parachute tangled in a pear tree. While he hung suspended, arms pinned to his sides and feet dangling above the ground, a German soldier had pulled the helpless paratrooper's commando dagger from its sheath and cut his throat. The soldiers' fury at the sad sight of their comrade was compounded upon seeing the contents of his pockets scattered around him. A deck of playing cards was strewn beneath his boots, discarded when other treasures such as cigarettes or candy might be had. The German who had committed the atrocity was dealt with quickly by some troopers who had seen him trying to get back to cover.

When Cooney arrived, the old man with the mustache stood in front of him and fired questions at the Red Devil: "What is your unit? Who is your commander? What is the situation?" As Cora watched, Cooney braced to attention and replied to all of the questions in a precise, military manner. The questioning lasted less than two minutes and ended with Cooney's words: "The Baltussens can be trusted."

In a good mood because of few casualties, Sosabowski's staff immediately became more talkative. Walking towards the village, they rapidly questioned Cora. The older, mustachioed soldier, now identified as "the General," told Cora in thickly accented English that his men needed a field hospital. He then gave instructions that the civilians were to stay in their homes, stay down when there was shooting, keep their windows closed, and not do anything beyond that. Cora was astonished by the Poles' knowledge of the local geography and impressed with their discipline and control.

When asked about the ferry, Cora replied that it was gone. Sosabowski kept repeating that the situation was surely critical, and that they must get across the river that night. Cora mentioned that there were usually some small boats tried up by the river, and, indeed, the British had been crossing during the past few days.

As the Polish officers turned to go to their assembly point, Cora Baltussen went off to organize a dressing station for their wounded. Aside from Dr. Van den Burg's "hospital" set up in the parish house, there was a parochial school in Driel. Until a week before the battle, it was occupied by priests who had been put out of their boarding houses in western Holland, so it already had beds. The school had not yet opened for classes because of the military situation that September, and stood empty in the center of the village.

When the headquarters group arrived at the Baarskamp farm, they found it deserted except for one of its workers, twenty-two-year-old Klaas Beukema. The Poles asked him for a horse and cart for the wounded. Beukem took it, with three wounded paratroopers, to the parish house. When he returned, the Poles fell back on their their instructions not to trust anyone and told him to remain in the farmhouse. Other wounded paratroopers were loaded on horse-drawn* wagons, to go with the rest of the Brigade to the river.

At the Baarskamp farm, Father Bednorz met the other Brigade chaplains. He told them about the loss of his kit bag with the field altar, but from his smock's breast pocket he pulled out a purple stole and bottle of oil; he still had the implements needed to perform the last rites. Bednorz then went off in the direction of the church steeple to meet the town's pastor.

The chaplain knocked on the door of the rectory and smiled at the thought of what the cellar might have in it. Father Poelman opened the door and looked in bewilderment as the man who stood before him in a camouflage smock and net-covered helmet, speaking in English, told him that he was a chaplain of the Polish Army. The shocked Dutch pastor asked, "What brings a Polish chaplain here?" Bednorz replied with a smirk, "The sky!" Father Poelman then understood: the paratroopers he had seen jumping were Polish. The priests then hugged and kissed each other's cheeks. The Dutch priest ran back into the rectory, shouting, "Wait!" He returned with a beautiful antique crucifix and pressed it into Bednorz' hands with the words "I give this cross to you, Father, as a remembrance of our liberation from the Nazis."

Now safely on the ground, the paratroopers marveled at the beautiful jump that the Troop Carriers had provided for the Brigade. This was in marked contrast to the training jumps that had been made during the summer, when far too many troopers were injured, and some killed, during exercises that left the units of the Polish Parachute Brigade scattered all over the English Midlands. Whatever doubts the Poles had had about their American Allies, particularly about their apparent lack of seriousness and maturity, were dispelled by the way the pilots doggedly held formation as they flew into the heavy German fire. That the Poles were grouped so well was a testament to this, the best jump the Brigade had ever made. Despite the normal confusion during the jump, the sight of two aircraft on fire still holding formation to give the paratroopers a

* Ten soldiers had received medical attention on the drop zone, and most of them returned to their units after having their wounds dressed. Those injured in the jump outnumbered the wounded in battle. The Polish Airborne Medical Company treated twenty-six men injured during the jump, ten of whom had broken bones. The others had sprained arms or legs.

chance to jump was engraved forever in the minds of those who saw it. In fact, two aircraft of the 315th Troop Carrier Group crashed in flames as they struggled south, killing the crews. Three more Dakotas were damaged beyond repair. Many others suffered battle damage and brought wounded airmen back with them.

Whatever good thoughts the Poles in Driel had about the American troop carriers, the sentiments were certainly not shared by the commander of the 1st Battalion, Major Marian Tonn. His aircraft landed in England at the same time the rest of the Brigade jumped at Driel. The scene was frantic at the Spanhoe operations room, while reports continued to pour in and the Major tried to sort out what had happened. Reports of aircraft that had lost the formation, or had been forced down in Belgium after dropping at Driel only added to the confused situation. Two planes carrying 1st Battalion troops did not return, and in their place two that had carried troops from the 2nd Battalion landed, one riddled with bullet holes. The assurances given by the Air Force that things would be all right carried little credence with the Major when he saw some of the Dakotas take off.

At 2000, Major Tonn returned to the empty Brigade Headquarters building in Stamford, where he learned that eleven 3rd Battalion aircraft had returned to Saltby. Tonn had the Polish supply officer attached to the Brigade headquarters send a report describing the confused situation to the Polish Chief-of-Staff in London. The cable went on to say that they could provide no information about General Sosabowski or the 1st Airborne Division. Tonn stated that he would try to join the rest of the Brigade, assuming that they had indeed jumped in Holland. This done, the major sent requests to have all of the returned Polish paratroopers assembled at one airfield and to have their parachutes exchanged. This last item especially disturbed Tonn: a damp chute will open very slowly, or incorrectly, if at all, and the parachutes had lain on the runways for three days in the rain and mists.

In Driel over 950 paratroopers had managed to assemble within an hour of the drop. Despite the crushing news that the ferry was gone, getting across the river was General Sosabowski's predominant thought. Alternatives were immediately sought, and the brigade sappers were sent to search the river bank for any boats that could be used. As the paratroopers began to move towards the river, they found the soft farmland difficult to traverse. The men, heavily burdened with personal equipment, also had to lend a hand with the heavy items recovered from the containers. Even the surgeons, whose skilled hands would surely be called upon to perform delicate operations, grappled with the awkward containers. It was even more difficult for the mortar crews to move the tools of their trade across the fields. The small wheels on the ponderous trollies kept bogging down in the soft earth.

For the moment, the Germans did not disturb the Polish movement towards the river. Their attack against the British in Oosterbeek was not only hindered by the British long-range artillery from Nijmegen that now supported the Red Devils, but also by the Allied threat from the Waal river. The German assault was diluted by the necessity of having to rush reinforcements south. Major Hans Peter Knaust's Panzergrenadier Battalion, reinforced with Panther tanks and Sturmgeschütze from the Hohenstaufen Division, was sent to Elst. They had been there less than an hour when the new wave of paratroopers landed in Driel. This event came as a shock to the Germans who, surmised that the newcomers' mission, aside from reinforcing the British, was to cut off the Frundsberg Division from Arnhem and to attempt to take the Arnhem bridge.

The Hohenstaufen Division commander, Lieutenant Colonel Harzer, was tasked with eliminating the new airborne landing. Harzer began transferring units that had either been used against the British in Oosterbeek, or had just arrived in Arnhem, to that end. First to receive movement orders were Flak Brigade Swoboda and Artillery Regiment 191 (including SS Werferabteilung 102 "Nickman," which fielded two batteries of Nebelwerfer rocket mortars) and a battalion each of machine guns, Luftwaffe ground personnel, naval infantry and Dutch SS troops. This motley group was collectively given the designation "Sperrverband [Blocking Group] Harzer," and was under the command of Colonel Gerhard of the Hohenstaufen Division.

The sun was already below the horizon as the Polish paratroopers approached the Driel dike. The impact of the events of the last days left Lance Sergeant Cadet Hrehorow shaken. The three nerve-wracking days of waiting, the flight and then the jump with the sights of the killed and wounded on the drop zone and the sounds of combat, all had taken their toll. Shaken and dry-mouthed, the platoon leader now regretted having filled his canteen with Scotch whisky, rather than black coffee or water. Not only was the occasion inappropriate for alcohol, it undoubtedly would have made the cadet's physical and mental condition even worse.

As Hrehorow passed by the neat farmhouses, he stopped before a pretty young girl and said, "*Wasser.*" The girl, some seventeen years old, scurried into a house and came back, not with a glass of water, but with one of cold milk. The fresh milk took Hrehorow by surprise, but then he remembered instructions not to trust any food or drink offered by the local population. Parched, the cadet motioned without another thought for the girl to take a drink herself. She put the glass to her lips and took a sip. As Hrehorow took the glass from the girl's hand he noticed a tear rolling down her cheek and hurt in her eyes. The cadet finished the milk in a few gulps and, without giving the girl another look, passed the glass to her and wordlessly rejoined the column.

Lieutenant Kaczmarek led his platoon directly to the ferry site. Reaching the dike, which stood 14 meters over Driel, the supply officer met Captain Piotr Budziszewski, commander of the Brigade's engineer company. His sappers had failed to find any usable boats. It was now 1900, and in the failing light the officers stood on the paved east-west dike road and observed the terrain. A small dike, 4 meters high and separated by 120 meters of sloping boggy polder, paralleled the main dike. The terrain beyond the small dike was a muddy flood plain that ran to the edge of the Neder Rijn. The river was tidal, and varied between 200 and 275 meters in width. Along the shore, stone flood spurs ran into the river to prevent erosion by the powerful current. The land between the village and the river was too boggy for growing crops, but was used either for grazing or for dredging clay to be baked into brick. A cobblestone road ran between the ferry site and road atop the Driel dike.

The rest of the Brigade reached the large dike one kilometer east of the ferry, near the De Nevel farm. General Sosabowski established himself in a barn on the north slope of the large dike. Across the river, Oosterbeek presented a spooky, foreboding scene. Columns of thick smoke rising from the village formed a black drape against the darkening sky. Orange tongues of flame were joined by the white flashes of explosions. The ripping sounds of Spandaus and Schmiessers, answered by the slower popping of Sten guns, drifted across the river.

At the ferry site, the two Polish officers carefully looked over the north shore. There was little sign of life, but indistinct voices drifted back across the river. On the bank opposite the Driel ferry dock, two vertical posts stuck out of the glassy surface of the river, and were thought to be masts for the sunken ferry (in reality these posts were the remains of the pier for the Arnhem-Heavedorp ferry).

Cupping his hands, Captain Budziszewski shouted as loud as he could toward the north bank. There was no reply. Budziszewski cocked the hammer of a flare gun, pointed it straight up in the air, and pulled the trigger. The same instant that the rocket whooshed into the sky, a stream of tracer bullets poured from the north bank onto the ferry site. The Polish troopers scattered like a flock of blackbirds as machine-gun bullets ricocheted off the paving stones. Lieutenant Kaczmarek lay curled up against the embankment thinking that "we would never come out alive."

After an eternal fifteen minutes, the fusillade stopped. With no urging, the soldiers scurried back to the main dike. To Kaczmarek's surprise, all made it unscathed. Moving east along the dike, the lieutenant ran into General Sosabowski. Kaczmarek reported that the ferry site on the north bank "seemed to be in the hands of the Germans." He wryly added, "Either that, or the British don't know we're here yet."

On the north bank of the river, the agitated Polish liaison team kept calling "Cuba" endlessly on their radio. Static or guttural German voices were the only replies coming through the headset. Hours had passed, and General Urquhart's orders to "contact the Polish Brigade as quickly as possible" weighed heavily on Captain Zwolanski. They had seen the Brigade land during the afternoon, but it might have never existed according to the airwaves. It was late. The group kept changing its location around the artillery positions, trying to obtain contact, but with no result. Finally, Zwolanski said, "I have to get across the river." Lieutenant Pronobis replied, "Why you? There are three of us here, we'll draw match sticks." Zwolanski chuckled. "That doesn't mean much. I received the order, I will carry it out." With this the captain took out three match sticks and let Pronobis and the correspondent draw. To Marek Swiecicki, "It seemed that he kept the shortest, confirming his mandate."

Cadet Tadeusz Herman was a prize catch for the Germans. Not only did they have a prisoner from the latest parachute drop, but he carried the equipment and had the bearing of an officer. After an unsuccessful interrogation on the spot, the captors realized that this prisoner would be of interest to higher headquarters.

Three guards were to escort the prisoner to Arnhem. None of them were SS troops. The man walking to the left of Herman showed himself to be a rather "decent" German. He had mentioned to Herman that he had spent time in England, and the two began to converse in English. Walking through Elden on their way to the bridge, Herman asked the man, "If I ran, would you shoot me?" The guard replied, "Well, I wouldn't kill you, but of course I'd have to shoot at you. The one in back of us,

I wouldn't worry about him, he's a musician, he won't shoot. But the corporal, he'd kill you for sure." The thought of the corporal cast away any of the cadet's intentions of escaping.

Reaching the Arnhem bridge, the party walked down a path cleared through the wreckage of SS AA 9's vehicles. As they moved down the long ramp on the Arnhem side of the bridge, Herman, despite the darkness, made out the sad sight of bodies, clad in Denison smocks, lying crumpled in the streets. Then, out of the darkness, came the roar of diesel engines and the clatter and screech of steel. Tanks were moving south across the bridge, fast and without lights. All along the bridge men quickly ran out of the way of the monsters. Cadet Herman did not stop at the bridge railing, but vaulted over it. Shots rang out while the cadet, not counting how many, scrambled over walls and ran down alleys. Cadet Herman had escaped, but was recaptured a day later. An Allied paratrooper had finally crossed the Neder Rijn over the Arnhem bridge.

The Germans started to react to the movements around Driel. They illuminated the polder with flares and started bombarding the south bank with mortars and artillery. While the fire was unobserved and caused no deaths or serious wounds, the shells screeching through the darkness invited terror among the many troops who had never before been under enemy fire. Spandaus from the north bank continued to sweep the dike with tracer. Fortunately, fear did not turn into panic, and the platoons on the dike and in the orchards awaited their further orders with a patience that was almost painful.

The British had promised Captain Zwolanski a dinghy, but there was no sign of it, or of the officer who made the promise. The Polish troopers sent to find a boat returned only with the useless information that all they discovered was artillery fire and German positions. Zwolanski went to the command post and stripped off his uniform. With Lieutenant Pronobis and Marek Swiecicki, he went to the bank of the Neder Rijn. After sitting silently a few moments, he rose and waded into the water, and was soon swallowed by the darkness.

At 2230 the artillery fire falling near Driel slackened. Captain Lorys was reconnoitering the river bank by the small dike. Suddenly, in the darkness a human form rose from the river. Startled, the operations officer stared at the unusual sight, and then recognized it to be Captain Zwolanski. Lorys drew his silver flask and the trembling liaison officer took "a couple of gulps" of Scotch, and then was led to General Sosabowski's command post. A blanket, pair of trousers and a mug of tea were brought for the shivering messenger.

General Sosabowski listened as Captain Zwolanski repeated General Urquhart's orders: "The ferry is in German hands—probably destroyed. . . .General Urquhart demands a speedy crossing—this will be done on rafts supplied by the 1st Airborne Division. . . .The British will launch a counterattack to secure the northern bank to allow the Polish Brigade to cross, after which the Poles will take over a section of the division's defensive perimeter."

After relaying the orders, Captain Zwolanski talked at length about how the battle was going and his experiences. The account was tragic. That morning, the battalion holding the bridge was overrun, and the rest of the Division was bottled up in Oosterbeek, where they lacked all supplies—food, water, medicine and ammunition. Help was desperately needed, and the Polish Brigade would have to get across the river as soon as possible. Zwolanski went on to confirm the tragic landing of the second glider lift, but described how the remainder of the anti-tank squadron, despite casualties, remained combative and was taking an active part in the defense.

General Sosabowski called together his commanders and made preparations for the crossing. The 3rd Battalion would be the first to go across as soon as the rafts arrived. They would be followed by the 4th Company, the Brigade Headquarters, the special units, and finally by the rest of the 2nd Battalion. All of the mortars and Vickers machine guns would be set up behind the dike to provide covering fire, but any fire would be *only* on Sosabowski's personal orders. As shells again began falling, the units made their preparations.

At the farm where he was sheltering, Benjamin Jansen prepared sleeping places for the villagers he had led from Driel. The women and children would sleep in the cellar and the men in the barn. After dark, there again came the sounds of explosions from the direction of Driel. The shelling became more violent as the night wore on. Refugees passing the farm told Jansen that the Poles had dug in. The farm hand worried about his parents, who had refused to leave the village. As the shelling continued, the men left the barn and went into the cellar to join the women and children. Cramped and fearful, nobody slept that night.

Across the river in Oosterbeek, the Polish Anti-tank Squadron had managed to maintain the same positions it had occupied since the day before. That part of lower Oosterbeek was crowded with troops, and had been under bombardment all day. Though no guns were lost, some of the gun crews had been wounded. While the German guns turned their attention to the sky when the Polish Parachute Brigade dropped, the gun crews improved their positions and left their cramped positions to try to find some food and ammunition. To Bombardier Nosecki, the drop meant that the rest of the squadron had landed. The exhausted gunner hoped that they would come to their assistance, but wondered, "How would they get across? The bridges were no longer in our hands." With the German artillery busy bombarding Driel, the area was now relatively quiet. Nosecki hoped that he might get an hour or two of sleep that night.

Not far from Nosecki, near the command post of the 1st Airlanding Regiment, Royal Artillery, Marek Swiecicki and the rest of the Polish liaison team occupied the corner of a cellar of one of the houses. The night was relatively peaceful; only mortar shells were falling on Oosterbeek. The Germans had shifted their artillery onto the Poles across the river.

The cellar was jammed with sleeping artillerymen. The correspondent and Lieutenant Pronobis sat on wooden boxes in an attempt to keep off of the earthen floor, which had turned into mud. A series of mortar shells fell nearby, shaking the house. Sitting in the dark, the Poles' thoughts were divided between the fate of Captain Zwolanski and the Brigade, and whether or not a shell would hit the house. Cadet Pajak came in to report that he still could not reach the Brigade with his radio. As he looked up at the cadet, Marek Swiecicki felt the top of the crate give way under his shifting weight with a crack and heard the sound of breaking glass. With a curse, the journalist ascertained by flashlight that the sticky substance covering the seat of his pants was jam. Shifting the light beam, Pronobis triumphantly announced that he was sitting on a crate of pickled cucumbers. The Brigade and the bombardment were forgotten as the men enjoyed their first meal since the previous day.

At 0100, an officer of the Royal Engineers crossed to the south bank and repeated the orders and information that had been brought by Captain Zwolanski. He further stated that rafts had to be built, and that one was almost finished. In reality, the information about the rafts was misplaced optimism; British engineers were trying to convert ammunition trailers into rafts by removing the wheels. The improvised vessels did not float long!

The officer returned to the north bank in the dinghy in which he crossed, taking Zwolanski and Lieutenant Colonel Stevens with him. As the Brigade continued to wait at the dike to cross, Captain Budiszewski informed General Sosabowski that one of his men had told him about some rescue dinghies he had purloined from the American Air Force. Now the problem was to find the container that they were packed in, somewhere on the drop zone amid all the other unrecovered containers.

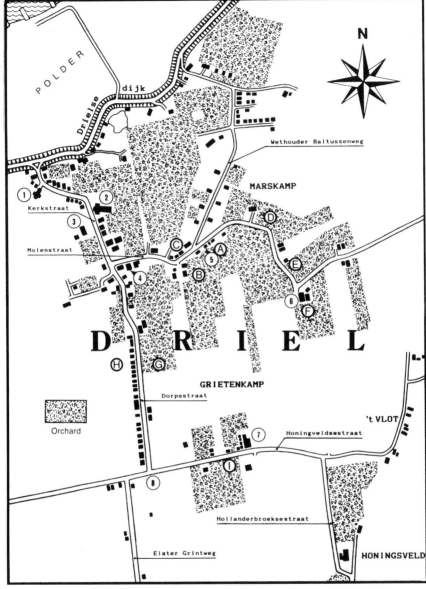

Map courtesy of Jan Bouman

POLISH POSITIONS IN DRIEL, SEPTEMBER 22, 1944

A Headquarters Company, Signals Co., Supply Co.
B Anti-tank Squadron
C 8th and 9th Companies (in reserve)
D 6th Company
E Engineer Company
F 2nd Lieutenant Tice's Platoon (7th Company)
G 5th Company
H 4th Company (platoons in a defensive screen on village's western edge as far north as the Driel Dike)
I 2nd Lieutenant Urbanski's Platoon (7th Company)

1 Dutch Reformed Church
2 Roman Catholic Church
3 Parish House (used as hospital)
4 Catholic Boys School (used as hospital)
5 The Beijer house (Sosabowski's headquarters)
6 The Baarskamp farm
7 The Baltussen house and factory
8 Intersection with anti-tank mines laid

14

And Then All Hell Broke Loose

0200 to 1330 Hours, September 22, 1944

As the black sky to the east began to show streaks of gray, the Polish paratroopers at the dike gathered their equipment for the march back to Driel. Led by patrols, the Brigade entered the village as the sun was rising and fanned out to prepare a hedgehog defense, waiting for whatever the day might bring. The Brigade Headquarters established itself in a house with an attached barn, the residence of the miller Beijer, on the Molenstraat. The headquarters would be at the center of the hedgehog, and ringed by rifle units.

The 2nd Battalion's rifle companies took positions in the village. The 5th Company was settled into positions in an orchard on Dorpstraat, 500 meters north of the street's intersection with Honingveldsestraat. On the 5th Company's right flank, platoons of the 4th Company were strung north, all the way to the Rijn dike, and formed a defensive screen on the village's western edge. The 6th Company dug into the orchards east of the Brigade's headquarters, and faced the Baarskamp farm 500, meters to the southeast.

The 3rd Battalion's 8th and 9th Companies were to dig into positions in the orchards between Molenstraat and the dike, and act a reserve. The two platoons of the 7th Company were to act as advanced outposts just beyond the village: 2nd Lieutenant Urbanski's platoon was to position itself in an orchard on Honingveldsestraat between the intersection with Dorpstraat and the Baltussen factory, and 2nd Lieutenant Tice's platoon would hold the Baarskamp farm.

As 2nd Lieutenant Tice marched his twenty-eight men on the tree-lined road to the Baarskamp farm, Private Lasek walked with his friend Private Chwastek. Passing a farm 150 meters away from their objective,

Lasek saw Polish airborne sappers preparing their defenses. Some of them, obvious combat veterans of the Polish and French Campaigns, were busy cutting the wire cattle fences behind their positions. Lasek, who had never seen combat, came to the correct conclusion that the sappers were making sure that they had a way out of their positions should they be forced to withdraw. Lasek hoped that his American platoon leader would provide the same cunning leadership. Walking a few meters farther, the platoon came to a bend in the road and there, ahead of them, stood the Baarskamp farm, a large brick farmhouse next to a gigantic brick barn with a smaller shed nearby.

The Polish paratroopers quickly took over the Baarskamp, setting up a 3-inch mortar in the yard in front of the farmhouse. In back of the house was a large orchard of plum trees, edged by ditches that ran south. Tice ordered his men to dig their foxholes at the edge of the orchard, just in back of the farmhouse. Lasek was disturbed by this deployment. Aside from an observer for the mortar at the southern edge of the orchard, nobody could see more than a few meters into the kaleidoscope of tree trunks and green leaves. Even the neat paths between the trees were obscured by the branches hanging heavy with ripe fruit.

Within Driel, there was a flurry of activity among the special units while the rifle companies dug in. The Brigade's chief medical officer, Major Dr. Jan Golba, sought the best possible location to set up his field hospital. During the night, the injured and wounded had been carried on farm carts to two temporary dressing stations that had been set up in the field, but these had been torn down as the Brigade moved back to Driel. Although Dr. Van den Burg's hospital did have thirty beds, it was primitive, and did not even have running water. The Catholic boys' school on Molenstraat had five large rooms, where the Polish doctors felt sixty wounded could be accommodated if the need arose. The parish house could serve several functions: as a dressing station for the lightly wounded, a place where the more seriously wounded could await evacuation, and for those beyond treatment to die in peace.

As the morning passed, more and more men straggled in from their units to the dressing stations with sprained limbs and even brain concussions suffered during the drop. The soldiers had tried to carry out their duties; only when their pain became unbearable did they leave their positions to have the injuries they had suffered the day before treated.

Shortly before 0600, the Brigade's signalers in Driel made contact with their comrades in Oosterbeek. From the barn attached to General

Sosabowski's headquarters, Corporal Ignacy Sas, working his WS18/68 radio, reached Cadet Corporal Pajak and the Polish signal team in the Hartenstein's cellar. After confirming General Urquhart's orders, the Polish signalers conversed. Private Wawiorko chattered with his comrades in the Russian slang learned in the Gulags to confuse any Germans who might be listening. The news from Oosterbeek was not good. Cadet Pajak detailed the disastrous glider landing, and ran down the Signal Company's casualties in killed and wounded, including the multiple wounds suffered by Private Bronislaw Paulski. But the conversation was cut short: Private Wawiorko was rousted from the signal center and sent to lay telephone lines. With telephone communications established between sub-units, the Brigade could free its radio nets and extend the life of the radio batteries.

At 0600 hours, Sosabowski ordered 2nd Lieutenant Jerzy Bereda-Fialkowski, commander of the 3rd Battalion's reconnaissance platoon, to take three men and try to contact units of the British Second Army, which should have arrived somewhere near Nijmegen. Bereda chose three men. After drawing hand grenades, they left Driel on bicycles to waves of their comrades.

Beyond the hamlet of Honingsveld, the patrol considered itself in enemy territory. The tense troopers kept watch in all directions, noting any places they could use for cover in the flat countryside. As they approached the crossroads outside of Elst, the patrol looked as four German tanks moved east towards Valburg and two armored cars drove north towards Driel. Watching the village, the patrol estimated that there were fifty Germans in the village itself. Knowing that the Brigade depended on their success in meeting the Second Army, Lieutenant Bereda ordered the patrol to move towards Valburg as quickly as possible.

The three Poles on bicycles cautiously entered Valburg and, to their great surprise, the citizens flocked into the street to greet the "liberation army." The Dutch made the sign of the cross and showered the Poles with joyous greetings. The patrol did not know how to react to the mixed laughter of young girls and the tear-filled faces of their elders. Bereda's sense of mission prevailed, however, and the Poles pedaled on through the town.

At the same time, General Sosabowski was giving his orders to 2nd Lieutenant Bereda, two miles south of the Nijmegen bridge, the 5 Troop, C Squadron, 2nd Household Cavalry Regiment turned over the engines of its armored vehicles. The evening before, the unit's commander, Captain Lord Richard Wrottesley, received orders to contact the Polish

Parachute Brigade in Driel. The Household Cavalry was the Guards Armored Division's reconnaissance unit, and had made the GARDEN force's first contacts with the 101st and 82nd Airborne Divisions. For the past two days, C Squadron had enjoyed the duty of escorting lorries carrying loot from the massive Wehrmacht supply dump at Oss. It was hoped that the troop (two Daimler "Dingo" scout cars and two Daimler armored cars) could take advantage of the morning mist, and by traveling west, bypass the German defenders at Elst to reach the Neder Rijn.

In Driel, General Sosabowski spoke with Cora Baltussen and strongly recommended that the Dutch evacuate the village. If anybody had to stay behind (he strongly emphasized these should not be women or children), they were to remain inside with the windows shuttered. Cora was struck with the seriousness of the General's questions about the village and the surrounding area. The paratroopers then borrowed wagons from the Baltussens and their neighbors so that they could gather supply containers, many of which were still scattered about the drop zone. While many of the citizens packed their most valued possessions and began leaving the village, Cora went with some of her neighbors to the parish house. There they made preparations at the improvised hospital for what might be the worst days the village had ever seen.

Having dealt with the Dutch, and finished his work at his headquarters, Sosabowski wanted to check on his men. With no other means of transportation available, the General pedaled off on a ladies' bicycle that he had found leaning against the Beijer farmhouse. Passing by the foxholes of Lieutenant Smaczny's 8th Company, Sosabowski was greeted by soldiers hooting at the sight of their commander traveling in such a manner, and followed by shouts asking if he had a license to operate the vehicle.

At the north end of the village, Lance Corporal Cadet Hrehorow and his platoon were turning a baker's house into a strongpoint. Besides barricading the windows and removing roof tiles for firing slits, the soldiers helped the baker carry some of the family's more valuable possessions into the safety of the cellar. While the cadet was inspecting his platoon's fields of fire, the General rode up on his impromptu transport. In a matter of a "few seconds," Sosabowski appraised the situation and countermanded the company commander's orders. The General told Hrehorow to get his men out of the building and onto the north face of the dike, where they could simultaneously close the road and keep a watch on the river.

2nd Lieutenant Kula's platoon from the 1st Battalion was ordered to occupy a house on the western edge of the village. Moving through the misty streets, Kula remembered Poland five Septembers before as he saw the frightened villagers leaving their homes, taking only what they could carry on their backs. When he reached a house on a small man-made hill, he opened the door without knocking and walked right in. The owners, an elderly couple, were still in bed. Without a word spoken, they quickly gathered a few possessions and joined their neighbors leaving Driel.

Some of the Drielenaren did not leave. Seventeen-year-old Henk te Dorsthorst and friend Anton Clappers helped the paratroopers dig slit trenches in the Greitenkamp meadow near Henk's home on Dorpstraat. Many of te Dorsthorst's neighbors also ignored the order to evacuate. They watched the young Dutchmen help lay M.75 mines on the intersection with Honingveldstraat, closing off the southern entrance to the village.

Lord Wrottesley's two armored cars, with the scout cars at the front and rear of the squadron, had skirted Elst. Several German soldiers had been seen through the mist, but they scurried away in fright and confusion as the swift vehicles pounded up the road. Moving through Valburg without stopping, the cavalry troop overtook Lieutenant Bereda's bicycle patrol. Bereda was disappointed when he learned that Wrottesley's group was, like his, only a reconnaissance patrol, and the British officer had no idea about the progress of the rest of the Second Army. The patrols parted, the Poles wanting to go south towards the Waal, and the Household Cavalry looking north towards the Neder Rijn.

Captain Wrottesley had already been briefed on the fact that the Polish paratroopers were in Driel, and took note of Bereda's warning that there were German tanks and armored cars in the area. The Captain decided to keep pushing west to Andelst, whereupon he turned north. Reaching the dike road beyond Indoornik, his troop turned and followed it through the village of Heteren. From their positions on the dike road, the men of the 4th Company heard the sound of engines coming from the west. General Sosabowski and his bicycle were still at the position. The General watched through binoculars as the vehicles approached unmolested. Seeing the yellow Celanese recognition panels draped on the front of the scout cars, he ordered the anti-tank mines pulled from the dike road. At 0850, No. 5 troop drove into Driel without having exchanged a shot with the enemy.

The British armored cars were escorted to the center of the village and parked near General Sosabowski's headquarters. Captain Wrottesley radioed a report and his route back to his squadron. The squadron commander then dispatched Lieutenant Arthur Young's No. 2 troop to Driel. The concealing mist was beginning to be burned off by the sun, but Young's orders were to join Wrottesley at all costs. Following Wrottesley's route, Young passed some Mark IV tanks near Elst, and picked up some pilots and aircrew who had been shot down over the Betuwe. On the dike road near Heteren, Young saw several Germans across the river. He dispersed them with bursts of machine-gun fire, and drove on towards Driel.

The center of Driel was quiet, and a grocery store near Brigade headquarters was open for business. Private Raschke, his mutton sandwiches now gone, purchased part of a loaf of bread and a piece of cheese. The merchant cheerfully accepted the Allied guilders with Queen Wilhelmina's portrait on them. Returning to the cypher section's corner in miller Beijer's barn, the cryptographer spotted a henhouse. He visited the feathered "grand ladies" and emerged with a few eggs. As he started to fry them on his Primus, 2nd Lieutenant Waclaw Jaworski appeared, smacking his lips, and asked Raschke where he bought the eggs. Raschke replied that he had "borrowed" them from the hen house. The pair shared a laugh, and then sat down to enjoy the fresh eggs.

With the coming of daylight, Marek Swiecicki had returned to the Hartenstein. Tree limbs and unburied dead now lay scattered across the hotel's grounds. The building's walls provided a false sense of security as bullets whizzed through doors and windows. Under the cover of night, German snipers had infiltrated the area, and now fired at any silhouette they saw moving in the hotel's rooms and corridors.

In the hotel General Urquhart saw sniper's bullets striking the walls. His men had made it through another night, but he doubted that they could take much more. He had signaled Browning during the night that his casualties were heavy, and that the Division's supplies were finished. Urquhart bluntly stated that it was "vital" that the division be relieved within twenty-four hours.

That morning, Urquhart had been handed a radio message that the 43rd Division had been ordered, at any risk, to effect relief of the Red Devils in Oosterbeek. The message was small comfort to the General— he was certain that XXX Corps was unaware of just how critical the 1st Airborne Division's situation really was. Urquhart told his chief-of-staff,

Lieutenant Colonel Charles Mackenzie, that he was to get across the river, get to Browning and Horrocks, and impress upon them in person just how desperate the division's situation was. He was to take the division's chief engineer, Lieutenant Colonel Edward C. W. Myers, to help in this difficult mission, and to give firsthand technical advice to XXX Corps on the matter of crossing the river.

In Driel, 2nd Lieutenant Zdzislaw Detko had just returned with a patrol of anti-tank men and a German Flak officer they had taken prisoner. The patrol had been ordered to reconnoiter east to try to find out the situation at the Arnhem bridge. At the railroad embankment, the patrol found the bridge across the Neder Rijn demolished, and too many Germans in the area to press on.

After making his report, Detko returned to the Brigade signal center and asked for volunteers to go to the drop zone and look for the company's missing containers. Having finished laying telephone line, just beginning to dig his foxhole, and "knowing that I would be 'volunteered' for something anyway," Private Wawiorko spoke up. The signaler liked the lieutenant, who had spent his time as a cadet in the signal company. Detko had always impressed Wawiorko as an "excellent officer." Aside from being hardworking and fair, Wawiorko admired Detko's "quiet dignity," and felt better about going out with him than staying behind and having to perform some other task for somebody else. A pipe-smoking farmer who lived across the road from the headquarters helped Wawiorko hitch a horse to a captured German wagon while the Dutchman's two young blond daughters watched with broad smiles on their faces.

At 1000, Lieutenant Smaczny received orders to take his 8th Company 7 kilometers west on the dike road to the village of Heteren. Aside from looking for any possible sites for river crossings, the company was to clear the village of any Germans, and bring out Allied soldiers and aircrew reportedly hidden by the Dutch underground there. Smaczny advised the forty-nine men of his command that he expected Germans. He stressed that they would have to move quietly, and keep alert.

The German forces comprising Sperrverbande Harzer had consolidated their positions along the Arnhem-Nijmegen railroad line during the night. They had completed their preparations, and were ready to carry out General Bittrich's orders that the paratroopers in Driel were to be attacked and wiped out. It was essential that the newly arrived Allies were neither to make it across the river to reinforce the British in Oosterbeek, nor to interfere with the Frundsberg Division as it attempted

Left: Sgt. Major Cadet Stanislaw Sosabowski,
Austrian Army, 1916.

Right: Lieutenant Colonel Sosabowski,
Polish Army, 1938.

May 3, 1939, Polish Constitution Day. As commander of the 21st "Children of Warsaw"
Infantry Regiment, Colonel Sosabowski led the annual parade through Warsaw.

Above: Despite being crippled by a poor economy, Poland tried to field as modern an army as it could. The 37mm Bofors anti-tank gun was produced in Poland under license.

Right: As the Germans approached Warsaw, the civilian population helped prepare the city's defenses.

With the defeat of France, the Polish forces evacuated to Britain. The overcrowded ABDERPOOL managed to reach the safety of Plymouth.

The strenuous training, as well as the Polish paratroopers' own view of Sosabowski, are well illustrated in the caricatures of Monkey Grove drawn by Lieutenant Marek Gramski.

Above: Parachute instructor Lieutenant Julian Gebolys, founder of the Polish Parachute School at Ringway. He and a group of students are reviewed by the commander of the Parachute Training School, Wing Commander Maurice Newman.

Right: The Polish paratroopers made up for the shortage of training aircraft by erecting a jump tower in Scotland.

The training the Polish
paratroopers received
in Scotland was
thorough in all
respects.

General Sosabowski
received much assis-
tance from the com-
mander of the British
Airborne Forces,
General Frederick
Browning, though their
relationship was to sour
after MARKET GARDEN.
This photo goes far in
revealing the different
personalities of the
two men.

Richard Tice is promoted to 2nd Lieutenant. The American volunteer did not have a
drop of Polish blood. He was to die in Holland.

Left: The Parachute Brigade provided an honor guard for the body of General Sikorski as it lay in state in Westminster Abbey. Winston Churchill is kneeling at the pew on the left.

Below: The new Commander-in-Chief of the Polish Armed Forces, General Kazimierz Sosnkowski, an old-line soldier, took command as both the political and military situations worsened for Poland.

A jeep and troops from the Brigade's Medical Company at Saltby airfield during the wait for the word to board aircraft.

Left: On March 13, 1944, Field Marshal Montgomery inspected troops of the Brigade.
Right: Sosabowski kneels before President Raczkiewicz of the Republic of Poland on June 15, 1944. This is the photo mentioned in the Foreword of this book.
Below: June 15 was the day Sosabowski was promoted to Major General, and the Standard made by the women of occupied Warsaw was presented to the Brigade. Also dipped in salute are the standards presented by the women of Fife, and the British 1st Airborne Division.

Above: The center of Driel, an ancient village located on some of the richest farmland in The Netherlands.
Below, left: Cora Baltussen, member of the Dutch Red Cross, came from a prominent Driel family. *Below, right:* Benjamin Jansen, like everyone in Driel, watched the paratroopers land by the Neder Rijn, and thought his village would soon be liberated.

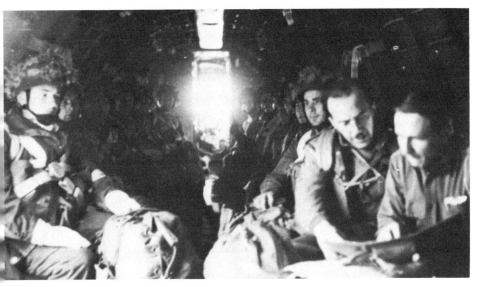

The journey to battle aboard a cramped C-47 "Dakota" transport.

Three of the Brigade's staff officers shortly before MARKET GARDEN (from left to right): Captain Jan Lorys, Operations Officer, Tactics; Lieutenant Colonel Stanislaw Jachnik, Brigade Deputy Commander; Lieutenant Jerzy Dyrda, General Sosabowski's former adjutant and interpreter.

A 6-pounder anti-tank gun during an exercise in the English Midlands. This was the heaviest weapon the Polish Brigade had on the battlefield.

Left to right: Lieutenant Albert Smaczny, commander of the 8th Rifle Company; Lance Corporal Boleslaw Kuzniar, 8th Company radioman; Bombardier Stanislaw Nosecki.

Left to right: Privates Mieczyslaw Chwastek and Michal Lasek of 7th Company, both graduates of Soviet labor camps; Private Piotr Wawiorko of the Signal Company.

Left to right: Captain Father Humbert Misiuda, 3rd Battalion Chaplain, left missionary work in Ceylon to join the Polish Army in France. His body was found on the Oosterbeek polder in May 1945; Lance Sergeant Cadet Zbigniew Hrehorow of 4th Rifle Company; Lieutenant Stefan Kaczmarek, supply officer, landed in Driel Sept. 21.

The morning after the Poles landed in Driel, they dug in and were soon under attack by SS Panzer units.

Above: A farmer's pigpen provided a ready-made compound for Germans captured in Driel. The irony was not lost on the Polish paratroopers.

Right: The face of liberation. After more than four years of Nazi occupation, there was something to smile about . . . for a while.

Above: The arrival of Household Cavalry Regiment vehicles in Driel not only provided relief to the hard-pressed Poles, it also opened a communications link between the 1st Airborne Division in Oosterbeek and the rest of the ground forces. *Below:* The Polish liaison team with the headquarters of 1st Airborne Division (left to right): Correspondent Marek Swiecicki, Captain Ludwig Zwolanski and Lieutenant Alfons Pronobis, here in good spirits after having reached "The Promised Land."

Above: The Driel Dike. The house was the location of General Sosabowski's command post the first three nights of the operation. In the background the demolished railroad bridge and the German front line can be seen. The dike road had been cratered after the 1st Airborne's withdrawal from Oosterbeek.

Below: A German Sturmgeschutz passes the body of a Red Devil as it moves through lower Oosterbeek. While German pressure continued to build, the Polish paratroopers were the only reinforcement that the British 1st Airborne Division received.

Above: Polish paratroopers who had missed the drop on Driel are landed on DZ-O, near Grave, between glide serials from the 82nd Airborne Division.

Below: On September 24, the Poles who had jumped at Grave waited patiently for orders to join the rest of their Brigade at Driel.

The family who lived in Stationsweg no. 8: (left to right) Mr. J.W. Kremer, Mrs. A.L.A. Kremer-Kingman, 12-year-old Ans and 11-year-old Sander.
Below: Stationsweg after the battle. On the right is the Kremer home. On the left is Stationsweg no. 6, Lieutenant Bereda-Fialkowski's command post in Oosterbeek.

Wearing his helmet and armored vest over his surgical gown, Lieutenant Dr. Janusz Mozdzierz treated casualties. Shortly after this photo was taken, the hospital was shelled and the doctor himself was wounded.

In May 1945, Polish paratroopers visiting the Oosterbeek battlefield examined a knocked out Tiger II "Konigstiger" tank in the lower part of the village.

December 27, 1944, Wansford England. With Lieutenant Dyrda on his right, General Sosabowski reviews his Brigade for the last time.

to push the Allies back across the Waal and then out of Nijmegen. On the north bank of the Neder Rijn, a battery of 20mm anti-aircraft guns had been moved west of Heavedorp to cover the river should there be any attempt at a crossing.

Kampgruppe Brinkmann, which had cleared Lieutenant Colonel Frost's paratroopers from the Arnhem Bridge, was now in Elst. The battle group was built around Aufklärungs Abteilung 10 (AA 10), the armored reconnaissance unit of the 10th SS Panzer Division Frundsberg. The Knaust Battalion, equipped with heavy Panther and Tiger tanks, was also in Elst; however, the Betuwe's fragile farm roads would not support the heavy vehicles. Knaust's Panzers were to remain in Elst as a counter to the Allied forces that had crossed the Waal. The German force preparing to destroy the Polish paratroopers in Driel would be built around the light-armored vehicles of AA 10.

2nd Lieutenant Bereda's patrol had finally reached the banks of the Waal. It found that the closest enemy positions were 400 meters to the east, and they were under heavy bombardment from the Allies across the river. The Poles watched with some pleasure the "hellish fire" falling on the enemy, and reasoned that there should be little threat to Driel under the circumstances. Bereda and his men cheerfully began pedaling back to the Brigade. As Driel's church steeples appeared in the distance, the paratroopers heard the hum of engines behind them. Looking over their shoulders, the men spotted German half-tracks moving across the flat countryside. The vehicles turned towards the patrol as the Poles rapidly pumped the pedals of their bicycles and sped toward the safety of the village. They were followed by several bursts of machine-gun rounds, one of which grazed a trooper.

As Private Lasek, a one-time farm boy from Przyworsk, dug his foxhole in the Baarskamp orchard he observed that the dark, rich soil was the most fertile he had ever seen. Lasek caught himself thinking that the soil was so beautiful, "you almost wouldn't mind being buried in it." Finishing his foxhole and feeling "tired as hell" after the night on the dike, the private lay back and dozed off. His rest was short-lived. Lance Sergeant Kurek roused the sleepers and told them to to look alive: "Who knows if Sosab or somebody else might drop in?"

Leaving his 2-inch mortar in his kit bag beside the foxhole, Private Lasek walked over to the Baarskamp farmhouse. Going past a neck-high hedge, he entered a large vegetable garden. Remembering the example of the sappers positioned down the road, Lasek thought that it might be a good idea to cut a break in the hedge; if the Germans overwhelmed them, it might be a good way to fall back from the orchard. Finishing chopping at the shrubs, Lasek filled his mess tin with water. The rifleman sat down in the vegetable garden and lit a fuel tablet to prepare some bouillon for breakfast.

Private Wawiorko proudly led the horse pulling the wagon full of signalmen as they passed through the hamlet of t'Vlot. The residents called out their greetings and made the "V for victory" sign with their fingers as they waved orange ribbons. Turning east, the wagon crossed a wooden bridge over a wide ditch, and after going another 250 meters, Wawiorko saw men from the Supply Company and other units gathering their containers from the drop zone.

As he led the wagon farther down the road, Wawiorko was startled by the ripping staccato of a Spandau, which was quickly joined by another from the opposite side of the drop zone. A soldier from the Supply Company came running out of the mist, pursued by tracer bullets, shouting, "Tanks and armored cars are attacking!" as a third machine gun started chattering.

The signalers leaped from the wagon and into a deep roadside ditch. The horse jumped and kicked in its traces, screeching in fright. Raised on a farm, Wawiorko took pity on the animal and ran back into the road to free it, fearing that the helpless animal would break its legs. Clawing at the sides of the ditch as they slid towards the water, the other soldiers shouted, "Stupid. . . fool. . . jackass. . . what are you doing?" The private finally released the horse and, giving it a hard slap on its rump, threw himself down on the road. "I wasn't trying to be a hero, I just like animals."

Private Wawiorko crawled towards the ditch and saw his comrades frantically trying to keep from sliding into the water. Wawiorko did not know what to do: "On the road I'll be shot. In the ditch I'll drown." The private crawled back towards the bridge and buildings they had passed on the way to the drop zone. From behind the buildings a loud voice boomed, "Sons of whores, get over here!" He got to his feet, ran five steps and threw himself down. This was part of their training, and Wawiorko and the signalers following him repeated the maneuver until they rounded the corner of the building. Out of breath, they saw 2nd Lieutenant Detko, who was also panting—but from laughter. The officer, in a voice filled with great dignity, asked Wawiorko, the only one whose uniform wasn't soaked with stinking ditch water, why he hadn't bathed like the others.

In the Baarskamp orchard, 2nd Lieutenant Tice was telling Privates Czarnocki and Chwastek where to position the platoon's Bren gun as a rumble of armored vehicles was heard to the south. Chwastek glimpsed soldiers moving between the trees and shouted that he thought there were Germans coming towards them. From deep in the orchard came shouts in English: "Don't shoot. . .Don't shoot!" The ghostly figures in the orchard were so close that the Poles could hear their footsteps. Standing to investigate, Tice told his people to hold their fire: "They might be British or Americans."

The ruckus in the orchard distracted Lasek as the water in his mess tin was coming to a boil. He heard the voice of his friend Czarnocki saying, "Sir, Lieutenant, maybe that's the Germans," and then in Lasek's words, "All Hell broke loose."

Peering over the hedge, Lasek saw a blizzard of leaves and twigs falling from the trees as Spandaus raked the orchard. A burst struck Tice in the chest, and Lasek heard him cry, "Help!" three times in English. Each time the lieutenant said the word, his voice became weaker. After a final moan, Tice was silent.

The platoon's return fire sputtered against the vicious blasts from the German weapons. From the south, machine guns from the from German half-tracks joined the fray and raked the northern end of the orchard. Lance Sergeant Kurek gave the order to withdraw, and one-by-one the men started pulling out. Cattle and horses in the fields galloped in circles, screeching in panic. Several lay shot, flailing with their legs in the air. A Holstein cow rolled over onto the Bren gun position, narrowly missing the crew but bending the weapon's bipod. Lasek heard the popping of Czarnocki's pistol as the Polish soldiers pulled back. Left behind in the orchard were the dead officer and the platoon's radio operator, who was taken prisoner with his cumbersome load.

Mortar shells started landing in the Baarskamp farmyard, killing a horse and a cow. As a haystack violently burst into flames, Private Lasek grabbed his Sten gun and ran. He got a few steps and then threw himself to the ground as another series of mortar shells exploded. A fragment struck the prone soldier in the wrist. The wounded man got to his feet and ran around the house, his hand with the phony wedding ring hanging limp and gushing blood. Lasek saw the 3-inch mortar standing abandoned as an aidman came up to him. As the medic slapped a field dressing on him, Lasek asked, "Who's still here?" Giving Lasek an injection of morphine, the medic replied, "Nobody, they're all gone. Let's get out of here."

The pair ran down the road, leaving the mortar and some Sten guns behind. As they reached the alerted sappers 200 meters beyond the Baarskamp, they were asked, "What about the Germans?" The medic replied, "For all I know, they could be right behind us." But there was no further shooting. The Germans had apparently held their advance at the farm. A fresh dressing was put on Lasek's wound, and he was sent on to the aid station in Driel.

Anton Verhoef, who had spent the past days helping the Driel Red Cross team, was told that there were wounded at Honigsveld. He decided to bring them to the hospital in the parish house, but got no farther than Honingsveldstraat. The Germans on the railroad embankment began shooting at him. Returning to the parish house, he tied his wagon horse to a tree by the church. When he went out a few minutes later, the horse lay in the street, shot dead. As he helped a wounded citizen into the hospital, an explosion blew off the building's back door.

A heavy bombardment of the center of Driel was unleashed from the railroad embankment as German half-tracks* approached the village from Elst in the south. They moved across the open country in a tight formation, passing through the hamlet of Honingsveld. At least six turned west at Honingveldstraat and approached the advanced position held by Lieutenant Urbanski's platoon opposite the Baltussen factory. The dug-in soldiers watched in horror as the vehicles approached their position. Lieutenant Pudelko gave Urbanski a hand signal to pull out. With German infantry behind them, the 7th Company abandoned their Piat anti-tank weapon and started falling back to the village. Cutting across fields, the soldiers reached Dorpstraat with the enemy at their heels.

From his house on Dorpstraat, Henk te Dorsthorst saw the half-tracks stop just in front of where he had helped the Polish paratroopers lay their anti-tank mines. He watched as the Poles retreated through the back-yards of the houses on the west side of Dorpstraat, heading for the 2nd Battalion's positions in an orchard 400 meters north of the intersection. The German infantry swung wide and followed through the pastures

---

*A number of the Polish paratroopers also remember PzKw II tanks in action this day. Supporting German documentation is very poor, other than the fact that the Germans did have such vehicles in the Betuwe during September 1944.

behind the houses on both sides of the road. The half-tracks, halted at the intersection, began firing their machine guns straight down the middle of the road and into the center of the village.

As tracers flashed up the street, te Dorsthorst looked out of his house and saw a Polish radioman who was struggling to keep up with Urbanski's withdrawing platoon. He repeatedly called on his radio as he moved, but apparently received no reply as his antenna kept getting caught on bushes. Henk called the radioman into the house, and tied his antenna down with a string so he might move more easily. A few moments later, the house was hit by a mortar shell. The men went in different directions, the Pole into the backyard and the Dutchman into the cellar. From his shelter, te Dorsthorst heard more explosions, and then the screams of the wounded radioman in the yard. He wanted to go out and help him, but did not dare.

There were many Drielenaren in the cellars of the houses on Dorpstraat. Piet Fischer was in his cellar with his wife, three-year-old son and some neighbors. After the explosions in the street stopped, the sounds of boot steps and the cellar door opening was heard above their heads, followed by shouts of "*Raus . . . raus.*" Fischer asked the German where they should go. One replied, "Arnhem." Fischer told him, "Go to Hell! If you want to get shot, you go to Arnhem." The civilians moved through the backyards as the Germans and Poles continued to shoot away at each other across the street and between the houses.

The Poles retreated until they came within 100 meters of the line held by the 2nd Battalion in the orchard on Dorpstraat. The 5th Company was on the east side of the road, with two platoons of the 4th on the west side. The Polish line began to crackle with a heavy and steady fire that hit the approaching platoons of Germans, stopping their advance cold. Private Michal Jakutczyk remembered seeing field-gray figures tumbling to the ground in the "hurricane of fire." A paratrooper in the foxhole next to Jakutczyk stood up and calmly fired his scoped sniper rifle, working the bolt and cursing between shots.

Throughout the morning, the Household Cavalry radios in Driel had sent back continuous situation and reconnaissance reports. These were relayed to Generals Horrocks and Browning, and to the 43rd Wessex Division, which had relieved the Guards Armored Division as the spearhead of XXX Corps. The reports generated more questions and requests for further information from the recipients. To find answers, the armored cars reconnoitered the river and reported on potential launching sites for amphibious DUKWs, which were being brought up to cross the Neder Rijn. The cavalrymen also observed fire and provided corrections for the 64th Medium Regiment, Royal Artillery, whose heavy guns had begun support fire for the Red Devils in Oosterbeek the day before.

While the situation in Driel became more and more intense, General Sosabowski continued going from unit to unit by bicycle. Since the attacks had begun Sosabowski vigorously pressed the Household Cavalrymen to engage the enemy with their armored cars. The British officers continued to decline, and could not convince the Polish general that their lightly armored vehicles were not designed to be used as tanks, but for swift reconnaissance. They also pointed out that their radios were the only link between the airborne forces and XXX Corps, and could not be risked in combat. Against the background of sounds of the heavy fighting on Dorpstraat, the general continued to badger the British officers. They again demurred, stating that their orders were to avoid combat.

The Germans had struck Driel with the boldness that was the hallmark of the Panzer SS. While the lightly supplied Polish paratroopers were running out of ammunition, the attackers used their machine guns lavishly. Sosabowski, barely keeping his historic temper in control, informed the cavalry officers that their radios would be a debatable asset if the defenders of Driel were dead or German prisoners. Lieutenant Young agreed to assist in the defense, but stated that he would not go chasing after the enemy. Sosabowski did not press the point further, but hopped on his bicycle and shouted in English, "Follow me!" as he led Young's armored car to the 2nd Battalion's position on Dorpstraat.

The dug-in Polish paratroopers watched the strange sight of their commander pedaling like mad on a ladies' bicycle as Colonel Kaminski, puffing, tried to run along beside him. The unlikely pair were followed by the armored car, as it jerked down the road to keep from overrunning the Polish general. Young's vehicle tucked itself into the edge of the orchard and cut loose with its 2-pounder at the German half-tracks at the intersection. The enemy was surprised at the sudden appearance of the armor and, after several rounds, its vehicles scuttled out of sight. The Daimler's machine gun then fired off an entire belt of ammunition, much of it tracer, as it traversed its turret, inspiring much caution on the part of the German infantry.

The situation was a stalemate for the moment. The Germans began going through the houses on Dorpstraat, chasing the civilians from their shelters. Anton Verhoef's wife, who had heard the terrible screams of the wounded radio operator, now saw the man dead. German soldiers were going through his pockets looking for cigarettes and chocolate.

Young Henk te Dorsthorst had tried to leave his house during the fighting, but a German soldier fired a pistol at him from across the street. During the lull, Henk crossed the road, but was beckoned over by a hostile German soldier. He demanded that the young man point out the "Tommies'" positions. One of te Dorsthorst's neighbors, a German-born resident of Driel, convinced the soldier, in fluent German, that Henk knew nothing. The Dutch civilians were then sent off in the direction of the Baltussen factory, across the Grietenkamp meadows. As he moved through the pasture, Henk saw many German wounded laying in the grass. Under the protection of a Red Cross flag, their comrades bound their wounds with torn bed sheets and pillow cases looted from the houses before carrying them over to the half-tracks, which then left for Elst.

On the other side of Driel, on the Rijn dike, the 4th Company's 2nd platoon sat in plain view of the Germans across the river, enduring shell- and machine-gun fire throughout the morning. The platoon had already suffered killed and wounded, and Captain Hojnor, the 2nd Battalion's deputy commander, decided that any further losses were pointless. He gave the order for withdrawal.

There were no smoke shells ready for the 3-inch mortars, so Lance Sergeant Cadet Hrehorow called out to his section, asking if anybody had a smoke grenade. Private Jakubowicz called back that he had one. As the cadet tried to shout his instructions through the bursting shells, Jakubowicz clambered, rather than crawled, up the side of the dike. To Hrehorow's further amazement, the bandy-legged private had his bright yellow identification panel tied to his arm. The cadet roared at Jakubowicz to "take that damned thing off your arm." As Jakubowicz huddled against the dike, pulling at the identification panel, Hrehorow called a target across the river for his Bren gunner. When the cadet looked back, "I did not know whether to laugh or to cry when I realized that Private Jakubowicz had contrived to wrap the yellow silk round his helmet, making it look like a funny hat." In disbelief he watched the spunky soldier standing on the dike lick his finger to check the wind direction. Hrehorow did not believe his eyes and the Germans "maybe laughed so hard that they couldn't shoot straight." Lighting the smoke candle, the private was not satisfied with its coverage. Jakubowicz picked the thickly smoking cylinder up and carried it to a spot where its haze covered the

Polish slit trenches. Happy with the results, he waved his arm, and the platoon scrambled across the dike, carrying their dead and wounded with them.

As morning faded into the afternoon, Private Wawiorko returned to the signal center after having crossed the drop zone during the course of the German attack. He was filled with admiration for his friend Adamowicz, and Lieutenant Detko, describing their conduct as "magnificent." Detko had led the signalers across the murderous field of fire "as if we were on exercise. Like rats we crawled through the barbed-wire fences. My helmet net got caught, and my helmet was pulled off of my head." The signalers passed through t'Vlot, finding the hamlet now deserted; gone were the people who had waved orange ribbons and greeted their liberators. The rest of the company greeted Wawiorko with laughter, and asked the "hero" what happened to his horse. The private went back to working on his foxhole, but this was interrupted by a call to repair telephone lines knocked out by the bombardment.

The Germans trying to take Driel licked their wounds as artillery from across the river and from behind the railroad embankment crashed into the village. The Polish paratroopers had held the attack, but now found themselves low on ammunition. General Sosabowski was worried about the situation. He did not have any idea when and how his men would get ammunition, or what form the next German attempt to wipe out his Brigade would take. The fact that his anti-tank artillery was across the river did nothing to increase his confidence. While German skirmishers continued to probe at the edges of the Polish hedgehog, Sosabowski continued his bicycle "tours." He showed up at many frontline foxholes to check on his "boys," and told them not to fire unless they had a definite target, and then only if they were certain of hitting it.

Many of the Drielenaren had found shelter at the Baltussen factory. Despite the fact that there were German armored vehicles parked outside, over 100 evacuees found a place in the factory or the warehouse. When Henk te Dorsthorst arrived at the jam factory, Frans Baltussen warned that the Germans were looking for a boy who was wearing riding breeches and boots, and whom they had watched helping the Poles lay anti-tank mines. The Germans had already taken away two innocent teenagers for interrogation; fortunately they had been released. Heeding Baltussen's warning, Henk and Anton Clappers found hiding places deep inside the jam factory.

Lieutenant Smaczny's 8th Company reached the edge of the village of Heteren, 7 kilometers west of Driel, at noon. The cautious soldiers, expecting Germans, were startled when they were met by the mayor, wearing the chain of his authority around his neck. Behind him stood a group of thirty citizens who carried flowers and shouted enthusiastically at the tense Polish paratroopers. The mayor signaled for silence, and made a speech, not a word of which was understood by Smaczny. He then bowed and presented the Polish officer with the key to the city hall. The Polish soldiers were mobbed by the Dutch, who hugged and kissed them. They forced fruit and flowers into the soldiers' hands, which minutes before had nervously gripped weapons ready for use. Smaczny's men were the first friendly soldiers that the town had seen in over four years, and the crowd was simultaneously laughing and crying from joy.

Though he was impressed by the welcome, Smaczny wanted to carry out his orders and get out of Heteren and back to the Brigade. It was obvious there were no Germans there. This was confirmed by the townspeople, who told him that they had left earlier that morning. The Polish officer was also advised that there were still Allied airmen and paratroopers hidden in the village, and that all of the collaborators had not yet left. It was decided that it would be better if the British remained hidden until after dark, lest the Germans return and punish those who sheltered them.

Smaczny collected cigarettes from his men and left them with the villagers. As the 8th Company formed for their return to Driel, Lieutenant Smaczny found it difficult to leave the village after its "almost childlike gratitude" during the brief liberation.

15

As Machine Guns Swept the Neder Rijn
1400 Hours, September 22, to
0400 Hours, September 23, 1944

At 1300 on the afternoon of Friday, September 22, two staff officers sent by General Urquhart, Lieutenant Colonels Mackenzie and Myers, dragged a rubber dinghy to the Neder Rijn and started paddling for the southern bank. The two staff officers attracted only some odd rifle shots and a few bursts of machine-gun fire that passed far overhead as they struggled in the swift river. Reaching the southern bank, the pair pulled the dinghy ashore and looked over the broad polder in front of the large dike.

The British officers had been told through the Polish radio link between the Hartenstein and Driel that they were expected in Driel, and that an escort of Polish paratroopers would meet them and form an escort to General Sosabowski's headquarters. Instead they saw nobody and heard the sounds of furious fighting coming from the other side of the dike. After long minutes of waiting in a ditch, the British officers caught sight of two steel helmets on the top of the dike. Not knowing whether the heads underneath belonged to friends or enemies, Mackenzie walked forward waving a white handkerchief, while Myers covered him with a pistol. It turned out that the helmets belonged to a British liaison officer in the company of a Polish officer. Mackenzie was pleased to find them waiting for him and Myers, but was a little put out that they seemed to be more interested in the course of the battle in Driel than in them.

Myers and Mackenzie pedaled to General Sosabowski's headquarters on bicycles that had been brought by their guides. Major Malaszkiewicz was shocked by the sight of the British officers. Their uniforms were filthy and their faces were haggard and unshaven. Even more shocking to the Polish Brigade's chief of staff was the fact that the divisional staff officers, rather than junior officers, had crossed the river as messengers. All of this underlined the straits in which the 1st Airborne Division found itself.

Lieutenant Colonel Mackenzie met General Sosabowski shortly after 1400. The British officer related the desperate situation in Oosterbeek. Mackenzie stressed the need for immediate reinforcement and added, "Every ten, or even five, men who will be able to cross the river will not only improve the morale of the already exhausted troops of the 1st Airborne Division, but will be welcomed as much-needed reinforcements in the defense line." The Polish general shrugged, and asked how his men would be able to cross without boats or rafts? Lieutenant Colonel Myers suggested rubber dinghies, which were part of the division's engineering stores. He laid out a plan for a hawser to be strung across the river on which the dinghies could then be hauled back and forth. Sosabowski called for Captain Budziszewski, commander of the Polish Airborne Engineer Company, to discuss the idea with Myers.

Lieutenant Colonel Mackenzie then approached Captain Wrottesley to get through to I Airborne Corps Headquarters in Nijmegen on his armored car's radio. Contact with the regimental headquarters of the Household Cavalry was quickly established and the microphone was handed over to Mackenzie. The airborne staff officer ignored security procedure and did not encipher his message to Browning. Speaking in the clear, his message for the Corps commander related the grave shortages of food, medicine and ammunition, and that the division could not hold out for more than another twenty-four hours without relief. He then turned to Wrottesley, who was stunned by the gravity of the radio message, and by the fact that it was not sent in code, and said that he had to get to Nijmegen. The Scottish airborne officer went on, stating that it was essential that he see Browning in person, and impress upon him the seriousness of the situation in Oosterbeek.

The German infantry were still in the area of the Baarskamp farm and, at 1400, supported by half-tracks, moved on the 6th Company's line at Marskamp. The Germans came within 250 meters of the Poles, but the 6th Company positions were well located, and the rifle platoons managed to catch the enemy skirmishers in a crossfire. One of the Household Cavalry's Daimlers was driven out to support the Poles, but found itself in the middle of the firefight and was forced to withdraw under heavy Spandau fire. Despite the distance, the Polish defensive fire was accurate, and brought the enemy to a halt. Under the protection of a Red Cross flag, the Germans gathered their wounded and then withdrew, leaving their dead behind.

An hour later, a German half-track came out the orchards and began machine gunning the 6th Company's lines from a distance of 300 meters. The armored vehicle was followed a few minutes later by a German tank. As the Polish soldiers watched, its turret began turning slowly to the left until it was pointing at the Engineer Company's positions. Despite being far out of range, paratroopers with Piats fired their weapons at the tank from their advanced positions in the hopes that fire from the weapons might deter the Germans from advancing. The clumsy anti-tank weapons were fired at maximum elevation in an attempt to throw the bombs the greatest possible distance. The bluff worked: the third round fired from a Piat miraculously landed a few dozen meters in front of the tank. The bomb's impressive explosion sent the tank into a retreat back behind the orchard.

Lieutenant Smaczny returned to Driel and made his report about the Heteren patrol to General Sosabowski. The lieutenant was told to take his company and dig in on Dorpstraat behind the 5th Company. Smaczny saw signs of heavy fighting throughout the village, and his brother officers filled him in on the 3rd Battalion's part in the fighting. Among the losses suffered was Lieutenant Slesicki, commander of the battalion's Headquarters Company. General Sosabowski had ordered the officer to send a patrol to the Baarskamp farm to recover the 3-inch mortar that had been left there. Slesicki personally took four men out, but the dying officer was carried back to the Polish lines by the only soldier who had not been shot by the Germans, who still held the farm. In addition to Slesicki, another soldier had been killed and two more wounded. The uninjured rifleman reported in disgust that the mortar had already been destroyed by the enemy.

Driel was quiet for the moment as Lieutenant Smaczny finished digging his foxhole. The company commander settled back to relax, thinking that for him it had been a strange war: he had been in action for twenty-four hours, and had yet to fire a shot. The officer's rest ended when a runner told him that he was wanted at Brigade Headquarters.

When Lieutenant Smaczny arrived at the Beijer farmhouse, he found General Sosabowski waiting for him in the front room. The General's face was serious, and he, "as was typical, came right to the point." Smaczny was to take his company across the river that night. He was specifically ordered to report to the 1st Airborne Division's headquarters at dawn and explain that the rest of Polish Brigade would try to get across that night. Going to a map, the General pointed out the location of the crossing. Smaczny was to take his men there at dusk and keep a watch for British in dinghies coming from the north bank. The Polish engineers had some rubber dinghies, and were building rafts to ferry the company's equipment across. Sosabowski stared intently at Smaczny for several seconds, and then extended his hand and wished the officer good luck.

The Polish sappers calculated that with four rafts promised by the British, plus the three they had recovered from the drop zone, they might get 200 men across the river before dawn. The sappers had also measured the river's current to be a very swift 1.4 meters per second. Sergeant Juhas was put in charge of building the rafts to float equipment across. He ordered his men to lash planks and doors from the houses and barns near the dike to ladders his men had found.

Across the North Sea, at Spanhoe airfield in England, Major Tonn had spent a frustrating day. He had returned to the vacated Polish headquarters in Stamford that morning, and tried to sort through the rumors about what had happened to his commander and the rest of the Brigade. Tonn was informed by Headquarters, I Airborne Corps, in England, that Sosabowski and much of the Brigade had landed in Holland, crossed the river and had joined with the 1st Airborne Division; that the bridges were held in the north by the British, and by the Poles in the south; and that Sosabowski had given orders for the Polish paratroopers who had been returned to England to rejoin the brigade.

More and more of the Dakotas that had dropped the Brigade the day before had returned to their home stations. Tonn was told to have his men ready at the airfields at 1200, to take off during the afternoon.

Major Tonn requested that all the returned Polish sticks be moved to one airfield, but the request was flatly refused. The Polish battalion commander then asked that his men's damp parachutes be exchanged as they had lain on the runways exposed to mist and rain for days. The British liaison officer noted Tonn's protest, stating that the parachutes were in good order, and then inquired whether the Poles would refuse to jump with them. The major said no, but that he would lodge a written protest holding the British responsible for any accidents that resulted from jumping with the damp chutes.

Major Tonn and the Polish paratroopers waited for half an hour in the bad weather at the airfield. At 1230, he received notice that the Poles would not be dropped on the Neder Rijn, but on drop zone "O," near Grave. The major immediately sent a protest to the American Group commander that his mission was to get to Arnhem and carry out the British orders. The American replied through the British liaison officer that he was no longer responsible. The British officers then handed Tonn maps of the drop zone, and told him that a liaison officer would meet them in Grave with further orders. The drop was canceled at 1300, and the 1st Battalion again returned to its quarters at Easton-on-the-Hill.

As the afternoon passed, the Polish troops in Driel felt less and less pressure from the enemy. Lieutenant Kaczmarek was in an orchard behind a house near General Sosabowski's headquarters, his platoon having spent the day sorting supplies recovered from the drop zone. Kaczmarek had just received word that a river crossing was planned for that night, and spread his subsequent instructions through the platoon. Corporal Bernard Wozniak had just emerged from an orchard and, holding out his left hand, said, "Look what a nice pear. Its for you, sir." The lieutenant sat down "serene and quiet," to enjoy the huge, juicy piece of fruit.

As the supply officer was taking out his knife, a large explosion burst a few meters behind Sergeant Antoni Salwuk, and was followed by five more in quick succession. Salwuk had been standing between Kaczmarek and the explosion, and now lay in front of the unhurt lieutenant, his body full of shrapnel. The sergeant moaned, "Lord, this is the end," and then lost consciousness. Nearby lay Corporal Wozniak; the hand that had offered a pear a minute before was hidden in a mass of shredded muscle and shattered bone hanging from the elbow.

The Germans began a heavy bombardment of Driel shortly before 1800. While the village was pasted by artillery and Nebelwerfers from across the river and from behind the railroad embankment, the reinforced armored reconnaissance battalion of the Frundsberg Division quietly withdrew to Elst.

The bombardment had lasted almost an hour, and much of it fell on the Supply and Signal companies' positions on the Molenstraat. Driel was a sorry sight, with many of the buildings badly damaged and the orchards torn and cratered. Quiet again, the Polish soldiers gathered their dead and took their wounded to the dressing stations. Cautiously they kept watch at the edge of the village for any signs of another enemy attack. All was quiet, except for the frantic activity in the dressing stations and among the men who were preparing to force the river.

In the rapidly fading light, paratroopers from the 2nd Battalion probed down Dorpstraat to see what had happened with the Germans. Having arrived at the intersection with Honingveldstraat without finding any, at 2000 they heard the rumble of powerful engines and the clatter of tank treads moving up the Elster Grindweg. Lieutenant Young's cavalry troop moved up to the forward Polish soldiers to investigate. Young had earlier been informed by radio that a relief column was moving towards Driel, but he had received no further notice about its progress. Sergeant Michal Iwaskow of the 4th Company listened to the rumbling as it came closer. It suddenly stopped just before reaching Honingveldstraat. The sergeant was afraid. "If those are Germans, they'll finish us off in the morning; all of our anti-tank guns are on the north side of the river." His fear was echoed by all of the men at the southern end of the village.

Henk te Dorsthorst had also heard the approaching tanks. In the twilight he saw them approaching Driel, but they did not look like any of the armored vehicles he had seen during the years of German occupation. He ran from the Baltussen factory as the tanks approached Dorpstraat and the anti-tank mines he had helped the Polish paratroopers lay. Running up to the lead tank, Henk waved his hands at the driver to stop. The driver, with a jaunty British beret on his head, smiled and waved as the tank clattered past the young Dutchman.

Sergeant Iwaskow watched Lieutenant Young move down Dorpstraat with Lieutenant Lucjan Zuchowski, deputy commander of the 5th Company. The lead scout car caught sight of the turret of a Sherman tank, and Lieutenant Young gave orders to fire yellow smoke cartridges as a recognition signal. The Poles started waving their Celanese recognition panels. The tank continued forward until there was a flash and an explosion from under its tread. Ignoring the yellow smoke, the Sherman's gun barked. The shot struck Young's armored car, blowing away its tool box and spare tire, and bowling Sergeant Iwaskow over into a roadside ditch. As the stunned troops started to react, the Sherman fired again, hitting a scout car in its front plate, decapitating the driver.

Lieutenant Zuchowski ran forward into the darkness, followed by some men with a Piat, thinking that the Shermans were manned by Germans. They were followed by Lieutenant Young, who heard English voices coming from the tanks, and managed to prevent any further tragedy. The tanks belonged to the 4/7th Dragoon Guards, which had spearheaded the 43rd Division's drive across the Betuwe to the Neder Rijn. Riding the tanks, and in carriers behind them, were infantrymen of the 5th DCLI (Duke of Cornwall's Light Infantry). At the end of the column were two DUKWs load with food, ammunition and medical supplies for the 1st Airborne Division.

As night fell over Oosterbeek, the 1st Airborne Division had survived its sixth day. The weather had prevented any resupply missions from being flown. Enduring bombardment and German attacks that had nibbled on all sides of the perimeter, the Red Devils hung on. General Urquhart was heartened that the Polish Brigade had landed in Driel, and had pinned his hopes on the Poles' getting over that night.

In their positions in lower Oosterbeek, the gunners of the Polish anti-tank squadron welcomed the falling night. At sundown they had moved their guns east, into positions around the Oosterbeek church. Early in the morning the squadron lost one of its two 6-pounders at the bottom of Kneppelhoutweg to a Sturmgeschütze that had come clanking down the Benedendorpsweg. Another Polish anti-tank gun, located 100 meters west, had spent a busy morning pumping high-explosive shells into a small copse of trees where the Germans repeatedly tried to infiltrate a machine-gun squad. Had they been able to take over the position, the Germans would have been able to cover the open polder with machine-gun fire right to the river's edge. German snipers then tried to set up shop in a brick building near the gas works, but the Polish gunners kept slamming away at it with armor-piercing shells. By afternoon, both the building and any plans the snipers had for it were wrecked. Now in new positions, the gunners rested tensely. They had seen two of their comrades killed that day, and more taken to the hospitals.

At the Driel dike, Lieutenant Smaczny led his men down the steep slope and across the polder to the small dike. The company was spread out and lay quietly waiting for the rafts to arrive. Smaczny ached for a cigarette, but knew that it would be impossible to strike a light in his exposed position. Reflecting on the situation, the lieutenant thought that "forcing" rather than "crossing" the river would be a more suitable term. The Poles had no artillery support. Much ammunition had been expended repulsing attacks during the day, and the Brigade's mortars and machine guns could not be counted on to provide any significant support fire.

A noise came from the dike road. Smaczny turned and saw a horse and cart silhouetted against the fading twilight. The quiet night was torn by a loud scraping noise as a large object was taken from the cart. Men then carried the bulky mass to the small dike and left it in the care of the 8th Company. Smaczny looked over the clumsy wooden raft, one of three that had been built. He ordered some of his men to put the raft in the water and start loading it with equipment. The soldiers waded a few meters into the river and lowered it gently so it would not make any noise. It sank immediately. On Smaczny's orders, the raft was then raised and set in the water again, and again it sank. The oak doors were too heavy to float.

From the small dike came the sound of hissing as sappers inflated the rubber dinghies with foot pumps. The Engineer Company had recovered three from the drop zone. One was large, and could carry two passengers and two rowers. The other two were small and would carry only one passenger and one rower. The dinghies had been made to save the lives of aircrew if their aircraft had gone down at sea, and were colored bright yellow. The sappers who had "borrowed" the dinghies from the Air Force had been unable to "borrow" any paddles, so shovels would be used in their place. All attempts by the British sappers to put a hawser across the Neder Rijn to pull the dinghies across had failed as the thick rope was swept away in the river's swift current.

Lieutenant Smaczny chewed on a piece of grass to stave off his craving for a cigarette. He had been waiting at the dike for almost two hours. Reacting to the sounds from the river, Smaczny stared into the darkness, and made out the faint shape of a man and a dinghy at the water's edge. Smaczny approached the man, who introduced himself as a lieutenant of the Royal Engineers. The engineer officer said that in addition to his two-man dinghy, another larger one would follow. He asked Smaczny how many men he had, and then briefed the Polish officer on the river crossing. Guides would be waiting for the Poles on the north shore to take them to the Oosterbeek church, where they would receive their orders. Smaczny nodded his understanding, and sent a signaler across with the Briton.

The crossing began at 2300, and Staff Sergeant Juhas rowed the first Polish dinghy across. The current was so swift the passenger had to help paddle with his hands to keep the boat on course. Despite Juhas's size and strength, the dinghy was very difficult to control. The rubber boat was designed to keep men afloat and prevent drowning, and not for navigation. The dinghies rode high in the water, and it was a constant struggle to keep the rubber boats on course. The British held only 400 meters of the opposite river bank, and the price to be paid for drifting downriver would be capture or death. By the time the boats returned to the south bank, they had drifted a good distance west of the fording site, and had to be laboriously hauled back across the muddy polder.

One wave had gotten across, and a second group waited behind the small dike for the dinghies to return from the north bank. Flares began to pop over the river and Spandaus started chattering from the north bank. Lance Corporal Kuzniar lay behind the small dike next to Lieutenant Smaczny. The signaler was to cross with the lieutenant. The officer decided to take a Bren gun with him, but then there was no room in the dinghy for the signaler and his radio. The lance corporal could clearly see the rubber boats on the river. In the light of the flares they looked "like white pastries floating on the water."

Lieutenant Smaczny paddled furiously with his hands as he crossed. Reaching the north shore, Smaczny met the glider pilots who were to guide the Poles to the church. About a dozen Poles had been assembled, and they had been ecstatically greeted by the hard-pressed Red Devils. A glider pilot asked Smaczny and three of his men to follow him to the command post of the 1st Airlanding Brigade.

Walking through the dark, littered streets, the soldiers heard the sounds of battle all around them. Several times British voices came from the ruined buildings of Oosterbeek, challenging the party. The glider pilot kept reassuring the Poles that he knew the way to the command post as Smaczny and his men passed through the positions of a platoon of British paratroopers who remained silent. They went up a narrow street flanked by houses. Hearing voices in the buildings, Smaczny listened alertly while he brought his Sten gun to the ready position. The language was not English . . . was it Dutch? The men followed their officer's lead, holding their weapons ready as they moved cautiously up the dark street, shattered glass and rubble crunching under their boots. After a few more steps, a voice from one of the windows barked sharply: *"Feldwebel. . . es sind Tommies!"*

Ahead, Smaczny saw the snout of an anti-tank gun farther up the street. The sound of clattering pots and pans crashed from the buildings as the Poles threw themselves flat on the street. Rifles and machine pistols banged and chattered from the windows as bullets crisscrossed the street amid more shouting in German. Smaczny cut loose with his Sten gun at the houses' upper floors, and then crawled over to his men. He told them that, on his signal, they were to throw a volley of grenades to each side of the street and then make a break for it. Smaczny shouted, "Now!" As the grenades burst, the Poles sprang to their feet and ran back down the street like "rabbits," their lieutenant firing a final burst from his Sten gun.

The fleet of dinghies made two crossings unmolested before the Germans awoke to what was happening on the river. More flares popped as machine-gun fire swept the Neder Rijn. The Germans in Oosterbeek called Werfergruppe Nickmann, and soon Nebelwerfers from the railroad embankment started bracketing the river. Tracer bullets from the northern bank churned the river's smooth surface, so that parts of it looked as if it was boiling. Multi-colored flares and star shells hung in the sky and cast their ghostly lights over the scene, as screaming Nebelwerfer rockets burst in bright flashes of orange light, throwing white columns of water high in the air over the black waters.

On the third trip, two of the rubber boats (one large, one small) sank. The paratroopers from the large dinghy swam back to shore, while the other men were swept away by the swift current. All the remaining dinghies miraculously survived the fourth trip without loss, but only one small boat returned from the fifth.

On the south shore, Lance Corporal Kuzniar saw the dinghy on which Lieutenant Smaczny had crossed sink, followed by another. The polder was well lit by the glare of flares as the mortar and machine-gun fire became more and more intense. Kuzniar pressed himself flat to the ground. The lance corporal's arms and legs flailed in the air from the explosive blasts as he was pelted by chunks of mud and gravel. The screams of the wounded competed with the wailing of the Nebelwerfers as the 3rd Battalion quit the river and returned to Driel at 0300 on the morning of September 23.

In Oosterbeek, Lieutenant Smaczny took stock of his situation. His three men were with him, one wounded in the thigh. One of the troops had seen the British glider pilot fall, shot and presumed killed. All agreed that it was a miracle any of them were alive. As the Poles moved back in the direction they had come, fire erupted in front of them. As the bullets flew overhead, Smaczny hugged the ground and thought they were hopelessly trapped. The Polish officer then remembered the British position they had passed through. Smaczny shouted in English, "Don't shoot, we're Poles. . . Polish!" The bullets continued to whizz overhead. The lieutenant became angry, and shouted at the top of his lungs: "DON'T SHOOT, YOU BLOODY FOOLS! WE'RE POLISH!"

The firing died down and then stopped. From the British position came a shout: "Approach!" Smaczny crawled along a ditch and identified himself. A British lieutenant told the Polish officer that he and his men were very lucky, as an entire platoon had been shooting at them. He then added that he didn't know anything about Poles crossing the river.

The British lieutenant had one of his men lead Lieutenant Smaczny to the Oosterbeek church. The Polish officer found some more of his men waiting there. After a few more arrived, Smaczny told them to get some sleep, then went into the church. Picking his way through the pews covered with sleeping men, the lieutenant found an empty spot under the pulpit. He curled up on the floor and shut his eyes.

In the parish house in Driel, Cora Baltussen heard the violent explosions from the river, and the roar of engines to the south of the village. The DUKWs that had followed the 43rd Wessex Division crawled along the narrow farm roads. But despite the efforts of the drivers and guides, the amphibious vehicles, heavily laden with supplies and ammunition for the Red Devils, slid off of the roads and bogged down in the soft verges. Cora had toiled throughout the day while Driel had been shelled and withstood German attacks. Now, in the early morning hours, more wounded flowed in. The gentle woman tirelessly struggled to ease the pain of the torn soldiers, and was amazed at their stoicism. She was deeply affected by men whose limbs had been amputated by bullets and shards of steel, and who spoke not of their pain but of their country and families so far away, wondering what future was in store for them.

16

Paratroopers Are Not Fond
of Sitting in Trenches

0430 to 1800 Hours, September 23, 1944

As the gray and damp dawn of September 23 broke over Oosterbeek, German artillerymen loaded the breeches of their guns to herald a new day with their "morning hate." A heavy drizzle soaked those sitting in their cramped muddy trenches.

After leaving the Polish paratroopers who had forced the river at the Oosterbeek church, Marek Swiecicki returned to the Hartenstein. The journalist weighed the impact the new arrivals would have on the battle. He tried to rationalize that relief would come the next day, especially with the news that XXX Corps had reached the opposite bank of the river. Stretching his thoughts further, Swiecicki believed that the 1st Airborne Division would hold out, particularly if they, like he, were becoming "used" to the shelling. Fellow correspondent Alan Wood could only reply laconically to the exhausted yet still garrulous Pole's hopeful arguments.

Under the pulpit of the Oosterbeek church, Lieutenant Smaczny awoke every half hour to see if any more of his men had showed up. At 0630, under heavy shellfire, a British officer escorted Smaczny and his soldiers to positions in the eastern part of the perimeter. Before leaving the church, Smaczny counted thirty-six men from his company. Others had crossed the river, but were not able to join their commander.

Dawn in Driel was quiet. The German gunners seemed to be giving the village a rest after their furious reaction to the river crossing. The DCLI had moved back from Driel to positions south of the village. The rest of the Wessex Division's advance had been held up by German armor in Elst. However, elements of another Wessex Brigade had begun to establish themselves near Homoet.

Coming back from the Driel dike, the remainder of the 3rd Battalion

181

reoccupied their old positions. The gap left in the line by the departed 8th Company was filled by troops from the Supply Company and some headquarters personnel. Lance Corporal Kuzniar went back to reclaim his former foxhole. Upon reaching the spot, the lance corporal found a fresh shell crater rather than his neatly dug slit trench. There was no sign of the friends who had taken over his position. He was informed that the cadet officer who had moved in after the signaler left for the river crossing had been blown to pieces. After a sleepless night, Kuzniar began digging himself another hole. Finished, he knocked on the door of a nearby farmhouse, hoping to wash and shave. The obliging Dutch occupants gave him some of their scarce water, and the tired soldier cleaned himself up while two children curiously watched his every move. Before leaving, the grateful signaler thanked the family in English. "They must have understood, they smiled so kindly."

Private Raschke returned to the farm shed that housed the Brigade's cypher section. After taking off his field equipment, he went to the chicken coop that had proved so bountiful the morning before, but this time returned empty-handed. Going into the orchard in back of the Brigade headquarters, he picked himself some large, ripe apples. In the shed he sliced the apples and some bread and put them together. Raschke wolfed down the sandwiches, and they "tasted like the finest torte." Minutes later, Lieutenant Jaworski stepped in, hoping he might repeat the previous day's breakfast with the cryptographer. Sour-faced with disappointment, the lieutenant told Raschke to "get some sleep. If there is no cypher work, there is no cypher work. If we get any, I'll wake you." The cryptographer, "under orders," happily stretched out on a pile of hay in a dark corner. Ignoring the distant rumble of artillery, he fell asleep.

The "morning hate" fell on Lieutenant Smaczny's new position. In Oosterbeek, the German fire was accurate, coordinated by the many snipers who had infiltrated the perimeter. By 0800 hours, neighboring positions had been evacuated, and the 8th Company, with several wounded, was also withdrawn. Moving back under heavy fire, the Poles retreated from building to building, seeking shelter from the bombardment. Moving ahead of his men, Smaczny was brought to a lieutenant colonel of the 1st Airlanding Brigade. Against a background of small-arms fire a few hundred meters away, the Polish officer was briefed about the local situation and told where to take his people.

Smaczny took his company to the building on the Benedendorpsweg, where they were to assume their new position. It was a large white manor house named the "Transvalia." A Border Regiment officer told Smaczny that his left flank between the river and the gas works was safe, but he could expect the Germans to attack down the road from Heveadorp. The Polish commander had his men dig foxholes in the large garden and around the greenhouses on the prosperous estate. While his men were digging, British soldiers would periodically appear and tell them the locations of friendly positions. The information was often contradictory, as the battle lines changed constantly. It seemed to Smaczny that "there were as many rumors as there were bullets flying. We only knew where the Germans were when they fired at us."

At 0900 hours, a Captain Watson, liaison officer from I Airborne Corps, arrived in Driel. He was tired from his journey, which had often been delayed by sharp fighting around Elst. The officer relayed information radioed to the Corps about the 1st Airborne Division in Oosterbeek. He then gave General Sosabowski the first concrete report about his missing troops: they had returned safely to England when the rest of the Brigade had jumped, and would be joining it as soon as possible.

Captain Watson was not the only visitor from I Airborne Corps in Driel. A Royal Army Medical Corps Brigadier, the Corps Chief of Medical Services, had also made the dangerous journey from Nijmegen. He met with the Polish Chief Medical Officer, Major Dr. Jan Golba, at the hospital. Golba requested more medical supplies. The Medical Company's heavy equipment and its main stocks of plasma, bandages and other first-aid and surgical supplies had gone in on three gliders on the 19th, and all supplies were becoming scarce. Against the busy background of casualties from the river crossing being treated, the British brigadier promised he would try to send the sorely needed supplies, and also try to eventually evacuate the wounded.

At that same moment in England, the gates of Spanhoe airfield once again swung open to receive trucks carrying Polish paratroopers. Major Tonn was pleased that the weather conditions finally seemed acceptable— he had no doubt that they would be taking off this day. The airfield bustled around the major as he walked to Operations for his briefing. The briefing itself was simple, and consisted of the usual information about anti-aircraft, flight paths and timings. A bit unusual was the revelation that the Polish drop zone would be receiving glider reinforcements for the 82nd Airborne Division both before and after the parachute drop. More disturbing to Tonn was the fact that there was no further news about either the 1st Airborne Division, or the Polish Parachute Brigade.

Private Wawiorko checked out a farm building near the positions his platoon had taken over from the 8th Company. Using bags of cement and sugar, Wawiorko and Adamowicz built themselves a protected spot under the eaves of a large shed. Taking off their armored vests and smocks, the signalers lay down to get some rest. The men, finally feeling relaxed, quickly fell asleep. Wawiorko's eyes soon jerked open at the sound of an explosion and the whine of a fighter plane's engine. Bullets beat on the tin roof as if it were a drum, and beams of light shown through the holes as the German fighter roared over and away from Driel. Wawiorko buried his face in his smock and "shook like jelly" from fear. It was again quiet in the shed. Adamowicz calmly talked to his friend until he regained his composure. Then a corporal's voice filled the shed, calling the men to repair telephone lines.

The elderly Dutch couple returned to their house, still occupied by Lieutenant Kula's platoon. They looked over its west wall, heavily pock-marked by bullets. The house had received an undue amount of attention. German machine-gunners had singled it out in an attempt to provoke a Polish reaction, and thus expose their positions. The couple was deeply moved when they saw the bedroom. A mortar shell had exploded there, leaving the floor caked with the dried blood of a mortally wounded paratrooper. As they looked at the officer, their faces reflected their mixed emotions of sadness and gratitude.

A British Bren carrier arrived at Lieutenant Kula's position and unloaded a machine gun, which began firing at the north bank of the river. The lieutenant was ordered to move his platoon to an orchard east of the village to help fill in the gap left by the 8th Company. Kula felt uneasy when he saw the green Westerbouwing heights sticking up over the dike and overlooking the Polish positions. As the soldiers fell out to dig their foxholes, a Nebelwerfer salvo screamed in. The shells burst mere meters from the line of men, who retreated farther into the orchard.

After the first salvos, the telephone patrol found a wounded paratrooper lying in a ditch next to their phone lines. A medic, who was already taking care of the man, handed the signalers the casualty's wire cutters. They had been bent by a large shell fragment that certainly would have killed the man had it not struck the heavy tool hanging from his belt. Another Nebelwerfer salvo came screeching in. Private Wawiorko ran for the shelter of a barn and pressed himself against the outside wall, while the corporal threw himself into the ditch. Wawiorko could not help bursting into laughter at the sight of his patrol commander's camouflage smock changing color as ditch water soaked into the fabric. The signaler's laughter was cut short when a shell exploded on the roof, surrounding him with a cloud of smoke and dust.

At 1000 hours, General Sosabowski called a staff meeting. The general was worried about preserving his fragile strength. Radio contact with the north bank was sporadic. There was no point in discussing further the crossing of the river without boats. Encoding the Poles' situation, needs and problems, and attempting to radio them seemed hopeless. Major Malaszkiewicz was instructed to contact the British infantry in Homoet. A jeep and driver were loaned by the 4/7th Dragoon Guards. This was the first assistance the armored formation had provided the Poles. A few kilometers south of Driel, the major and his freckle-faced, "carrot-haired" driver ran into some British medics caring for four wounded soldiers too badly wounded to transport. They told Malaszkiewicz that the enemy had tanks dug in just south of a nameless hamlet on the way to Homoet. Heeding the warning, the jeep skirted the area by driving through tulip fields. Major Malaszkiewicz did indeed see three dug-in tanks, but no Germans were seen around them, nor did he care to find any.

Reaching the British positions, Malaszkiewicz was shocked by the contrast with Driel. Well-dug positions surrounded tents among the orchards. The headquarters of the 43rd Wessex Division's 130th Infantry Brigade was easy to find: "There were so many telephone lines and tents, it looked like a peacetime maneuver." The Polish major was quickly taken in to the 130th's commander, Brigadier Ben Walton, who gave him a hearty welcome.

Brigadier Walton struck Malaszkiewicz as "combative, and wanting to continue the advance rather than sitting dug in between the manure piles, but didn't have any orders." The discussion immediately went to the problem of the lack of boats. Malaszkiewicz and Walton reached an "understanding." Walton said that he had eighteen large boats, each capable of holding twenty-four men, and the Poles could expect them at 2000 hours that night. Canadian sappers attached to the Wessex Division would man the vessels, allowing Polish sappers to secure the north bank where the troops would be landed, and then help turn the boats around. The Polish officer then complained about the lack of artillery support. Walton replied that XXX Corps and his brigade artillery would try to shoot by the map, along with fire observed from the Driel dike.

Bombardier Nosecki no longer knew how long he had been in Holland, or even what day it was. That morning, the Anti-tank Squadron had lost another gun to shellfire at the intersection of Benedendorpsweg and Kneppelhoutweg. The gun's commander, Lance Sergeant Stanislaw Horodeczny, was wounded, but he refused evacuation and took command of the gun across Benedendorpsweg and aimed north, straight up Kneppelhoutweg.

Nosecki loitered by a badly wounded friend, Gunner Jozef Ratowski. Ratowski had never totally recovered his health after release from Soviet labor camps. The sickly soldier knew his wounds were fatal, and made his farewells with the world. Taking leave of his friend, Nosecki crossed the road to join Horodeczny at the gun.

Lieutenant Smaczny's 8th Company was now the anchor of the perimeter's southwest corner. His line ran north from Benedendorpsweg into the woods. The lieutenant was worried; his men were very short on ammunition, and they could hear German voices coming from a group of houses, across and ninety meters west on the Benedendorpsweg. Any movement near the road brought German fire. It was with difficulty that his men managed to lay a daisy chain of M.75 mines across an exposed portion of it. Meanwhile, from the manor's cellar came screams and moans that were almost as unnerving as the shelling.

Smaczny saw a woman looking out of one of the dormer windows on the Transvalia's rooftop. She stepped back as bullets chewed up the manor's roof tiles. Apparently the Germans had also been keeping an eye on her. When the firing stopped, she again appeared. Watching, Smaczny thought her "either very brave, or very foolish," and went to investigate.

The cellar was filled with British wounded, some quite seriously. The woman came down to the cellar and told the Polish officer the locations of the German positions. Smaczny was grateful for the information and was relieved that her performance at the window had a purpose, and that she was not merely watching the battle. The woman was in her thirties, and the Pole guessed that she was a housekeeper at the manor. Helped by her teen-aged daughter, the woman cared for the wounded with whatever humble means she had on hand. Smaczny gathered morphia from his men and, after showing her how to inject it, gave it to her to use on the seriously wounded. Another Polish paratrooper gave her a large slab of meat he had carved from a dead cow.

Marek Swiecicki left the Hartenstein hoping that he might get a bite to eat at the headquarters of the Airlanding Brigade. There, he could not even find so much as a "smell of breakfast." Moving on during a break in the shelling, the correspondent reached the 8th Company's positions. Not only did they not have any food with them, but the soldiers answered his request with the question, "Under such fire, who wants to eat?"

Crawling into a hole with a Polish 2nd lieutenant, Swiecicki's journalistic instincts provoked him to ask, "How do you feel over here?" The officer, face incredulous, replied, "Paratroopers are not fond of sitting in trenches." The atmosphere lightened after the correspondent asked the new arrival what had happened across the river. Swiecicki was amused by the descriptions of "Old Sosab" charging the Germans on a ladies' bicycle. The tone then became bleak when the subject turned to 2nd Lieutenant Richard Tice. The correspondent shared everybody's shock and sorrow on hearing about the death of the American so universally known and liked both by the Scots and the soldiers of the Brigade.

Across the river in Driel, the shells continued to fall. German gunners on both sides of the Neder Rijn gave particular attention to the steeple of the Catholic church, being used as an observation post for the Polish 3-inch mortars. Three shells slammed into the tower just moments after the 3rd Battalion's mortar platoon sergeant climbed down from it. In the churchyard cemetery, Father Mientki, who had been supervising the burial of the Brigade's dead, threw himself to the ground as more shells began to land. The soldiers in the burial detail sheltered behind gravestones and in freshly dug graves as the chaplain counted ten shells from the east and twelve from the north strike the church steeple. One of the soldiers in the burial detail was himself killed as shrapnel flew through the once peaceful graveyard. The hospital in the parish house was showered with fragments from the shells that missed the steeple. Wounded streamed into the main hospital set up in the schoolhouse, despite shells from the north bank landing all around. A large Red Cross flag, 10 meters square, had been stretched across the building's roof, but provided no protection from the shells.

A nearby explosion brought Private Raschke out of his sleep and to his feet. Running outside, he saw the chicken coop, its back wall blown into splinters, its occupants just piles of blood and feathers. Some of the neat, well-kept houses that had lined the streets when the cryptographer went to sleep were now heaps of rubble and ashes.

The telephone patrol tried to maintain communications between the units. Private Wawiorko found some of the telephone cables, their insulation blown off by the bombardment, bright copper. The lines had not only suffered from the shelling but now too the vehicles that were moving through Driel had been breaking the lines to pieces. At a crossroads the cables were strung across the road on the village's telephone poles. Wawiorko clambered up a wet pole and hung on to the crosspiece with his left arm while grabbing for the lines to be spliced with his right.

A loud warbling "moan" announced another salvo of Nebelwerfers coming in. The men below scattered for cover as Wawiorko clung to the top of the pole. Not having climbing spikes, he did not want to scale the wet post again. Holding on tightly, the signaler tried his best to shrink himself behind the protection of his armored vest and helmet. Howling in imitation of the rockets, he shouted at them to explode somewhere else. Passing overhead, the high-explosive rounds landed in the meadows beyond, which erupted in geysers of earth. The patrol's corporal passed Wawiorko a line, which he quickly spliced. Private Wawiorko smiled when a voice from the switchboard at the Brigade's headquarters came through the handset.

The 2nd Battalion lost one man killed as they changed positions early in the morning. In front of their new lines the Baarskamp barn was burning as a result of the shelling. A patrol was sent out under General Sosabowski's orders to find any supply containers still on the drop zone. The ammunition situation was highly critical, so that when the day's general orders were issued, "No. 8: Conserve Ammunition" was literally underlined for emphasis by Sosabowski.

From his forward position, Sergeant Iwaskow's 1st platoon, 4th Company, had chased off an enemy patrol with machine-gun fire as the Germans probed through the orchards. Another patrol appeared from behind a single house across the road from a group of buildings less than 150 meters in front of the platoon's position. They had a screaming Dutch woman with them. The astonished Polish paratroopers held their fire, not wanting to bring any harm to the innocent female. The Germans pushed her in front of them as they scurried across the road, then ran between the houses and disappeared into an orchard. Shaken by the incident, Iwaskow thought of the children who might have been left orphaned by the enemy tactic.

The 8th Company's positions were under bombardment all morning. At times the men in the foxholes could hear the German gun commanders yell, "*Feur!*" before the Nebelwerfers shrieked into the Oosterbeek perimeter. Between shellings, skirmishers and snipers tried to infiltrate the Polish positions. Short of ammunition, the Poles had to respond with aimed shots, and only when they were certain of their targets.

Two German tanks now came clattering up the road from Heveadorp. The daisy chain of mines stretched across the road were exposed, because Lieutenant Smaczny was ordered not to conceal them should more reinforcements appear. The men girded themselves to fight the steel horrors with whatever means they had on hand. From behind them, an anti-tank gun appeared, pushed by its crew down the Benedendorpsweg. They stopped and fired a single shot, which with a clang struck the lead tank, leaving it damaged. Without hesitation, the other tank reversed, retreating to the sound of its grinding transmission. The savior gun was pulled by its crew back up the Benedendorpsweg as quickly as this had appeared. The 8th Company's ammunition crisis was partially resolved by a sympathetic British officer who remained in the area. He would vanish for hours and suddenly reappear with haversacks filled with bullets, sometimes managing to find enough to give each man twenty rounds.

As morning passed into the afternoon, a cold-weather front pushed across The Netherlands. The skies began to clear, but the sun brought little respite to the Red Devils holding the Oosterbeek perimeter. The once prosperous town was now a shambles around them. Neat lawns and gardens were gored with foxholes, slit trenches and shallow graves. The stench of the burned houses, the unburied dead and excrement mingled with the sour, sulfurous odor left by the tons of expended explosives hanging over the area. The soldier's mouths and nostrils were painted with the putrid stink. The many wounded were being cared for in crowded dressing stations and hospitals set up in hotels and houses in the perimeter. For all, ammunition, food, sleep and especially water were desperately needed.

On this seventh day of battle, it seemed that the enemy bombardment was even heavier than on preceding days. When the shelling shifted to other parts of the perimeter, small groups of German infantry, supported by Sturmgeschütze and tanks, attacked limited objectives. The combat was usually platoon-sized struggles with grenades and machine pistols over a few houses, as the Germans maintained pressure and tried to compress the perimeter in bits and pieces. Many of these small but vicious assaults fell on the northern "fingertip" of the perimeter commanded by Brigadier Hackett.

In England, the chimes of the church tower near Spanhoe airfield announced 1315 hours as the engines of the Dakotas burst into life. A half hour later, the wheels of the first of forty-one aircraft left the runway. Major Tonn's lift was finally airborne. Leveling off at 1,500 feet, the formation made its way east to the Channel.

Compared with the planeloads of apprehensive paratroopers who had taken off two days before, the atmosphere within the airplanes was much lighter. With the tension of the past days finally broken, the paratroopers joked and smoked. The Poles were not the only troops flying to Grave: from the windows they saw many of the 230 Waco gliders, towed by a like number of Dakotas. The Poles would be rejoining the rest of their Brigade, and through the minds of many of the men ran the thought that, at last, the time was approaching to extract some vengence for what had been done to their homeland.

Around Driel the Poles had spent much of the day in their wet foxholes with shells bursting around them. A respite came as two Allied fighter planes appeared and then orbited over the battlefield. The shelling petered out while the planes flew in lazy circles high above. A half hour later they were relieved by a squadron of rocket-firing Typhoons. After several passes, the fighter-bombers dived. The enemy artillery came to a complete stop as the planes attacked the railroad embankment and the German lines around Oosterbeek. The Polish paratroopers in Driel climbed out of their holes to watch as sparks winked on the broad wings of the diving airplanes. The dull popping of their cannons reached the ears of the paratroopers through the humid air. The Typhoons came around again and this time used rockets. The planes looked as if they were standing on their noses. The howling of their engines became higher and louder as they dived. The sight made the paratroopers' faces beam with sheer joy as they watched the rockets streak onto their tormenters. Private Raschke's "heart rose," imagining the enemy "nailed to the ground, huddled like rats." The Poles not only felt a sense of relaxation for the end of the bombardment, but also that "their" aircraft were overhead.

Behind the fighters the heavy drone of the fleet of multi-engined aircraft grew louder. At 1530 the black specks in the southern sky turned into 72 four-engined Stirlings in tight formation. The earth shook as the black-bellied bombers passed overhead, and on over to Oosterbeek. Puffs of gray smoke and fiery streaks of tracer began appearing around the ungainly bombers as more and more German anti-aircraft crews manned their guns. Suddenly, the sky bloomed with hundreds of multi-colored chutes. The paratroopers watched the spectacle in awe. Then one of the Stirlings started losing altitude in a slow curve after it had released its cargo. Another caught fire and left a smokey arc in the sky as it fell towards the earth in flames.

Minutes later, the Stirlings were followed by a formation of fifty-one RAF Dakotas. The German gunners' fire was now even more concentrated and furious than that which greeted the Stirlings. The tight formation passed over Oosterbeek, again filling the skies with the silken "spring flowers." One Dakota, with containers still slung under its belly, purposely swung around in a wide arc for another pass over Oosterbeek. Every Pole stood transfixed as the plane began a solo run over the perimeter.

Lance Sergeant Cadet Mieczyslaw Jurecki of Lieutenant Kula's platoon watched as it again went through the dense flak. "Suicide," Jurecki thought, then swiftly re-assessed: "No . . . hero! Everybody held their breath as the plane made circles, both pathetic and magnificent, dropping supplies in a sky full of bursting shells. Eyes and mouths wide open, everybody wanted to shout at the aircrew, 'Jump! Save yourselves!' " The brave Dakota did not make it. Jurecki watched as, in a fraction of a second, "Its wings folded up, as in prayer, and the machine hurtled down. Everything became quiet."

Some of the supplies were released over Driel. Private Wawiorko looked over these treasures, searching for the tapered cans that contained corned beef. Many of the tins were unlabeled. Those with "CANADA" stamped into their lids contained potato soup. Other were full of pudding. Wawiorko looked at the unnourishing fare and glumly thought, "What stupidity . . . the fliers risk their lives to bombard us with potatoes and pudding!" It did not take the German gunners long to get back to their work after the Allied aircraft disappeared. Only minutes later, Driel was again under heavy fire. Some of the shells were air-bursting at rooftop height, leaving Wawiorko shaking, "as if I had malaria."

At the Hotel Hartenstein, Marek Swiecicki watched a duel between German snipers and the Red Devils who occupied the slit trenches that ringed Divisional Headquarters. Two snipers had been brought down "like large pears from the trees" by Sten guns. The British paratroopers launched "punitive expeditions" that slowly worked the grounds around the headquarters, much like hunters after elusive partridge in Scotland. Those birds would take to the wing in an explosion of feathers if startled. But the young fanatics in spot camouflage, raised on a steady diet of Nazi mysticism, were sly, and would sooner shoot than panic – frequently shooting first. Fortunately, the snipers watched the supply drop with the

same curiosity that the beleaguered troops did. The crack of rifles and
the chatter of Sten guns could be heard over the drone of the supply
planes. Movement outside the hotel was now possible.

After the correspondent saw a sniper, clad in spotted camouflage, his
young face streaked with blood, led past the hotel entrance to the prisoner
cage, he decided to visit his friend from the Glider Pilot Regiment,
Sergeant Cotterill. Besides, the sergeant might even have something to
eat! Finding his friend in a slit trench, the correspondent crawled in.
Cotterill had nothing to offer but his company, until Swiecicki spotted
a London newspaper in the bottom of the dugout. The veteran journalist
quickly forgot his stomach when he saw the paper. It was dated the day
before, and had arrived in the supply drop. Bold print below the headlines
about the battle now going on in Holland cried, "MORE FLYING BOMBS
OVER LONDON," and distracted the correspondent from the news about
the airborne operation. Marek now thought about Krystyna Kuratowska,
whose name he had chalked on the nose of his glider. She was his fiancée,
and was in London.

The Dutchwoman emerged from the cellar of the Transvalia with a
large pot containing stew made from the meat given her by the Polish
soldiers. After feeding the wounded, she distributed the remainder to the
men entrenched in the garden. Lieutenant Smaczny was not happy about
the situation with the wounded in the cellar. Certain that many would
die if a doctor did not look at them, Smaczny sent a runner to find one.
The situation was deteriorating; contact had been lost with the Border
Regiment troops holding positions to the north of the 8th Company's.
Two German machine-gunners had worked their way between the two
units, and snipers on the Benedendorpsweg were so active that Smaczny
was forced to pull back his positions there. The men who had been
withdrawn were sent to reinforce the company's north shoulder.

The Polish Parachute Brigade's seaborne tail was still stuck in
Flanders. The day before, its ambulances had been pulled from the column
and given a road priority to reach the Brigade's units on the Neder Rijn.
That night, Major Tokarz called the men together for a short com-
memoration of the Brigade's fourth anniversary. After a roll call of the
men killed during training, Tokarz gave a short speech to the assembled
troops on their obligation to deliver the supplies and equipment needed
by their fighting comrades. The speech was not necessary—this was
already well understood. The Polish column had only moved a couple

of kilometers the day before, but that had been its last movement. At this point nothing was moving. The GARDEN corridor had been cut by a vicious German counterattack above Eindhoven. For the last twenty-four hours, units of the 101st Airborne had been locked in furious combat with the German forces that were trying to keep the corridor severed. The men loitered near their vehicles waiting for orders to move again. Overhead they saw hundreds of aircraft and gliders flying north at low altitude. The powerful sight of so many airplanes on the Brigade's Holy Day left the troops with the feeling that there would be a good end to this affair.

The forty-one planes carrying the remaining Polish paratroopers had crossed the Channel and flown over the Continent. The formation descended to an altitude of 300 feet. Europe was glorious in its autumnal splendor, and morale was high.

In plane 13, Corporal Boleslaw Wojewodka of the 3rd Company's headquarters section reflected on his journey to this time and place. It had started in 1939. As a teen-aged volunteer with the Polish cavalry, and after release from Soviet captivity, he served together with his father in the same Polish service unit in Egypt. Together the two men pondered the fate of Boleslaw's mother and sister, who had been deported to Russia, and from whom there had been no word for years. Wojewodka looked at his company commander, Lieutenant Zbigniew Ziemski. The highly intelligent lieutenant had been one of the Brigade's original officers. He was a tough professional soldier, a fact belied by his gentle nature, soft-spoken manner and the careful attention that he had always given his men. The atmosphere was almost joyful with the men joking and singing. In the distance, flak started to rise from by-passed German positions. The happy atmosphere on plane 13 came to an abrupt halt when a tracer bullet flashed past the Dakota, leaving its passengers in sober silence.

Just after passing over Eindhoven, the red lights flashed, bringing the paratroopers to action stations. The men stood hooked up and ready for the jump. Tensely they waited as the aircraft gained altitude, and many minutes went by without the lights changing to green. At landing zone "O," the Waco gliders carrying the 82nd Airborne's 325th Glider Infantry Regiment were already skidding to a halt. The glider men quickly assembled and cleared the LZ. The Dakotas carrying the Poles appeared over the LZ at 1647. Twenty minutes after the red lights went on, they finally flashed green and the impatient troopers tumbled out of the planes like "potatoes pouring from a sack."

The high-pressure weather front that cleared the skies over Holland brought with it strong winds. Corporal Wojewodka's parachute opened neatly, but before he could release his kit bag, the chute began oscillating wildly. In the kit bag were extra batteries for the company radio. The chute hit the ground before the corporal, and slammed him down too. Landing on the bank of a raised road, he slid, head first, down the slope, pushed by the heavy kit bag. Many men were injured before they could collapse their parachutes. Wojewodka reached for his commando knife and cut himself and the kit bag free of his tangled parachute lines. The first man Wojewodka saw was Lieutenant Ziemski. Together they walked towards the blue smoke that marked the assembly area of the 3rd Company.

The Poles had to move swiftly to clear the landing zone, and began dragging their containers off the field. Just seven minutes after the last paratrooper had landed, more gliders were released over the same field. Almost one hundred Wacos, carrying more troops and anti-tank guns for the 82nd Airborne Division, landed.

An hour after the drop, a jeep with an American officer and a British lieutenant colonel from I Airborne Corps sought out Major Tonn. The British officer told him to accompany them to the 82nd Airborne's headquarters for orders. Tonn was instructed to proceed to a wood outside of Malden, and was cautioned about the presence of the remnants of a German parachute company outside of Mook. The major returned to his men, who were sorting out the contents of their containers. While briefing his officers about the march route, an American officer interrupted Tonn to tell him that a Polish liaison officer from I Airborne Corps was looking for him. Tonn eagerly received Captain Kazimierz Dendor, who gave him the latest available information about the Brigade in Driel, including the fact that part of it had crossed the river. Tonn asked Dendor to secure them transportation so they might join the rest of the Brigade in Driel. Dendor replied that he could not arrange anything at the moment, but would have more substantive information the next day. Before parting, Tonn asked the captain to inform General Sosabowski that the rest of the Brigade was in Holland.

Lieutenant Smaczny alerted his Piat crew as a Char B tank* clanked

---

*Most of the armor used by the Germans on the western flank of the Oosterbeek perimeter were French Char B tanks, captured in 1940 and put to use by their captors. The 35-ton, slab-sided vehicle had a 47mm gun and co-axial machine gun in a turret. The 75mm gun that had originally been fitted in the hull was usually replaced by the Germans with a flame thrower.

slowly up the Benedendorpsweg towards the Transvalia. The ugly vehicle ground to a halt 120 meters from the Polish positions, out of range of the anti-tank weapon. The paratroopers crouched as the tank fired several rounds at the Poles. From the vehicle's deck, a man with a rifle patiently shot at the mines stretched across the road. They all blew up after a single bullet found its mark.

The Polish Airborne Anti-tank Squadron continued to suffer through the shelling and mortar fire. Snipers had established themselves in the trees, and Lieutenant Mleczko prayed for nightfall: "You could not get out of a trench or building without getting hit by some kind of lead." With dark there might be a letup in the bombardment, and permit the gunners to move out of their cramped positions.

German tanks and Sturmgeschütze probed, but did not press their attacks. The tanks moved very slowly and carefully from cover to cover. From a hull-down position they would spray the area with machine-gun fire, and then blindly fire their main guns. The fire was inaccurate, but in the crowded sector the wild fire eroded the exhausted defenders' morale. One tank took Corporal Pawalczyk's gun under fire at the corner of Kneppelhoutweg and Benedendorpsweg. The corporal and his crew pushed their gun closer to the tank for a better shot. The Polish gunners quickly fired four rounds at the vehicle and, though not hit, the tank decided it had had enough, and pulled away.

An hour after the attack by the Char B, British medical jeeps flying Red Cross flags arrived at the Transvalia. Lieutenant Smaczny was astonished as firing from all sides stopped, "as if by magic." When the jeeps bearing the wounded from the Transvalia's cellar disappeared from sight, the battle resumed. But the jeeps again worked their "magic," returning to clear the rest of the wounded from the manor. Once more the shooting began after the jeeps left, as the Poles hunkered in their holes awaiting night. The 8th Company had suffered several killed and wounded during the day, including a lance sergeant who had complained about the discomfort of the armored vest that Smaczny insisted be worn. He was found dead after a bombardment, his vest beside him. A small fragment had torn through his spine, which would have been protected had the vest been worn.

As light faded, jeeps towing anti-tank guns for the 82nd Airborne Division sped past the Polish paratroopers marching north. Major Tonn was told that his men would provide security for the American anti-tank crews and, until further orders from I Airborne Corps, would remain under the 82nd's command. Tonn requested vehicles to transport his heavy containers, and rations for his men. In these uncertain circumstances, he did not want his men breaking into their 24-hour emergency rations, which was all the food they had with them.

As the sun started to descend behind the Westerbouwing, the situation had become quiet on the Benedendorpsweg by the Transvalia. Lieutenant Smaczny turned his attention to the German machine guns, which separated his 8th Company from the Border Regiment troops to the north. A patrol was sent out to make contact with the British troops, and to hit the enemy machine-gun positions from the north. At 1730, Smaczny and a dozen men broke cover. They drew heavy fire from the machine guns. The chatter of the Spandaus was joined by reports of Enfield rifles and Sten guns and the blasts of grenades. The ripping sound of the machine guns ceased. Taking a few men with him, Smaczny worked his way towards the source of the machine-gun fire. He found the machine-gun nest with other men from his patrol already examining it. Both weapons were in a shallow pit that had been cleverly concealed by bushes. The Polish lieutenant lit a cigarette and turned back towards the Transvalia, wondering what the night would bring.

17

Hold On To Yourselves and Everything Will Be All Right

1900 Hours, September 23, to 0400 Hours, September 24, 1944

Major Malaszkiewicz returned to Driel at 1900. Immediately after receiving the major's report, General Sosabowski gathered his staff and gave his orders for the coming night. Because the boats were to arrive at 2030, preparations had to be made swiftly. As the ferrying was to be done by British sappers, Captain Budziszewski's Engineer Company was to be responsible for organizing the crossing. In addition, some of the Polish sappers would go with the first wave to the northern bank to provide security for the landed troops and ensure a speedy turnaround for the empty boats. The unit commanders were told to prepare their troops for the impending crossing and to report to Brigade Headquarters at 2130 hours for orders.

A Royal Artillery officer from XXX Corps attended the meeting at Brigade Headquarters. He would coordinate the Corps and Divisional artillery support for the crossing. The Englishman made it very clear that the ammunition supply was critical, and the support fire would have to be sparing. Looking over the north bank from the dike, the artilleryman became even more reticent about close support because the British and German positions were visibly intermingled.

General Sosabowski issued the priorities for the crossing. The 3rd Battalion units remaining in Driel would cross first, followed by Brigade Headquarters, the 1st Battalion mortars, the special units and the 2nd Battalion. Last to go would be the sappers, who would be directing the crossing from the south bank. Returning to their units, the commanders relayed their orders to the company and platoon commanders. The boats would carry eighteen men each, so the companies would have to be divided accordingly. In the 3rd Battalion area, Lieutenant Kula heard that they would be joining the British in Oosterbeek. Captain Gazurek concluded his "happy news" by saying that, "across the river our skins will be better thrashed than here."

It was already dark when 2nd Lieutenant Relidzinski awoke in his corner on the second floor of Brigade Headquarters. The sounds of boots pacing the floor below were accompanied by the General's voice. Speaking mostly in Polish, with some sentences in English, Sosabowski stated his worries about matters other than the technical details concerning the crossing. He was concerned about the state of fatigue suffered by his troops, and their lack of supplies. They had not eaten properly for three days and were short of ammunition. The General's voice rose, "Unless supplies come today, it's difficult to even talk about crossing. The soldiers cannot go hungry. . . . we cannot even guess about anything on the other side." A soft and very tired English voice replied with the promise of supplies that evening.

Lieutenant Szczygiel was in charge of staging the crossing. As soon as it was dark enough to move freely behind the dike, the sappers marked the routes to the two loading areas on the river bank with white tape. Several waded into the cold water to check the river depth at the crossing sites. Captain Budziszewski set up his command post in the now ruined house on the north side of the dike. 2nd Lieutenants Skulski and Grünbaum were in charge at the site of the previous night's crossing, and Lieutenant Dawidowicz was to be in command at a new site 500 meters to the west. The Brigade would stage in the orchards behind the large dike, divided by units, then further divided into boatloads. They had already moved into the village, where they expected the boats to soon arrive.

While the Poles waited for the boats, Captain Watson was in Nijmegen preparing his report about the situation for General Browning. His report summarized the Polish Brigade's part in the operation to date, starting with the three-day wait at the airfields, through the various landings and drops, and recounting the fighting the Brigade had taken part in. The report concluded with evaluations of the situation from General Sosabowski: "The state of the German defenses at the main bridge is unknown." The 1st Airborne Division's relief demanded a division-sized crossing "with full artillery support and smoke." DUKWs would be impracticable due to the nature of the terrain, and he recommended "the large-scale use of assault boats." The Germans held the high ground and this "must be neutralized by all artillery available."

The promised rations and ammunition arrived and were distributed to the waiting men in Driel. There was still no sign of the boats. Lance Corporal Kuzniar received a tin of sweets and a cube of pemican (compressed dried meat). The signaler was also given an American ration that consisted of a block of vitamin-enriched hard chocolate, with strict instructions to consume this only when ordered. Mixed in with the normal military rations were locally canned preserves; the soldiers looked them over and chose the most appetizing. The already overburdened paratroopers left the rest of the heavy jars and cans in the street. At 2230 the Brigade slung its weapons and marched to the dike, leaving behind some men to guide the boats, when they arrived, to the crossing sites.

In the parish house, where the critically wounded awaited either death or evacuation, Cora Baltussen looked at her charges. Horribly maimed, they lay quietly on the forty stretchers spread across the floor: "I have never been under the impression of such courage. You did not hear one sound of screaming or crying. These were people from hundreds of miles away waiting for a doctor to operate or amputate. A people very earthy, so honest and with a sincerity that has always impressed us."

There was a tension among the troops that Cora could feel. "The situation was very critical; everybody was very nervous." Cora had not slept for two nights, and it did not appear that she would this night. The Red Cross team cared and comforted the wounded as best they could, communicating with them in whatever English they had learned. A soldier whose arm had been shattered during the fighting told Cora of his life on a farm in Poland, then of how his father was killed when the war broke out. Afterwards, his family was deported to Siberia and he had not heard from his mother or sister since. Cora could scarcely comprehend his tragic story, "just incident after incident. After all, he had just one question, 'Do you think that there is a farmer who would want me with just one arm?'"

The door swung open. A heavily armed paratrooper came in and walked over to one of the medics. He stayed less than a minute. Pressing a piece of paper into the medic's hand, he said: " Write my wife and tell her where I went."

In the woods outside of Malden the 1st Battalion troops settled down for the night. Except that fires or cigarette smoking were forbidden, the bivouac was almost like a scout camp. The quiet and peaceful woods had a calming effect on the men after their exertions and tensions of the past days. The 82nd Airborne Division provided rations, and these were distributed to the men. Major Tonn puzzled over the many questions that had emerged that day. How long would he be under American command? How were the rest of the containers going to be recovered from the drop zone? Would I Airborne Corps give him orders and transportation to Driel? What was happening with the rest of the Brigade in Driel? Tonn wondered if he would ever see them again. The woods were peaceful, but there was a war on. The paratroopers in the dark, quiet woods heard gunshots from the direction of Mook and artillery fire from Groesbeek throughout the night.

The paratroopers marched down the muddy road from Driel to the Neder Rijn. The night was pitch dark, but the men managed to maintain an exemplary quiet. In the glow from the burning Baarskamp farm, paratroopers saw colored supply parachutes draped in the trees. Hanging tantalizingly below them were white containers, dropped in error on this side of the river during the afternoon. Nobody paused to collect them. When the column reached the large dike, the previously assembled boatloads fanned out behind it, into the orchards to await the arrival of the boats.

Lying in the wet grass on the reverse slope of the dike, Private Raschke wondered what had happened to the boats. Over the dike the bright fires across the river were reflected by the river's mirror-smooth surface. Shells continued to land on the Oosterbeek perimeter throughout the evening. Seemingly not satisfied by the bombardment they had given the Poles throughout the day, the Germans continued to fire harassment rounds into Driel at intervals.

The weary men in the wet grass around Raschke were half asleep. The Private looked at his watch; it was now past midnight. Still no boats. Pressing his eyes shut to "forget about people, the world and all this insane shooting," Raschke dozed off. His rest was short-lived. The cryptographer was awakened by cold and precise whispered instructions. The boats had finally arrived, but they were smaller than promised, and the boatloads would have to be rearranged.

DUKWs began arriving in Driel at 0023 on the morning of September 24. They brought with them fourteen FB Type-3 assault boats that had survived the 82nd Airborne's forcing of the Waal three days before. Consisting of a plywood floor, the vessels had impregnated canvas sides that folded up and were held in position by wooden braces that formed the gunwales. The boats could carry twelve passengers rather than eighteen as expected. The drivers of the DUKWs knew nothing about the sappers who were to do the rowing, and hurriedly left after their cargo was unloaded. Four Polish sappers would now have to row each boat.

The intricate planning, accomplished so carefully during daylight, now had to be reworked in pitch darkness. The boatloads had to be rearranged so that platoons and fire teams, signal sections and mortar crews would not be separated from one another. To maintain quiet, orders had to be whispered. Section leaders groped in the darkness for soldiers who had fallen dead asleep from exhaustion. In the black night no one could even recognize faces under helmets, as company commanders tried to sort out their men.

It was almost 0200 when Captain Zwolanski shook Marek Swiecicki awake. General Urquhart was speaking over Cadet Pajak's radio set. Both the rain and the German shelling had stopped. Leaving the Hartenstein, the two Poles tried to make their way to the river, stumbling through the torn woods and tripping over shattered limbs and fallen tree trunks. With the correspondent holding on to Zwolanski's belt, the pair fell into a trench, whose sleeping occupant expressed his appreciation in terms that would make an East End dockworker blush. They pushed on in the "Egyptian darkness." Reaching a clearing, they recognized nothing—the day's bombardment had changed the landscape. The correspondent wished aloud for some light, and the Germans granted his request, as shells again began bursting in the Oosterbeek perimeter.

It was 0300 hours when the guns of the Dragoon Guards' Sherman tanks began to bark. The 3rd Battalion troops lifted the 200-pound assault boats and manhandled them over the dike. They carried this burden in addition to the 60 to 80 pounds of personal equipment that burdened each paratrooper. The river was almost 300 meters away. The awkward boats had to be hauled down the steep, slippery slope, across a boggy meadow and over another dike. The open polder was illuminated by fires blazing on both sides of the river. On the north bank, the Germans had opened a main at the gas works and ignited it.

On the Driel polder, Lance Corporal Kuzniar watched the conflagration across the river in Oosterbeek. He helped put the boat he had carried across the polder into the water. But before he could grab his kit bag packed with communications equipment, the boat was full and had pushed off. As soon as the next boat was put into the water, he jumped into it.

Private Chwastek, amazed at the flimsiness of the boats, watched his company commander, Lieutenant Pudelko, leave with the first wave. Chwastek hid behind the small dike and waited until another boat was available. Peering over the top, the rifleman felt "sick to his stomach" as he watched arcs of tracer rising from the northern bank.

Finally reaching the Oosterbeek polder, Marek Swiecicki and Captain Zwolanski saw the orange glow over Driel. On the south bank a brickworks was blazing. Its roof beams had "a strange nightmare appearance, like an apocalyptic cross," until they crashed to the ground, "sending a thousand orange fireflies flitting up into the night." Flares popping in the sky bathed the smooth river in multi-colored light. As the liaison officer and correspondent huddled against an embankment, they watched a clumsy boat steadily making its way across the river. Lines of tracer pouring from both banks followed the pathetic vessel. It hit the bank, and its passengers hopped over its sides into the sticky mud. The machine guns had followed the boat's progress to shore until the bright flashes were whizzing over Swiecicki and Zwolanski's heads. The tracers then swung out to the river and converged on another boat that had left the opposite shore.

Lance Corporal Kuzniar's crossing was unhindered until his boat reached the middle of the river and the first boat hit the far shore. A volley of machine-gun bullets then flashed over the flimsy craft as a flare popped overhead. One of the canvas sides burst into flames as tracer bullets riddled the boat, and the soldier next to Kuzniar slumped over with a bullet in his arm. Stunned, everybody in the "burning boat in the middle of a pitch black night" stopped rowing and stared in shock at the wounded man. An angry voice from the rear shouted "Row!" and the men set to the task.

Hitting the shore, they jumped out onto the mud flats and pushed through a wall of reeds and into a ditch. Looking across the polder, the Lance Corporal spotted a few buildings, and a church—the assembly point. Crawling up the ditch, Kuzniar started finding German corpses, some of them badly mutilated. Though the repulsive discoveries made movement difficult, they gave the corporal some satisfaction that "somebody had done a good job."

On the north bank, the wounded and the sappers whose boats had been sunk were loaded into those that had survived. They pushed off for the southern bank to pick up more men. The German artillery and mortars joined the machine guns in raking the river and the polders. Shells landed among the troops waiting to cross, causing further confusion and casualties. The sappers took cover behind the stone flood spurs, where they were safe from the machine guns; but they cringed as the mortar shells screamed through the air. From them there was little protection. Whenever the fire slackened or shifted, the sappers went back to work; boats were still being brought forward.

More 3rd Battalion men packed themselves into the boats as they were put into the river. Father Misiuda was refused permission by Captain Gazurek to go across because, "If you are not carrying a weapon you are just taking away a place in the boat." Not wanting to leave his soldiers in the face of such a severe trial, the priest snuck aboard. The next wave pushed off. Enemy fire rose and fell in intensity as the machine-gunners paused to change belts. A soldier sitting in front of Lieutenant Prochowski slumped as a bullet went through him and lodged in the officer's leg. Using shovels and rifle butts, the passengers helped paddle to keep the boats on course in the strong current. Private Chwastek paddled with his hand, soaking his smock to the elbow.

As the Anti-tank Squadron prepared to cross, Lieutenant Bossowski assigned one of his men as a messenger to Captain Wardzala. He told him to stick to Wardzala and take care of him, no matter what. The incoming fire had slackened as Bossowski's boat loaded and pushed off. The boat carrying Wardzala and Lieutenant Colonel Rotter was carried downriver by the current. The men got out when it reached the north shore. Only after the boat had departed for its return to Driel did the newly landed contingent find themselves staring down the barrels of German rifles.

Reaching the north bank, Private Chwastek found British soldiers dug in. They looked tense, but not frightened, and they pointed the Poles east along the bank. By 0400, the bulk of the 3rd Battalion had crossed and was assembling by the dike below the Oosterbeek church. One of Lieutenant Kula's platoon reported that he was wounded when a bullet struck a grenade in his pocket. It did not explode, but pieces of the shattered bullet and grenade had lodged in his leg. He was taken to the hospital.

Lieutenant Prochowski pulled out the bullet that had struck him in the leg with his fingers. The wound seemed slight, and he could still move his leg with little discomfort. After applying a field dressing, the lieutenant pulled off his wet boots. One sock was soaked with water, the other with blood.

Under the cover of darkness, Lieutenant Smaczny's 8th Company gathered and buried the dead. With the Germans only 100 meters away, the troops took the opportunity provided by night to get out of their cramped holes and stretch. The rest of the night was spent improving their positions, watching and sleeping. Artillery and mortar fire continued sporadically all that time. It was very intense at moments, especially during the early-morning hours by the river. The men of the 8th Company did not speculate on what the commotion was all about; they just considered themselves fortunate that it was not landing on them!

The sapper corporal who rowed Captain Wardzala across the river returned to the south bank. He sought out Sergeant Juhas and reported, "Chief, I'm sure that there is something wrong. The current pulled us downstream and I'm certain that there were Germans there. They took our soldiers and let us go." Juhas believed that the enemy had wisely let the boat return, hoping that it might bring them more easy prisoners. Juhas took the corporal to Captain Budziszewski. After listening to the sapper corporal's report, Budziszewski replied, "You must row harder." He dismissed the men as the shelling increased. As another sapper finished his report with a salute, Budziszewski instinctively raised his fingers to the rim of his helmet to return the honor. Before he could complete the gesture, a shell burst nearby and mangled his hand.

The strong current added further delays to the crossing. Many of the boats had drifted downriver by the time they had made the northern bank, and by the time they had returned to the starting point, they had drifted farther still. The boats had to be hauled around the flood spurs and back to the staging area before loading more men. Already the sky to the east was beginning to lighten. The boats' wakes were beginning to fluoresce, and the German bombardment was increasing. The Headquarters and Signal Companies were scheduled to go next, while the 2nd Battalion waited its turn patiently.

Waiting behind the dike, Private Raschke wondered when the Brigade Headquarters would begin crossing. With him were his friends Lance Corporal Cadet Franciszek Oleksow and Lance Sergeant Tomasz Lepalczyk. The three had been with the Brigade Headquarters since the early days, and considered themselves the "old guard." It was now almost 0500, and the cryptographer had heard the scream of shells and of men for almost two hours. 2nd Lieutenant Waclaw Jaworski called his men together and spoke: "We are separated from the river by 200 meters of meadow. The quicker you get across it, the better. Its under heavy enemy fire. The rest should go easy." Minutes later, they were carrying their boat over the dike.

Lieutenant Grünbaum had energetically toiled through the entire night to keep the crossing going. His shouts and curses were heard in between explosions by the men waiting on the dike. Grünbaum briefed a group of signalers, "We go over the dike; after 200 meters, we will stop. After that we go for the river. We will have to work fast, the whole area is under German machine-gun fire."

As mortar shells burst, 2nd Lieutenant Relidzinski kept his eye on Corporal Cadet Adam Niebieszczanski, who would be crossing on another boat. The cadet was charged with the trolley that held the headquarters radio set. Grünbaum gave the word, and the twelve men carrying the boat went forward between lines of paratroopers awaiting their turn to cross.

In the ghostly half-light, the next wave took their boats over the Driel dike. Private Wawiorko, his shoulder helping to bear the weight of Cadet Niebieszczanski's boat, hit the ground with the rest of the men as a pattern of six Nebelwerfer rounds burst around them. One shell landed where his friend Private Filipowicz was standing. Wawiorko crawled over to the spot where he had stood and groped for him in the darkness. The signaler's hand recoiled as it felt something warm and sticky. Around him the other paratroopers were lying next to their boats. Standing, Lieutenant Grünbaum shouted, "Damn it! Get moving, we're too good of a target!"

Reacting to Grünbaum's tirade, 2nd Lieutenant Relidzinski's men rose, but there were fewer of them. One slipped in the mud. The following man fell over him, and pulled the boat and the soldiers carrying it down with him. Grünbaum shouted, and the men again moved forward. And so it went until the third wave reached the small dike, where Grünbaum called a short break: "Still 50 meters to the river. Hold on to yourselves and everything will be all right."

Private Raschke found the going tough. "Every few meters we fell to the ground and sought cover behind the boat. We could not run across the meadow in such a situation. With every shell burst or scream of Nebelwerfers, we hit the ground, and a few seconds later we were on our feet like madmen . . . forward . . . forward . . . before the next salvo tore into the earth." With dry mouth and pounding heart, Raschke prayed to the Blessed Virgin for protection from the bullets. Another salvo slammed into the ground, bowling over the paratroopers. An agonized cry came out of the darkness, "Help me . . . help . . . my legs!" Cadet Oleksow shouted: "That's Lieutenant Mroz . . . We have to help him!" "No! No! Leave him!" shouted Lieutenant Jaworski, "The medics will take care of him. Forward!"

The headquarters men threw their boat into the water, clambered in, and pushed off. 2nd Lieutenant Jaworski was in the prow rowing. Ahead of them, Private Raschke saw other boats. "A cold wind blew off of the river," he remembered. "The night was 'pregnant' with the curse of battle. Everybody was helping with the rowing to get across the Rijn as quickly as possible. Behind us the incoming artillery shells and mortar rounds sowed death on the banks."

The boat reached the center of the river, where the current was stronger, and the men exerted themselves accordingly. The German artillery adjusted, and soon great fountains of white water rose from the black water, following loud explosions. A flare burst over the center of the river. Tracer bullets flashed out from the north bank, meeting in a crossfire. The boat in front of Raschke's entered the fiery 'X' and then vanished. The fire shifted to another boat, but the evil sparks did not touch it. The tracers now turned towards the crytographer's vessel. At the bow, Lieutenant Jaworski was riddled and the deadly stream worked its way down the boat. Kneeling in front of Raschke, Lance Sergeant Lepalczyk was rowing with his rifle butt. Shot in the head, he fell backwards and lay inert on the breast of his friend.

Grünbaum barked, "Go!" and the men rose quickly from behind the small dike. "It was as if the Germans were waiting for us to show ourselves. The Spandaus went totally crazy. Tracer bullets flew around us like bloody streaks," recalled Lieutenant Relidzinski. The men hesitated, and Grünbaum started pushing them off the dike. At that moment, a stampede of paratroopers came running back over the dike from the river, knocking over the men trying to get their boats over it. Grünbaum grabbed one of them, who reported that, on orders, the crossing site had been moved.

Under fire, the signalers moved behind the small dike to the new launching point, hoping they would not receive the attention from the Germans they had received at the former one. They arrived very much frightened but with no further casualties, except for Relidzinski's Sten gun, which had been pierced by a shell fragment. The boat was put in the water and the men began jumping in. Private Wawiorko ran back to his trolley and grabbed the kit bag with the radio, threw it in the boat, and then jumped in after it. But the boat was overloaded and the sappers were throwing people out of the vessel. One grabbed the collar of Wawiorko's Denison smock and pulled. The signaler jumped, landed with one of his legs in the water, and did not stop moving them until he was behind the shelter of the small dike.

The boat with the signalers pushed off, and then got stuck on a mud shoal. The men fell to the bottom of the boat as shrapnel pierced its sides. A stricken man howled. Lieutenant Grünbaum stood, shouting, "Get into the water and push!"

Jumping into the river, the lieutenant was alone as the boatload of stunned men looked at him. "Get out and push, you sons of whores!" That profanity, so shocking coming from the lips of an officer, broke the trance. Men went over the side and pushed the boat free. Taking his place in the prow, Grünbaum rowed as the boat moved across the river. As the boat hit the north bank, a Polish sapper fell shot, and in his pain begged his comrades to finish him off. Nobody gave a thought to the sapper's request as they scrambled out of the boat looking for cover. 2nd Lieutenant Relidzinski ran for the protection of a dike. Collecting his thoughts and his breath, he glanced at his watch: the time was 0500.

The sky was becoming translucent and the black night gave way to a landscape outlined in soft grays. German machine guns continued to pour tracers onto the south bank. Lieutenant Grünbaum managed to row the two wounded men back across the river. As he got out of the boat, a shell burst, and a fragment struck the gallant officer in the face, smashing his cheek and the eye above.

In the morning twilight, Colonel Kaminski shouted through the bursting shells to break off the crossing and get back. The sappers moored the remaining six boats to the flood spurs.

Private Wawiorko reasoned that if he went by the straightest route back over the polder to the main dike, he would have too much company, and be exposed to most of the unceasing German fire. He thought better of trying to get to the brick ruin, where Captain Budziszewski had directed the crossing. Hoisting a kit bag full of communications equipment over his shoulder, the signaler ran across the polder to the cover of a ditch. Wawiorko rested a few minutes to catch his breath and "let fear subside, and reason return." Feeling collected, he threw the kit bag on his shoulder and bolted for the ruined building.

With a few men following him, Wawiorko was confronted by a familiar silhouette running towards him out of the darkness: "Coward! Coward! Why are you running?" Private Wawiorko stopped before the familiar form and could well imagine the glaring eyes. Bringing his arms to his sides, he reported, "Sir, General, Colonel Kaminski has given orders to stop the crossing and withdraw." The shadow replied, "Well done, well done," and continued to run in the direction of the crossing area. With shells exploding on the polder, Wawiorko ran across the dike road and squeezed through a gap in the wire livestock fence, tumbling down the other side. Moving back to Driel, he saw vehicles, including some tanks, in the distance. The Tommies of the DCLI were starting breakfast, and were brewing their morning tea on their Primus cookers. The peaceful scene contrasted with the inferno a half hour before on the opposite side of the dike. Staring, Wawiorko thought, "A hell of a war. Such firepower sitting here, and they push us off blind."

Among the last to leave after the crossing was called off, Sergeant Juhas and Father Mientki had evacuated the wounded Lieutenant Mroz. In the dark the priest had bandaged Mroz's badly mangled legs while Juhas dismantled one of the failed homemade rafts that still lay by the river. They placed the wounded officer on a ladder recovered from the raft, and put his haversack under his head as a pillow, and carrying him to the dike road. Juhas returned to collect equipment while the mists could still provide some cover. As he hiked back up the dike draped with ammunition bandoliers, rifles and Sten guns, he was pleased with himself. He believed that the Brigade would need every possible round.

The remainder of the Brigade once again returned to Driel. Most of the 3rd Battalion was across the river, but in the confusion, only the mortar platoon's officers had managed to get across. The mortar men, with others remaining from the battalion, and ten men from the Anti-tank Squadron, were put under Lieutenant Tadeusz Rembisz' command and sent to join the 2nd Battalion.

Of the Headquarters and Signal Companies, fourteen men had reached the north bank fit for combat. Of the Brigade staff, only the quartermaster, Lieutenant Colonel Rotter, had crossed; but he was now a prisoner. While Private Wawiorko's impression of total inactivity on the part of the British tanks may have been false, the sparse support fire provided by XXX Corps and the 43rd Division was due to an ammunition shortage. They were further hindered by fear of hitting British positions in Oosterbeek. The unobserved support fire was targeted on the German rear and failed to provide much relief for the men forcing the river.

After a heartbreaking night at the dike, the Poles on the south bank trudged back to their old positions in Driel.

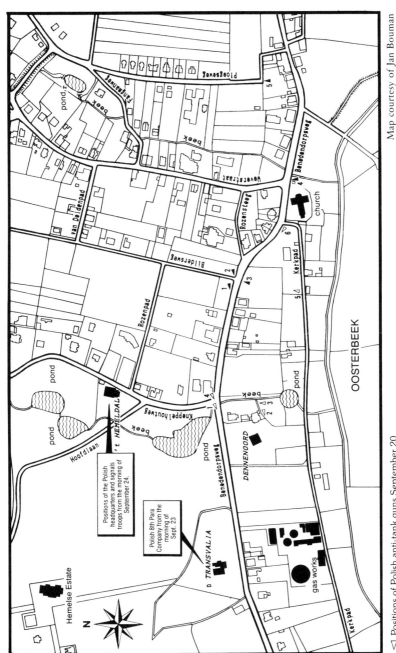

OOSTERBEEK

Map courtesy of Jan Bouman

▽ Positions of Polish anti-tank guns September 20
▼ Positions of Polish anti-tank guns September 22

Positions of the Polish headquarters and signals troops from the morning of September 24.

Polish 8th Para Company from the morning of Sept. 23

Hemelse Estate

TRANSVALIA

DENNENOORD

gas works

church

Benedendorpsweg

Kerkpad

Bildersweg

Rozenpad

Hoofdlaan

Kneppelhoutweg

't HEMELDAL

Van De Idenpad

Weverstraat

Rozensteeg

Ploegseweg

beek

pond

N

18

The Finest Sons of England
Are Dying There in Vain

0400 to 1130 Hours, September 24, 1944

On the open polder by the north bank of the Rijn, Father Misiuda prayed as the body of Lance Sergeant Lepalczyk was lowered into a hastily dug grave. Private Raschke's attention was divided between fear of staying in this exposed place, and the thoughts of his two close friends stricken during the night: Lepalczyk and Lieutenant Jaworski. Jaworski had been taken, barely alive, to the field hospital located in the ter Horst house. There he died. The words spoken by Father Misiuda, "From ashes you came . . . and to ashes you shall return," spun in Raschke's brain. They reverberated, drumming up memories of his close companions, and how "to ashes went all of their hopes, their fears, and their knowledge."

After the shallow grave was covered, the men of the Brigade headquarters company hurried towards a small wood across the polder. As they passed a foxhole at its edge, they were greeted by a grinning British paratrooper, who joyfully gave them the thumbs up. Raschke glanced around and spotted comrades from the signal company waiting in a small group of trees, which were "very well trimmed by German bullets."

Twilight revealed the cost of the Polish Parachute Brigade's bloody attempt to reach the north bank of the Neder Rijn. Polish officers who had survived the river crossing took stock of their losses, and assembled what was left of their platoons. The Anti-tank Squadron's men were to join their comrades who had landed with their guns by glider. The 3rd Battalion had managed to muster almost 100 men, but was short of Bren guns and had only one Piat with them. Together, the Headquarters and Signal Companies had managed to gather less than twenty men.

General Urquhart had decided before the crossing that the situation on the eastern side of the perimeter was much more critical, and that the new reinforcements would be given to Brigadier Hackett. On hand to help organize the new newcomers was Captain Zwolanski. As Hackett had been critically wounded that morning, Zwolanski's orders now were to have the newly arrived troops wait in the 1st Airlanding Brigade area before moving them into the 4th Parachute Brigade's lines. The Polish liaison officer led them to the area around the ponds on the grounds of the Hemelsche Berg estate.

Captain Zwolanski guided the column through the thick woods. After a few dozen meters, the soldiers came to a two-story convalescent home, the "Hemeldal." Beyond the Hemeldal, the woods opened to reveal a pond, and further yet another that was slightly smaller. The area was lovely. The ponds were ringed with beech trees, and these in turn were towered over by oaks. Zwolanski stopped and pointed to a stand of tall trees, "Signals dig in there, and hurry, the Germans will be 'sprinkling' soon."

The 3rd Battalion group was taken even farther into the woods. The troops fell out and occupied the abandoned foxholes and slit trenches that scarred the ground. After crossing, 2nd Lieutenant Kula had searched for stragglers among the British artillery positions. Hearing the order "Fire at enemy positions!" called to the British gunners, he stopped and watched the shadowy artillerymen load and lay their guns. The methodical whispers of the crews and the sounds of breechblocks opening gave Kula the impression of almost parade-ground precision. After two stubby 75mm howitzers each barked once, the order "Cease fire!" was called. Obviously, the ammunition situation did not permit any further fire.

Kula found some of the Polish anti-tank men from the glider lift near their weapons. The lieutenant was saddened as the gunners gave a day-by-day report of their comrades who had been killed. They spoke in a monotone, "everything unemotional, as if it was a natural everyday routine."

Corporal Stanislaw Lewicki, a squad leader in Lieutenant Bereda's reconnaissance platoon, was gladdened by the joyful greetings that the Red Devils had given the Poles. He sat at the edge of a foxhole that he shared with his friend Konstanty Wesolowicz, and waited for further orders. The battalion commander, Captain Gazurek, was away, being briefed about what role his men would take in the Division's perimeter. Lieutenant Jan Kutrzeba, commander of the 3rd Battalion's mortar platoon, was without a command—the carts carrying the heavy 3-inch mortars had bogged in the spongy polder, and their struggling crews could not get them to the boats before the crossing was called off. Taking advantage of the quiet, Kutrzeba visited the signalers nearby.

The signalers had fallen out and taken positions in the woods, which were already full of foxholes and slit trenches. The Brigade signal officer, Captain Julian Karasek, took his staff to the Hemeldal. Lance Sergeant Marian Blazejewski entered the building's cellar. He carried a haversack full of medical supplies he had found after crossing, and put it to immediate use; the cellar was full of civilians, some of them badly wounded. Lieutenant Relidzinski selected a deep hole, and covered it with a tarp from a wrecked jeep. As the officer shoveled a layer of dirt onto the tarp, he wondered what Zwolanski had meant by "sprinkling."

Private Raschke dug in near his friend, and fellow cryptographer, Lance Corporal Cadet Oleksow. Their positions, with those of the other headquarters personnel and signalers would form part of the 1st Airborne Division's reserves, and occupied defensive positions 600 meters southwest of the Hartenstein. Save for the chirping of birds, the woods were very quiet. Raschke looked through the leafy canopy at patches of gray sky and was overcome with sad memories of Lieutenant Jaworski. Fighting back tears, he lit a cigarette and began improving his position, knowing that the "peace" would not last forever.

2nd Lieutenant Bossowski waited with his men from the Anti-tank Squadron for instructions. That night, thirty-seven of them managed to gather on the north bank of the river. Lieutenant Mikulski had spoken with Lieutenant Mleczko, who told him that since he had only four guns left, there was no work for the Polish gunners who had crossed that night. Besides, added Mleczko, the British glider pilots had ignored their officers; they had adopted the guns they had delivered, and refused to leave. Two men were taken to help man the anti-tank guns, and three Bren gunners were assigned to the 3rd Battalion by Captain Zwolanski's orders. The rest of the anti-tank men were to man perimeter positions as infantry.

In the woods outside of Malden, 20 kilometers south of Oosterbeek, the Polish paratroopers of the 1st, and the rest of the 3rd, Battalion awoke, cold and hungry. The soldiers cooked breakfast over small fires as Major Tonn pondered how he would reach the rest of the Brigade in Driel. At 0900, he gathered all of the 1st Battalion's bicycles and put them under command of 2nd Lieutenant Jerzy Racis of the reconnaissance platoon. The lieutenant's orders were to ride north and contact the Brigade as soon as possible. Shortly after Racis left, Tonn received a message from the 82nd Airborne that the Poles could expect some vehicles to help with gathering the containers that remained on the drop zone. Tonn wondered what information Captain Dendor would bring, and when his men might be released from the 82nd's command.

The Poles who were dug in around the Hemeldal offered cans of pudding, dropped on Driel, to the Red Devils dug in around them. There were no takers among the British. Even if dry wood could be found, the enemy was so close that lighting a fire was unthinkable. It seemed to Corporal Cadet Niebieszczanski that "the British would rather starve than eat the pudding cold." The Poles had no such objections and willingly choked down the mixture of cold lard and oatmeal. The cadet seemed satisfied with his meal, because "when he got some cold pudding down his throat, he was stuffed for twenty-four hours."

Mortar officer Lieutenant Kutrzeba joined the signalers in their meal. He opened a tin with his commando knife and ate the heavy paste with its blade. Between swallows he related his adventures crossing the river. Private Raschke watched him eat and saw determination in the sharp-featured officer's large, dark eyes. Kutrzeba stood and stretched and, yawning, complained of his exhaustion. He went over to a narrow slit trench and pulled some paving slates over it. He told his comrades that if things got rough, or if he was needed, to awaken him. The lieutenant crawled in. After moving the flagstones until only his face was visible so that he might breath, he fell fast asleep.

Waiting for orders, Lieutenant Bossowski looked around at the quiet woods and wondered, "Where is the bloody battle?" Troubled, the anti-tank officer sought out Lieutenant Mikulski and told him he was going to have the men dig in. As he moved back to the head of the group Bossowski gave his orders and the men incredulously pulled out their entrenching tools. One soldier stared at the officer with eyes that said, "Are you sure you know what you're talking about?" Bossowski angrily barked, "Never mind, it won't cost anything. Just do it!" Dirt flew over the hunched soldiers as they started scraping holes in the earth. Just as the foxholes were beginning to take shape, the men looked up, reacting to the whistle of an incoming shell. They dived into their fresh con-structions as more and more shells began to burst in the fields and trees around them.

Lance Corporal Grzelak and Corporal Kuzniar were carrying WT 38 radio sets to the Hemeldal as the bombardment began. Buffeted by shell blasts and surrounded by whistling fragments, the signalers sought cover in the underbrush. As the pair made a break for the building, the microphone was torn from Grzelak's hand by a bush, in branches of which it remained hooked. It was only when the open door of the building was in sight that the pair realized that the microphone needed to operate the set was hanging in the underbrush in a hurricane of shrapnel. Captain Karasek was waiting for them at the doorway of the Hemeldal. Karasek placed his hands on his hips and replied with only a stern stare as the signalers asked if there was another microphone. The captain ordered the pair to dig in and fight as riflemen after they took the radios inside.

After a half-hour, there was no letup in the shelling. Lieutenant Bossowski cringed, confident that every shell whistling in was going to be the last for him. The officer remembered the stories he had heard as a child from old veterans about the bombardments at Verdun. Bossowski was certain this was worse!

The chirping of birds ceased as the howl of Nebelwerfers echoed through the cool woods. The soldiers around Private Raschke were paralyzed in their holes as the cryptographer prayed, "preparing his soul for its afterlife journey." Between explosive blasts and the groaning of trees being split apart, Raschke heard a penetrating yowl from a nearby foxhole. The plaintive and pained cries continued.

Raschke looked to his neighbor, Cadet Oleksow, whose face was buried in a missal, and said, "Come. We have to help." Moving towards the tortured crying, the two Poles saw dead and dying British paratroopers. One Red Devil, with thick, dark blood gushing from his chest, sat wide-eyed. The soldier's lips moved, mouthing silent words. He then convulsed and fell back dead. Shells were no longer falling, but continuing cries led the pair to a hole where a Polish paratrooper was doubled over in pain from a wound to the stomach. Raschke pulled him from his hole and carried the wounded young soldier to the aid station in the cellar of the Hemeldal. The man's cries softened into moans. As the moans became weaker, Raschke and Oleksow had him down on the trail. The soldier weakly protested when a morphine syrette was produced. In a whisper he spoke of his love for his mother in faraway Lwow. His body jerked twice, then lay still in the arms of his would-be rescuers.

When the shells stopped falling, the Poles entrenched near the ponds got out of their holes. A Red Devil walked among them, waving a five-pound note for anybody who would sell him a hand grenade. An optimistic Polish paratrooper figured that he would live to spend the fantastic sum, and traded one of the precious explosives that he had brought across the river with him.

Cadet Oleksow was deaf from the shell bursts, and was sent to the Hemeldal aid station despite his protests. The Poles then made a horrible discovery: Lieutenant Kutrzeba lay dead in his trench, his face blue and his tongue pushed horribly out of his open mouth. A small shell fragment had entered his well-protected hole and struck him below the chin. The fallen officer's platoon sergeant, who had lived and worked with him for many years, took a beret that had been hanging on a tree and covered his respected commander's face with it. He then pulled a piece of sheet metal from a wrecked jeep and with a piece of wood fashioned a cross. On it he wrote: "Lieutenant Kutrzeba. Polish Paratroopers. 24-9-44."

Lance Corporal Kuzniar and Cadet Grzelak sought a place to dig in among the large old trees on the grounds of the Hemeldal. British paratroopers greeted the new arrivals, and asked the inevitable question, "Do you have any cigarettes?" The Poles pulled some out of their pockets and passed then out to the Red Devils who, between puffs, suggested that they dig in quickly. Kuzniar borrowed a long-handled spade, and quickly dug himself a foxhole. While gathering branches to cover it, the whistle of shells prompted the lance corporal to dive into his brand-new shelter with the spade still in his hands.

For over an hour, exploding mortar and artillery shells ripped the air around him. A shell exploded nearby, and the lance corporal felt internal pain from the explosion. Trying to catch his breath despite his aching chest, Kuzniar felt an apprehension that something was descending towards him, coming nearer and nearer. The memory of his father telling him, "When you do not hear the sound of a falling shell it is heading towards you," flashed through his brain. The wait seemed to be forever, and ended without a sound. Dazed, the soldier felt his arm throbbing, and thought to himself, "This is the end." Another thought followed: "If I am thinking, this cannot be the end." Again, the words of his old soldier father came to him, "When seriously wounded, you don't feel the pain." Kuzniar did not want to look at what felt like his shattered arm. He slowly tried to move his fingers, and they worked! Opening his eyes, the signaler saw that he had been hit by a large lump of packed earth that had been ripped from the side of his hole by a shell that lay nearby, unexploded.

Among the many rumors that flew around the men of the 8th Company dug in by the Transvalia between bombardments was the news that as many as 200 Poles would be crossing during the night, and would be taking positions in the woods to the north. Lieutenant Smaczny worried about his men; the lack of food and water was acute, and wounded began to pack the Transvalia's cellar. Taking advantage of a lull in the bombardment, the lieutenant went around his positions and was relieved when he discovered that morale was not at all that bad. Reaching the hole shared by Lance Sergeant Cadet Bielawski and a corporal, he found the two rubbing out an inscription on a sheet-metal cross. Noting that both men had their names on it, the lieutenant listened with amusement when they explained that they had their grave marker already prepared but were changing the date, seeing that they had survived the night.

Lieutenant Smaczny called over to the hole of the British officer who kept bringing the Polish 8th Company ammunition and asked if he would like a cigarette. The officer, his own cigarettes long gone, eagerly sprinted the 10 meters to Smaczny's foxhole. As the offered cigarette was lit, shells again started falling in the area. The two officers smoked several in succession as they huddled in Smaczny's cramped hole. When the bombardment ceased, the Briton thanked the Polish lieutenant and hurried back to his foxhole. Seconds later, he was back with tears running down his dirty cheeks. He asked the Pole to look at his position. It was gone, except for the bent remains of a Sten gun and the shreds of a haversack sticking out of the freshly churned earth.

A salvo of British 3-inch mortars at 0830 signaled the start of the 3rd Battalion's move to its assigned positions. Captain Gazurek was to take his men and occupy a group of houses on Stationsweg just north of that street's intersection with the Utrechtseweg. With Gazurek in the lead, the column moved east into Lower Oosterbeek, and then north through the devastated town. The advance was slow, harassed by sporadic German sniping and shelling. Flanked by smoking buildings, the streets were littered with the crumpled bodies of British paratroopers. Among the corpses, a gray beret or an eagle stenciled on a steel helmet marked a Polish countryman. The smell of roasted flesh mingled with the stench of burnt buildings and expended high explosive. Red Devils' heads popped out of garden foxholes or wrecked window frames. Their filthy and exhausted faces brightened at the sight of the reinforcements. Swollen lips broke into broad smiles, followed by requests for cigarettes and any news about XXX Corps. The Poles tossed some of their now scarce cigarettes to their British comrades, but could only reply with shrugs of their shoulders to the requests for any news about the ground forces, before they moved on.

The anti-tank men who had crossed the river moved through the woods of the Hemelsche Berg estate and took positions vacated by the Border Regiment, facing Valkenburg on the wooded western edge of the perimeter. The Poles dug foxholes and slit trenches a dozen meters inside the forest, facing a farm road. On the opposite side of the road was pasture land, separated by hedges from the comfortable villas that ringed Oosterbeek. The digging was interrupted by the appearance of curious German soldiers moving across the pasture. The enemy vanished, along with their curiosity, as a few bursts of Bren gun fire swept the green field.

Lieutenant Bossowski walked over to the British positions that ran at a right angle to those of the Polish. He was pointed to the command post, located in a villa that was missing all of its doors and windows. From these openings flowed light notes of piano music. The villa was surrounded by a hedge with British soldiers dug in behind it. There were also foxholes on the other side of the hedge, some of them filled with the corpses of German soldiers. Bossowski discussed with British officers, except for one with a young face who remained at the piano, the tactical situation. After confirming the locations of friendly and enemy positions, the Polish officer quickly rejoined his men.

In Driel, General Sosabowski inspected what was left of his Brigade following the long and difficult night. After looking over his defensive positions, he went to the hospitals, where the surgeons, with steel helmets and armored vests over their surgical garb, sutured and struggled with the torn and wounded men, trying to keep down the harvest reaped by Ruhr lead and steel. At 0900 the General returned to his headquarters and drank a mug of tea. He then went to sleep, hoping to redress a little the abuse to mind and body he had suffered over the past several days.

Sosabowski's respite was short, for he was awakened only an hour later. The Polish commander was told that a British general wanted to see him. General Brian Horrocks, XXX Corps commander, had come forward to this, the most advanced position of the GARDEN half of the Operation, with whose success he had been charged. Horrocks, only a battalion commander in 1940, had had much experience fighting in North Africa and had become one of Montgomery's favorite officers. A vigorous leader, Horrocks had a way of speaking to people as if they were the only ones in the world. He gained their confidence, and infused them with his own enthusiasm. This served him well in his work after retirement from the military, in a second career as a television personality. But this day Horrocks was anything but beaming. For eight days, XXX Corps had only advanced slowly, blaming German resistance and the terrain.

General Sosabowski was both surprised and pleased that such a high-ranking officer had come this far forward, and greeted Horrocks warmly. In a private discussion, the Polish general outlined the situation on the northern bank of the river and the results of the crossing the night before. He stressed that the British were cut off from the bridge, and needed support from heavy weapons. Supplies and ammunition had to be brought to them lest they be totally destroyed. The only other alternative would be a very careful withdrawal south across the river. Horrocks replied that one battalion of the Wessex Division, with supplies for the 1st Airborne, would cross that night. The rest of the Polish units in Driel were to cross at the same sites they had used the previous two nights. Horrocks then told the Pole that all of this would be discussed and planned at a meeting at the 43rd Division's headquarters.

In once-lovely Oosterbeek, thousands of wounded had been taken to dressing stations set up in the hotels and large houses of the town. There, the wounded British, Polish and German soldiers were joined by scores of wounded Dutch civilians. All lay and waited for the battle to end. The civilians had endured over four years of humiliation, deprivation, robbery and the threat of deportation by their occupiers.

After the outburst of joy that liberation was at hand, they had taken to the cellars, and had been there for days as the battle raged above them. They huddled through explosions, screams, the clatter and squeal of Sturmgeschütze treads, and the crash of buildings falling into the streets echoing over their heads. The battle entered their candle-lit worlds when the crunch of hobnails grinding broken glass on the floor above left them breathless in terror. The civilians did not know if it was their would-be liberators, bringing a wounded comrade or looking for a place to hide, or Germans demanding to know who was sheltering in the cellar.

The Dutch were killed and wounded when they were forced from their hiding places by thirst, hunger, fire or at the point of a gun, but the injured soon saw their countrymen in the hospitals, helping the British medical staffs toiling over the wounded, without bandages, morphia, food or water. Everything was in desperately short supply. Though they themselves were parched, hungry and exhausted, civilians and medical orderlies alike selflessly succored their fellow men. They were so overburdened in caring for the maimed that they paid scarce attention to the armed enemy soldiers walking around and through the dressing stations; the dressing stations at the Schoonoord and Vreewijk hotels, on the corner of the Utrechtseweg at its crossing with Stationsweg, had been overrun that morning by the Germans.

In the Hartenstein, an exhausted Marek Swiecicki tried to function, gathering information to fulfill his journalistic duties. A divisional staff officer tried to put the best face on the situation by talking about the numbers of enemy troops the Red Devils had engaged. The reporter had heard snatches of conversation about planned counterattacks all around the perimeter. With Spandaus chattering less than 100 meters from the hotel, the correspondent was not convinced. The cellar was packed with wounded, and the journalist was called over by a British medical orderly to a Pole, who asked to speak to one of his countrymen. The man had been hit in the spine. As the correspondent helped the gravely injured soldier rearrange his hands, the man spoke to Swiecicki. He told him that his name was Wiktor Chmielewski, and that the journalist was to write that he was fighting in Holland so he could return to Wilno.

Still, there was some sense of order in the crowded hotel. The Division staff toiled unceasingly, and there was constant activity in the corner of the cellar where the Polish signalers worked continuously to keep their radios functioning. A sergeant major was the king of the building. With a toggle rope around his waist and a swagger stick under his arm, the sergeant major directed traffic in the crowded headquarters and distributed the dwindling rations. With unquestioned authority, he cleared the premises of able-bodied soldiers who had sought shelter there. In the midst of it all, General Urquhart carried on. Marek Swiecicki observed the towering Scot, who seemed quite unflappable, and even cheerful. To the reporter, the man in his quiet way seemed a distillation of the stubbornness, dogged determination and perseverance of the men he led, who wore the red beret in this handful of hectares of Hell.

In Driel, the conditions in the field hospitals had become desperate. The sterile dressings that had been brought with the parachute lift were nearly exhausted. Still the casualties came in. As a result of the river crossing, forty new wounded were brought for treatment. One was already dead as the result of a head wound, and two more died shortly after arrival. As the situation began to look hopeless, ambulances rolled into Driel. They were from the Brigade's seaborne tail, which, along with others from XXX Corps, were given a road priority to get through to the village. The medical supplies so carefully packed and sent to the Continent over a month before, on the Brigade's vehicles, were broken out and put to immediate use.

Plans to evacuate the wounded were set in motion without delay. As the vehicles were emptied, they were refilled. The drivers waited patiently for a letup in the bombardment and machine-gunning before setting off for the comparative safety of Nijmegen. By the end of the day, seventy wounded had been evacuated. Another seven, in too serious a condition to be moved, remained in Driel. The medical staff was considerably relieved that their charges were out of danger, but knew that there would be more to take their places.

Lieutenant Dyrda was on the Driel dike when a runner from headquarters came with orders for him to report to General Sosabowski immediately. When Dyrda asked what was happening, the runner replied that a British general had been at the headquarters that morning and had had an animated conversation with the brigade commander. Sosabowski was waiting for Dyrda when he arrived at the farmhouse, and told him to get his Sten gun and some hand grenades. A few minutes after 1030, a British jeep pulled up in front of the Polish headquarters. Its driver hopped out, left the jeep and ran off to rejoin his unit. Dyrda realized that he would be going somewhere, and shuddered, thinking about Myers' and Mackenzie's experiences two days before.

The fact that Sergeant Juhas climbed into the driver's seat did little to raise Lieutenant Dyrda's confidence; the burly ex-ski instructor had long had a reputation as a crazy driver. Dyrda and Lieutenant Colonel Stevens climbed in back. After General Sosabowski climbed in next to Juhas, the jeep took off. The Polish lieutenant was not disappointed, as the jeep careened down the narrow farm roads at speeds of 90 kilometers per hour. The two passengers in back hung on to the grab handles, white-knuckled with fear. At one point, tracer bullets whizzed past the jeep, but neither Stevens nor Dyrda would release their grip to grab their weapons, for fear of falling out.

Outside the village of Valburg, British military police gestured the jeep into a large pasture with many parked vehicles and a large tent. A group of British officers, collars marked with scarlet collar flashes, gathered around Generals Browning and Horrocks. General Sosabowski reported to the commander of the 43rd Wessex Division, General G. Ivor Thomas.

Thomas returned Sosabowski's greeting in a cool, almost bordering on cold, manner. Lieutenant Dyrda was puzzled that a commander coming straight from the front should be received so poorly. Horrocks had been in Driel that morning, and a river crossing had been discussed; perhaps there would be a mass crossing involving all units?

General Horrocks came forward and said, "Please go in. We were waiting only for you before we begin the meeting." Sosabowski replied, "Sir, I wish that you permit my adjutant to come. This will be a very important matter." He nodded to Lieutenant Dyrda, who stood two meters behind him. Horrocks snapped, "No, this will not be necessary. You know English. Just this morning I talked to you. You didn't need an interpreter then, and you won't need one now." Sosabowski repeated his request and added, "Sir General, this will be an important matter, I beg you." Horrocks again said no, and walked off in the direction of the tent.

Lieutenant Dyrda went to General Browning, and asked, "Sir, do you not think it better that I interpreted, rather than that the General speak for himself? You know the General."

Browning was as familiar with Dyrda as he was with Sosabowski. On many occasions, Dyrda had been with the two men when matters on the highest levels were discussed. The immaculately uniformed Browning nodded, and walked over to Horrocks. After a few quiet words, Browning returned to Dyrda and told him that he could also attend.

The interior of the tent was divided by a long table. One side of it was lined with seated British generals and staff officers. Lieutenant Colonel Stevens also took a seat with them, leaving Sosabowski to a single empty chair on the opposite side of the table. The Polish general took his seat and told Lieutenant Dyrda to sit next to him. As Dyrda looked for a chair, Horrocks, seated opposite and flanked by Browning and Thomas, said, "No, your interpreter can stand behind you." All of this struck Dyrda as very odd; it seemed to him to be a court-martial, where on one side sat the judges, and on the other the accused—and not a meeting of allied officers.

Horrocks convened the conference by saying that he had spoken with General Dempsey, Second Army commander, that morning, and he had been ordered to open a strong bridgehead on the north bank of the Neder Rijn. There would be two river crossings under the overall command of General Thomas. The agenda was then turned over to Thomas, who rose. Despite a curt and acrid manner in dealing with people, Thomas was considered to be a model British officer, with a reputation as a "driver" who got the job done. His command, the 43rd Wessex Division, was the spearhead of XXX Corps, and had had a long, hard war since landing in France.

To Lieutenant Dyrda, the contrast between his own commander and General Thomas could not have been greater. Thomas, like the other British officers, was resplendent. His scarlet cap band and collar gorgets shone brightly on his smartly tailored and crisply pressed uniform, anchored by brilliantly polished boots of fine leather. The two Polish paratroopers, who had jumped into Driel four days before, though freshly shaven, looked rather shabby; the entire time he had been in Holland, General Sosabowski had not taken off his boots, and would have been lucky if he had slept a total of twelve hours.

Thomas spoke, as Lieutenant Dyrda translated, and repeated that there would be two river crossings that night. A battalion of the Wessex Division, with supplies for the 1st Airborne Division, would cross at a point just to the west of the ferry landing. They would be followed by the Polish paratroopers who had jumped at Grave, and who were soon expected to arrive in Driel. The remainder of Sosabowski's men would cross the river at 2200 hours, at the same crossing site used the two previous nights.

To Dyrda, the meeting was surprisingly unmilitary, without answers to the usual questions: How many boats would there be. . .? When would the boats arrive, and how many men would they carry. . .? What kind of artillery support could be expected. . .? What cover would the British tanks provide. . .? Nothing, just the blunt statement that the 1st Polish Parachute Brigade would cross. The Polish lieutenant was disturbed, and could feel his commander getting angry. The Polish Parachute Brigade was being dismembered, without a word of explanation. With one battalion already across the river and Thomas taking another, Sosabowski, ever so proud of his brigade, was now in effect a battalion commander.

General Sosabowski listened in disbelief. The fate of one battalion was a small matter in the face of a greater objective. In this sixth September of world war, the Western Allies had twice as many soldiers as the Germans, fifteen times as many tanks, thirty times as many aircraft. Listening to an apparent briefing for defeat was becoming hard to bear.

General Thomas continued, stating that the commander of the crossing would be Brigadier Walton, commanding the 130th Infantry

Brigade. Sosabowski kept silent, even though his units were un-ceremoniously given to the command of a junior infantry brigadier. After Thomas spoke, a silence transpired. General Sosabowski stood up and spoke:

"The situation on the north bank of the river is very serious. If there is a larger and stronger effort, we can win all of this. . . . Crossing one British battalion and the remains of the Polish Brigade will change nothing. This is without an objective. I propose the crossing of an entire division, and at another crossing point between Renkum and Heteren. I am certain that this will lead to the success of the entire MARKET GARDEN operation. I, over the past few days, have carefully watched the Germans. They don't have any reserves, they are running out of ammunition, their fire against us is starting to slacken. They are not weak, however, they are strong and have tanks. This plan helps neither the British 1st Airborne Division nor us. I would attack beyond the Westerbouwing, which overlooks the entire Rijn, and this is very impor-tant tactically. I am certain that General Urquhart's Airborne Division will not be able to take that position, and that one British battalion will also not succeed. This is an unnecessary sacrifice of soldiers."

Before taking his seat, Sosabowski added: "I, as Brigade commander, can best select which one of my battalions should cross the river with the British."

The apparent lassitude of the senior British officers disturbed Dyrda. To them, everything was straightforward. Thomas stood and said, "The crossing will take place as I said, at the locations I stated, and will begin at 2200 hours."

Sosabowski could no longer stand this, and rose. His English fluency was proportionate to his anger, and at this moment the words came to him easily: "General, don't sacrifice your soldiers. You won't gain anything by this. One battalion will not change the situation there. Help, we must help . . . to lead to a victorious end to this operation. The entire division must cross."

The audience was impassive, and this further increased Sosabowski's aggravation. As Thomas tried to interrupt, Sosabowski raised his voice and, speaking directly to him, added: "Sir General, remember, since eight days and nights, not only Polish soldiers, but also the finest sons of England are dying there in vain, for no effect."

General Horrocks interrupted: "The conference is over. The orders given by General Thomas will be carried out." Turning to General

Sosabowski, Horrocks continued, "And if you, General, do not want to carry out your orders, we will find another commander for the Polish Para Brigade who will carry out orders."

Seeing that there was nothing further he could do, Sosabowski sat down. The former staff college professor was seething. He had not uttered a single syllable implying that he would not carry out his orders. He felt himself senior to all of the officers present, in age and experience, if not in rank; and he could not convince his audience. The fiery Pole had failed to impress the seemingly casual retinue that MARKET GARDEN must be won. The thought of being defeated by the Germans at this stage of the war was intolerable.

The stormy meeting broke up. General Browning asked Sosabowski to mess at his headquarters in Nijmegen. Outside the tent, General Thomas was giving Lieutenant Colonel Stevens verbal orders for the Polish Brigade. General Sosabowski walked over to the officers, but was ignored by Thomas, who would not even look at him while he continued to give instructions to the Brigade's British liaison officer. When Stevens rejoined Sosabowski for the first time since entering the tent, he was met by a penetrating stare. Sosabowski asked, "Well, Colonel, when will you be taking command of the Brigade?" The liaison officer blurted, "What?" and looked at the Polish general in surprise. Eyebrows hooked, Sosabowski glared at Stevens and crisply told him, "You took the orders. You did not say anything except 'Yes, Sir' instead of referring to the commander of the Brigade, General Sosabowski."

The officers all then climbed into jeeps, and left for Nijmegen.

19

May Poland Appear in Your Dreams

1200 Hours, September 24, to
0500 Hours, September 25, 1944

Lieutenant Colonel Ian Murray of the Glider Pilot Regiment had taken over command of the 4th Parachute Brigade from the wounded Hackett. As noon approached, he found himself personally leading Captain Gazurek and the Polish 3rd Battalion to their assigned positions at the intersection of Utrechtseweg and Stationsweg. As the Poles reached the wide street, they saw their objective ahead of them. At the corner a jeep belched bright orange flame, and at intervals tracer bullets streaked from the German lines and down the length of Utrechtseweg. Open-mouthed, the leading troops watched chips of brick and masonry fly off the walls of their final destination: the nine houses that lined the west side of Stationsweg.

The intersection overlooked by the Polish riflemen was the 1st Airborne Division's front line, facing the Germans pressing in from the east. The divisional headquarters at the Hartenstein was less than 400 meters away. The troops in the Oosterbeek perimeter referred to it as "MDS (Medical Dressing Station) Crossroads" because of the facilities set up in the hotels Vreewijk and Schoonoord, located on the opposite, eastern corners of the intersection. The row of houses that was the Polish objective were held on the northern end of the block by British glider pilots, while those at the crossroads were held by No. 1 Platoon, 21st Independent Parachute Company. In back of the houses was open terrain with vegetable gardens and fruit trees.

German snipers and machine gunners, who had managed to infiltrate the positions of the remnants of the 156th Parachute Battalion, occupied some of the houses in the area, and took the backs of the houses on Stationsweg under fire. The glider pilots at the north end of the block had beaten off several attempts over the past few days by German tanks to move down Stationsweg. The day before, the pathfinders had stopped a German attack that had swept through the positions of the 10th Parachute Battalion to the southeast, and that left one of the houses they were defending a heap of ashes and rubble.

In Stationsweg no. 8, the fourth house from the corner of Utrechtseweg, lived the Kremer family. The large, three-story brick house reflected the prosperity of the Kremers, who had done well with coffee plantations in the Dutch East Indies. The Sunday before, the Kremers had reveled in their liberation as they watched the Germans speed out of Oosterbeek, steps ahead of the British paratroopers who had fallen from the sky. The cellar of the sturdy building now provided shelter for Mr. and Mrs. Kremer and their twelve-year-old daughter, Ans, and son Sander, age eleven. The Kremers also opened their doors to many of their neighbors. Mrs. Kremer remained cheerful despite the fact that the Red Devils had taken over her house after the British advance had bogged down. Even when Stationsweg had become the front line, the vibrant woman took snapshots of the airborne soldiers and had them sign their autographs in the family ledger. But on this Sunday, September 24, the eighth day of battle, even Mrs. Kremer was getting a little weary. German snipers in the trees across Stationsweg had killed two pathfinders in her house. The cellar of no. 8 now held thirty-three people after more neighbors had come to the Kremers to escape the fire that had claimed the house three doors up the street.

While the Poles were collecting themselves for their dash across Utrechtseweg, Colonel Graeme Warrick, chief medical officer of the 1st Airborne Division was returning to Oosterbeek after having met with his opposite at the headquarters of the II SS Panzer Corps. There he had arranged a cease-fire so the many wounded could be evacuated to the German-held hospitals in Arnhem for treatment. The Germans agreed; they had moved relatively unhindered in the area of the hospitals in Oosterbeek, which in fact had changed hands several times over the course of the previous days. They promised to lift the mortar fire in the area, and even help with the evacuation of the casualties, some of whom had been wounded again, or killed when shells struck the buildings where they lay.

Near the head of the column, Corporal Jan Towarnicki watched the bullets hitting the pavement and ricocheting up. He suggested to Captain Gazurek that they cross the road some 20 meters west, where most of the spent bullets would not be accurate or fly up, above a man's height. The decision was taken to cross Utrechtseweg one man at a time. There was still enough movement and confusion in the area, with the Hartenstein down the road and the British medical aid stations at the intersection, to allow an individual to sprint across the road without attracting too much enemy attention. Captain Gazurek planned the crossing: Lieutenant Pudelko's 7th Company, consisting of two platoons led by 2nd Lieutenants Urbanski and Kula, would be first, followed by 2nd Lieutenant Bereda-Fialkowski, leading the battalion headquarters. The rear would consist of the two platoons of the 9th Company led by 2nd Lieutenant Leon Prochowski.

Up with the command group, Corporal Towarnicki grabbed his section's Bren gun and covered the first two men as they went across the street, and then quickly joined them. The three moved in back of a wall behind the houses on Stationsweg. Towarnicki took cover behind an oak tree. As he peered around it a burst from a Spandau slammed into its thick roots and sent bark and splinters flying. Towarnicki pulled back, telling Captain Gazurek that the gardens were under heavy machine-gun fire. They went into the backyard of Stationsweg no. 2, a stately building named "Quatre Bras" on the corner of Utrechtseweg. After identifying himself to the pathfinders holding the building, Gazurek waited for more men to come across. As Urbanski's platoon was crossing the road, a bullet tore into the stomach of a medical aid man, Private Mikolaj Bzowy. His comrades dragged him with them. As the rest of the 7th Company gathered in the rear of the Quatre Bras, Captain Gazurek prepared to lead them in an assault up the street.

In Stationsweg no. 8, the Kremers spent the relatively quiet late morning talking to the men of the 21st Independent Parachute Company holding their house. Even the redoubtable pathfinders were beginning to show the strain of the ordeal. Mrs. Kremer waited with them for the arrival of Second Army, and it was becoming clear to the civilians that something was going wrong. A hurricane of small-arms fire broke out around the house and there were shouts from upstairs, "Germans are attacking!" Outside, shouts in an unknown language were heard amid the shooting, as the civilians scurried back into the cellar.

The Poles moved north through the backyards. With Gazurek in the lead, the shouting Poles burst into the Kremer house. Following the battalion commander, Lance Corporal Kuzniar ran through a long corridor to the other side of the building. With grenades exploding in the street, the Poles ran out the kitchen door and into the yard. Standing in the midst of branches from shattered fir trees, Gazurek looked at the thick brick wall, almost two meters tall, that blocked the way to the next house. Pulling off his helmet, the captain started to climb the wall, and shouted for Kuzniar to go back and show the way to the men following. The signaler-turned-rifleman ran back through the corridor and, looking across the alley at the house he had just left, saw a Polish lance corporal at the door. At Kuzniar's hand signal, the corporal's face broke into a broad smile, and he led his section into the Kremer house. The corporal ran forward to the garden and was greeted by a horrible sight: Captain Gazurek's helmetless head rested on a stump, skull laid wide open by a bullet. Gazurek's jaw moved twice, and there was no further motion from the fiery captain.

Stunned, Kuzniar gaped at the man who had never permitted the paratroopers to remove the uncomfortable helmets during training. 2nd Lieutenant Bereda arrived. In a moment Lieutenant Pudelko caught up with him. Bereda reported the death of Captain Gazurek to Pudelko, and that *he* was now ranking officer. The lieutenant cut Bereda short, "You know the orders and the terrain. There is no time to brief me; I will follow your orders."

The embroiled Poles swept around the wall to the next yard. By now, there was fire all around. The British defenders, getting over their confusion at the violent outburst of shooting and the shouts in a strange language, fired at the enemy-filled woods across Stationsweg. From the upper floor of the next house glider pilots laid down fire, as a Spandau raked the backyards. A burst of machine-gun bullets sent fountains of dirt and vaporized brick in front of the running lance corporal, so "they looked as if I were chasing them." Over his shoulder, Kuzniar saw a rifleman fall, shot through the legs. The corporal who had smiled at Kuzniar grabbed him under his arms, and pulled him into the nearest building, and then followed the lance corporal into the last building on the block.

2nd Lieutenant Bereda supervised his men in taking up the defense of the houses on Stationsweg. There was a burnt-out house opposite the Polish positions. Facing the Quatre Bras was a large hotel, the Vreewijk, which housed a dressing station. Aside from a few small houses near the intersection with the Utrechtseweg, the area across the street was heavily wooded and was known as the "Dennenkamp." This was held by the tough sappers of SS Panzer Pioneer Battalion 9, who had been sniping from the tall trees at the British in the houses with some success. The Quatre Bras was occupied by a platoon of the 9th Company commanded by 2nd Lieutenant Kowalczyk, and led by the experienced Corporal Towarnicki. The next house (Stationsweg no. 4) was occupied by 2nd Lieutenant Prochowski, with the other 9th Company platoon. The large house next door was occupied by Bereda and the battalion headquarters troops. The Kremer house beside it was held by the 1st Battalion troops commanded by 2nd Lieutenant Kula. Stationsweg no. 10 provided positions for the commander of the 7th Company, Lieutenant Pudelko, and 2nd Lieutenant Urbanski's platoon. Of the next three houses, one was a heap of rubble, and the other two were held by British glider pilots. Six Polish paratroopers with a Piat were sent to reinforce them.

Among the Poles who reinforced the British in the corner house at the end of the block were Lance Corporal Kuzniar and his friend and fellow signaler, Lance Corporal Karol Matlak. The house showed the effects of the German attempts to push down Stationsweg: The ceiling hung down in sheets and the corner of the building facing the Germans was completely demolished. There was even a large hole in the wall that formed the corridor between the rooms. The house had been defended by seven British soldiers, commanded by a captain. Everybody was soon taking turns at guard, at posts in the upstairs and ground-floor windows, and at the hole where the building's corner used to be.

The pathfinders in the houses on the lower part of the street turned over their positions to the Poles. After a short rest, they dashed across the Utrechtseweg in a group, behind the cover of smoke grenades. Lieutenant Kula's platoon took over Stationsweg no. 8 from the British. In the ground-floor dining room, a sick woman lay on a bundle of blankets. The young woman had been very pregnant, and had miscarried a few days before. Unseen by a doctor, the poor woman was in no condition to enter the crowded cellar. Cared for by a teenager, the pair had become comfortable in the relative shelter of the Kremer's dining room, located in the middle of the house.

Mrs. Kremer came out of the cellar to see the new defenders. From the doorway watched her daughter Ans. The new soldiers were different from the phlegmatic British pathfinders. A group of Polish paratroopers sat in the hallway, backs to the wall and their weapons on their laps. To the Dutch, the soldiers looked stunned, just staring blankly at the civilians. Mrs. Kremer looked at the men, and picked out one soldier with a "nice, frank face that gave me confidence." Speaking some words of Polish she had learned as a teenager, Mrs. Kremer told the man she had visited Warsaw, Krakow and Lwow. Lance Corporal Cadet Jurecki looked at the woman, and then decided he was not interested in conversation; the events of the past six days weighed a little too heavily on his body and his soul.

When 2nd Lieutenant Bereda came to inspect the Kremer house, he noticed the cellar and told the men that if the Germans entered, they were to make their last stand there. Mrs. Kremer understood enough Polish to realize what was being said, and pleaded for the helpless civilians. Bereda was eventually made to understand their plight, and agreed to respect the cellar sanctuary.

The Poles took their positions at the windows of the upper floors. Outside the cellar door lay a Polish paratrooper with his Bren gun pointed towards the back window. The situation looked serious to Mrs. Kremer as the soldier seemed to expect the enemy to come in the window at any moment. She realized that this was the man she had tried to talk to. She told him what happened with "the Polish commander." Not taking his eyes from the window, Cadet Jurecki let go of the Bren with one hand and took Mrs. Kremer's: "I'm lying here near the cellar door, and I give you my word that none of us will enter the cellar." The pair were silent for a few moments, until Jurecki took the woman into his confidence: "I am still young and I have my life ahead of me. . .and now I have to die."

Mrs. Kremer looked at the young soldier who had come from a country so far away. He was tense, and would not take his eyes away from the window and the green gardens beyond. The woman tried to comfort him, telling the young paratrooper that he would live, as they all would. When she got no reaction from him, she asked him to sign the family ledger as remembrance. Jurecki turned towards the woman, and with a sad smile, said, "Tomorrow, when I'm still alive."

On arrival at I Airborne Corps headquarters in Nijmegen, Lieutenant Dyrda, owing to his junior rank, was pointed to the officers' mess. General Browning then went with General Sosabowski to the staff officers' mess. With the sounds of battle in the distance, the generals sat down to dine. As waiters served the meal on china plates, Browning's staff asked Sosabowski question after question about the state of the battle. Following the meal, Browning asked Sosabowski to his caravan. Despite the sad incident with General Thomas, Sosabowski harbored the hope that he would finally be able to approach Browning on the question of a mass crossing that could save the operation.

After an hour and a half, a staff car delivered Sosabowski back to the officers' mess. Lieutenant Dyrda saw that the General was quite agitated as he related to Dyrda what had happened at the meeting with Browning. General Browning had immediately come to the point, and stated that he and his corps headquarters were now subordinated to XXX Corps. The main task now was to keep the road between Eindhoven and Nijmegen open, and to bring up as many combat units of XXX Corps and the sea-lift vehicles of the airborne forces as possible. The situation in the corridor was very serious, and the Germans had in fact cut the road. Sosabowski stated that there should be a mass crossing of the Neder Rijn, to relieve 1st Airborne Division as soon as possible—more of Urquhart's men were being killed and wounded every minute. Browning replied that there was no equipment for a river crossing. Sosabowski, remembering the losses during the Polish river crossings, became bitter. He pointed out that there were hundreds of vehicles in Nijmegen, and even ambulances had gotten through to Driel—and now there were no boats? Frustrated, he stormed that a Polish company commander, assigned to cross a single river, would have made sure that boats were available. MARKET GARDEN called for six rivers to be crossed, and what kind of carelessness on the part of the British generals had caused them to forget boats?

An experienced and ever-diplomatic negotiator, Lieutenant Dyrda thought of the damage that might have been done during Sosabowski's meetings with Browning. Both generals had been under tremendous pressure over the past days, and Dyrda bluntly warned the Polish general that by exposing a mere suggestion of reluctance to come to the aid of the 1st Airborne Division, he might no longer have any friends among the British generals, and indeed might have created some enemies. Sosabowski, self-righteously convinced of his correctness, was displeased with Dyrda's frank assessment. Not another word was spoken between the officers as they returned to Driel.

At noon, Major Tonn was visited by Captain Dendor, and told that the Polish paratroopers who had dropped at Grave the day before would be provided with motor transportation to Valburg. Dendor then provided more information about the rest of the Polish Brigade in Driel. Tonn was surprised when told that he would be under the orders of the British 43rd Division. Tonn gave his command orders to prepare: trucks were expected to arrive at 1530 hours.

In embattled Oosterbeek, Private Raschke looked at his comrades dug in around him. Sergeant Wojcik had lapsed into a sullen silence after the morning mortar and artillery bombardment. As the wounded were cared for and the dead buried, the angry drone of aircraft engines ripped through the air, followed by the whine of falling bombs. The Poles threw themselves into their holes as the bombs exploded. Raschke lit a cigarette to calm himself, and watched the tobacco smoke drift in the soft breeze before explosions hurled tree limbs, rocks and earth onto the Polish foxholes and slit trenches.

Wojcik's dust-covered face appeared from his hole. The sergeant broke his silence by shouting, "May the Devil take them." The dead from the air attack lay where they fell; there was no longer the time or the will to bury them. "Time," the cryptographer thought to himself, "victory was a matter of time, but how to hurry it?" Raschke thought about the grenade that had been sold for five pounds; time had better pass fast, "before the price of grenades skyrockets!"

At the Quatre Bras on the corner of "MDS Crossroads," the Polish defenders went through the kitchen and cellar, looking for something to eat. The only thing edible was a large bag of bran, probably feed for chickens. The soldiers were hungry, and many had not eaten for a day. There was no water in the house, so Corporal Towarnicki asked Lance Corporal Konstanty Welsolowicz to try and get some water. As Wesolowicz moved through the yard of Stationsweg no. 6, he was struck by a burst of machine-gun fire. The occupants of the house pulled him in, but there was little they could do. Corporal Stanislaw Lewicki stared at his dead comrade from the reconnaissance platoon. Just hours before, they had shared a foxhole after crossing the river. Bidding his friend farewell, Lewicki hummed the old Polish soldiers' dirge to himself: "Sleep, Friend in Your Dark Grave, May Poland Appear in Your Dreams."

Mortar and machine-gun fire continued to hit the houses on Stationsweg. The only good thing about being so close to the German front line was that the men there were spared the artillery and rocket mortars that were blasting the perimeter behind them. Some of the Polish soldiers braved going into the yards and, stretched out on their stomachs, dug shallow communications trenches so they might move between the houses with some security from the ever-present snipers. In Stationsweg no. 10, Private Mikolaj Bzowy, the 7th Company aidman, died from his stomach wound. Upstairs, Private Emil Mentlik moved just a little too carelessly and offered his silhouette to a sniper sitting in a tree. The shot entered the window and hit Mentlik squarely in the chest. The paratrooper's armored vest gave no protection against the high-velocity bullet, which knocked him across the room. The stricken soldier curled up against a clothes closet by the wall, and then lay still. The Poles responded by spraying suspected green leafy treetops with automatic-weapons fire.

At the Hotel Schoonoord, the proprietor's daughter, Hendricka van der Vleist, had been caring for the many wounded who had flowed in. There were so many that all of the rooms, the hallways, and the reception area were filled. They even lay on the veranda. Among the wounded were Poles, who at times translated for the British doctors and orderlies as they tended to the German wounded. German combat troops with weapons in hand had been arrogantly parading through the emergency hospital for days, but the young Dutch woman had ignored them. She had slept only a few hours each night and had eaten what little could be spared after feeding the wounded. With all the broken and bloody men to care for, she had no time to listen to the boasts of young SS men.

The German soldiers had also used the protection of the Red Cross flags around the Schoonoord and Vreewijk to move through the area. The armed enemy, brazenly violating the laws of war, were taken under fire by Lieutenant Kowalczyk's men. The Germans had stuck the barrel of a machine gun out of one of the upstairs windows of the Schoonoord. This drew a burst of fire from across the street. As Hendricka van der Vleist watched a bullet fly through the window and bury itself in the ceiling, a British doctor knocked the machine gun down. Hendricka and the doctor told the Germans that there were Poles nearby. The word "Poles" seemed to get their attention, and they quickly pulled all their weapons from the windows.

At 1500 hours, the mortar fire in the area of the crossroads stopped. British jeeps, flying Red Cross flags, and German ambulances began evacuating the wounded from the medical stations around the intersections. Up the Utrechtseweg from the Schoonoord, the Poles opened a vigorous fire every time the field-gray or spot-camouflage-clad figures exposed themselves. They did not take time in the heat of battle to check whether the objects they carried were stretchers or Mausers. A German next to an ambulance outside the Schoonoord drew a burst of Bren-gun fire from the Quatre Bras as he stood, pointing his machine pistol at the upper floor of the building. The British medical officers were frantic that these outbreaks would ruin this limited solution to the misery of the wounded.

Lieutenant Colonel Dr. Arthur Marrable managed to shoo the armed Germans out of the dressing stations, then went to speak to the Poles in the Quatre Bras. Marrable did not have an easy task in either endeavor, but he did get his point across to 2nd Lieutenant Kowalczyk. This was the first that the Poles had heard of a local cease-fire. 2nd Lieutenant Bereda was informed of the situation by Kowalczyk, and the acting commander of the 3rd Battalion then passed strict orders to his men in the houses up the road not to fire in the direction of the aid station.

As he watched the now uninterrupted evacuation of the Schoonoord and Vreewijk dressing stations, 2nd Lieutenant Kowalczyk was surprised. He had never seen the enemy this close, and was amazed at the discipline and self-control of the German medics. Here he saw dreaded SS, wearing Red Cross armbands, "quietly and efficiently, and with great tenderness, attend to their charges regardless of nationality."

In the house at the corner of Paul Krugerstraat, Lance Corporal Matlak stood guard at the attic window. Matlak spotted the German ambulances moving at the end of the street. Focusing his binoculars, the soldier clearly saw Germans moving about without any shooting. Matlak's curiosity was aroused. As he leaned his head out the window for a better view, a bullet crashed into the brick in front of his face.

The truce was soon over. The Germans established and consolidated positions around the crossroads, and were now south of the Polish positions on Stationsweg. The Poles were now under fire from all directions. In Stationsweg no. 6, where Lieutenant Bereda had his headquarters, Corporal Franciszek Wieczorek stood guard in an attic window. He felt good about the house; it was large and solidly constructed. As he was watching through binoculars, a Spandau burst crumbled the plaster wall above his head. Keeping low at the windowsill, the corporal scanned the park across the street and, 100 meters away, spotted a clump of bushes with wisps of smoke rising from it. Wieczorek emptied an entire Bren magazine into the shrubs. The chastened corporal then returned to watching the park. A quarter-hour later, a pair of Germans with Red Cross arm bands and curious white helmet covers moved swiftly across the park. They paused at the bushes that Wieczorek had fired on, and dragged away a body. A few minutes later they returned and carried away a second.

During the afternoon, the 8th Company was asked by the Border Regiment to provide a reconnaissance patrol. Smaczny told Lance

Corporal Cadet Bielawski to take ten men and report to the Border Regiment headquarters. Bielawski was told that his task was to reconnoiter the area west of the road. The cadet did not like the idea, certain that he would find the area strongly held by the Germans. A British major took the Poles to the jump-off area by the road, and in doing so, attracted lively sniper fire. Bielawski and his men hustled across the road and into the woods. They pushed on through the deep forest, slightly spread out but keeping an eye on each other. After moving quietly 400 meters west, heavy machine-gun fire tore through the woods, killing the point man, Private Mieczyslaw Krzeczkowski. The patrol fell back, leaving the soldier behind, but not before noting the location of the enemy position. Bielawski led his men back to the Transvalia, where he reported to his company commander. While Smaczny sent the report of the reconnaissance to the Border Regiment, the exhausted patrol tried to get something to eat, but even clean water was not to be found.

In a wood outside the town of Malden, a column of thirty-three trucks arrived. Major Tonn glanced at his watch; it was a few minutes past 1530. The Polish paratroopers loaded their heavy equipment and themselves onto the trucks. They joked among themselves about how it was such a pity they had to ride: "After all, paratroopers so love to walk." It was almost a pleasure trip, the Polish soldiers playing tourist as they drove through the 82nd Airborne Division's area and then on to Nijmegen. The column wound through the devastated city and then crossed the wide Waal river over the road bridge, and into the Betuwe.

A formation of Dakotas flew north over the Betuwe and crossed the Neder Rijn. Lieutenant Smaczny's men got out of their holes and waved their Celanese identification panels at the supply planes, hoping that a container or a pannier might be dropped into their hands. The 8th Company soldiers watched in frustration as the twin-engined transports flew past them, shortly before colored parachutes blossomed over the woods north of the Transvalia.

Due to bad weather over the British Isles, no supply missions were flown from there on September 24. However, twenty-one aircraft from the RAF's 46 Group had moved to Brussels to provide better support for the 1st Airborne Division. These Dakotas comprised the only supply mission flown that day in support of the desperate men in Oosterbeek.

Two supply containers drifted through the trees and came to earth, watched by the Polish troops dug in near the ponds. Private Raschke was "tempted like the Devil" by the sight of the containers, and by the promise that the contents would fill empty magazines and stomaches. They lay in a place covered by the fire of two German machine guns. The odds of retrieving them were not very good, but temptation gnawed at the men looking at the white cylinders a hundred meters away. From the cover of the trees, two Red Devils, who had already suffered eight days in this Hell, crawled towards the treasure. Hearts in their throats, the Poles watched the pair crawl meter by meter to them. After agonizing minutes, they reached them and undid the retaining bands. As they started emptying the contents, the German machine guns "cut loose a wall of bullets from both sides that chopped the 'jokers' to pieces. Around the dead lay scattered tins of food and ammunition. Maybe some other 'joker' might pick them up after dark. . . maybe."

The day passed for the Anti-tank Squadron men, fighting as infantry on the western edge of the perimeter. The enemy no longer moved in the open, but a bullet from a sniper did kill one of the Poles. For much of the day the Germans kept the area under heavy mortar and machine-gun fire, wounding one soldier, who was evacuated to an aid station. Lieutenant Bossowski and his men crouched in their narrow foxholes, curled in fetal positions. Throughout the long day, falling earth, pebbles, branches and shell fragments drummed on Bossowski's helmet as he huddled in his hole, chin tucked between his knees.

At 1700 hours in General Sosabowski's headquarters in Driel, the unit commanders were briefed on the plans for the night's river crossing. The 2nd Battalion would lead, and the remaining Brigade units would follow, using the old crossing point near De Nevel. At the same time, the trucks carrying the 565 Polish paratroopers who had jumped at Grave approached Valburg. They passed some British heavy-artillery positions, and then came to a halt. The sound of unrelenting artillery fire came from the direction of the Rijn. Four trucks would remain with the Poles to carry the heavy weapons, ammunition and signal equipment that were still packed in containers. Major Tonn went ahead to the Wessex Division's headquarters to find out the situations of both the friendly and enemy forces. Tonn met Lieutenant Racis on the road. He had gone ahead to contact the Brigade in Driel, and was returning to make his report.* Tonn

---

*Earlier in the day, Lieutenant Detko of the Signal Company had left Driel on motorcycle to contact the missing troops. Passing near Elst, the gallant officer was machine-gunned. He was later found by British soldiers and evacuated to Nijmegen.

tried to raise Sosabowski by radio, but received no reply.

As the sun descended in the west, Lieutenant Smaczny organized an expedition to recover some of the supply containers that had landed in the woods. Cadet Bielawski and his recently returned patrol were to hold the 8th Company's positions. Smaczny took six men to create a diversion, while another patrol was to move in the direction of the containers in case any could be recovered. The energetic officer led his group west, where they crashed into the woods, firing bursts from their Sten guns and throwing their precious grenades. The search party managed to locate three containers. The raid was not without loss; in addition to the containers, they brought back two men wounded in the attempt. At the Transvalia, the soldiers eagerly removed the retaining bands and unsnapped the buckles. Their disappointment was acute; one of the containers was full of Sten-gun ammunition and the other two were packed with M.75 mines without detonators. The men had hoped for hours that they would be rewarded for their efforts with food or cigarettes.

At the crossroads of Stationsweg and Utrechtseweg a British medical officer from the Schoonoord walked towards the Polish positions a few minutes before 1800. He came to see 2nd Lieutenant Bereda, and carried an ultimatum from the Germans to evacuate the house overlooking the crossroads. The Germans claimed it threatened the hospital, and they would bring up tanks and level the house if the Poles did not leave. Bereda consulted Captain Zwolanski in the Hartenstein by radio. Zwolanski rejected the ultimatum and told the lieutenant, "You cannot surrender, you cannot withdraw, and we cannot give you any help."

2nd Lieutenant Bereda went to the Quatre Bras to tell the defenders of the ultimatum, and to also expect German tanks. Corporal Towarnicki asked Bereda if there was any water anywhere, and told of the losses suffered in the search for it. Bereda replied that there was a well up the street, and he would send some up. A half-hour later, a half-filled pail of water appeared at the house. Everybody took a quick swallow, and then the bran was dumped into it. A fire was lit, and bran cooked. Towarnicki could not take more than a spoonful since it was without salt. The few people who could stomach it ate the horrible gruel. Towarnicki went to his haversack, where he had hidden three cans of ox-tail soup. He started passing it to his men. Each would get a gulp of the liquid, and maybe a fatty bone. Private Jan Jaszkiewicz asked Towarnicki, "Will we return to

England?" The corporal looked at the young soldier and focused on his eyes. The blue pupils were surrounded by seas of red. He reassured the soldier and then gave him half a can of the hoarded soup.

In failing light, Major Tonn's group made its way on foot to join the rest of the Polish Parachute Brigade. The equipment trollies were useless—over the days, military traffic had rutted and torn apart the Betuwe's fragile roads. The soldiers carried not only their personal weapons and equipment but also shared the burden of the ammunition and supplies that did not fit into the four trucks provided by the Americans. The sound of artillery drifted across the fields to them. Some of the soldiers, having their first taste of combat, looked at the dead cattle along the sides of the road and grimaced. Corporal Wojewodka thought back to 1939, when he saw people lying in such obscene positions, and saw a pall of smoke and flashes of flame ahead of him. The troops were tense, and Wojewodka didn't know why, but "we all sensed that we were going to be doing something that was almost impossible."

In the Kremer house, those civilians remaining on the ground floor were sent into the cellar. The Poles did not totally trust the Dutch, and feared the damage a single collaborator might do. In this desperate situation, 2nd Lieutenant Bereda bluntly issued strict orders that the civilians cover the cellar windows, not use any kind of light, or speak a single word—they were to stay totally silent. The soldiers rummaged through their pockets and managed to find a few pieces of candy and chocolate to give to the children. As she went to the cellar, Mrs. Kremer asked Cadet Jurecki, "Do you think that the English tanks will reach us?" Forcing a smile, Jurecki replied, "I believe yes."

As darkness approached, the Polish soldiers prepared for the night. With a loud explosion, a hole was blown in the thick brick that separated Stationsweg no. 10 from no. 8. The blast was so strong it blew out the remaining windows in both buildings, but it completed a shallow communication trench system that linked the first five houses on the street. The paratroopers then left the upper floors of the houses and took positions in the slit trenches that had been dug by the previous British occupants. 2nd Lieutenant Bereda continued going from house to house, checking on the defenses, giving orders, and keeping up morale. He had also made it very clear that they were surrounded, and that they would fight, and if need be, this would be their grave. The tough and resourceful commander seemed to take no rest. The troops were amazed; during his daylight forays, he had been barely missed by several shots fired from distances as near as 40 meters.

The Poles holding Quatre Bras had prepared for the tanks the Germans had promised if their ultimatum was rejected. Corporal Towarnicki had gathered all of the Gammon bombs and had pulled plastic explosive from each. He had managed to assemble one that weighed several pounds. Towarnicki would occupy the second floor with some men, and hope to throw the Gammons on top of the tanks, should they get close enough. The large Gammon was placed on the end of a long plank, and left outside. The plan was to push it under any tank that entered the intersection. Lieutenant Kowalczyk and seven men would occupy the slit trenches dug into the narrow lawn.

The Polish anti-tank gunners in Lower Oosterbeek had endured another day of shelling. There was no change of positions from the day before and no guns had been lost, but men had been killed and wounded. After Lance Sergeant Horodeczny was wounded a second time, Bombardier Nosecki was sent to a gun on the grounds of the Oosterbeek church, its barrel pointed north up Weverstraat. He joined Corporals Waldemar Gasior and Waclaw Hajduk, who manned a gun together with a wounded man Nosecki did not know. There were British soldiers in the houses along Benedendorpsweg and dug in along the side of the road. Shells had stopped falling in the area of the church and all seemed quiet. The Polish gunners stared through the gathering darkness and awaited the enemy.

On the grounds of the Hemelsche Berg, Private Raschke waited to take his turn on guard at a British machine-gun position a few dozen meters from his slit trench. Sergeant Wojcik had taken his turn, and had returned two hours later when relieved by Cadet Niebieszczanski. Wojcik stretched out on the ground next to the foxhole and immediately fell into a deep sleep. He tossed and turned, his snoring echoing throughout the forest. Raschke was agitated by the performance, but he did not awaken the sergeant from the "only pleasantry in this situation." The crytographer, half asleep himself, kept one eye out for the enemy and the other on his watch so that he could relieve Cadet Niebieszczanski.

A combined growl of diesel engines and rumble of treads came to the ears of the anti-tank gunners from the darkness. In the ghostly twilight caused by fires appeared the silhouette of a large German tank. Its gun cracked, and then everything happened so fast that Nosecki could scarcely comprehend. Amid shouts coming from the surrounding night, Corporal

Gasior yelled, "Run, I'll take care of him myself." The crew ignored him as Gasior aimed down the barrel and cut loose with a round. Seeing the crew still behind him, Gasior told Nosecki to load and Hajduk to pass. Nosecki closed the gun's breech as Hajduk held another round ready. With a crack, the 6-pounder fired again as the gunners wondered whether they would be hit or crushed by the steel monster, or whether they would stop it.

Gasior shot "passionately, quickly and without halting." In the span of a few seconds, four more rounds were fired at the tank. Ears ringing, Nosecki saw the tracers of the anti-tank rounds striking the steel mass through the 6-pounder's smoke. The Panzer came to a halt and its crew scurried about the vehicle. A quick succession of sparks came from one of them. Nosecki grabbed a Sten and replied to the German tanker's machine pistol. With a lump in his dry throat, the bombardier waited for any further movement, but saw none. The gun crew was shortly relieved, and Nosecki crawled into a cellar and fell dead asleep on a pile of coal.

General Thomas' men prepared for the river crossing to take place that night. The first wave was to be made up of the 4th Dorset Battalion, commanded by Lieutenant Colonel Gerald Tilly. The Dorsets were already in their staging area west of Driel. Their objective was to cross to the area of the Heveadorp ferry, and break into the 1st Airborne's perimeter. Six DUKWs, loaded with supplies, were to accompany two companies of the 7th Royal Hampshires. The plans were straightforward, but the boats had not yet arrived. Two trucks of a Royal Canadian Engineer field company column, loaded with assault boats, made a wrong turn near Elst and were captured when they entered German lines. Other trucks slid off the narrow roads and bogged down in the soft soil of the Betuwe.

The Polish paratroopers in the yards and gardens of Stationsweg heard the throaty throb of a large diesel engine and the clatter of tracks as a tank approached the intersection below. The soldiers wondered whether, as if by some miracle, this might finally be the British ground forces. . .or was it the Germans making good on their threat? From a trench in front of Bereda's house, Corporal Lewicki saw 2nd Lieutenant Kowalczyk approach the dark form with several of his men.

The tank stopped opposite the Schoonoord, just short of the intersection. The turret hatch opened and the accented words, "Do you speak English?" were heard over the sound of the idling engine. The men in the slit trenches strained their eyes and ears to catch fragments of conversation in which both parties spoke a language not their own. A voice, in beer-hall German, boomed, telling "Fritz" to shut up. A Gammon bomb exploded, and the tank shifted into reverse. The tank fired a dozen machine-gun bursts up the Utrechtseweg and into the Quatre Bras as it withdrew. Lewicki was dumbstruck in astonishment as Kowalczyk and his men, muttering among themselves, slipped back into their slit trenches.

As Major Tonn led his column to the outskirts of Driel, he was met by Lance Sergeant Boguslaw Horodeczny. The ever-cheerful former parachute instructor informed Tonn that General Sosabowski wanted to see him, and that he would take him to the General. Tonn, with his adjutant and Captain Sobocinski, 3rd Battalion commander, reported to Brigade headquarters just before 2300 hours. There Sosabowski briefed them about the crossing. The newly arrived troops would follow the DUKWs, led by the remnant of the 3rd Battalion, with the 1st Battalion following. The crossing was expected to be halted at morning twilight, around 0430. Passing four DUKWs loaded with supplies, the Major returned to the battalion, dispatching soldiers from the reconnaissance platoon to reconnoiter the crossing areas and routes. Tonn then summoned his company commanders to give his orders for the crossing, and gave instructions that the troops were to have a short rest.

At the Driel dike near De Nevel, the site of their previous crossing, the Polish sappers prepared for yet another. The command of the Engineer Company passed to Lieutenant Wieslaw Szczygiel, who had taken over after Captain Budziszewski had been wounded. The early-morning bombardment had caught the lieutenant after he had left his slit trench for a nearby house to wash and possibly have a spot of breakfast. He was shaving as a barrage started falling. He grabbed his runner and they threw themselves into the water closet. The sturdy brick farmhouse shook as it took a direct hit. By the time the bombardment had ended, they were both soaked with water that had splashed out of the toilet. As night fell, Szczygiel considered himself lucky that there were no casualties from his platoon, "but we were sappers, and always dug our trenches deeper . . . and had nicer shovels to do it with."

Lieutenant Szczygiel now waited in the dark by the dike for the promised boats. Tied to the flood spurs, the Poles had three of the assault craft that had survived the day's bombardments and previous night's crossing. Sappers were on the flood plain marking the approaches with minefield tape when the boats arrived. They were being readied to be taken to the base of the dike when a British captain came up to the Polish officer and said: "You are to give up the boats." Surprised, and a little aggravated by the stranger appearing in the middle of staging and giving orders, Szczygiel radioed headquarters. Not coding his message, he asked for the wounded Captain Budziszewski. When his commander answered, Szczygiel said, "Our friends are wanting us to give up the toys, is it okay?" Budziszewski replied, "Yes, it is all right, give up the boats."

General Sosabowski had received a radio message from the Wessex Division that its crossing would be delayed. The Polish Brigade was asked to turn over its boats to the Dorsets. At 2245, the Polish 2nd Battalion's crossing was canceled. British soldiers loaded the boats onto Bren-gun carriers, and drove west. Lieutenant Szczygiel led his exhausted men back to their slit trenches. The engineer officer went to the cattle barn where his company headquarters was located and decided that he, too, needed some rest. He looked at a concrete trough cut into the floor and decided that this was the safest place. The Lieutenant stretched out in the trough and quickly fell asleep.

As the hands of his watch showed 0100, Private Raschke awakened Sergeant Wojcik so the Germans would not get him as he lay snoring, and went to relieve Cadet Niebieszczanski. The cryptographer carefully picked his way through the cold, dark woods, not wanting to fall into a foxhole or a slit trench. He groped ahead, guided by the scant light of flares that burned in the skies and filtered through the leaves of the trees. As he went forward, his leg hit a soft obstacle, and Raschke fell flat on the ground. Angry, the private cursed and put his hand out to raise himself up. A damp paste oozed between his fingers. Raschke shook with an icy shudder, and shuddered again when he realized he had tripped over a corpse. He did not know whether the remains were those of a British or a Polish soldier. As he wiped the sticky mess from his hands on the grass, he was filled with sadness that he had sworn at a dead friend. Looking around, Raschke saw another corpse, and then a third. The private silently apologized, "Sorry. . . I am your comrade in arms, tomorrow I might suffer the same fate. . . Rest in peace," and then he continued on his way to relieve his friend at the machine gun.

At 0100 on the morning of September 25, the Dorsets still waited for more boats. Brigadier Walton had earlier told Lieutenant Colonel Tilly that only half of his battalion could be transported across the Neder Rijn. Meanwhile, the Polish soldiers who had jumped at Grave moved forward to Driel to cross in the wake of the Dorsets. Corporal Wojewodka met some of the Polish paratroopers who had been in the village for four days. They told him, "You are entering Hell." Wojewodka passed out cigarettes, and as matches flared in a sheltered corner, saw their faces. He needed no further convincing of the soldiers' seriousness.

Lieutenant Szczygiel woke when heavy artillery rumbled through the air over his company command post in the barn. The officer listened; the shells were going from south to north. Closing his eyes, the Lieutenant went back to sleep. The massed artillery of XXX Corps and the Wessex Division had begun their covering bombardment.

It was after 0200 when the Dorsets completed assembly. The Polish troops who were to follow the Dorsets lay in ditches filled with cold, muddy water, and were made even more miserable by a continuous drizzle. The men were tense and tired. Their officers wondered what the next few hours would bring; their only orders were to follow the Dorsets across. There were no further instructions on what to do or where to go once they were across.

The Dorsets crossing the dike were illuminated by the brightly blazing Hevea rubber factory, set on fire by the Germans. The fifteen boats were immediately subjected to the same punishment that had marked the river crossings of the previous nights. Mortar shells again burst on the south shore and German machine guns raked the river. Some men never left the bank, and those who did spun and drifted in the swift current. The DUKWs gunned their engines and went forward, but three bogged before reaching the dike.

At the British machine-gun position, Private Raschke heard the intense exchange of explosions that marked the river crossing. Something was happening on the river, but what? At 0300, a Red Devil came to relieve Raschke at the machine gun. The man told the cryptographer that there was one hell of a battle going on at the river, and a few men were getting through: "The rest seem to be waiting for some kind of a miracle to get over to us. . . So you had better say your prayers, it's going to be one whopper of a day." As Raschke picked himself up to return to his foxhole, the British paratrooper cheerfully added, "Good luck!"

The Poles holding the houses on Stationsweg were tense and nervous. They waited, fingers on their triggers, for the Germans. Fortunately, the enemy remained inactive, and there was no further sign of the tank. Other than the large-caliber shells from XXX Corps landing behind the forward German positions, the night was comparatively quiet. In the cellar of

Stationsweg no. 8, the situation seemed "grimmer and grimmer," to twelve-year-old Ans Kremer. There were thirty-three people crowded in the dark cellar. They sat in silence and fear, unable to speak, able only to listen, trying to make some sense of the situation taking place in their streets, and praying that "soon this will all be over."

Most of the Dorset boats had landed far west of the perimeter and their passengers were taken prisoner. The three DUKWs that managed to get to the river crossed, but then bogged to their wheel hubs in the muddy polder far west of the perimeter. German machine guns shot the massive vehicles to pieces. The Dorsets who did manage to reach the north bank by the ferry landing were immediately taken under fire from Westerbouwing. The German paratroopers who held the height had an easy job as they threw and rolled hand grenades down the slope. Only a handful of the Dorsets reached the 1st Airborne Division's perimeter. At 0430, the crossing was halted.

20

Savouring the Final Gulp

1530 to 1530 Hours,
September 25, 1944

As dawn of September 25 broke over Holland, the skies were clear and the air chilly. The German mortars and artillery for a change did not greet the rising sun with their now traditional "morning hate." The artillerymen, like the enemy snipers and machine-gunners, prepared their morning meals from captured British rations before they began their day's work. The Poles holding Stationsweg left their slit trenches and went back to positions in the houses. They no longer had any food, and no ammunition had been brought up. Sleep had been impossible. Their commander was blunt: the houses would be held to the last man. There was no questioning the situation, or 2nd Lieutenant Bereda: "It would be defense as usual."

Early in the morning, a survivor of the disastrous river crossing had made his way to the Hartenstein. Lieutenant Colonel Myers had crossed on one of the DUKWs, then staggered along the shoreline to reach the perimeter. He reported to General Urquhart at 0605 with letters from Browning and Thomas, and verbal instructions from General Horrocks. The letter from Browning began by stating that it would be brought to Urquhart by General Sosabowski, and consisted mainly of reassurances that XXX Corps was doing all it could to relieve the 1st Airborne Division. The letter from Thomas had been written later, and was in code.

Myers sadly told his commander that the Dorset crossing had been a total failure. After the Valburg meeting, General Horrocks had consulted with Browning, and then met with General Dempsey, Second Army commander. They had made contingency plans for the evacuation of the 1st Airborne Division from the north shore of the Neder Rijn if a bridgehead could not be established by the Dorsets. The Thomas letter was decoded, and the contents confirmed Myers' report. The letter spelled the end of Operation MARKET GARDEN. The instructions for the evacuation of the Oosterbeek perimeter were spelled out under the ironic title "Operation BERLIN."

Unaware of the events in the cellar below them, Marek Swiecicki stood at a window of the Hartenstein with his American friend, Lieutenant Bruce Davis. Swiecicki took a liking to the brave and optimistic Air Force officer, who was to be part of the ground control link for the tactical air support that should have been provided to the 1st Airborne Division. Davis looked across the littered lawns at the blue sky and said, "Its going to be fine." He gave the Polish journalist a cracker from an American field ration, and told him that it was his last one as he slapped Swiecicki on the back. He returned the correspondent's smile and said, "When its gone we'll starve, won't we, Mark?"

Swiecicki extended his hand and, shaking Davis', agreed not only with the Yank's analysis of the rations, but also with his analysis of the situation. Though Swiecicki could not even keep track of what day it was, or decide whether the lack of sleep was worse than the lack of food, he felt optimistic. This was the first time in several days that the correspondent had taken off his steel helmet. The morning was quiet, and the long-awaited Second Army was just across the river.

Private Raschke had managed to get a few hours sleep after his stint at the British machine-gun nest. He awoke to the tweeting of swallows and the chatter of magpies as sunbeams poked through the green canopy and mottled the forest floor with buttery spots of light. The cryptographer, like the birds, was hungry. Raschke was not alone in his situation: it was so quiet that he heard the sounds of stomachs rumbling nearby.

The deeply religious man turned his thoughts to the earthly situation around him. He wondered whether the Allied forces across the river would rescue them, or. . . ? He pinned his hopes this day on the chance that a Dakota or Stirling might drop a container with some food on this corner of the perimeter. An hour passed, and a British officer walked among the dug-in men with a helmet full of apples. "Better than nothing," thought Raschke as he reached into the helmet and took two large ones. Taken aback by the Pole's greed, the British officer smiled and said, "Sorry, sir! Only one apple, please." The irritated Raschke complained to Sergeant Wojcik, who replied in amusement, "Angry? How? For supper they will give a pear, or maybe two."

Lance Corporal Kuzniar took his turn as guard by the hole in the front wall of the house on the corner of Stationsweg and Paul Krugerstraat. His weary eyes tried to focus as he saw a helmeted man in a British Denison smock emerge from the Dennenkamp and saunter towards the house. The lance corporal thought that the man must be one of theirs, but could not imagine what he was doing in the park. He kept coming in the direction of the house, but a mere 20 meters away, the man turned his head as if startled, and leaped into the bushes. "Something must have frightened him," reasoned Kuzniar, but the characteristic coal scuttle shape of the German helmet on his head was imprinted on the corporal's brain. When relieved from his post, Kuzniar reported the intruder to a British sergeant, who said he would keep an eye out.

The morning quiet that was enjoyed by many people in the Oosterbeek perimeter was not shared by the Polish 8th Company at the Transvalia. Throughout the night, shells had fallen around the manor house and nobody had gotten any sleep. Lieutenant Smaczny noticed that they were being shelled from the north and west, but some large-caliber shells coming from the south had landed dangerously close to his position. Just before daylight they were hit with a long and potent mortar barrage.

The mist rising from the river and flood plain was intensified as smoke shells started popping around the Transvalia. In the past days, Smaczny felt that the Germans had not seriously pressed their attacks, but rather were "simply biting at the edges, and savoring the final gulp." Fearing that the "final gulp" might be coming, the lieutenant alerted his men, and gave orders not to fire unless they had the enemy dead in their sights. In a matter of minutes shadowy forms were seen running through the mist straight at the manor house. Rifles and Sten guns popped sporadically until they reached a crescendo, the entire Polish line crackling with fire. The attack came as close as 20 meters to some of the foxholes before the Germans fell back in confusion.

Across the river in Driel, the Polish paratroopers were consolidated in the village. The new arrivals who had jumped at Grave passed out cigarettes and ammunition to their comrades, who had been in the village since September 12. Many of the sturdy houses of the once neat village were now crumbling into rubble. Dead livestock lay around pathetically, their legs pointed to the sky, and affected many of the men who themselves had been raised on farms. Lieutenant Rembisz had taken command of what was left of the 3rd Battalion and the 1st Battalion's mortar platoon in Driel, and had been attached to the 2nd Battalion the day before. He was told that Captain Sobocinski and the lost platoons from the 3rd Battalion were now in Driel, and that he was to rejoin them. Rembisz was happy for, until this moment, he had feared the missing troops had jumped into German hands, and were either dead or prisoner.

In the cellar of the Hartenstein, Marek Swiecicki watched as a medical orderly passed out cigarettes. They were only given to the wounded, and each was to be shared by two men. In a corner a wounded Polish corporal savored the smoke and, when the cigarette was half finished, passed it to a bandaged man lying next to him. The man took it and replied, "*Danke.*" The German had been a sniper, shot and taken prisoner the day before.

The Polish corporal shook his head and told Swiecicki, "If anyone had told me I'd be giving a shit from the SS a cigarette... Idiotic war." The correspondent thought again about his rucksack, which was in Zwolanski's jeep. There was a small fortune in it: two twenty-four-hour rations, a thousand cigarettes and a sweater that was made for him by his fiancée, Krystyna. The jeep was only 30 meters east of the hotel. Swiecicki had thought of this treasure for several days, but the German fire had been too intense for him to attempt to cover the short distance. He thought he might have a chance now.

Walking through the hallway of the hotel, General Urquhart passed the Polish correspondent. The General had taken a walk around the grounds of the Hartenstein, whose lawns were now criss-crossed with slit trenches and littered with tree limbs and unburied dead. The operational orders had stated that his division would be relieved in forty-eight hours. On this, the ninth day of the operation, he had already lost almost 70 percent of the Division's strength, either killed, wounded or taken prisoner. The remaining 2,500-odd defenders, fighting outgunned and at close quarters, were starved and exhausted beyond human comprehension. The aid stations were full again. Urquhart's soldiers asked no questions, they just numbly fought on. The tall Scotsman, a soldier for twenty-four years, made his way to the coal cellar and gave orders for the signalers to contact General Thomas. Corporal Cadet Pajak's radio tried to raise anyone in Driel.

As Marek Swiecicki stepped out of the Hartenstein, an explosion sent part of the veranda's glass roof crashing to the ground. The German gunners were back at work. The correspondent squatted behind the remains of a marble statue, and then made a break to where his jeep had been parked. The fallen trunk of a large tree had smashed the jeep flat to the ground. Part of a wheel, a canvas cover and bent sheet metal were all that was visible of the vehicle. With none of his treasures recovered, Swiecicki sprinted back to the shelter of the hotel.

The Germans had become impatient with the course of the battle. They had lost the bridge at Nijmegen, and Elst was seriously threatened. The Allied troops holding Oosterbeek had been there too long, and had fought too doggedly. Germany's reinforcement pipeline was beginning to run dry, and the Hohenstaufen Division's valuable survivors had to be conserved for other tasks in the days ahead. They decided that it made no sense to press further attacks; it would be more economical to grind down the defenders with the large amount of artillery at their disposal.

It was 0808 when General Urquhart was called to the Polish radio set; Pajak had gotten through to General Thomas. Urquhart's message was simple: "Operation BERLIN must be tonight." The Airborne general was not certain his soldiers could even hold out until night. The hazards of getting across the river had been pointedly borne out by the Polish and Dorset attempts. Urquhart had much to think about; in twelve hours it would be dark enough for his men to move.

There was much activity in the village of Driel. The 3rd Battalion troops dug in just outside the village, facing west, with the rest of the Brigade east of the village's center. Major Tonn moved his men into the fields and orchards inside the village. There were already some foxholes dug, and these were quickly occupied, as those men not so lucky started digging their own. Tonn was not happy about the situation; there were too many people packed into a relatively small area for his liking. The 1st and 2nd Battalions, as well as the Engineer Company, were all packed into an area that measured 500 by 500 meters.

Corporal Wojewodka dug his foxhole and sat back to relax. Lieutenant Ziemski, inspecting his company, paused by Wojewodka. Looking at the corporal, the officer asked, "You think you'll survive in this? I suggest that you go a little deeper."

Wojewodka, "being a lazy man by nature," was unhappy with the remark, but knew his company commander's advice was always good. He picked up his entrenching tool and started scraping at the bottom of the hole as the bloodcurdling howl of a Nebelwerfer echoed through the morning air. The corporal threw himself face first into his shallow shelter as an explosive blast announced the start of a bombardment that would last the entire day—the worst that Driel had yet experienced.

Corporal Marian Stopczynski, of Lieutenant Kula's platoon, located his newly arrived company. He was pointed to the house where company commander Lieutenant Jan Pic had his command post.

Stopczynski became uneasy when he saw the 2nd Company taking positions in an orchard as he made his way to the house. The corporal reported to Pic that one man had been killed the first day in Driel, and that Lieutenant Kula and the rest of the platoon were across the river in Oosterbeek. Stopczynski, having spent days in the village, warned his company commander that it was dangerous to have his positions under the trees. Before Lieutenant Pic could reply, shells started landing. One of the first burst in a tree and killed a rifleman digging below.

At the Hartenstein, Captain Zwolanski's head ached from fever and lack of sleep. His parched throat felt even worse than his head. The little water available in the hotel's cellar was reserved for the wounded, and Zwolanski had not had so much as a sip for thirty-six hours. The liaison officer decided to chance going to a well in the garden of a nearby house when there was a letup in the shelling. He listened, and when the explosions outside were not so near or as frequent, he thought he had a chance. Not wanting to go alone, Zwolanski stood up and, banging two canteens together, announced his intentions. Two British soldiers volunteered. Zwolanski led them upstairs, and in a corner of the hallway, laid out his plan.

The house was 400 meters southeast of the hotel, and there was much open ground. The grounds of the hotel were well-covered by snipers, and the three would have to rush out the door together. If they went one by one, the chances were good that the second or third person out the door would be hit. The men burst from the back door and headed for the shelter of the trees in back of the Hartenstein. Accompanied by the wasp-like buzzing of bullets around them, Zwolanski led the men in bounds from tree to tree, through slit trenches, and eventually to the scant cover of the shrubs surrounding the well. The group crawled over to the well and lowered a bucket. As the full bucket was pulled up, another was lowered. One of the Red Devils fell over, struck by a bullet in his arm, but fortunately the wound was slight. The canteens were filled quickly, and the soldiers made their way back to cover. The group followed their earlier path to get back to the hotel. When the once grand building, now looking more and more like a ruin, was in sight, the shelling began anew.

The German Sturmgeschütze were active on Stationsweg, and took some of the houses under direct fire. The Poles reasoned that the Germans were firing anti-tank ammunition, as many of the shots went straight through the sturdy brick walls without exploding. Not all the fire in the area was German; XXX Corps' heavy artillery was also hard at work, and some of the large-caliber shells had landed uncomfortably close. All along Stationsweg, the soldiers in the houses cringed as the buildings trembled around them, fearing that they would collapse. A shell impacted on a green brocade sofa in the parlor, sending burning stuffing all over the room. No one was injured, and the fires were quickly stomped out by boots.

Corporal Lewicki looked sadly at the once beautiful room, now smashed and filthy. Among the litter was a shattered crock of old Genever (gin) that had been given to the Poles the day before. The contents, neither tasted nor enjoyed, soaked into the plaster that covered a once luxurious rug.

In the house on the far corner of Stationsweg, the British glider pilots prepared for the burial of one of their own, killed while standing guard. Lance Corporal Kuzniar watched as they stuck a large Red Cross flag out the door, and the German fire ceased. Under the protection of the flag, the soldiers took their comrade outside and buried him in a corner of the garden. Once back inside, the flag was withdrawn and the machine guns started again.

Thoughts of food now became loud and unanimous, and the soldiers started a collection. Kuzniar gave all he had, a hard bar of vitamin-enriched chocolate that composed his emergency ration. Another soldier pulled out a Pemmican cube, another found a handful of small green potatoes, and so it went. The next problem was to get water from the well in the garden. A soldier put his helmet on the end of a rifle and stuck it out the door. While the machine guns and snipers turned their attention to the distraction, a glider pilot sprinted to the well and filled a bucket. The helmet was again stuck out the door to draw fire as the soldier ran back inside.

As the men gathered around the pot waiting to eat, the British sergeant who had relieved Kuzniar told one of his number that a soldier had passed the house and gone into the woods wearing a British camouflage smock. Unsure whether the man was a friend or foe, he let him go. The stew was soon ready, and Kuzniar's irritation disappeared when he was served the very watery, but warm soup. To him it "was a treat, something warm after such a long time!"

At 0940, Marek Swiecicki saw General Urquhart and a staff officer come out the door that led to the sub-cellar where he had his command post. With the pair was the Chief Medical Officer, Colonel Warrack. The correspondent noticed the doctor had "sad eyes and a melancholy smile on his face." Swiecicki did not know it, but Warrack was the first officer outside of headquarters to receive the news that the 1st Airborne Division was going to withdraw across the river. Despite the fact that they had been cleared out the day before, the aid stations were again crowded with casualties. Warrack was told that the medical personnel would have to stay behind and see to the wounded. General Urquhart then had his field commanders report to him at 1030 to give his orders and lay out the withdrawal plan.

At noon the 43rd Wessex Division notified the Polish Parachute Brigade's headquarters that the 1st Airborne Division would be withdrawn across the Neder Rijn that night. The Poles were also to make preparations to leave Driel for "other tasks" the next morning. The Brigade was to be ready to move out at 0900, at which time further orders from I Airborne Corps would be given. What equipment could not be carried would be destroyed. This came as a complete shock to General Sosabowski. Within the hour, the dismayed general informed his battalion commanders of the new orders. The Polish paratroopers had until then the (foreboding) thought that there would be yet another attempt to cross the river and reinforce the Red Devils that night.

In the early afternoon, one supply drop was attempted over the Oosterbeek perimeter. Seven Dakotas had taken off from Brussels. They began releasing their loads of food and medical supplies in the region of the Heveadorp ferry, hoping they would land in the ever-diminishing perimeter. One aircraft did not return from the mission.

Some of the containers came to rest in the center of the green pasture in front of the line of Polish anti-tank troops near Valkenburg. The troops had located seven enemy machine guns facing them. One by one the Poles concentrated Bren fire on them, and the German fire noticeably lessened. Lieutenant Bossowski was proud of his men, who held their line without complaint except for one, who could not stand the thirst anymore. He had left his foxhole and was never seen alive again. However, Bossowski waited for dark, tormented by the containers lying in "that bloody clearing." The veteran of the French underground was hatching plans to recover them after dark.

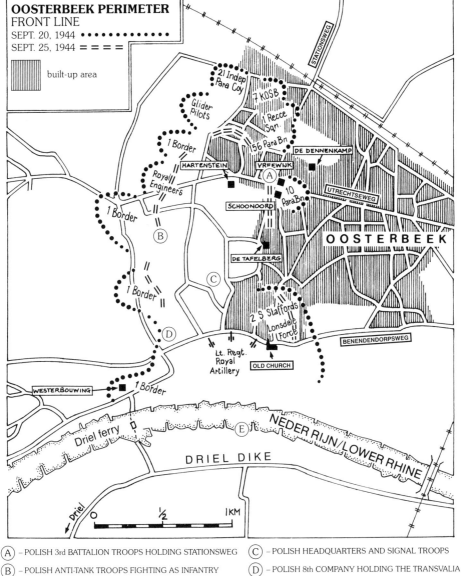

OOSTERBEEK PERIMETER
FRONT LINE
SEPT. 20, 1944 ●●●●●●●●●●●●
SEPT. 25, 1944 ═ ═ ═ ═

built-up area

STATIONSWEG

21 Indep
Para Coy
7 KOSB
Glider
Pilots
1 Recce
Sqn
156 Para Bn
1 Border
DE DENNENKAMP
Royal
Engineers
HARTENSTEIN
VREEWIJK
A
10
Para Bn
1 Border
SCHOONOORD
UTRECHTSEWEG
B
OOSTERBEEK
DE TAFELBERG
C
1 Border
D
2 S Staffords
Lonsdale
Force
BENENDENDORPSWEG
Lt. Regt.
Royal
Artillery
OLD CHURCH
WESTERBOUWING
1 Border
Driel ferry
E
NEDER RIJN/LOWER RHINE
DRIEL DIKE
Driel
0   ½   1KM

(A) – POLISH 3rd BATTALION TROOPS HOLDING STATIONSWEG   (C) – POLISH HEADQUARTERS AND SIGNAL TROOPS
(B) – POLISH ANTI-TANK TROOPS FIGHTING AS INFANTRY   (D) – POLISH 8th COMPANY HOLDING THE TRANSVALIA
                    (E) – SITE OF POLISH RIVER CROSSINGS

The Polish anti-tank gunners manning their 6-pounders in Lower Oosterbeek cringed under the day's heavy bombardments. One after the other, their guns were disabled or destroyed. The gun positioned the farthest east, aimed up Ploegscheweg, was destroyed and a gunner killed. Bombardier Nosecki's gun had its elevating mechanism damaged, leaving its barrel now pointed uselessly at the sky. The gun crew stayed in their position as infantry, armed with rifles and Sten guns. The gun at the corner of Bildersweg, pointed west down Benedendorpsweg, was also destroyed. Its crew grabbed Piats and moved 200 meters east up the road to maintain their watch against German tanks. A glider pilot serving with the squadron was killed, but not before his gun had knocked out a Sturmgeschütz. By afternoon, Lieutenant Mleczko had no guns left.

Private Raschke supplemented the apple he had eaten at daybreak with a bunch of grapes that a smiling signaler had taken from a greenhouse in a nearby garden. Raschke's thirst was slaked by the delicious fruit, and he was filled with admiration for the man who brought them. There was a Spandau dug in nearby, and the Polish soldier had crept under the machine-gunners' noses, so he might raid the greenhouse before the enemy did.

During the afternoon, the German artillerymen hitting the positions in the Hemelsche Berg adopted a curious tactic. First, they slammed the area with heavy artillery joined by mortars. Then, after fifteen minutes of intensive bombardment, there would be a break during which only single shells fell. Suddenly, the heavy barrages were repeated. Private Raschke, with the rest of the Poles, was well dug in. The cryptographer realized that they were holding the approaches to the river, over which he still expected the ground forces to pass after crossing the river that night.

At the Hemeldal, Sergeant Cadet Blazejewski cared for the growing number of wounded. Lance Corporal Cadet Niebieszczanski had been hit by shrapnel in the arm, and after having the wound dressed, helped Blazejewski in the impromptu aid station. A young Dutchman kept bringing water to the station and tea was brewed for the occupants. The wounded were no longer evacuated from the Hemeldal as they had been the day before. Since that morning, the jeeps carrying them through the hospital behind the German lines were not returning. It was difficult to find anyone willing to drive.

The shells continued to whistle into Driel from both the north and the east. Much to his relief, Major Tonn had received orders at 1000 to move his battalion farther south in the village. Still, despite the fact that they had a chance to spread out, more men were wounded and killed by the shells. At noon, Captain Stasiak told Tonn to move even farther southward. The bombardment continued, and an hour later Tonn requested a further move, to the area of the Baltussen factory.

Meanwhile, Corporal Wojewodka had taken Lieutenant Ziemski's advice, and energetically dug deep holes each time he had moved during the day. After digging down one meter, water would start seeping into the foxholes. The paratroopers threw tree branches or hay into the holes, and then spread out their rain or gas capes to keep their bottoms dry.

The 1st and 2nd Companies had moved to their new positions when the Headquarters Company left its foxholes to follow. The 3rd Company sat tight as the area was again bracketed with bursting shells. Killed were two of the men who had gone ahead of the battalion to reach Driel — Lieutenant Racis and Lance Sergeant Cadet Horodeczny.

The wounded continued to flow into the Polish field hospital in Driel. This day, a total of thirty-four casualties came in, adding to those whose condition had been too critical to have been evacuated. This day, six paratroopers were beyond doctor's care and died in hospital. Ambulances belonging to the Brigade and XXX Corps continued to evacuate the wounded from Driel.

Supply officer Lieutenant Kaczmarek was in the corridor of the schoolhouse converted into a hospital, helping move some of the heavy plasma containers to a safer location. Hearing the whistle of incoming artillery, the lieutenant pushed his way into the water closet as a large-caliber shell struck the building. He opened the door and checked to see if the plasma was still all right. He could not see anything through the thick cloud of plaster dust and cordite smoke. From the choking white soup he heard Dr. Mozdzierz's voice boom, "Take a hand!" Kaczmarek looked down and saw a wounded man just out of surgery lying on a stretcher. Kaczmarek grabbed the handles and helped the doctor carry him outside. After putting him against the wall of the building, they both went back in. The supply officer grabbed a plasma container and went outside to breathe and compose himself.

As the smoke and dust cleared, the hospital presented a miserable sight. The ceiling was curled down into the main hall. Two Polish ambulance drivers had been killed by the bombardment and their vehicles were destroyed. By a miracle, the only wounds suffered by those inside the hospital were slight. Dr. Mozdzierz himself was struck by a small fragment on the side of his head, just below the rim of his helmet. He took off the helmet and squeezed the fragment out with his fingers, then treated the wound and bandaged himself. Still wearing his armored vest under his surgical smock, and weaving slightly, Mozdzierz went back to tending the wounded.

In the parish house hospital, Cora Baltussen looked at her smock. She had been hit by shrapnel in her head, shoulder and thigh. Though the wounds were painful, Cora continued tending the wounded. She was concerned about her blood-stained smock, and did not know how much of the blood was hers and how much came from the people she had so tenderly cared for. The exhausted woman wanted to go home and change, perhaps get a little rest. She hopped on her wooden-tired bicycle and started pedaling towards her house. On the way, she was caught in the bombardment and was blown off her bike into a ditch. She lay there some minutes after the shells stopped falling, then got back on her bicycle and covered the last of the short distance home. Upon arrival, she threaded her way through the many refugees who sheltered at the Baltussen factory and home, and washed. After changing her dress, she looked for a place where she might lay down to get a little rest. The only spot she found was on the floor. Cora fell immediately into a deep sleep. She did not stir, even though people were stepping over her all night. Her body was trying to make up for the four nights of effort helping the Poles who had dropped from the sky.

The unit commanders of the 1st Airborne Division made the dangerous trip to the Hartenstein for General Urquhart's orders group. The general told his officers that the Division would be withdrawing across the river that night. The men would follow two routes, down the eastern and western sides of the perimeter, to the river. Lieutenant Colonel Myers' sappers would mark the trails with minefield tape and strips torn from the colored supply parachutes, and be responsible for the embarkation. The artillery would continue firing during the evacuation, in an attempt to deceive the enemy that all in the perimeter was normal. Detachments would be left as rear guards, and the troops would not be informed of the coming evacuation until absolutely necessary. Captain Zwolanski had received the details during the afternoon.

21

The Promised Land

1600 Hours, September 25, to
0830 Hours, September 26, 1944

As the sun was setting, Corporal Cadet Niebieszczanski came to Private Raschke's dugout with the report: "The remnants of the 1st Airborne Division, together with units of the Polish Parachute Brigade, will begin evacuation in the late evening. The wounded will be the first to leave, then the Red Devils, and finally the Poles, who will act as rear guard. The majority will be passing by these positions. There are strict orders to avoid engagements, and do not fire, the area will be full of our people. The last unit should pass at around 2100 hours. This will be your relief, and after they pass you are to join them."

It was still five hours until 9 o'clock, and "a lot could happen by then," thought Raschke. The cryptographer lit a cigarette to kill time. The Germans for the moment were as quiet "as rats in their burrows." He speculated on how the river crossing would go, and remembered how pleasant the German mortars and machine guns had made it when he had crossed the river coming over.

Just before 1800 hours, Captain Zwolanski and three British officers arrived at 2nd Lieutenant Bereda's command post on Stationsweg. One of them was a Scot. Private Jan Szubert looked at him, and thought him to be attired rather strangely for battle in a tartan kilt and steel helmet. The radioman listened as Zwolanski told Bereda that the division would be evacuating that night, and the Polish 3rd Battalion would be the rear guard for the northeastern part of the perimeter. Zwolanski ordered that all packs, gas masks and other field equipment that could not be carried would be left, neatly lined up in rows to send a message to the Germans when they occupied the position.

Private Szubert watched the officers leave. An English officer paused by the door and stared at the Polish soldiers for a few seconds. He said, "God help you," before walking into the twilight. Bereda immediately gave orders that there was be a count of the number of Poles in each house and an inventory of any remaining food. He then ordered that his men bury their dead.

Next door, 2nd Lieutenant Kula received the news from Bereda that the 1st Airborne Division would be withdrawing from Oosterbeek that night. Kula was told to make his preparations, and given strict instructions not to let the civilians know anything about the withdrawal. Only with difficulty was the woman who had suffered the miscarriage persuaded to leave the ground floor to go into the crowded Kremer cellar.

Up the street, Lance Corporal Kuzniar watched his house's commander whisper instructions to the British soldiers. He then gathered the Poles. Glancing at his watch, the British officer told the Poles that when it got darker, they would have to go to the house next door, and from there make their way to the lower houses on the street to rejoin the rest of the Polish paratroopers.

Across the river, in Driel, the soldiers of the 1st Polish Independent Parachute Brigade made its preparations to leave. Others, in small groups, made their way to the dike to guide whatever men came back across the river, *if* any men came back. A tired and frustrated General Sosabowski reflected on the consequences of MARKET GARDEN. Had the Allies only established a bridgehead over the Neder Rijn, the strategic damage to the enemy would have been immense. The Germans had thought of Arnhem as a gateway to Germany. Beyond Arnhem there were no fortifications or major rivers or mountains. Sosabowski imagined waves of Allied armor outflanking the Ruhr and rolling across the Lower Saxon plains. The Germans could never allow such a situation go unchallenged, as they had showed the past nine days. But where would they get the manpower to prevent any more of this? They were heavily committed on all fronts, with the Allied armies pressing in on the borders of the Reich.

The General returned to his headquarters; the need for sleep was more important than any angry speculation. The staff officers were busy in the farmhouse's main room, so Sosabowski found a corner in an upstairs room and shut his eyes.

Against the background of explosions that had almost become normal, the Polish Parachute Brigade's staff labored. They had to prepare contingencies for the yet unknown orders that they would receive in the morning from I Airborne Corps. As Captain Lorys was typing an entry in the Brigade's war diary, the sound of explosions came nearer. Everybody except the captain paused as the whistle of shells was heard. As they exploded nearby, a large chunk of plaster fell from the ceiling onto Lorys's typewriter. The captain cursed, because he was almost finished, and left the table to join the other officers crowded around the cellar door. Seconds after the room was cleared, a direct hit struck the building. Matches were struck and candles lighted as the officers called for their general. Sosabowski opened his eyes and saw orange glimmers through the thick dust. Once again, as in Grochow, he had slept as a shell exploded in the room he had occupied, without awakening or suffering a scratch.

Lieutenant Bossowski's plan to retrieve the container in the pasture was interrupted by the appearance of two British officers. The lieutenant had already gathered a few volunteers, but the raid was forgotten when the British notified the anti-tank men of the coming evacuation. Bossowski was given vague directions about the path they would take to the river. The only firm instruction was that the Poles would be informed when they could withdraw.

The evacuation began at 2015 from the north end of the perimeter. The first troops to begin their trek to the river were the survivors of the 156th Parachute Battalion. The last handful of men from this badly mauled unit had been pushed out of the buildings west of Stationsweg, leaving the Poles virtually surrounded. On the dot of 2100 hours, the massed artillery batteries of XXX Corps and the Wessex Division began a covering bombardment.

Lieutenant Relidzinski heard the British machine guns start giving cover fire from across the river. He reasoned that there must be quite a few, as "their roar did not slacken for a moment." From the Hemeldal's nearby cellar, Relidzinski heard children crying. As a cold wind picked up, British soldiers moved swiftly and silently towards the river, and the lieutenant was impressed with their discipline. To him, they looked like a "human hedge," slowly moving just outside his position as he waited for the word to join the evacuation.

As the British units withdrew from around the 8th Company's positions, a Royal Engineers major gave orders for Lieutenant Smaczny to hold his positions and cover the evacuation. Smaczny was told that his company would withdraw at 0030 hours—but only on orders to be brought by a runner. Smaczny then requested that the major take one of his men with him, so that the 8th Company could be sure that someone would come for them. The British officer replied that that was un-necessary, that he would come himself if he could not find anybody else to do so.

Smaczny was not happy about any of this. To him, the order in such a situation was "a virtual sentence of extermination." The Polish commander did not convey the order to any of his men and, bearing this burden, tried to project an image that everything was in order.

The Polish soldiers in the Hartenstein made their preparations. They had been briefed by the British on the rules for evacuation, and told that the route would certainly pass near German positions, but combat was to be avoided at all costs. Those lightly wounded during the withdrawal would be treated and taken along, while those badly wounded would be given aid and left behind. "God, don't let me get wounded in this situation," Lieutenant Pronobis thought to himself. He turned to Zwolanski and asked, "Where is Marek? I have to tell him to maintain silence during the march. The way he stomps his big feet, you could hear him a kilometer away. He could spoil the whole business. . . . And tell him to keep his helmet fastened this time."

In the anti-tank positions, Lieutenant Mleczko apprised his men of the coming withdrawal. The squadron was to start pulling out from its positions at 2200. Mleczko took Bombardier Nosecki aside and repeated the instructions, then told him to go tell the men in the outlying positions and also remind them to remove the guns' breech blocks. Despite the darkness, and drawing some machine-gun fire, Nosecki found the remaining crews. They had already heard about the withdrawal from neighboring British soldiers.

Captain Zwolanski collected Lieutenant Pronobis, and together they left with one of the first groups. The only arms they carried were pistols and grenades. Pronobis was sorry to leave the shelter of the cellar. He moved through the familiar flower garden, through the iron fence and down the road to the glider pilot guides. Moving down a trail marked by minefield tape, Pronobis heard a machine gun off to the right. The group ahead of him squatted on the trail. Pronobis wondered what the delay was, and went forward looking for their commander. The Polish lieutenant found the man and cursed him for his carelessness and delay, got the men going, and then followed. Passing by a cottage, a shell whistled by, causing everybody to throw themselves to the ground. Farther down the trail, tracer bullets came flashing at the group from straight ahead, but they were high and passed harmlessly overhead.

Pronobis' party reached the British artillery positions in lower Oosterbeek, and passed through them to the river. There they found the end of a long line of people waiting their turn to get into the boats.

Going to check on his wounded at the Transvalia, Lieutenant Smaczny met Father Misiuda. The chaplain had delayed leaving until he finished whatever duties had to be done in Smaczny's positions. When Smaczny walked in, the devoted priest was helping the Dutchwoman nurse the wounded.

The two men quietly conferred, and Smaczny told Misiuda of his orders. He asked the chaplain to take his walking wounded to the river. Then, choosing some of his men to help them, Smaczny watched the group of seven wounded leave for the river. Father Misiuda paused to say goodbye to Smaczny and departed with the words, "I will pray for you."

Two British Bren gun teams arrived to reinforce the Polish rear guard. The lieutenant positioned them by the Benedendorpsweg, and told them to fire a few bursts at intervals to keep the Germans off balance. Returning to his foxhole, Smaczny sat down and thought, "Now we wait."

An hour after the briefing, Lance Corporal Kuzniar and the other Poles in the corner house slid out the back door. Besides being dark, it had started to rain, further concealing from the enemy what was happening in Oosterbeek. Moving quickly and quietly past the scarred and spooky houses, the Polish paratroopers found the communications trench and made their way to Stationsweg no. 8, which had guards posted all around it. As Kuzniar entered the building, a terrific outburst of small-arms fire broke out on the northern end of Stationsweg. A Bren-gunner, positioned on a staircase, started shooting over the gardens at the racket. 2nd Lieutenant Kula stopped the man, explaining that the firing was the way the British were covering their retreat; blowing off any surplus ammunition and at the same time keeping the Germans confused. Looking into the gardens, Kuzniar saw the shadowy forms of the British glider pilots being swallowed by the black night as they headed towards the river.

2nd Lieutenant Bereda entered the Kremer house and gave the paratroopers there his plan for the withdrawal. The Poles would assemble at Lieutenant Kowalczyk's house at the corner of Utrechtseweg at 2200. From there they would make their way to the river to be evacuated by boat. Bereda went on, insisting that the dead be buried before leaving, and saying that unfortunately the wounded would have to be left behind. He ordered them gathered. They would be left under the protection of a Red Cross flag. The orders were to travel light, leaving behind anything that would make noise. Each man was to tie his Celanese marker panel to his back. The soldiers then wrapped their heavy boots in rags to deaden the noise of their hobnails.

The Poles on Stationsweg hurried with their final preparations. As the paratroopers lined up their discarded equipment and haversacks neatly against the wall, gunfire broke out up the street, followed by guttural shouting. Lance Corporal Kuzniar thought the Germans "went mad," as they circled one of the abandoned houses, firing rifles and machine guns and throwing grenades. The Poles returned fire, cooling the Germans' enthusiasm, but a Spandau took the Kremer house under fire. A Polish Bren-gunner replied. The machine guns duelled, both weapons firing simultaneously until the Spandau fell silent. The Poles continued their nervous wait for further orders.

At 2130 began the inevitable attack on the Quatre Bras. Under heavy support fire, the German infantry came forward. Illuminating the house with flares, the SS men made lavish use of hand grenades and machine guns. Kowalczyk's soldiers fought like madmen, not only for their own lives, but for those of the Polish soldiers in the other houses. As grenades flew from the windows and the garden into the intersection, the Poles opened a heavy return fire. From the corner window of the cellar, Corporal Towarnicki fired off magazine after magazine from his Sten gun. A young soldier, Private Marian Nowak, kept passing the corporal fresh magazines or loaded Sten guns as Towarnicki swept the street with bullets from left to right and back again.

As the flares sputtered into embers, the Germans broke off their attack. 2nd Lieutenant Bereda gave the word for everybody to move into Stationsweg no. 4. Taking hold of the belt of the man in front, the line of soldiers held weapons ready in their right hands and moved unhindered into the house. There, they waited for the word to go next door.

The Polish Paratroopers were ready to begin their move to the Quatre Bras. The soldiers stood in line, as if waiting to jump out of a Dakota. 2nd Lieutenant Bereda led, leaping into the yard through a hole where a window had once been. There were shots and a terrified shout, "Lieutenant Bereda has been killed!" The soldiers in the house froze in shock and fright. The paralysis was broken by Bereda's angry demands from across the garden that the men get over to him. With their leader obviously unhurt, the paratroopers bolted out of the house as if they were cats on fire. One man fell, shot as he jumped from the window. Nobody would risk this fate, or worse, by stopping to help him, but moved quickly on to the corner house. There, everybody who was leaving was assembled.

The Polish Paratroopers waited at the Quatre Bras for the enemy activity to die down. The German positions were very close, and it was difficult to judge the enemy's possible reactions. The Germans, too, had taken casualties, and besides, they habitually hated night combat. They were also confused by the fact that some of the houses were apparently empty while others offered incredible resistance. The Germans could well afford to wait until daylight to deal with the Poles on Stationsweg.

Silently, the Polish Paratroopers crossed the Utrechtseweg and moved through the woods and parkland opposite the Schoonoord. The wood looked like a fresh clear-cut. The soldiers tripped and stumbled over the fractured trunks and branches, which grabbed at their trousers and boots. The rain and the darkness helped cover their movements and muffled their muttered curses as the men staggered and bumped their way through the obstacle course.

Lieutenant Mleczko had gathered together his men from the Anti-tank Squadron's glider lift at the Oosterbeek church. It was pitch dark and rain was pouring down. The lieutenant gave his men final instructions before leaving for the river. If no boat came by 0300, everybody was on his own. The gunners would either try to swim across the river individually, or take a chance and wait for whatever might happen. Mleczko recommended swimming; that was what he planned to do himself.

Private Raschke again looked at his watch: 5 minutes to 11 o'clock. He lit a cigarette in anticipation of moving to the evacuation site. The hours had passed, and still British soldiers moved by on their way to the river. They were in such a close, continuous stream that they reminded Raschke of a "giant gray caterpillar" moving south. The appointed time had long past, but there was no sign of the promised relief. Another "human snake" came out of the woods. To make certain they saw him, Raschke stood up in his slit trench. The group passed wordlessly. Without any further hesitation, the cryptographer joined the end of the line.

Armed with his Sten gun and a single grenade, Lance Corporal Kuzniar snaked his way through the tangled woodland, and wondered how far ahead were the glider pilots whose retreat the Poles had been covering. Behind him, Kuzniar heard angry shouting in German coming from the houses on Stationsweg. Within moments, enemy flares popped in the sky, and the withdrawing Polish Paratroopers hit the ground and froze as sizzling magnesium illuminated the area "as if it was daylight." Mortar bombs bracketed the shattered wood, and the soldier lying next to Kuzniar was hit in the neck. The wound was serious, and the unfortunate man was wrapped in a rain cape and left behind.

Lieutenant Pronobis surveyed the situation at the river bank. It was unusually quiet, and Pronobis was convinced the Germans were not aware of the situation. The number of boats seemed few. As their queue reached the river bank, it became the turn of Pronobis and Captain Zwolanski to cross. They got into the boat and pushed it off to make their way across the river to "the promised land." In minutes it ground on the opposite shore and the evacuees got out. They watched the sappers turn the boat around and again it headed to the north bank.

In celebration of their deliverance, the two Polish officers shared their last cigarette. They followed a white minefield tape to the large dike. Zwolanski recognized the terrain from his mission of four nights before, and expected to find the Brigade momentarily. The pair entered a barn where other men who had returned from Oosterbeek were collected. They were given a ladle of hot stew and a jigger of rum. Pronobis thought the rum was the best he had ever had in his life. The evacuees were then pointed to trucks, which drove them south to Nijmegen. To Lieutenant Pronobis, the trip in the back of the crowded truck was "comfort" after his eight days in Oosterbeek.

At 2345 hours, Correspondent Swiecicki slipped out of the Hartenstein. The village was burning and shells were bursting. Having spent the day in the cellar, his eyes were dazzled by the "glaring, terrifying, crimson light." Fallen trees made the going difficult, and detours had to be made around the shell craters. The group's guide fell, ripped by shrapnel. Another man came forward to take his place, but met the same fate. As more shells burst around them, the group dissolved between those seeking cover, and those who kept moving south. The journalist ran towards the shell bursts.

The Red Devils passing the 8th Company's positions became fewer and fewer. Lieutenant Smaczny still waited for the runner who would bring him word to join the evacuation. Some of the passing British asked the Poles sitting in their holes, "Why don't you leave?" Smaczny was relieved when his men ignored the suggestions.

To the Polish anti-tank troops near Valkenburg, the order to evacuate seemed at least an hour overdue. Lieutenant Bossowski was getting impatient, and he went to the villa that had the piano, but found it deserted. A little disgruntled over the "misunderstanding," Bossowski discussed the best way to withdraw with the other officers in his unit.

They finally gathered their men and began moving to where they thought the evacuation was to take place. In the dark, rainy night, they moved out in a long column. After bumbling through the rain-soaked woods, Bossowski felt something was wrong. He was sure that they had missed their turn. He called the column to a halt and, retracing his steps, found the road that led to the Neder Rijn. It was so covered with branches and leaves that it was virtually invisible. About to enter German lines, the column turned around. They were again moving towards the river when the anti-tank men finally caught up with the end of the queue awaiting evacuation.

It was late, already past midnight, and the soldiers of the 8th Company were becoming apprehensive. An hour had gone by and no more British soldiers were moving past the Transvalia en route to the river. Still there was no sign of the runner. Lieutenant Smaczny pondered the reason for his absence. Was he killed? Did he lose his way? Was the 8th Company to be written off as a rear guard? Smaczny and his company maintained their positions, fully conscious that every minute they waited lessened the hope they might get across the river.

The entire area was quiet and the sky began to show gray to the east. Smaczny sent Lance Corporal Cadet Bielawski to a British battalion command post. Bielawski found the building deserted, except for two medical orderlies and a group of wounded. The medics were unable to provide any information as to the location of the crossing site. They had no further revelations other than that the British troops in the area had left more than two hours before. On hearing Bielawski's report, Smaczny gathered his men and started towards the river.

In the driving rain and near gale winds, Lieutenant Relidzinski heard the insect-like hum of motors from the river. The path to the river was still marked by minefield tape. At the waiting area, groups of men lay in the mud stirred up by hundreds of boots. Some of the groups sat exposed on the river's wide polder. The Germans were becoming aware that some sort of major event was taking place on the Neder Rijn, so, braving British bombardment, they began to react. As flares arced into the sky and mortar salvos began to bracket the polder and the river, more of the waiting evacuees were killed and wounded.

Running through the explosions, Marek Swiecicki caught up with another group, only to lose it in the dark. After dashing forward dozens of meters, the correspondent stopped to orient himself. In the dark, he saw men huddling under fallen trees just ahead of him. Seeing men move past him in the dark, Swiecicki started shoving and shouting at the prone men to move. They did not respond; they were dead. The journalist resumed his dash to the river, passing the burning houses of Oosterbeek. The torn woods gave way to the broad polder at the river's edge.

Covered with mud and the blood of dead men, the correspondent stopped to survey the scene. People were lying in the mud on the riverbank, waiting for boats. Terrified cattle galloped among them as bursting shells threw fountains of mud into the air. Multi-colored necklaces of tracer bullets flew from the south bank into the German lines. A burst from a Spandau kicked up spurts of mud near the correspondent and he threw himself down. Quickly, a hand stretched out from behind a dead cow, and pulled Swiecicki to cover. The tracers from a pair of Spandaus meshed in a crossfire over the men's heads, while behind them on the river a boat burst into flames.

Private Raschke moved along the western edge of the perimeter towards the river. Nearing the burning gas works, he spotted two British officers armed with Sten guns. One pointed the withdrawing soldiers towards the river, while the other continually kept watch on a German mortar position less than 50 meters away. A few dozen meters down the trail was the queue for the boats. The signaler joined the end of the "living wall." Then a flare burst over the open field. "Don't move! Stay where you are!" a British officer shouted. Raschke kept repeating the Hail Mary as shells exploded around the line of soldiers. After several salvos, it again became quiet. Stepping over the bodies of the killed and wounded, Raschke reached the polder. He found dozens of dispirited British paratroopers sitting in the mud, waiting their turn for boats while the wounded were loaded first.

The British and Canadian sappers labored under numerous difficulties to keep the evacuation going. As dawn approached, the deadly enemy fire increased in intensity and accuracy. The river current was strong, as always, and again played havoc with the light craft. The sappers used two different types of boats. The Canadians had motor-powered wooden storm boats. Unfortunately, the rain kept stalling the motors, leaving the craft at the mercy of the river. Again, therefore, the canvas-sided assault boats were used, and, despite their obvious faults, those who were evacuated in them had little room for complaint. Aside from carrying more men, they did, in fact, handle better in the swift current than the smaller wooden storm boats.

The Poles marveled at the Red Devils' discipline as they waited patiently in queues for evacuation, glider pilots acting as guides. As a boat came ashore, it methodically filled with waiting soldiers and then immediately pushed off for the southern bank. At 0200 Lieutenant Mleczko, Bombardier Nosecki and a dozen other survivors of the Anti-tank Squadron's glider lift, climbed into a boat and crossed the Neder Rijn.

The shelling continued to make casualties of the men waiting patiently on line. A glider pilot pointed Marek Swiecicki toward an embarkation point. A British captain kept repeating, "Don't panic, don't panic," in a calm, full voice. As the orderly soldiers filed past the man, Swiecicki was reminded of "a bobby in the middle of Oxford Circus."

Wading waist-deep in the river, Swiecicki climbed into a boat, took a paddle and rowed with the rest of the passengers. They crossed without interference until reaching the middle of the river. There, the enemy fire shifted towards the boat, and rocket mortar shells arced overhead. While nearing the southern shore, a large piece of shrapnel tore open the back of the canvas boat and spilled its passengers into the water. After swimming the last few meters, Swiecicki scrambled up on the muddy ground. Crawling through machine-gun fire to the top of the dike, he ran into a British soldier. Recognizing his voice, Swiecicki realized this was the man who had pulled him to safety behind the dead cow. As the pair walked towards Driel, the British soldier discovered that the man he saved was a Pole. He introduced himself as a Scot, and the two men walked to the village talking about Scotland.

The men who had fought at Stationsweg kept moving towards the river. The woods thinned as they approached the polder. Tangled in a stand of young trees a group of bodies was discovered; Lance Corporal Kuzniar recognized the face of a glider pilot who had been in his house on Stationsweg.

Rain came down harder as the group neared the river. The crowds became larger, the shelling heavier and the boats fewer as the hours passed. Officers supervising the evacuation maintained order and prevented panic with words alone as they filled a boat and dispatched it to the south shore. Kuzniar watched what he believed to be the last boat push off. Recognizing the futility of getting his men across as a unit, 2nd Lieutenant

Bereda turned to them and said, "Men, each one is on his own. We shall meet in Driel." The 3rd Battalion dispersed into the waiting mob on the polder.

The defenders of Stationsweg fell into small groups and weighed their possibilities for getting across. Some of 2nd Lieutenant Kula's men called to him that they had found a boat. As he climbed in, Kula wondered what kind of mercy the SS would show the wounded and the civilians left behind.

In the cellar of Stationsweg no. 8, the thirty-three civilians spent a horrible and hungry day, and most of a night, in their dark, damp and uncertain shelter. After midnight, the British artillery south of the river started working over what had been the northern part of the Oosterbeek perimeter. Large-caliber shells burst around the Kremer house, and the sturdy building shook as the Dutch huddled together in a group, as far as possible away from the cellar door. None among them had the nerve to leave their shelter to see what was going on in the world above their heads.

Lieutenant Bossowski's group reached the end of a long queue. It kept starting and stopping. With each halt, it took longer before it again started moving. While they sat in the grass and waited, Bossowski took a drink of water from a ditch. He strained the filthy water with his fingers, as "there wasn't *anything* that wasn't floating in that water." After ten of Bossowski's group were taken in the boats, the line stopped, and did not move for almost an hour. When he went forward to find the guides, Bossowski discovered they had already left.

Lieutenant Bossowski went back to his group and said, "Get ready, we're going to go—*running*, not walking." They ran south, through artillery and mortar fire behind their lieutenant, towards the Neder Rijn. When they reached the river bank, it was deserted and swept by heavy fire. Some of the men threw themselves to the ground to take cover. "No going down!" shouted Bossowski. The embarrassed troops stood up. Suddenly, two boats appeared in the mist. The anti-tank men waded into the river and clambered into them. Looking back, Bossowski saw that the river bank had not been deserted, and angry British soldiers arose from bushes where they had sought cover, shaking their fists. Apparently these were the last boats headed for the group of men standing on the mud flat.

When the men of the 8th Company were still 200 meters from the river, they heard terrible screaming and shooting. Of the thirty-six men he had managed to collect after crossing three nights before, fewer than twenty were left. Smaczny gave orders that each man was to try and save himself. Many could not swim, and Smaczny refused to leave them. Lance Corporal Bielawski bid Smaczny goodbye, and stripped off his uniform. He waded into the river, regretting having to leave his brave commanding officer behind.

Lance Corporal Kuzniar was successful in his search for a way to get across. Under a small ridge of earth on the riverbank the signaler found a boat. Kuzniar, Lance Corporal Grzelak and two others pushed it into the water and jumped in. Paddling with two small shovels they had found in the craft, they headed for a red boat that had been pulled up onto the south bank. A machine gun picked at them, but the tracer bullets went high over their heads. But the farther they went across the river, the closer to the river's surface the tracers came.

Before reaching the bank, the men jumped into the water, which reached up to Kuzniar's ears. Swimming ashore, they caught their breath behind the red boat on the polder and examined their situation. The area in front of the dike was swept by machine-gun fire. Watching, they spotted a machine gun that seemed to be paying particular attention to their area. The tracers methodically swept the section of dike in one direction, and then came back over it. The paratroopers timed their movements till the machine guns worked past their position, and then scrambled up the dike. Happy to be alive, Kuzniar and Grzelak somersaulted down the muddy embankment, until Kuzniar and his Sten gun accidently crushed his friend's leg. Cadet Grzelak was very annoyed!

The Polish paratroopers on the south bank who were to provide support for the evacuation huddled in their foxholes behind the dike. The night of wind and rain had filled the holes with cold water and the troops shivered. The sounds of the bombardment, the machine guns, the buzz of motors and the screams of men gave the only clues to what was happening on the river. As the morning grew brighter, the horrible sight of the soldiers evacuated from Oosterbeek became visible: They were wearing remnants of uniforms or were wrapped in blankets or ladies' dresses found in houses. Their faces showed their exhaustion, and they were filthy. Many of them wore bandages that had not been changed for many days. To Sergeant Iwaskow they looked like "a procession of ghosts walking out of Hell."

Meanwhile, Private Raschke sat plaintively on the northern bank with the other men of his unit. They seemed to be waiting for some kind of miracle to happen. It was becoming light. What were the choices? Death?

Captivity? The cryptographer got up from the ground and jumped into the river: life and freedom. He was in such a taut state that he did not think the water felt cold. Raschke kept repeating the Hail Mary as his arms and legs seemed to weaken with each stroke. But then, finally, under his feet he suddenly felt the sticky river bottom. Trying to walk, Raschke staggered as if drunk. A British soldier pulled him from the water in the gray morning light. Raschke wanted to shout for joy, but was too tired. A tear rolled down his cheek, and he thanked God that he was free.

On the northern bank the remaining soldiers were running out of choices. Another boat came ashore and dumped a pile of captured German life vests on the bank. The boat was almost capsized by all of the men who tried to get aboard. A total of thirty-six wounded were evacuated in this last boat. Though he was not a strong swimmer himself, Lieutenant Prochowski thought he could make it. The officer weighed the fact that some of his men were wounded or could not swim, and he decided that he would share their fate.

Corporal Lewicki surveyed the scene around him. Enemy tanks had added their guns to the cannonade that was falling on the polder. More and more heads were swallowed by the river, never to reappear. The screams and moans of the wounded were more piercing than the exploding shells. Lewicki waded into the river. Reaching the southern bank he looked around. The scene was almost comical. Next to a uniformed soldier stood a completely naked man. Another wore an undershirt, and nothing else. Some were in women's dresses, others in athletic clothes. It was "like a scene from the morning after a bizarre masquerade." He found 2nd Lieutenant Bereda gathering together what he could find of his remaining soldiers. There were not many.

The Polish Airborne Engineer Company stood by behind the Driel dike to lend any possible assistance in the evacuation. They had waited all night without receiving any requests for help. The redoubtable Sergeant Juhas watched the night's events from the dike road. To him, the sky was lit up like day all through the night. At dawn, he could see hundreds of men still on the polder. They were throwing off their uniforms and jumping into the river or walking along the polder naked. The Germans were raking the whole area with fire, even from the railroad bridge. Juhas felt like crying, but the sight was so absurd he perversely had to laugh. He watched, as fountains thrown up by the bullets surrounded the bobbing heads, till the bodies stopped swimming and simply floated away with the river's current.

Private Szubert watched as the last boat left. "Everything falls apart. Soldiers start doing everything for themselves. They were jumping in the water, some knew how to swim, others didn't. People were drowning, getting wounded. You could hear the groans and cries of drowning soldiers. I wanted to jump in, but when I saw how miserably they died, I decided that I would rather die with a gun in my hand." Szubert stayed on the polder. It had become a little quiet: "All of those in the river had either made it or not. We were on our own. Nobody was giving orders."

The Germans continued to fire machine guns and mortars, but they did not attack. After an hour, a British soldier hung a white rag on his rifle and stood up. "I wasn't too far from him, I saw it all," recalled Szubert, who watched as a staff sergeant walked over to the Brit and said, "'Soldier, put it down or I'll shoot you.' The soldier put it down." After another fifteen minutes, a tall, older man with a large, sandy-colored mustache stood up. Szubert could only understand some of what he was saying, but listened as the man identified himself as a battalion commander. He thanked everybody for their good service and performance, but lamented that there was no point in fighting further. He, as senior officer, was taking all responsibility.

The British officer then turned to the man next to him: "Soldier, raise the flag to surrender. That's an order."

As Germans approached, Szubert did not know what to do. He had thrown down his Sten gun, but kept his .45 automatic in his hand. From his left, he heard a voice telling him: "Throw down the gun and give up." He looked up and saw a young SS lieutenant standing on an embankment, in "a uniform cleaner than a whistle." Next to him were a few soldiers with rifles. They weren't shooting.

The SS man again said, "Throw down the gun." Szubert complied, and started walking towards him. He had taken a few steps when the officer motioned with his Luger that he was to follow the rest of the defeated paratroopers being rounded up on the polder.

The radio man moved quickly to catch up to the column of surrendering paratroopers. He suddenly felt something hit his arm, but in his exhaustion paid no attention. He felt it again and, looking up, saw a teen-aged German soldier poking him with a bayonet. The adolescent put his finger in the trigger of his rifle and said, *"Hände hoch, oder ich schiesse."* Szubert looked at the young soldier and, "in the eyes of this German I saw fear. He was more afraid of me with a gun on me than I of him." Szubert smiled and put his hands in the air.

The Germans had started moving towards the river bank from both sides of the perimeter. Lieutenant Smaczny saw men falling, both British and German. With their backs to the river, some British soldiers were shooting at the approaching enemy. The explosions and screams were reaching a greater intensity. White flags started appearing on the polder, and more men were now standing up with their hands in the air. Smaczny told his men to move back into the woods. As they turned, they saw two tanks, less than a 100 meters away, moving towards them. The Germans ordered the trapped men to lay down their arms. Lieutenant Smaczny and the remains of the Polish 8th Parachute Rifle Company were taken prisoner.

Sergeant Juhas kept watching from the dike road. He had spent the night bellowing and waving instructions to the evacuees who had made it to the south bank of the Neder Rijn. Their ordeal was not over, for they still had to cross the open polder and climb up the Driel dike, both of which were swept by German fire. Sergeant Cadet Blazejewski, who had run the aid station in the Hemeldal, himself had to be carried over the dike after catching a machine-gun bullet in his leg. The survivors from Oosterbeek were becoming fewer and fewer. Soon, there was nobody left in the river. With the Brigade withdrawing the same morning, the sappers left the dike to make their own preparations.

A heavy, gray and wet day broke over Driel. In the village, Lieutenant Kaczmarek had tried to get some much-needed sleep. All night he had heard explosions, trucks and shouting. Then, the melodic but thickly accented words: "Roll out the barrel. . .we'll have a barrel of fun. . ." flowed in through the window. Kaczmarek stuck his head out to see who was singing. Coming down the street, clad only in underpants, were three of the Brigade's paratroopers. Happy to be alive, their faces were black with a grime that contrasted with the scarlet of their deeply bloodshot eyes. They smiled and waved at the supply officer as they passed his command post.

After crossing the river to Driel, Marek Swiecicki was given tea, a sandwich and a large glass of rum. Handed a blanket, he was packed with a group of some twenty-five people into a large truck. Swiecicki settled down for what he expected to be a pleasant drive to Nijmegen after the events of the past week. A few kilometers after leaving the collection point, the truck overturned at a sharp bend in the road and the men were thrown into a big tangle of arms and legs in one corner of the vehicle.

Some seconds went by, with everybody in a heap either trying to think of what to do, or just too tired to care. A calm and full voice repeated, "Don't panic. . . Don't panic," in imitation of the evacuation guides in the Oosterbeek perimeter. In no time the heap of soldiers was shaking with laughter.

Stationsweg was wrapped in the strange quiet of the dawn, in the aftermath of a battle fought to the end of its tether. No longer was the deafening drum-fire of explosions and machine guns part of the background. Instead, the echo of a vehicle or rifle shot sounded puny compared to the "orchestra" that had played for the last week. From the windows of Stationsweg no. 6 came the sounds of static, punctuated by the words, "*Hallo Pudelko. . . Hallo Pudelko,*" and then again the crackling of empty airwaves, before the Poles in Driel again repeated their attempts to raise anybody who might have remained.

Next door in the Kremer house, young Ans opened the cellar door and looked around the ground floor of the home she had grown up in. Outside, the bodies of Captain Gazurek and another Polish soldier lay in the communications trench. As she turned the corner into the front room, the girl heard laughter. Looking up, she saw a large Polish paratrooper, one of his feet wrapped in a huge bandage, sitting at the table and laughing at her. He said something to her in Polish, but Ans did not understand. In a moment, German soldiers stomped into the house. In front of Ans, they hauled the wounded Pole from his seat. Shoved by his captors across the room, the man limped and looked over his shoulder. He gave the girl a smile and winked before he was pushed out the door. The Germans and their captive disappeared into the yard of Stationsweg no. 6.

As more people came out of the Kremers' cellar, shots were heard outside. When no more Germans were seen on the street, Ans went into the next yard. The haversacks that the Poles had left behind so neatly were turned inside out and thrown all over the place. There in the garden lay the body of the paratrooper with the bandaged foot.

Lieutenant Smaczny was marched to a park. An angry SS officer shouted for all Poles to step forward. Everyone and everything became quiet. The British officer who had shared Smaczny's cigarettes at the Transvalia took off his red beret and put it on the Polish lieutenant's head. He asked Smaczny how to say "There are no Poles here" in German.

After Smaczny told the man, his soldiers asked their commander what was going on. Smaczny told his men to shut up while the British officer repeated the phrase in absolutely atrocious German. This further angered the SS officer. Smaczny feared that they would be made to take off their Denison smocks, as their battledress jackets bore Polish insignia.

Then, the situation suddenly changed. Shells started bursting around the park. The Germans shoved and herded the prisoners out of the park, and sent them on to Arnhem. Smaczny found himself in a group locked up in a warehouse near the river. The Polish officer thought the surroundings were somehow familiar, even though he had never been there before. It then dawned on him that had MARKET GARDEN gone according to plan, this would have been his company's original objective on September 19.

The Germans, who again occupied Oosterbeek, made it clear to its inhabitants that they would soon be expelled from their town. As the families gathered their belongings for a journey into the unknown, Mrs. Kremer sent her daughter to fetch some jewels that had been hidden upstairs. The jewelry shared the same room with the body of Private Mentlik. The twelve-year-old looked at the man, curled up against the wall with his head bent back. The position looked painful to her, and the girl started pulling at the man's legs to put him into a more comfortable position. She pulled at the heavy boots, but was unable to budge him. Ans suddenly realized the man was dead and not suffering any pain anyway. She got the jewels and left.

The rain was stopping as Lieutenant Mleczko joined the column of men for whom there was no room on the trucks to Nijmegen. His mind was working overtime, trying to make sense of his role in the battle he had fought for over eight days. By its end, the Anti-tank Squadron had lost all of its guns. In exchange, Mleczko was certain they had destroyed only one tank, a few armored vehicles, some enemy soldiers, and that was all. He rationalized that his guns were essential for the survival of the British in Oosterbeek, and with the rest of the Polish Brigade holding the south shore, allowed for their evacuation.

Mleczko's thoughts then traveled to a lofty strategic plane. He thought of all the exceptionally bad luck that had plagued the operation, and how with a little "guts" the Allies might have been rolling across the plains of northern Germany. Reaching Nijmegen, the lieutenant's freshly realized conviction was reinforced. "The town was full of all kinds of troops. . . vehicles. It was as busy as Picadilly Circus on V-Day parade. . . only a few miles from Arnhem."

He was shaken from his thoughts by a voice: "Sir, the showers are in that gray building." Mleczko went in, "to wash everything off, and start anew."

Many of the Poles who had come out of Oosterbeek succeeded in rejoining their Brigade. The others were taken to the British reception area in Nijmegen. Lance Corporal Kuzniar and his friend flagged down a jeep driven by a British corporal. He took them to Driel, but the Brigade had already left. They were then taken by truck to the reception center for evacuees in Nijmegen. There a large queue was formed for a hot meal. The sun had come out and, not wanting to stand on line, Kuzniar loitered in the courtyard. He glanced at a large window that reflected everything in the yard. In the window he saw a pathetic figure. The man was, "black with dirt and grime, terribly tired and tattered. I felt sorry for that man. I wanted to know who he was." Kuzniar turned around, and saw no one behind him. It was then that the Polish soldier realized he had been looking at his own reflection.

22

Hey, Polish Paratroopers, You Fought at Arnhem!

September 26 to October 30, 1944

At 0900, the Polish paratroopers in Driel slung their weapons, picked up their equipment and began their march to Nijmegen. An hour earlier, the Germans had given Driel another taste of their artillery, causing losses in equipment and leaving more men wounded. It was quiet again as the troops moved out in a widely spaced column under cloudy skies. The Poles were to march south to Slijk Ewijk, and then east to the Nijmegen bridge.

At the Baltussen house, Cora woke up. She realized it was already late morning and rushed to the hospital, where she was sure to be needed. She was puzzled when she got there: rather than seeing the Polish soldiers she had cared for, and for whom she had acquired such affection, Cora found the hospital and streets deserted, abandoned, wrecked by shellfire and littered with medical waste. The only signs of life came from a handful of British soldiers with a jeep in the village center.

Most of the Tommies still around were scrounging through the houses looking for something to eat. A soldier sitting in the jeep told Cora that everybody was gone—the Poles from Driel and the Red Devils from Oosterbeek. From the shattered steeple of the Catholic church, Cora heard the bell that she had heard chime practically every hour of her life. It continued to ring irregularly as she walked toward the church. In the steeple she saw a British soldier who was responsible for the noise. She called up to him, "Why are you ringing the bell?" The Tommy sheepishly looked at Cora and shrugged his shoulders and said, "It seemed like the right thing to do."

The Poles marched out of Driel in the numerical order of their battalions. The soldiers chafed under their heavy loads of equipment, and cursed as they threw it, and themselves, to the ground as the Germans continued to harass the withdrawing troops with artillery and mortar fire. Though not generally accurate, it did seriously wound some men, and frayed the nerves of those left untouched. At 1200, the 1st Battalion reached Slijk Ewijk. Lieutenant Colonel Jachnik arrived to tell the Battalion to wait and let the rest of the column catch up.

The 1st Battalion began moving an hour later, the first Poles reaching the Nijmegen bridge at 1500. They crossed it under German artillery fire. Entering the city, the Polish paratroopers found it jammed with soldiers and military vehicles. Private Wawiorko and some of the telephone platoon forgot their fatigue and marched through the streets swinging their arms and singing a variation of the "work song" (in heavily accented English) from the Walt Disney film *Snow White*: "Hi-ho, Hi-ho, to MARKET way we go. . . ." They passed a brick building out of which poured war correspondents, amazed at the procession, which they dubbed the "bloody Polish SS."

General Sosabowski went ahead to General Browning's headquarters to receive his promised orders. Told to wait, he sat down in a soft chair and promptly fell asleep. The General met briefly with Browning and reported the Brigade's status. The Polish Parachute Brigade had lost almost 400 men, a figure that represented 23 percent of its officers and 22 percent of its other ranks. Browning said that he knew of the Brigade's difficulties during the battle, and that it would eventually be withdrawn to England, but that due to the situation it was still needed in the area.

Sosabowski then received his new orders from one of Browning's senior staff officers. The Brigade was assigned the mission of defending airstrips established in the area of Neerloon in order to provide security for the Allied lines of communication against German troops located in the region of s'Hertogenbosch and Oss. The shocking part of the orders was the clause stating that Sosabowski and his men were to be subordinated to Brigadier Russell, commander of the British 157th Infantry Brigade. The unit was the sea column of the 52nd Lowland Division, which was to have been airlifted into Holland as part of the original MARKET plan. The airlift for the 52nd Division had been canceled, and Russell's brigade were the only Lowland troops on the Continent at this time, as well as the only unit besides the Polish Parachute Brigade under Browning's command.

Motor transport took the Poles to their new positions at 1830. The

1st Battalion went to Herpen, the 2nd to Ravenstein and the 3rd to Overlangel, with the Brigade headquarters established at Neerloon. All of the units quickly began digging field positions, sending out patrols and establishing communications with their neighbors.

After his troops had occupied their positions, the livid Sosabowski fired off a letter of protest to Browning. He could not believe that his unit, though it had been roughly handled, was in such a state that it should be necessary to subordinate it to another formation. The Polish Parachute Brigade was a functioning "independent" formation, and there was no reason that it, and he, a major general, should be subordinated to a brigadier. Sosabowski felt the order was a deliberate slight on the part of Browning. This done, the General began his written report on the battle for the eyes of General Sosnkowski, his Polish Commander-in-Chief.

The next day, September 27, what remained of Oosterbeek's population gathered what possessions they could carry and left their shattered town. The Germans had expelled the civilians and begun fortifying the ruins of Oosterbeek for the inevitable time when the Allies would again try to force the Neder Rijn. In the meantime, southwest of Nijmegen the Polish paratroopers strengthened their defenses and continued patrolling. Patrols from the 2nd Battalion clashed with patrolling Germans, and returned with three prisoners at no loss to themselves.

At noon, Major Aleksander Tokarz, commander of the Brigade's 1st seaborne lift, reported to General Sosabowski. His 200 men, with the supplies and heavy vehicles that had landed in France over a month before, were welcomed back to the ranks. Throughout the day, more and more Polish paratroopers returned to the Brigade from the reception area in Nijmegen. The returning soldiers told the dramatic and horrible stories of the epic struggle that had taken place on the north side of the Neder Rijn.

That night, a jeep brought Marek Swiecicki from Nijmegen and delivered him to the Polish Parachute Brigade's positions in Neerloon. Directed to the Brigade's headquarters in a brick farmhouse, the correspondent knocked on the door. It swung open and he saw General Sosabowski illuminated by a paraffin lamp.

The General looked up. His face first registered shock, but then beamed with joy. "Swiecicki, you're alive. You're alive! Man, they told me you were dead!" The tough old soldier threw his arms around the correspondent and kissed him on both cheeks. Swiecicki was taken aback by all of this; the General had never paid much attention to him before. The journalist came to attention and saluted, "Reporting, sir, I have returned from the other side of the river."

Sosabowski's voice boomed, "Come here my good man, we have something to discuss. You must get to London immediately, so our history will not be plundered."

Sosabowski's instructions to the reporter were straightforward and easily understood. In September 1944, the Anglo-American affair with the Soviets was still a loving one, and the Polish victories and sacrifices at Cassino and Normandy had been muted in the press. Sosabowski spoke of the killed and wounded the Brigade had suffered, facts that needed no explanation to the correspondent. He charged the journalist with getting to London as fast as possible, so "that there might be some propaganda benefit from our sacrifices."

Swiecicki was more than willing, and asked how he might get there. General Sosabowski retorted, "You have a head, Mr. War Correspondent, I can't help you. All I can do is have a jeep take you to the nearest airfield. After that, you're on your own." The journalist asked for any specific instructions. In response, the General told him, "I have no instructions. I don't want to tell you anything. Write what you want. You were there, you know what you saw. You know these matters better than me, I'm only a general," he said, as he broke into a chuckle.

Dismissed, Swiecicki went into the kitchen to begin working on his notes. He remembered listening to a BBC radio broadcast that morning, praising the "heros of Arnhem." His instructions from General Sosabowski were underscored when the correspondent realized he had not heard any mention of the Poles in the broadcast.

The dawn of September 28 saw a ship, one of hundreds in the English Channel, approaching the port of Arromanches. It carried the light artillery battery and the remaining vehicles and supplies of the Polish Parachute Brigade that could not be flown into Holland because of the shortage of gliders.

The 332 Poles on board now looked at the Continent. They had boarded ship three days before and waited at the dock. The ship finally sailed on the previous day, but these Polish paratroopers did not know they were to spend another night on board before they could disembark. They would occupy themselves, as they had since leaving their barracks on September 23, with talk and endless games of bridge, all the time wondering what was happening to the rest of the Brigade.

Shortly before noon, a Brigade jeep delivered Marek Swiecicki to an airfield near Grave. The field was buzzing with activity. Dakotas disgorging supplies and passengers arriving from England were also carrying the survivors of the 1st Airborne Division back on their return leg. Swiecicki began inquiring as to how he might be able to get a place on an airplane. The magic words were, "I came from Arnhem." A New Zealand Air Force officer arranged a ride in the toilet compartment of a Dakota for the correspondent.

When his aircraft landed at Northolt, Swiecicki got out and joined the line at Customs. The Polish war correspondent was in a bit of trouble: he was out of uniform. He had left his steel helmet in the toilet of the Dakota, and his beret had been lost long before in Oosterbeek. Bareheaded, he explained to the military policeman where he had come from. Once again, "Arnhem" proved to be the magic word. The journalist got a ride to Picadilly, then was left on his own.

Swiecicki's next thought was to call his fiancée, Krystyna Kuratowska. He had a few tattered Occupation guilders in his pocket, and asked a passing Londoner if he might spare a few pennies so he might make a telephone call. The Englishman stared at the correspondent – bareheaded, speaking with a strange accent, clad in a disheveled battle-dress jacket and with maniacal front-line glimmers in his eyes. The man handed him the coins.

When the phone rang at Miss Kuratowska's busy desk in the Polish Ministry of Information, she was trying her best, with difficulty, to carry on with her work. The day before, her telephone had rung and correspondent Alan Wood told the young woman that Marek Swiecicki had given him the phone number in the Hartenstein. He was sorry to say that he had not seen the Polish correspondent during the evacuation, nor later in Nijmegen. The woman fought off thoughts that her fiancé was dead, or at best a German prisoner. The voice at the other end of the phone was now Marek's – back from the dead and asking the astonished woman to call the Polish Telegraph Agency and have a stenographer ready. He had to prepare a radio broadcast.

The Polish soldiers in Holland continued to improve their defensive positions through the day. The British provided four 6-pounders with jeeps to replace the losses suffered by the Anti-tank Squadron. Two, under 2nd Lieutenant Bossowski's command, were sent to provide support for the 2nd Battalion, while two under Lieutenant Mleczko went off to the 3rd Battalion.

At 1900, on the evening of September 28, General Sosabowski finally received a reply from General Browning concerning the subordination of the Polish Parachute Brigade to the British 157th Infantry Brigade. Browning explained that the Polish Brigade had been disorganized by the dispersed drops and the casualties suffered during the battle. The Lowland Brigade, occupying a critical sector, was understrength and needed a ready reserve. The situation now permitted the Polish Brigade to revert to the command of I Airborne Corps, effective the next morning at 0800 hours.

The message from Browning also stated that the Poles were to provide two companies for a bridge-security assignment. One was to relieve the Americans of the 82nd Airborne Division at Heumen; the other was to reinforce the British soldiers at the road bridge over the Waal at Nijmegen. There were special worries about the road bridge: the German front line came as close as 500 meters to it, and enemy tanks were sometimes seen from the structure. There were fears that the Allied forces on the Betuwe might be cut off.

At 0600 on the morning of September 29, the 3rd Battalion troops went to their assignments guarding the bridges. The 7th Company, with the mortar and reconnaissance platoons and one anti-tank gun, left for the bridge at Heumen. The rest of the Battalion drove to Nijmegen. Reaching the city, the Polish troops were shocked to find that the railroad bridge had been demolished the night before. The threat had been realized not from German ground forces, but from enemy frogmen, who swam downstream and attached charges to both bridges. The road bridge suffered some damage when the charges were detonated, but remained open. The railroad bridge, however, had dropped one of its spans into the river.

In London, Marek Swiecicki broadcast his report on the BBC. It told of the Polish Parachute Brigade's part in the battle of Arnhem. It was broadcast not only to Poland, but was translated into the other languages of the BBC World Service. The next morning, Swiecicki had an appointment with Professor Stanislaw Kot, the Polish Minister of Information.

Kot was delighted to see Swiecicki, for he too had heard the message from Alan Wood, and knew the odds were very poor that the correspondent might have survived. The ministry, like all the offices of the Polish government, was becoming frantic in the deteriorating political situation. The man who was in charge of Polish propaganda efforts told Swiecicki, "You must write, and write quickly, so this Polish blood is not wasted . . . you must write a book that might awaken some sense of justice in the English." Kot loaned the correspondent his secretary to this end. The work began immediately, the correspondent speaking from memory while Miss Kuratowska wrote everything down.

General Sosabowski, meanwhile, was chafing at having his Brigade guard bridges in Holland. His men were specialists—trained paratroopers—yet his elite assault unit was being used to guard bridges. The Brigade's mission of taking part in the liberation of its Motherland was still preeminent in Sosabowski's mind when the General met with Lieutenant Colonel Grudzinski of the Polish liaison mission with 21st Army Group. He told of his recent subordination to the 157th Infantry Brigade, and hoped Grudzinski might bring up the matter with Field Marshal Montgomery of the Brigade's withdrawal to England.

The war diaries and after-action reports of the Polish Parachute Brigade reported that September 30, 1944, was a day of little activity. The units remained in the same positions they had held the day before. Except for some artillery falling around the Nijmegen bridge, the troops watched the military traffic go by, and with the help of the Dutch Oranje Battalions they checked the papers of civilians who wanted to cross the bridge.

However boring those days were for Sosabowski's paratroopers in Holland, there was much excitement among the Poles in London. On September 1, General Sosnkowski had signed "Order 19," in which he reproached the Western Allies for betraying Poland by giving inadequate aid to the soldiers of the AK in Warsaw. The conservative Sosnkowski had always been viewed by the British as a key factor in the Polish Government-in-Exile's inability to come to an accommodation with Stalin. On September 30, the Polish government bowed to British pressure and dismissed Sosnkowski from his position as Commander-in-Chief.

The Polish paratroopers in Holland maintained their watch on the bridges over the Waal and Maas rivers through October 2. On the final day, on the shores of a river many kilometers to the east—the Vistula—the AK had finally laid down its arms in Warsaw. At the end of sixty-two days of fighting, with over 200,000 men, women and children dead, the last districts held by the anti-German insurgents surrendered. After protracted negotiations with the Nazis, the Polish soldiers of the AK were accorded the rights of combatants subject to the Geneva Convention, rather than immediate execution as partisans. The AK men dismantled their barricades and marched into the German lines by unit, where they stacked their arms before going into captivity. Over 800,000 civilians who had survived the hunger, the bombardments, the murder and the fear were then expelled from the city with what they could carry in one suitcase. They were herded into transit camps outside the city. From there, many were deported to Germany as slave labor.

Warsaw, after its depopulation, was then looted in a fashion that the citizens of Oosterbeek and Arnhem would have understood. On the specific orders of Hitler, special demolition squads next began total destruction of the city. They started with any structure of cultural value, and would stop only when every building was either gutted by fire or left a pile of rubble.

In Holland, the day of October 3 passed with the Polish para-troopers – unaware of Warsaw's fate – carrying on at their posts at the bridges and airfields. German air activity intensified, and a few anti-personnel bombs fell on the Brigade's positions, without causing any casualties. Dogfights provided a distraction for the troops, and they watched as a twin-engined German aircraft was knocked down in flames by the British guns defending the Nijmegen bridge.

October 4 went by with the Polish paratroopers busy with inspections and continuing improvements to their defensive positions. The day was quiet, but during the night the Heuman bridge was shelled. The next morning, General Sosabowski and Lieutenant Dyrda met with American General James Gavin, commander of the 82nd Airborne Division. Gavin's troops were still holding the Groesbeek heights, and were in continuous contact with the enemy.

Gavin asked Sosabowski to provide two ten-man patrols. The American said he wanted the Germans to think Polish paratroopers were in his area with the Americans.

Sosabowski asked Gavin, "How would the enemy know they were Poles?" In reply Gavin just gave a sly smile. The Polish general was not happy about the idea, but Lieutenant Dyrda remarked that it might be politic to help the Americans and added, "Besides, our boys can take care of themselves."

The 3rd Company provided a patrol, which left the 82nd Airborne's lines after dark on the night of October 5. The soldiers waited for a preparatory artillery barrage to finish, and then moved into the Reichswald forest, inside Germany itself. Happily, not only did the Polish paratroopers return from their patrol without loss, they also managed to bring back a Waffen SS prisoner. But though the Poles did not suffer any casualties, the dangers of the area were underlined by the death of an American paratrooper. He was a sergeant of Polish descent and, speaking their language, had led the Polish troops to the 82nd's front-line foxholes. When the patrol returned, they saw him lying facedown on a stretcher, shot dead by a sniper.

General Sosabowski began receiving indications of subtler events. On October 1 he had received notification that General Browning was to be decorated with the Star of the Order of Polonia Resitituta for his assistance in raising the Polish Parachute Brigade. Sosabowski had been invested with Britain's equivalent order when he was made Commander of the British Empire in December 1943. Although Sosabowski had not met Browning since arriving in Nijmegen on September 26, there had been constant communication with his Corps headquarters though liaison officers. The Polish general wrote Browning a congratulatory note in the name of the Brigade. A few days later, Sosabowski received a reply from Browning; the British general wrote that he regretted the award came at such a time, and was "unfortunate" in light of the unhappy relationship between himself and Sosabowski and his Brigade. Sosabowski immediately sent a letter regretting any part he may have personally had in this situation, and affirmed his "soldierly loyalty."

For the Polish paratroopers, October 6 passed with the usual rumble of military traffic back and forth across the bridges they guarded, along with the checking of civilians' papers. As the sun was setting, orders came that the Brigade was to prepare for movement south. It appeared that at last the Brigade was to be withdrawn to Britain.

The packing and preparations were interrupted by a report that was received by Brigade Headquarters at 2200. The British 157th Infantry Brigade reported that German "gliders" had landed 9 kilometers southwest of Grave. The Polish rifle battalions were notified, and watches were doubled and patrols stepped up. Unknown to the Poles, the 1st Battalion, Grenadier Guards, had two companies deployed, looking for the "German gliders."

Now, near the Polish Brigade's positions, British soldiers riding Sherman tanks spotted figures ahead of them wearing paratroop helmets. The Guards challenged the shadowy figures once, and then again. When the shadows replied in a foreign language, the Grenadiers opened fire, killing two soldiers from the Polish Parachute Brigade's Supply Company and leaving two others wounded. The British unit, in its report, stated they were informed there were no friendly troops in the area. Two days later, one of the Polish wounded died in a hospital.

The report about the "German gliders" was followed a half-hour later by an order confirming that the Polish Parachute Brigade was to move to Louvain, in Belgium. There, further orders would follow for movement to England.

At 0945 on the morning of October 7, the units of the Polish Brigade assembled at Reek to await transport. The first elements of the convoy left for Louvain at 1215. The tail of the convoy arrived without incident eight hours later, and the troops were quartered in a former German barracks. The next morning, the Brigade's airborne element was to go to Brussels airport, and from there fly back to England.

In France, the Brigade's 2nd seaborne tail boarded ship to return there. Arriving as late as it did, and unable to get a road clearance, the vehicle-bound paratroopers waited in a transit camp for seven days. They were returning to England eleven days after they had embarked on the Continent, having accomplished nothing.

In London, Marek Swiecicki had accomplished much. As soon as a chapter met his satisfaction, it was taken immediately for translation into English. He had worked day and night on his book, but he was not going to work during the day and night of October 7; he had other priorities. In a simple ceremony at the Polish church on Devonia Road, he married Krystyna Kuratowska.

On the European continent, at 1000 the Polish paratroopers arrived at Brussels airfield and waited for the order to board aircraft. They looked at the grumbling gray sky and reflected on how similar it looked to that seen during the horrible days of waiting at Saltby and Spanhoe. They loitered in the on-again, off-again drizzle and inspected abandoned Focke Wulf fighters at the recently liberated field. The hours passed, and the promised aircraft did not arrive. On one Dakota, the Brigade quartermaster, Lieutenant Colonel Stevens, and a few officers flew to England. The rest of the lift was canceled at 1600, and the troopers were transported back to the barracks at Louvain.

The paras spent another night sleeping on the damp concrete floors of the barracks, and at 0815 again boarded trucks for Brussels airfield.

The sky was the same as it was the day before. The soldiers again killed time by the runways and waited. At 1400, two Dakotas did take off with two loads of paratroopers, along with Major Malaszkiewicz and another officer. The rest of the men still waited until, three hours later, they were informed that their flight orders were canceled. This was followed with a message that the Brigade would have no air-transport priority in Brussels for the next two days.

The Polish paratroopers sat at the airport throughout the night. At 0340 on the morning of October 10, trucks began transporting the Poles to Ostende, where they were to board LSTs to return to Britain. The first trucks reached the docks at 0930. There they were reunited with the Brigade's seaborne tail. The 3rd Battalion was embarked almost on arrival of the boats. The rest of the troopers were billeted for the night in (again) former German barracks. But there an unexpected surprise welcomed them: the barracks had bathing facilities, and many of the paratroopers enjoyed their first hot bath since the start of MARKET GARDEN.

The following morning, the troops again went to the bombed and blasted docks of Ostende. The 1st Battalion was next to embark and their ship weighed anchor at 1230, almost the same time that the 3rd Battalion was arriving in England. The vehicles from the seaborne tail were sent to a transit camp to await the rest of the Brigade. The balance of the paratroopers were transported by train, and reached their old billets around Peterborough at 0100 during the night of October 12.

As the third LST, carrying the Brigade Headquarters, and the Supply, Signal and Medical Companies, weaved its way between the masts of scuttled ships in Ostende harbor, a mine exploded. Apart from frightening the men and showering the decks with water, it caused no damage. The two ships arrived in Tilbury the next day, October 12, at which time the last LST, carrying the 2nd Battalion, left Ostende. By 0200 on the morning of October 15, all of the Brigade's units had arrived in their garrisons in the Midlands.

In the Anti-tank Squadron's old billets in Blatherwyck, Bombardier Nosecki and Corporal Gasior looked at one another. Their quarters had fourteen beds, but the two men were the only ones to have returned from Holland. They stood among the empty bunks in silence. Then Gasior, a Pole who had been born in the Ruhr, and who was a veteran of both the Spanish Civil War and the French Foreign Legion, cried out in a choked voice, "What about Warsaw? What's this all about? We were being killed, and nobody helped us, and they died in Warsaw . . . and nobody helped *them*. Let's get the Hell out of here and be among people."

The two gunners snuck out of their compound and started down the road to town. As they walked, an American truck barreled past them and then screeched to a halt. The face of its black driver popped out of the window and called, "Hey, Polish Paratroopers, you fought at Arnhem! I'm going to Northampton, hop in!"

The pair soon found themselves at a hotel in the company of an RAF sergeant, his wife and mother-in-law. The five had a quiet dinner, during which the Poles hung out their memories of the past month and talked about their experiences—helped by a few peaceful glasses of Scotch whisky. They stayed at the hotel that night and returned to Blatherwyck the next day, missing morning roll call.

In the following days, the Brigade's soldiers who had jumped during Operation MARKET GARDEN handed over their diving-eagle parachutist badges together with the insignia's award document. These were returned to them the next day at unit formations by General Sosabowski. The badges now had a gilded wreath attached to the eagle's talons, identifying the wearer as a participant in a combat jump. Sosabowski then authorized the soldiers a ten-day leave.

An overnight train full of Polish paratroopers arrived in Edinburgh from the Midlands. As there was a wait of several hours for a connecting train to Leven, Lance Sergeant Cadet Hrehorow took a group of the men for breakfast at a Polish Forces canteen on Moray Place.

Hrehorow was still troubled by memories of the battle. He kept seeing the tears rolling down the Dutch girl's face as she sipped from the glass of milk. But he was most shattered by the thought of the death of his friend, Cadet Boguslaw Horodynski. The two men had both been a part of the tightly knit group of parachute instructors. Horodynski, who was known to the British cadre as "Bob," was especially popular at Ringway. Curiously, he did not spend any of his free hours with his comrades, and they wondered if perhaps he might have a girlfriend, and was busy "improving his English." It turned out that the Cadet had spent all his free time pestering English and Polish offices in London to have his parents and sister brought to Britain, for they were still in the Middle East after having come out of Russia. "Bob's" secret was revealed when he told his friends that he had succeeded. But he did not get to see his family. They arrived in Britain while the Parachute Brigade was locked in camps in the English Midlands, waiting to fly into Holland.

As the queue approached the counter, a young girl in uniform, with an attractive head of blond hair, watched the men in gray berets, who wore the diving-eagle badge on their breasts. After some hesitation, she walked over to Sergeant Cadet Hrehorow and asked if they had just returned from Holland. Receiving an affirmative reply, she introduced herself as Miss Horodynska, and asked Hrehorow if he had known her brother, Boguslaw, and how was he?

Hrehorow felt sick to his stomach and weak in the knees when he replied that he and the others did not know him, they were from a different battalion. As she walked away, the Cadet no longer felt hungry. His only consolation came when his companions admitted they would have done the same thing.

23

A Precious Gem Called Freedom

November 1944 to December 1992

By autumn 1944 the Battle of Arnhem had already passed into legend. A bloody defeat for the Allies, it achieved only the creation of a 100-kilometer corridor to nowhere in Holland. Montgomery's ambitious plan to try to end the war by Christmas had resulted in Hitler's last victory on the Western Front. Nobody attempted to analyze the failure, but instead the heroism involved vaulted the battle into the Pantheon of noble failures of British arms—alongside those of Gordon at Khartoum, Ishandalwana, and the Charge at Balaklava. The outstanding conduct of Urquhart's 1st Airborne Division ensured that it had earned its place in an outstanding chapter in the annals of military history.

While the Polish Parachute Brigade was starting to rebuild itself, the Polish Government-in-Exile's situation was becoming more bleak by the day. The relationship between the Anglo-American Allies and the Soviet Union had become strained as a result of Stalin's refusal to help the Poles during the Warsaw Uprising and his obstruction of American supply drops to the beleaguered city. The destruction of Warsaw and the bloody defeat of the AK after sixty-three days of titanic struggle left the Poles with a legend of noble and heroic failure, but little else. The underground army that had been so painstakingly built, and functioned under such difficult conditions for years, had all but been destroyed. The Red Army was on Polish soil, and a Soviet-sponsored "Committee of National Liberation" was already in place.

On October 13, Polish Prime Minister Stanislaw Mikolajczyk met with Churchill and Stalin in Moscow. Stalin pressed his demands for Poland to cede its Eastern territories to the Soviet Union. Mikolajczyk protested this loss of 47 percent of Poland's territory. Afterwards,

289

Churchill lost his temper with the Polish leader and accused the Poles of being petty and narrow-minded; they were, he said, setting out to "criminally" destroy the peace of Europe. The Western Allies no longer discussed Stalin's demands on Poland's eastern territories, or looked upon the Polish Government in London with any seriousness.

The 1st Independent Polish Parachute Brigade immediately began the task of reconstructing itself. An intensive training program was undertaken by the Polish Parachute School to replace the men who had been killed or wounded in Holland. Many of the new volunteers came from the vast harvest of German prisoners taken in Normandy that August; this allowed many Poles who had been conscripted into the Wehrmacht to rejoin their countrymen-in-exile. The first course for Polish paratroopers at Ringway since June began on October 21, 1944, and graduated 93 paratroopers on November 8.

In The Netherlands, the citizens of Arnhem and Oosterbeek had been expelled. The Betuwe itself was also evacuated by the Allies, and Cora Baltussen had her wounds finally treated in Nijmegen, days after they had been inflicted. However, on October 2, the U.S. 101st Airborne Division started moving onto the Betuwe, and would stay there until the end of November. This fertile and lovely part of Holland soon had all of its trees denuded, both by shelling and by the cold of autumn. There was much more rain than sunshine, and the robust American paratroopers soon came to hate the Betuwe as they cringed under constant bombardment. Artillery in both directions across the Neder Rijn further reduced the wreckage of Driel and Oosterbeek to utter devastation. The American paratroopers suffered from the same problem as the Poles, in that low-lying Driel was under constant observation from the high ground across the river, and any movement immediately brought German reaction.

The fighting in the Betuwe was often vicious as the Germans tried to push the "Screaming Eagles" from the area. In one attempt German paratroopers were slaughtered as they tried to force the Neder Rijn in rubber dinghies.

It is sad to say that American looting there was widespread, and not only of items from abandoned houses that were intended to make life more comfortable in the field. The American "bazookas" proved to be better at opening safes than destroying tanks, and the safes in the Catholic church and the Baltussen jam factory were so opened. Of course, the American soldiers were under British command, and the British supply system, and the GIs despised British rations. The 101st Airborne Division's records, and memories of the soldiers who fought in Driel, all give testimony as to how the jam from the Baltussen factory made their food, and thus their lives, a little more bearable. When the division was finally withdrawn, a truck loaded with Baltussen preserves went with it. In the bleak days of December 1944, the truck managed to get into Bastogne before the 101st was cut off. While the Screaming Eagles were writing their own legend during that epic siege, the jars that were filled with the glorious Betuwe sunshine of the summer of 1944 were passed among the frozen foxholes of American paratroopers.

General Sosabowski received a short, but direct, telegram from General Browning on November 4, 1944. The telegram stated that, despite the original agreement that the Polish Parachute Brigade would only be used during one operation, it would remain under command of the 1st Airborne Division. The same day, a message was received from General Urquhart confirming that the Polish Brigade would remain under his command, and that they should meet to discuss training matters. Sosabowski immediately replied to both British generals that he must refer the matter of the Brigade's subordination to Polish General Headquarters in Britain. Sosabowski then reported the matter to General Stanislaw Kopanski, Polish Chief of Staff in London.

On November 18, General Browning was decorated with the Order of Polonia Restituta in the Polish General Headquarters in London's Hotel Reubens. The decoration honored Browning's great contribution in helping raise the Polish Parachute Brigade. General Sosabowski attended, and saw Browning for the first time since the evacuation of Driel. There is no historic evidence that either said anything to one another.

On December 1, Sosabowski was informed by General Kopanski that Browning had suggested his removal from command of the Parachute Brigade. The next day General Sosabowski met with Kopanski at Polish General Headquarters in London. The Chief of Staff handed him a letter, dated November 20 (see Appendix B). It had been written by General Browning, and was addressed to Lieutenant General Sir Ronald Weeks, Deputy Chief of the Imperial General Staff. On it was a notation that a copy had been sent to Field Marshal Montgomery. The copy that Sosabowski held in his hand was another that had been forwarded to Kopanski.

The timing of the Browning letter is, itself, curious. Kopanski had a meeting with General Weeks on November 16, concerning the Polish Parachute Brigade's subordination. It was agreed that the Polish Brigade would remain under the command of the Polish Commander-in-Chief for the meantime. This took place four days before the Browning letter was dated, and is all the more curious in light of a coded message uncovered by Richard Lamb during research for his book *Montgomery in Europe.* Dated October 7, 1944, Montgomery reported to the Chief of the Imperial General Staff, Viscount Alanbrooke, that the Polish Parachute Brigade fought poorly, and he did not want it under his command, suggesting that it be sent to Italy to join the Polish forces there. Written in October, it can be assumed that Browning and Horrocks were the key movers behind Montgomery's (the chief architect of MARKET GARDEN) sending the letter to Alanbrooke.

The letter that Sosabowski read contained a summary of Browning's dealings with him after the Polish Parachute Brigade was mobilized into the ranks of I Airborne Corps in July, but mainly addressed the allegation that General Sosabowski had caused constant difficulties in the period before action, and during Operation MARKET GARDEN was argumentative and wanted everything for his unit. It went on to state that he undertook his part in the fighting only reluctantly, and that there would be further difficulties in any future dealings with him. Browning recommended that the Brigade undergo a change in command.*

After receiving Browning's letter, it was obvious that the Polish military authorities were obligated to comply with these wishes, despite the fact that this was a matter of individual conflict, rather than one of misconduct, incompetence, or negligence. General Kopanski asked Sosabowski for his suggestions for further service not involving the Parachute Brigade.

The situation was obvious to Sosabowski: the British wanted a more pliable commander. He replied to Kopanski, in a letter dated December 4,

---

*What is most unusual about these accusations is that they were leveled outside the normal chain of command. In September 1988, General Urquhart stated to this author that he, General Sosabowski's immediate superior during Operation MARKET GARDEN, was in no way consulted as to his opinion of the Polish Parachute Brigade's conduct before or after the prejudicial reports were submitted to the Imperial General Staff. In fact, General Urquhart said of the Polish paratroopers: "I could not fault them for cooperation. I never had any worries about that. Everything I asked was done, unless there was a very good reason."

that the call for his dismissal was on personal, rather than military, grounds. He called for an examination of his service to the Polish Army as a Polish general and the Brigade's commander, and for Kopanski to take his defense.

On December 7, Sosabowski was granted an audience with the President of the Polish Republic, Wladyslaw Raczkiewicz. The President told the Parachute Brigade commander he had studied the letter and had discussed the matter with General Kopanski, and said he was very sorry, but that there was nothing to do except comply with the request. The removal would be without prejudice, and he would try to find satisfactory work for him. Raczkiewicz then made the analogy that if a host country found an ambassador unsuitable, it would ask for his recall, and so this similar request must be complied with. Sosabowski replied that his honor as a soldier was at stake, and that he had taken the same risks as any parachute rifleman. What would he tell his men — that he was dismissed for carrying out the Polish point of view?

The same day, he received a letter from Kopanski. The Chief of Staff stated that despite the fact that he saw nothing wrong with Sosabowski's tactical decisions during Operation MARKET GARDEN, he could not change the matter, whether or not there was actual merit to the charges in Browning's letter. Kopanski's letter went on to say he could not think only of the future of the Parachute Brigade, but of the whole world of Poles in exile, which now depended on the goodwill of the British.

On December 9, President Raczkiewicz informed General Sosabowski that he was relieved of command of the Parachute Brigade and appointed Inspector of "Guard and Staging Units." As the month of December passed, Sosabowski continued to write letters to President Raczkiewicz and General Kopanski, requesting a board of inquiry. The only reply he received to any of these requests was a letter dated December 20, from the Chief of the Military Cabinet of the President, General Dembinski. Dembinski simply stated he had not received any disposition in the matter.

The news that General Sosabowski would be leaving the Brigade on Boxing Day spread quickly through the units' billets. The soldiers, ignorant of the politics between the generals, were stunned. The Brigade's Christmas card had already been printed and sent. It featured a caricature of their commander in combat gear on a ladies' bicycle, shouting, "Follow me!"

On Christmas Eve, Brigade units garrisoned in Wansford and Peterborough refused to enter their mess halls. Sosabowski went to these units and spoke to them, telling them that, though he felt as they did, they should not "do anything foolish" and bring further problems either to him or themselves. The General, who so loved his soldiers, entered the mess halls and invited them to eat with him. The men dined with their commander, who was cheered not only by this show of support, but also by the fact that their behavior was beyond reproach through a difficult and emotional period.

On December 27, 1944, General Sosabowski appeared for the last time before his Brigade. At Wansford, Sosabowski read the letter from President Raczkiewicz, and announced his final order as commander of the Parachute Brigade. It ended with the words:

> I was not only your commander, but was also, and still hope to be, the one who guides your souls.
>
> If God permits, that all of these fears and sorrows will end, and your hearts and faces will again smile when our strong legs will again stand in our own homes, I will smile with you— because I always was happy during those times when things went well for you.

General Sosabowski then turned over command of the Brigade to Lieutenant Colonel Jachnik and left for London.

By the time this sad event had taken place, General Browning was also packing his bags. He was leaving for Ceylon, where he was to be Chief-of-Staff to Lord Louis Mountbatten, the "Supremo" of South East Asia Command. The command of I Airborne Corps passed to Major General Richard Gale.

It was a new year, 1945. While the 1st Polish Parachute Brigade was rebuilding, step by step, the Red Army resumed the offensive that had stopped across the Vistula River from Warsaw the previous August. On January 17, the Red Army entered the city. With them were Polish soldiers of the Soviet-sponsored "Kosciuszko" Army. They, and the civilians following in their wake, entered a totally destroyed metropolis, the bodies of tens of thousands of its citizens buried beneath the frozen rubble. Taking the salute at the "victory parade" was a group of Poles not known to any of their countrymen. They were Stalin's puppets, known as the "Committee of National Liberation," and they now referred to themselves as the provisional government of Poland.

As the Nazis were being driven out of Poland, that nation's fate was not being decided by guns, but with fountain pens. Roosevelt, Churchill and Stalin met in Yalta on February 4, 1945. The ailing American president believed that Stalin was a man of honor, and agreed to Soviet annexation of Poland's eastern territories, for which Poland would be compensated with land to be ceded by Germany. The Anglo-American Allies also recognized the "Committee of National Liberation" as a legal entity and declared that free elections would be held, with participation of the constitutional government in London. The head of the election commission would be Soviet Foreign Minister V. I. Molotov, the man who had negotiated the division of Poland with the Nazis in 1939.

The Poles in exile were not naive, and could well imagine any "free" election sponsored by the Soviets. In London they denounced the Yalta Agreement as yet another partition of their suffering nation. In Italy, General Anders' II Polish Corps, consisting in the main of men from the Eastern Territories who had spent two years in the Gulags, feared that they would never see their homes again. They grumbled and even threatened to leave the front lines, since they had nothing to fight for. Their commander, who had led them out of Russia, prevailed on their sense of honor as Polish soldiers to continue the fight against the Nazi enemy, with the hope that their excellent performance on the field of battle might bring justice for their country from the Anglo-Americans.

Early in March 1945, Lieutenant Colonel Jachnik was badly injured in a jeep accident. Major Tonn, who had left the 1st Battalion to take Jachnik's place as deputy Brigade commander, took command of the Brigade while the colonel was hospitalized. On March 27, General Kopanski called Colonel Jan Kaminski to London. Kaminski, one of the original Polish paratroopers who jumped at Kincraig on September 23, 1941, was offered command of the Brigade, and told it would shortly be sent to the Continent for operations. However, he was subsequently informed, three days later, that the British considered him unsuitable for command because of his close relationship with the Brigade's "former commander." On April 13, Antoni Szczerbo-Rawicz, who had seen previous service with the Parachute Brigade, took command of the unit.

Meanwhile, the noose was tightening around the Third Reich. The Western Allies had crossed the Rhine in force and were pushing to the Elbe. In Italy, the soldiers of the Polish II Corps were driving across seven rivers toward Bologna in the final battles of that campaign. With them, still wearing his gray paratrooper beret, was war correspondent Marek Swiecicki. He had already published one of the first books about the airborne invasion of The Netherlands: *With the Red Devils at Arnhem.* The book had enjoyed reasonable commercial success, but it, like the final battles by General Anders' men, did not awaken a "sense of justice" for the Poles in the eyes of their allies.

The Red Army had now surrounded Berlin, and no one doubted the war would be over in a matter of days. Behind the German lines elsewhere, however, thousands of people waited for deliverance from the Nazis. There were no accurate statistics, but between 120 and 160 Polish paratroopers had been taken prisoner in Holland. Their British comrades watched over them so that their captors would not single them out for "special treatment" because of their nationality. The prisoners suffered from the shortages of everything in the Third Reich during these last months of the war. Those who were capable were put to work according to the Geneva Convention, and labored under the whistle of bombs as the Allied Air Forces continued to punish the country that had set the world on fire.

The Drielenaren, though free and not facing the trials of their countrymen north of the Neder Rijn, waited to return to their homes and farms. The river had been a battle line for months, and the flinty farmers had to wait for the war to end. Nature, however, did not wait. Already the shattered fruit trees were blooming, and there was no one to trim the damaged branches and put the summer crops into the welcoming earth.

North of the Neder Rijn, the Nazi occupiers had severely punished the Dutch for the enthusiastic welcome they had given their failed liberators, and for a nationwide railroad strike that paralyzed the German war effort. They looted The Netherlands, allowing the country to starve. The evacuees from Oosterbeek moved in with relatives, friends or strangers, and waited for the chance to return to their town. On April 12, Canadian and British forces began a short but vicious offensive to clear the area north of the Neder Rijn.

In London, a disappointed General Sosabowski still tried to find justice among his people, in an exile that apparently would never end. Sosabowski's appointment, which he had announced to his friends in the British Army as "Inspector of Light Units," in actuality became "Inspector of Salvage and Disposal of the (Polish) Ministry of Defense." Further appeals to General Kopanski were spurned. Early in March, Sosabowski appealed to General Anders, who (in addition to commanding the Polish II Corps in Italy) was appointed acting Commander-in-Chief, for a board of inquiry by his peers. Anders responded to the former commander of the Parachute Brigade that he would take up the matter after he returned from Italy. Sosabowski could only sit back and wait.

By the end of April, the 1st Independent Polish Parachute Brigade had been reconstituted. The Brigade's depot in Scotland, and the school at Ringway, were closed after a final class was graduated on April 19. Since the end of Operation MARKET GARDEN, a total of 1,653 paratroopers had been qualified, and the majority were assigned to the Brigade, which now mustered 250 officers and 3,919 others. Despite assurances given to the Polish General Staff concerning the Brigade's subordination, it had begun training exercises with the British 1st Airborne Division.

The dawn of May 3, 1945, Polish Constitution Day, found the Brigade waiting at the airfields for a training jump with the British 1st Airborne Division. The jump was canceled due to bad weather, and the troops were delivered by truck to their drop zone. On the second day of the exercise, the Polish paratroopers were told to return to their barracks immediately and await orders for sea transportation to the Continent. The Polish Parachute Brigade was to relieve Allied units besieging the Germans who still held the port of Dunkirk.

While the Brigade were preparing to embark for the European continent, the war in Europe came to an end; the Brigade left England on May 8, and while it was at sea the news that Germany had unconditionally surrendered was received. The scourge of Nazism had been destroyed, but it had taken with it the lives of millions of people from around the world. After landing in Ostende, the Polish Parachute Brigade received a change in orders. It was now to proceed to Germany and join the British I Corps.

As truck convoys carried the Polish paratroopers to Kleve in northwestern Germany, hundreds of thousands of people wandered about the ruined continent trying to return to their homes, hopefully to reunite with loved ones and begin their lives again. Those people who had lived in Arnhem and Oosterbeek, and had not died of starvation during the final winter of the war, returned to their shattered homes. Oosterbeek was a pitiful sight. Not a building escaped damage during the battle or in the months of bombardment afterwards. Though there were hundreds of graves throughout the town, the corpses of hundreds of paratroopers still lay where they had fallen eight months before. Everything and anything of value that remained in the houses after the fighting was either stolen or vandalized. Across the river in Driel, the villagers returned to find the same devastation. Among the Drielenaren who did not return was Cora Baltussen. She now wore the uniform of UNRRA (United Nations Relief and Recovery Organization), helping the many Netherlanders who had found themselves among the ranks of the slave workers deported to Germany.

The Brigade settled in at Kleve. It was ironic that it was posted to this city, which was only 45 kilometers away from Arnhem. Had Operation MARKET GARDEN been successful, the Allies would have swept through the area to cut off the Ruhr.

Kleve had been almost totally destroyed during the bitter fighting for the battle of the Reichswald Forest in March 1945. Despite the devastation, the Polish soldiers wondered why there were so few German civilians on the streets. It seems the British soldiers, previously in the area, had terrorized the remaining population with tales that the "Polnische Fallschirmjägers" were coming, and what they could expect.

On June 1, however, the Brigade celebrated the Feast of Corpus Christi with traditional religious processions and celebrated mass under the clement spring sun. The Germans, seeing this unexpected manifestation of "civilization" in their occupiers, no longer hid in terror from the Polish soldiers who now patrolled their streets.

Through the destruction and desolation of Europe in the spring of 1945 wandered hundreds of thousands of "Displaced Persons": former prisoners of war, political prisoners, concentration-camp inmates, and liberated slave laborers from most European nations. Many of them were Poles, unable to return to their homes because of the destruction of transportation systems, or because their birthplaces were now under Soviet occupation. Most found themselves wandering through Germany. Treated worse than animals during their captivity, the sick and starved DPs were herded into camps and relief centers, where the most basic needs were provided by the military government and UNRRA, which, for all their efforts, were swamped by the magnitude of the task.

The Polish Displaced Persons in the region of Kleve were surprised when they met their paratrooper countrymen. The horrors of deportation and starvation, of explosions and fire, and the memories of fear, death and the terror of war were imprinted on these people's hearts and minds. The traumas were softened by the soldiers who spoke their own language and extended their hands, in sharp contrast to the men in other uniforms, who had for years brutalized and humiliated them. The fact that this help was given by strong men who wore the Polish eagle on their berets was almost a miracle: their Polish Army still existed after six years of unbelievable horror and dislocation!

In their area of occupation, the Polish paratroopers were moved by the plight of their countrymen and immediately began to help these pathetic people, stranded in the shattered landscape of the former Third Reich. All units of the Brigade helped their forlorn compatriots. The sappers built bunks for the people in the hastily set-up camps, the Medical Company constantly visiting to treat the sick and suffering. The paratroopers wrote to the people who had shown them such memorable hospitality in Britain, and soon their Scottish and English friends responded. The British Red Cross sent money and parcels of much-needed clothing to help those whose lives had seen so much misery. These were first steps that made the Displaced Persons begin to feel like people again. In Kleve the Brigade even sponsored dances, where young men and women could forget their wretchedness and humiliation, and speak to each other without having to use flattering words in a language only recently learned. Now they laughed and stepped to music that had long been part of their souls.

The Polish paratroopers took the opportunity to go to nearby Driel and Oosterbeek to visit the battlefields and recover any usable equipment. They found a devastated landscape, and the bodies of comrades who had disappeared during the fighting. Lieutenant Mieczyslaw Jurecki, recently released from a prisoner-of-war camp and promoted, visited Stationsweg no. 8. He found the Kremers, busy putting their lives and their grand house back together after having spent the awful winter in Apeldoorn. The officer, still alive, looked at the woman whose ledger he had not signed. She mentioned with a smile that, when she received his response to her question about whether the British would reach them, she knew then that their situation had, indeed, been hopeless.

As the Polish paratroopers walked through the streets of Driel, the citizens of the wrecked village took time from their rebuilding to greet the visitors who had so surprisingly fallen from the sky only months before. When the Polish soldiers went to the churchyard to pay their last respects to friends who lay there, they were greeted by a great surprise: the graves had neat white crosses on them and were surrounded by freshly planted red and white flowers. The Drielenaren, with so much to do, had cared for the resting places of the men from so far away who had been killed on the fertile soil of the Betuwe.

The interlude in Kleve lasted a few weeks. By the end of June, the Brigade received orders to proceed to the area of Osnabrück, Germany, where it would form one of the brigades of the Polish 1st Armored Division for administrative and command purposes, and carry on with occupation duties. The Brigade's headquarters was established in the town of Bersenbrück, and the three rifle battalions were stationed in the towns of Bramsche, Fürstenau and Ankum. The Brigade's other units were quartered in nearby villages.

The Polish Parachute Brigade settled into the role of occupier in this quiet northern backwater of Germany. The German civilians gave the Polish soldiers little trouble in this primarily agricultural area. The paratroopers' military duties were not strenuous, and they spent much time attending courses to help prepare them for civilian life. Among the varied skills they studied were courses in mechanics, electrical installation, carpentry, dairy farming and forestry. Many of the youngest had had their basic education disrupted by the Nazi invasion and subsequent odysseys before reaching the Brigade, where learning to collapse a parachute and shoot accurately took precedence over basic reading and mathematical skills. Life in this calm corner of the world permitted many men to catch up with what life had denied them for years.

Nearby German POW camps held women soldiers of the AK who had been captured during the Warsaw Uprising. These women and girls had seen front-line service in some of the most vicious house-to-house combat during the Second World War, and it was sad to see such heroic (and often pretty) soldiers sit behind barbed wire while the Allies decided what to do with them.

Female personnel had served for years in the Parachute Brigade's Soldiers' Welfare Platoon, and it was decided to accept more into the ranks. Issued mens' battle dress, they took the jackets apart seam by seam and, after tailoring the waist and padding the shoulders, reassembled them into a garment that had not only a distinct military appearance, but one that was much more attractive than the shapeless drab uniform as issued. The baggy battle-dress trousers were pulled apart, and by the time the seamstresses were done they had matching wool skirts. The young women, who had been in combat for over sixty days in filthy camouflage smocks, and months in tattered rags in prisoner of war camps, now wore crisply tailored ensembles with parachute collar tabs and the crimson "POLAND" titles on the shoulders, crowned with the Brigade's gray beret.

By the summer of 1946, the Brigade's Women's Auxiliary Service Company, as it was by now called, numbered sixty. The women quickly won the respect of the paratroopers, who had often been cynical in the beginning. They worked not only in the telephone exchange and canteens, but were on the administrative staffs of battalion and Brigade head-quarters. Many eventually married men they had served beside.

Within a few hours' drive of the Polish Parachute Brigade's billets were eighteen Displaced Persons camps, with almost 25,000 Poles among the people interned there. Donations, given willingly by the comparatively wealthy Polish paratroopers, went out to those who had suffered and lost so much. Bread and soap, leather and marmalade, shirts and cigarettes were passed out. The Brigade's Field Post Detachment established mail service between the camps. Mail was now easily forwarded to Polish military units throughout Europe, and to the Polish Red Cross, allowing people, torn and blown by winds of war, to seek each other and hopefully reunite.

Among the DP camps were children, deported with their parents. They only had memories of war, and their education had been curtailed as part of the Nazi design to keep the Poles slavish and ignorant. The paratroopers provided schools, opened in the DP camps, with almost 6,000 books and hundreds of items of school supply, so that these totally innocent boys and girls might learn the fundamentals of writing and mathematics. On St. Nicholas Day, a paratrooper with a long, false beard and his beret replaced with a mitre cap gave a present to each child in Bramsche. The young Poles in the camps who had participated in the Polish Scouting movement before, or during the time it had to go underground, now, too, looked to the Brigade, which provided scout masters and sponsored several troops.

Back in England, General Sosabowski never received the board of inquiry regarding his dismissal. In September 1945, the General received word that his son, Stanislaw, had survived the war. Blinded during the Warsaw Uprising, the young man did not go into captivity with the rest of the AK, but remained in hiding in various places in Poland while the

Germans demolished the city. Sosabowski went to General Crawford, former commander of Scottish Command, and now Deputy Chief of the Imperial General Staff. With his help, father and son were reunited in London in December 1945.

The role Poland played in the ranks of the Allies in the defeat of Germany was quickly forgotten in Britain. The United Nations had convened in San Francisco, but without Polish representation. Despite the fact that Poland was one of the charter members when the organization was formed, it was not allowed to participate until the question of whether the "London" or the "Lublin" Poles constituted the "legal" government was settled. By the end of 1945, there was pressure in Great Britain to commence repatriating the Polish soldiers in the West back to their homeland. For many Poles, this was not possible. From both justifiable pride and justifiable fear, the Polish soldiers who had fought so hard, for so many years, could not bring themselves to return to a homeland dominated by Stalin.

On May 8, 1946, a grand victory parade was held in London. Representatives of all the Allied armies and even police from the smallest British colony paraded through the capital. The Poles were not invited, except for fifteen officers and others from the Polish Air Force. RAF Fighter Command, mindful of the Poles' contributions during the Battle of Britain, extended the invitation, which was declined. The Polish airmen kept faith with their countrymen, rather than celebrate a victory in which their country could not participate.

The same month, a Polish Resettlement Corps was organized as a vehicle to demobilize the Polish armed forces. The Polish soldiers were given the choice of joining the Corps, where they could take courses in civilian trades, or return to Poland.

The choice was difficult. Despite homesickness for their country, many could not bring themselves to return to a devastated land where one occupier had been exchanged for another. The majority of Poles who opted to return were those who had been conscripted into the Wehrmacht, or had been deported as slave labor; they had had the most recent contacts with their families, although they had had no experience with the "workers' paradise" to the east. Still, others chose to return, not only because of their families, who were in great need, but also with a firm belief that their presence in their homeland could make a difference. Very shortly after their departure came reports that Polish soldiers, particularly officers, who had served in the West were being arrested and imprisoned. The NKVD-sponsored Polish security police murdered a number of the returnees, and tortured many more.

In the meantime, in Driel the Polish graves had been moved across the river to the Commonwealth War Graves Commission cemetery established in one of the former supply-dropping zones in Oosterbeek. This greatly upset the villagers. They had cared for the graves, marked with crosses bearing names so foreign to the Betuwe, as if their own flesh and blood reposed there. Their official appeal, with the words "Leave them in our midst, it is our duty to care for these graves!", was in vain. When the Polish paratroopers went to pay their respects to their comrades who now lay in the War Graves Commission cemetery, they found red and white geraniums on the graves, planted by the Drielenaren.

On September 21, 1946, the second anniversary of the Polish Parachute Brigade's landing in Driel, a group of veterans attended a memorial service in the village. The Brigade's commander, Lieutenant Colonel Szczerbo-Rawicz, unveiled a memorial built by the Dutch to the Polish paratroopers. It was simple, as postwar circumstances allowed, and bore the Polish coat-of-arms.

That same week, on September 23, 1946, the Brigade celebrated its fifth anniversary. All units attended mass under the open sky, and then were reviewed by Lieutenant Colonel Szczerbo-Rawicz. This was the last time the entire Brigade was together under arms. Already plans were afoot to commence Operation LAPWING. This operation was to withdraw the Polish forces from the British Army of the Rhine and transfer them to England. The Polish army in the West was being demobilized and absorbed into the Polish Resettlement Corps.

On May 19, 1947, Szczerbo-Rawicz gave his farewell order to the 1st Polish Independent Parachute Brigade Group. During the past year, weapons and equipment had gradually been turned in, and more and more of the soldiers had been absorbed into the Polish Resettlement Corps or had returned to Poland. By July, the only Polish paratroopers remaining on the Continent were those who were at the depot in Fürstenau or at the Military Family Camp in Bramsche. Soon these centers would also be liquidated. On June 12, 1947, paratroopers, among the last Polish soldiers in Britain still with arms, provided an honor guard at the funeral of President Raczkiewicz. Their weapons were then turned in, and on July 10, 1947, the Brigade's standards – including the precious one made by the women of occupied Warsaw – were deposited in the Sikorski Institute in London.

Each September, British and Polish veterans have returned to Holland to walk the streets and fields where they left so much of themselves in 1944. For a veteran of the battle, or his parents or children or widow, there has never been a question of having to pay for accommodation in a hotel or pension. Dutch families consider them honored guests. In September 1949, General Sosabowski visited Driel for the first time since he floated down from the sky five years before. The school, which had served as a hospital, was now rebuilt, and renamed after Saint Stanislaw Kostka, Poland's patron saint of youth. On a subsequent visist to Driel, in 1954, the former commander of the Polish Parachute Brigade was given the high title of "Freeman of the Municipality of Heteren."

Stanislaw Sosabowski, former Major General of the Polish Army, veteran of thirty-three years of service, entered civilian life with a savings of £300. With this savings, the fifty-seven-year-old man made a downpayment on a London boarding house. Himself working at times in the kitchen, he was soon forced to sell the enterprise at a loss. Sosabowski then entered a partnership with another former Polish officer in a furniture-refinishing and upholstery business. In the unbalanced postwar economy, there were few customers, and, when there were, materials could only be obtained through the black market. When that business failed, the former general found himself penniless. Through the labor exchange, Sosabowski obtained work in the supply department of an automotive electronics factory. The year was 1949, and the talented soldier was making six pounds a week. For years, Sosabowski lugged heavy rolls of brass and copper wire. None of the workers in the factory knew the identity of the quiet and at times sour man who kept to himself in the supply room, except as "Stan." Fellow workers who had been veterans of the Polish Army honored Sosabowski's request to keep his identity secret.

Sosabowski was kept busy trying to earn a living, but took every opportunity to be with his former soldiers at their reunions. At the urging of Brigade veterans, he wrote a history of the unit entitled *Najkrotsza Droga* (The Shortest Way), which was published in 1956. With the aid of a former British paratrooper, this was revised and translated into English as *Freely I Served* in 1960. A Dutch edition of this book appeared under the title *Ik Vocht Voor de Vrihjeid* (I Fought for Freedom). That year, a monument to the Polish Parachute Brigade was unveiled in Driel. For it, the Dutch sculptor, Jan Vlasbom, designed a modern statue of "youth, holding freedom like a precious gem," with a stone rising above it like a parachute. Inscribed on the pedestal are the words "SURGE POLONIA" (Poland Arise), the same words that were embroidered on the Brigade's standard by the women of Warsaw during the bleak days of the occupation.

In Poland, the era of Stalin was over. Those officers and other soldiers who had been imprisoned on their return to Poland had by 1953 been released and "rehabilitated." The Polish People's Republic had raised the 6th "Pomorska" Airborne Division, and adopted the diving-eagle badge that was worn by Polish paratroopers during the war. It was during this hopeful period that veteran paratroopers living in the West began gathering funds to raise a monument to the Polish paratroopers – in Warsaw. On September 18, 1965, after a mass celebrated by Father Mientki, the large memorial was dedicated in Warsaw's Powaski Cemetery. Below the large diving eagle, on a massive block of stone, were the names of all the paratroopers and *Cichochiemni* who had died for their country between 1941 and 1945. This was the first and, for a long time, the only monument behind the Iron Curtain to soldiers who had fought in the West.

On December 30, 1966, Stanislaw Sosabowski found himself unemployed. His firm had released all workers older than sixty-five years of age. At seventy-five, the former general found himself having to exist on a small old-age pension. He had just completed a final book of remembrances, which was being printed when his heart gave out on September 25, 1967. In the final chapter of his book, *Droga Wiodla Ugorem* (The Way Wound Through Desolation), Sosabowski wrote that he did not know how much longer he would live: "Maybe tomorrow, maybe after ten years. . . That does not worry me. But one thing does, and that is a life without perspective. Hard and desolate was my entire life. In the midst of all these miseries there were also bright times. These I had witnessed with my own eyes, that through my efforts, and through the efforts of those who believed and followed, that they did not go for nothing."

The General's last published words were: "There is no feeling like the one that the soldiers have for their 'Pops.' It is a sign that I am theirs, and they own me. For that it is worth living."

General Sosabowski's coffin lay in London's St. Andrew Boboli church, flanked by the standards of the 1st Polish Independent Parachute Brigade, the 21st "Children of Warsaw" Infantry Regiment, the Polish Paratroopers Association and the Polish Scouts in Exile. From the

Netherlands came the Mayor of Heteren, J. A. Bolt, and the Polish paratroopers' longtime friend, A. J. Baltussen. On October 10, his ashes were taken to Warsaw by his son. General Sosabowski finally returned to his beloved Poland. After a mass said by Father Mientki, the former general was interred in the family grave in Powaski Cemetery. The Army of the Polish People's Republic provided a full honor guard for the burial, which was attended by former paratroopers and veterans of the 21st Infantry Regiment who came to bid farewell to their "Pops."

In Poland, history has always been alive, and has been devoured eagerly as a counterpoint to the lies that were forced on its people during almost fifty years of Soviet domination. As during the earlier partition periods, history and character were taught at home as a foil to the way the themes were covered in state-sponsored institutions. Despite many difficulties, an independent Scout movement managed to flourish in Poland. Even before the fall of the communist People's Republic of Poland, almost thirty Scout Troops were named after the Polish Parachute Brigade or the heros of Arnhem, Driel and Oosterbeek. While the majority of paratroopers never made it home by the "Shortest Way," memory in Poland is long, and the Brigade served as an example of dedication, courage and perseverance.

Even before the end of communism in Poland, the curator of the Museum of the Polish Army in Warsaw told this author that the most popular exhibit in the museum was the case that contained General Sosabowski's uniform. He went on to say that there was always a crowd of schoolchildren in front of it, looking at it in awe.

There were changes afoot in Poland even before free elections were held in 1990. The Polish Post Office issued a series of stamps commemorating the country's military leaders during the Second World War. In 1989, a stamp bearing Sosabowski's portrait and a map of the battlefield in Holland had been issued. That same year, the crushing defense expenditures that Poland had to pay as a member of the Warsaw Pact led to a reorganization of the 6th "Pomorska" Airborne Division into a brigade-sized formation. At this time, the Brigade was renamed after General Sosabowski.

In November 1990, free elections were finally held in Poland and, not surprisingly, the communists were defeated. The following month, the Polish Government-in-Exile, which had continued to maintain offices in London, brought the Polish Republic's constitution and the Seal of

State back to Warsaw. Since the restoration of the Polish Republic, monuments to the paratroopers of old have appeared all over Poland. Until recently, such memorials had only been permitted in churches. Today, however, there is a monument to Captain Gazurek in his hometown of Bielsko, and a beautiful bust of General Sosabowski now graces Krakow. In 1992, the Polish Republic sponsored a reunion of the soldiers who fought for her. They came from all over the world and paraded through the streets of a free Warsaw for the first time since 1939. While Poland still faces great problems in becoming an economically viable nation, after the abuses of having an artificial and exploited economy for so many years, the veterans marched with a satisfaction that the struggle for freedom that they had embarked on over 50 years before had come to a victorious end.

The paratroopers, like many other former Polish soldiers, were scattered across the Western World. Their reward for their long and seemingly endless fight and exile, ironically, was freedom. The men who suffered countless humiliations savored their new homelands with an appreciation frequently more acute than their British, American, Canadian or Australian neighbors—who were born there. The former paratroopers were not afraid of hard work, or of seemingly impossible odds, and energetically carved out new, and often satisfying, lives in their adopted countries. As the years passed, they raised families and tried to instill in their children the devotion to the "God–Honor–Country" motto they had been raised with. They have never forgotten their motherland as they watched her trials of repression and despair, along with the periods of brilliance when her sons and daughters electrified the world with their accomplishments.

In The Netherlands, now one of the world's best-educated countries, with one of the world's highest standards of living, solemn and touching ceremonies every September commemorate the battle of so many years ago. But there is something being done to create new memories, besides preserving the old ones. Each year young Poles are brought to Driel, and young Drielenaren visit their new friends in Poland. This is an insurance that the intimacy, welded by the flames of war between their grandparents, shall remain in future generations. It is on the young that we pin our hopes, and these friendships shall not only continue, but be as strong as those between the now gray-haired people who remember the horror and the courage of years past.

The Polish Paratroopers Association was formed in London in January 1948 as the last Polish soldiers hung up their gray berets. Chapters were established throughout Britain and the United States. The comradeships formed in prison camps, on foreign seas, in barracks and on battlefields have been maintained over the decades. At yearly reunions, former riflemen, mechanics, machine gunners, radiomen and quarter-masters greet each other with broad smiles. Now retired accountants, factory workers, shipping clerks and truck drivers, they pull out photos of daughters and sons who are teachers, doctors, engineers, computer programmers or grocers, and begin to exchange lies about their grandchildren. The mood turns somber as the one-time paratroopers remember their own youth, especially the friends they buried in the mud of Holland, as well as the faces of those friends they will no longer see— men who survived German shells but succumbed to the ravages of time since the last reunion. After a tasty meal, over drinks with friends, come the reminiscences of whisky shared years before. Between popular songs, the hall is filled with the melodies of mazurkas and obereks, familiar to Poles for centuries. Muscles that were hardened by the impossible exercises at Monkey Grove still pull to the lively tunes that go on into the night. Little thought is given to the difficult times of the past. Yes, how long ago that was.

The Polish Paratroopers Monument in Driel, Holland.

Photo: B. de Reuss, Oosterbeek

1st POLISH INDEPENDENT PARACHUTE BRIGADE
Table of Organization

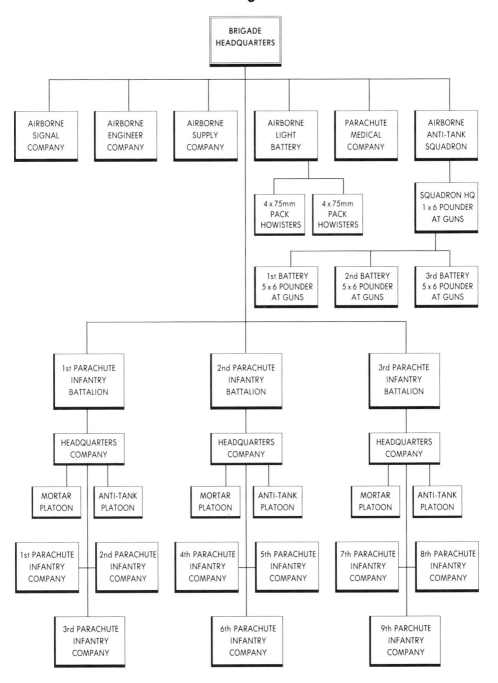

*The following is the text of Lieutenant General Browning's letter to the Imperial
General Staff stating his dissatisfaction with Major General Sosabowski.*

COPY   PERSONAL AND CONFIDENTIAL

                                  Headquarters Airborne Corps,
                                  A.P.O. England.
                                  20th November, 1944.
Sir,
        Report on Major-General St. Sosabowski, Commanding 1st Polish
                        Parachute Brigade Group

        I have the honour to bring the following facts to your notice with regard to
Major-General St. Sosabowski, Commander 1st Polish Parachute Brigade Group,
before and during operation "MARKET."
        During the weeks previous to operation "MARKET," a period which entailed
detailed planning for three other possible operations, the 1st Polish Parachute
Brigade Group formed part of the force envisaged.
        Both during this period and, in fact, ever since the 1st Polish Parachute
Brigade Group was mobilised in July, Major General Sosabowski proved himself
to be extremely difficult to work with. The "difficulty" was apparent not only
to Commanders under whom he was planning but also to staff officers of the
other airborne formations concerned.
        During this period he gave me the very distinct impression that he was raising
objections and causing difficulties as he did not feel that his brigade was fully
ready for battle. When the brigade was first mobilised I made it absolutely clear
to this officer, and in no uncertain terms, that I was the sole judge of the
efficiency of his brigade and it was merely his duty to get them ready and train
them with all the determination of which he was capable.
        It became apparent during this training period that, capable soldier as this
officer undoubtedly is, he was unable to adapt himself to the level of a parachute
brigade commander, which requires intimate and direct command of his
battalions. He left too much to his Chief of Staff and attempted to treat his
parachute brigade as if it were a much higher and bigger formation.
        During operation "MARKET" the brigade was unfortunate in being dropped
in parts owing to the weather. However, during this period of operation
"MARKET" great difficulties were being overcome hourly by all formations of
the Second Army in their efforts to reach the 1st Airborne Division at Arnhem.
This officer proved himself to be quite incapable of appreciating the urgent nature
of the operation, and continually showed himself to be both argumentative and
loathe to play his full part in the operation unless everything was done for him
and his brigade.

Subsequently, when the 1st Airborne Division had been withdrawn, and the Polish Parachute Brigade Group reverted to my command South of the R. Waal, this officer worried both me and my staff (who were at that time fighting a very difficult battle to keep the corridor open from inclusive Nijmegen to Eindhoven) about such things as two or three lorries to supplement his transport. I was forced finally to be extremely curt to this officer, and ordered him to carry out his orders from then on without query or obstruction.

Both Commander 30 Corps and Commander 43 Division will bear out my criticism of the attitude of this officer throughout the operation.

Major-General Sosabowski has undoubtedly, during the three years in which I have been connected with him, done a very great amount for the 1st Polish Parachute Brigade Group under disappointing circumstances. He was mainly responsible for the whole of the raising, organisation and training of the brigade. However, this good record cannot be allowed to interfere with the present and future efficiency of the brigade.

I am forced, therefore, to recommend that General Sosabowski be employed elsewhere, and that a younger, more flexibly minded and cooperative officer be made available to succeed him.

There are, to my knowledge, two possible candidates now serving with the brigade. The first is Lieut-Col. S. Jachnik, who is at present Deputy Commander. This officer has had practically no opportunity to display his powers owing to the somewhat overbearing nature of General Sosabowski's personality. The appointment of this officer would, in my opinion, be essentially in the nature of an experiment.

The second candidate is Major M. Tonn, who commands 1 Parachute Battalion. This officer has trained his battalion well and, in my opinion and in the opinion of the G.S.O.1. Liaison (Airborne) Lieut-Col. Stevens, he possesses the requisite drive and administrative ability to fulfill the appointment.

However, this appointment must remain largely a matter for the Polish Army itself to make, and it will probably be better in the long run if new blood be brought in.

Finally, I wish to emphasise again that I consider Major-General Sosabowski is a knowledgeable and efficient soldier and up to the average of his rank, but owing to his outlook, temperament and inability to cooperate he should be given a change of employment.

> I have the honour to be, Sir,
> Your obedient Servant,
> (Sgd) F.A.M. Browning
> Commander Airborne Corps.

Personal and Confidential.

Lieut-Gen. Sir Ronald Weeks, KCB, CBE, DSO, MC, TD,
Deputy Chief of the Imperial General Staff,   Copy to:
The War Office, Whitehall, S.W.1   Commander-in-Chief,
21 Army Group, B.L.A.

Select Bibliography

Acherson, N. *The Struggles for Poland.* New York: Random House, 1987.

Anonymous (L. Hagen). *Arnhem Lift.* London: Pilot Press, 1945.

Anonymous (A. Pronobis). *GO . . . Album Wyspomien Spadochroniarza.* Germany: publisher unknown, 1947.

Bauer, C. *The Battle of Arnhem.* London: Hodder & Stoughton, 1966; New York: Stein & Day, 1967.

Bieganski, W. *Poles in the Battle of Western Europe.* Warsaw: Ksiazka i Wiedza, 1971.

———. *Arnhem.* Warsaw: Ksiazka i Wiedza, 1977.

Blair, C. *Ridgway's Paratroopers.* New York: Doubleday, 1985.

Devlin, G. *Paratooper!* New York: St. Martin's, 1979.

———. *Silent Wings.* New York: St. Martin's, 1985.

Dover, V. *The Sky Generals.* London, 1981.

Essame, H. *The 43rd Wessex Division at War.* London: Clowes & Sons, 1952.

Farrar-Hockley, A. *Airborne Carpet: Operation Market Garden.* New York: Ballantine, 1952.

Garlinski, J. *Poland, SOE and the Allies.* London: Allen & Unwin, 1969.

———. *Poland in the Second World War.* London: Macmillan, 1985.

Gavin, J. M. *On to Berlin.* New York: Viking, 1978.

Green, A. *The Border Regiment.* Kendal (UK): The Museum of the Border Regiment, 1991.

Hackett, J. *I Was a Stranger.* London: Chatto & Windus, 1977.

Heaps, L. *The Evaders.* New York: Morrow, 1976.

Hey, J. A. *Roll of Honor, Battle of Arnhem.* Oosterbeek: Friends of the Airborne Museum, 1986.

Horrocks, B. *Escape to Action.* New York: St. Martin's, 1960; *A Full Life.* London: Collins, 1960.

———. *Corps Commander.* London: Sidgwick & Jackson, 1977; New York: St. Martin's, 1977.

Infield, G. B. *The Poltava Affair.* New York: Macmillan, 1973.

Jansen, B. *Ein Drielenaar in oorlogstijd.* Driel: privately published, 1990.

Joslen, H. F. *Orders of Battle, Second World War, 1939–1945.* London: H.M. Stationery Office, 1960.

Kaminski, J. *Od Kon i Armaty do Spadochronu.* Warsaw: Pax, 1985.

Korthals Altes, A., K. Magrgry, G. Thuring, and R. Voskuil. *September 1944: Operation MARKET GARDEN.* Houten: De Haan, 1987.

Krolikiewicz, T. *Szybowce Transportowe.* Warsaw: MON, 1985.

Lorys, J. J. *1st Polish Parachute Brigade Group – Polish Airborne Forces in World War II at Arnhem–Driel 1944, List of Participants (Materialy– Dokumenty Zrodla Archiwalia, No. 3).* London: The Polish Institute and Sikorski Museum, 1987.

Maassen, G. H. *Oosterbeek Verwoerst 1944–1945* (Book 1). Oosterbeek: Meijer & Seigers, 1981.

——. *Vijf gesteisterde dorpen: Opheusden, Kesteren, Randwijk, Heteren, Driel.* Oosterbeek: Hoog, Laag & Seigers, 1984.

——. *Oosterbeek verwoerst 1944–1945* (Book 2). Oosterbeek: privately published, 1985.

Mientki, Father F. *Bog i Ojczyzna: Wspomnienia Kapelana Wojska Polskiego.* Warsaw: Novum, 1985.

Orde, R. *The Household Cavalry at War: The Second Household Cavalry Regiment.* Aldershot (UK): Gale & Polden, 1953.

Powell, G. *The Devil's Birthday.* London: Buchan & Enright, 1984.

Ryan, C. *A Bridge Too Far.* New York: Simon & Schuster, 1974; London: Hamish Hamilton, 1974.

Sosabowski, S. *Droga Wiodla Ugorem.* London: Veritas, 1967.

——. *Freely I Served.* London: Kimber, 1960; Nashville: Battery Press, 1982.

Swiecicki, M. *With the Red Devils at Arnhem.* London: Max Love, 1945.

——. *Ostatni Rok Wojny.* Glasgow: Ksiaznica Polska, 1946.

Urquhart, B. *A Life in Peace and War.* London: Weidenfeld and Nicolson, 1987; New York: Harper & Row, 1987.

Urquhart, R. E. *Arnhem.* London: Cassell, 1958; New York: Norton, 1958.

Interviews and Correspondence

Polish Ministry of Information
Kuratowska-Swiecicki, Krystyna

Polish Parachute Center, Ringway
Janiga, Lieutenant Kazimierz
Kruszewski, Lieutenant Stanislaw

Brigade Headquarters
Dyrda, Lieutenant Jerzy
Gramski, Lieutenant Marek
Holub, Sergeant Cadet Edward
Jakubowicz, Lieutenant Wiktor
Lorys, Lieutenant Jan
Mazurek, Lieutenant Ludomir
Raschke, Private J. Zbigniew
Swiecicki, Corporal Cadet/War Correspondent Marek
Szegda, 2nd Lieutenant Janusz
Szygenda, 2nd Lieutenant Jan

1st Battalion
Drewienkiewicz, Corporal Wojciech
Jurecki, Lance Sergeant Cadet Mieczyslaw
Kula, 2nd Lieutenant Jozef
Paszkiewicz, Corporal Marian
Platta, Private Franciszek
Rojewski, Lieutenant Tadeusz (Ted Roy)
Wilkojc, Lance Corporal Waclaw
Wojewodka, Corporal Boleslaw
Ziemski, Lieutenant Zbigniew

2nd Battalion
Chichon, Lance Corporal Tadeusz
Gozdecki, 2nd Lieutenant Leonard
Herman, Lance Corporal Cadet Tadeusz
Hrehorow, Lance Corporal Cadet Zygmundt
Iwaskow, Sergeant Michal
Lampert, Lance Corporal Cadet Tadeusz
Paluch, Lance Sergeant Tadeusz
Stopczynski, Corporal Marian

3rd Battalion
Chwastek, Private Mieczyslaw
Dabrowski, Lance Corporal Kazimierz
Dobroczynski, Private Jan
Gasowski, Lance Sergeant Cadet Zbigniew

Lasek, Private Michal
Lucki, Lieutenant Jerzy
Smaczny, Lieutenant Albert
Szubert, Private Jan
Towarnicki, Corporal Jan
Urbanski, 2nd Lieutenant Waclaw

Anti-Tank Squadron
Bossowski, 2nd Lieutenant Zbigniew
Mleczko, Lieutenant Wladyslaw
Nosecki, Bombardier Stanislaw
Oprych, Bombardier Jozef
Romaniszyn, Corporal Jozef

Signal Company
Blazejewski, Sergeant Cadet Marian
Kuzniar, Lance Corporal Boleslaw (3rd Battalion)
Nowak, Corporal Roman
Soloniewicz, Lance Corporal Stefan (3rd Battalion)
Wawiorko, Private Piotr (Telephone Platoon)
Wilk, Lieutenant Jan

Supply Company
Kaczmarek, Lieutenant Stefan

Medical Company
Spilakowski, Private Mikolaj (Michael Rorison)
Sztuba, 2nd Lieutenant Dr. Florian

Engineer Company
Szczygiel, Lieutenant Wieslaw (George Harvey)
Kurasz, Sapper Stanislaw

Netherlanders
(Driel)   *(Oosterbeek)*
Baltussen, Albert   Kremer, Ans
Baltussen, Cora   Kremer, Sander
Beukema, Klaas
Dorsthorst, Henk te
Fischer, Peter
Harn-Hensen, Janna van
Jansen, Benjamin
Verhoef, Anton